IDEOLOGY IN A SOCIALIST STATE

SOVIET AND EAST EUROPEAN STUDIES

Editorial Board

SOVIET AND EAST EUROPEAN STUDIES

IDEOLOGY IN A
SOCIALIST STATE

POLAND 1956–1983

RAY TARAS

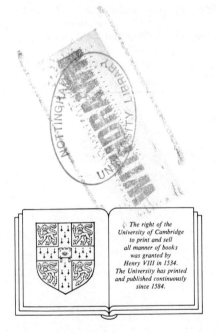

The right of the
University of Cambridge
to print and sell
all manner of books
was granted by
Henry VIII in 1534.
The University has printed
and published continuously
since 1584.

CAMBRIDGE UNIVERSITY PRESS

CAMBRIDGE

LONDON   NEW YORK   NEW ROCHELLE

MELBOURNE   SYDNEY

Published by the Press Syndicate of the University of Cambridge
The Pitt Building, Trumpington Street, Cambridge CB2 1RP
32 East 57th Street, New York, NY 10022, USA
296 Beaconsfield Parade, Middle Park, Melbourne 3206, Australia

First published 1984

Printed in Great Britain at the University Press, Cambridge

Library of Congress catalogue card number: 84-4970

British Library Cataloguing in Publication Data
Taras, Ray
Ideology in a socialist state. – (Soviet and
East European studies)
1. Poland – Politics and government – 1945–
I. Title   II. Series
320.9438   JN752

ISBN 0 521 26271 2

C

301485

For Małgorzata and Michał

Contents

Preface

This study sets out to examine the role of ideology in a socialist state and the way it may change over time. More specifically, it focuses on ideological developments in Poland. The period covered is from October 1956, when Gomułka acceded to power, to the end of 1983, when both Solidarity and martial law were treated as history by the Jaruzelski leadership.

Research for this study was carried out in Poland in the period between October 1977 and June 1982, whilst the author was completing a doctoral programme at the University of Warsaw. The present monograph is a shortened version of a dissertation submitted to that University in October 1981. Two new chapters – on the Solidarity and martial law periods – have been added since. I would like to emphasise that responsibility for the overall content of the present study is mine alone.

The analytical framework of the study focuses on official discourse of party rulers and was adopted well before the birth of Solidarity. Theoretically it would have been possible to adjust the research design after August 1980 to include Solidarity's discourse as well. But the enormous scholarly interest that the movement provoked, and still inspires, allows the author to rest easy that what he did not undertake in this study has been more than adequately undertaken by others. Moreover it is my belief that not enough attention has been paid to the rulers' view of the events between 1980 and 1983; this monograph seeks to fill this gap.

Chapters 1 and 2 review conceptual and methodological approaches to the study of ideology. These include the views of Western social scientists and their Polish counterparts. Chapters 3 to 8 present empirical findings on the functioning of ideology in Poland between

1956 and 1982 in selected issue-areas. Finally Chapter 9 interprets these findings, discusses ideological developments after martial law was ended in mid 1983 and considers the relevance of ideology to the modern socialist state.

I would like to acknowledge the assistance extended to me by a number of institutions, in Poland and elsewhere, which permitted the completion of this study. Firstly I am grateful to the Institute of Sociology, University of Warsaw, and its members who aided and encouraged me during the period I was registered in the Institute.

Secondly I am indebted to the Social Science and Humanities Research Council of Canada, which awarded me a doctoral fellowship enabling me to remain in Poland and observe its political and ideological developments at first hand.

Thirdly I wish to thank the Center for Russian and East European Studies, University of Michigan, and its Director, Professor Zvi Gitelman, for providing resources to update this study during the 1982–3 academic year.

A number of individuals helped immeasurably to improve this work. Professor Jerzy Wiatr (Institute of Sociology, University of Warsaw) gave invaluable advice whilst I was completing earlier drafts. Professors Jean Laponce (Department of Political Science, University of British Columbia) and Franciszek Ryszka (Institute of History, Polish Academy of Sciences) provided constructive critiques at a later stage. I also received much intellectual inspiration for this study from Professor Winicjusz Narojek (Institute of Philosophy and Sociology, Polish Academy of Sciences). At the most crucial, final stage in the preparation of this typescript, an anonymous reader of Cambridge University Press offered the professional advice needed to transform a dissertation into something more scholarly. I am grateful to my editors at CUP, Stephen Barr and Michael Holdsworth, for constant encouragement and interest. Finally I would like to thank Professor David Lane (Department of Sociology, University of Birmingham) for the intellectual and practical help he has given me over the past ten years.

It is my hope that this monograph will contribute to an understanding of recent events in Poland by looking at how its leaders have perceived and interpreted the world around them.

Lexington, Kentucky,
January 1984

I

The concept of ideology and Western sociology

The great political and moral crisis that societies are now undergoing is shown by a rigid analysis to arise out of intellectual anarchy. Whilst stability in fundamental maxims is the first condition of genuine social order, we are suffering under an utter disagreement which may be called universal. Until a certain number of general ideas can be acknowledged as a rallying-point of social doctrine, nations will remain in a revolutionary state, whatever palliatives may be devised; and their institutions can be only provisional.

Auguste Comte, *Cours de philosophie positive*

A central element in Marx's theory of social formation is his structural model of society, said to consist of an economic base and a political and ideological superstructure. This model has inspired considerable research into economic relations, political systems, and their interdependence, both in capitalist societies and in those undergoing socialist transformation. Inexplicably, systematic research into the role of ideology, especially in socialist states, has lagged behind.

If we focus on ideology as the principal element in the base–superstructure model, we may follow a Marxist approach to determine the ideological importance of Marxism. If we conduct this analysis in a society attempting the construction of an advanced form of socialism, then we can suggest not only what the principal features of the dominant ideology are, but also what role this ideology itself plays in the process. When this analysis is carried out for a certain time span, then it is possible to discover not only how elements of the dominant ideology are operationalised and change over time in response to their dialectical relationship with the economic system but also what effect its prescriptive value has had in society generally. Thus it is not precluded that such a Marxist-based approach may

reveal the inadequacies of Marxist ideology as it has been operationalised in a socialist state.

The definition of ideology as false consciousness, given by the
young Marx in *The poverty of philosophy*, was the source of one of the
first, and subsequently one of the most bitterly contested, controversies surrounding this concept. For Marx the definition was an attempt
to relate ideology to class conflict in society, more specifically, to the
way in which social consciousness could be deformed by such conflict.
Later, for example, in his Preface to *A contribution to a critique of political
economy*, he used the term to denote the whole range of legal, political,
religious, artistic and philosophical values. The confusion which
followed among Marxologists in trying to arrive at a 'correct' interpretation of his concept of ideology originated in the incorrect
assumption that the two definitions must, or ought to, have something in common. In fact Marx knowingly used the term to describe
two quite different phenomena. Initially he contended that ideology
was the result of a 'limited material mode of activity' which produced
contradictory relations and, simultaneously, distorted reproductions
about them. Ideology unified consciousness and reality into one
phenomenon.[1] In his later works he made it clear that his intention
was to construct an ideology free of deformations and false consciousness, one which would constitute an influential force in a given
historical epoch and in which social classes would internalise as well
as express the world outlook, or set of beliefs about reality, which this
ideology contained. As Engels noted in his Introduction to *The
eighteenth Brumaire of Louis Bonaparte*, Marx was the first to see all
forms of struggle – whether political, religious, philosophical, or in
other spheres of ideology – as examples of class conflict.[2] Whereas
earlier Marx treated ideology as a passive element, deformed by this
conflict, he later saw it as an active factor in this process, playing a
constructive historical role. In this way the later Marxian concept of
ideology is functional: social values and directives to action are
stressed, not elements of deformation.

Western critics of Marxism rarely consider the latter use of the
concept; it is more dominant in the approaches to ideology taken by
scholars in socialist states. Western critics either attack the 'ideology
as false consciousness' thesis, or they point to the general inconsistencies alleged to be found in the writings of Marx and Engels on the
subject. Thus Gurvitch attributes to Marx eight different uses of the
term 'ideology',[3] whilst Seliger concludes: 'Marx did not use "ideol-

ogy" according to a uniform definition, and the term itself did not occupy a central position in his work. He used interchangeably *Ideologie, Ideen, Anschauungen* and *Doktrinen.*'[4]

That the term was not used consistently throughout Marx's writings is undeniable. What can be claimed is that a logical evolution occurred in his thought on the subject. This is most clearly seen when relating the notion of ideology to science. For ideology was identified with false consciousness so as to distinguish it from science – the objective analysis of the real world which excluded all forms of deformation. Historical materialism was initially regarded by Marx and Engels as a world outlook based on a scientific socialism. Thus it was not an ideology. Later they understood historical materialism in broader terms: it was a systematisation and rationalisation (but not necessarily an aggregation) of outlooks on morality, religion, law, politics, science and art.[5] The method it used was to treat these aspects of historical development in a philosophical way; its content consisted of the social and political values of social groups. With Lenin historical materialism came to be regarded as a 'scientific ideology' and as the ideology of the proletariat. Whereas other ideologies were still characterised by the false consciousness they expressed and the non-scientific method they employed to view the world, historical materialism presented an objective analysis of social development in all its aspects. Also, it was devoid of false consciousness. Thus, whereas for the young Marx historical materialism was a scientific discipline and could not, as a result, be considered an ideology, for Lenin it constituted a unique unity of scientific and ideological elements.

The confusion surrounding Marx's use of the term also originated, according to Larrain, in his application of the concept of ideology within a double perspective. On the one hand he stressed the relationship between consciousness and practice; on the other he emphasised the relationship between base and superstructure. The logic and consequences of each perspective were not exactly the same:

Under the base–superstructure relationship, ideology appears as a secondary ideal structure which is directly determined by the economic structure. Under the practice–consciousness polarity, ideology appears as the free and conscious product of a subject, as a false consciousness which protects some class interests. While for the former ideology is necessary, for the latter it appears illusory. The emphasis upon the necessity of ideology under the first polarity produces a tendency to consider it, at least partially, as a positive fact of social life, as performing a necessary function for society. On the contrary, ideology, considered as a false consciousness or illusion, is always contingent and negative.[6]

A related dichotomy was described by Parekh. He imputed to Marx a view of ideology as a body of ideas systematically biased towards a particular social group. It displayed at one and the same time idealist and apologist features. The idealist strand was based on the Marxian assumption that consciousness could be detached from concrete socially situated subjects. The ideology which followed from such consciousness was, accordingly, also autonomous and self-sufficient. Such an idealist approach was, for Parekh, bound to view the interests and values of a particular social group as universally valid. Idealism always led, therefore, to an apologia for the pursuit of these interests and values (although not every apologia had to involve idealism).[7]

These are two general, seemingly contradictory tendencies characterising the Marxist approach to the concept of ideology. However, it would be a gross oversimplification to conclude that the use of the term by Marx was limited solely to two imputations. Indeed, given the absence of a precise definition, it may be deduced that for Marx ideology signified a philosophy, a political programme, a form of social consciousness, a set of norms or values, a political theory legitimising a particular type of social order, a 'spirit of the age' and a scientific discipline. Since most ideologies, historical materialism included, consist to a greater or lesser degree of all these aspects, such generality in Marxian thought is by no means unique. For Marxists his contribution lay not in his concept of ideology but in his being able to situate it in a historical context and to assign it a historical role. If ambiguity arises in usage of the term, less unclear is its place in the Marxist model of social formation. Ideology is a product of the economic relations of a given epoch; it may continue to exist after these relations have become outmoded or replaced; likewise it may exert a considerable influence on future social development.

Ideology has been very widely interpreted by non-Marxist thinkers as well. A long list of definitions of ideology current among social scientists was compiled by Naess and his associates as early as 1956.[8] Since then further entries could doubtless be added. As the Polish political scientist Wiatr wrote: 'There are few terms in the social sciences which are as equivocal and possess such different substantive and emotional associations as the term "ideology".'[9] But the non-Marxist approach to ideology is not only characterised by divergent definitional and conceptual views. It also lacks a consistent interpretation of the role and function performed by ideology in social development. In the latter half of the nineteenth century, largely in reaction to the views propounded by Marx and his followers, ideologues of the existing social order attempted to formulate a rival doctrine which could explain how capitalism arose and under what conditions it might prosper. English economists underlined the positive role which the ideology of *laissez-faire* was to perform in promoting the kind of social and human relations needed for capitalism to flourish. Throughout the first half of the twentieth century, various ideological offshoots and modifications of *laissez-faire* and the private economy (most notable of these being Keynesian economics and social democracy) continued to pose as alternative ideologies to historical materialism. The world was a place of ideological struggle in which rival ideologies sought 'to win over the minds of men'. Neither side denied the importance of winning this confrontation and imposing its own ideology, which would in turn determine in what direction society would evolve. But ideological victory over one's rival was not an end in itself. As Marx wrote in *The eighteenth Brumaire of Louis Bonaparte*, just as in warfare one fights with the use of arms but not for these arms, so in the ideological struggle one fights with the help of an ideology but not for the ideology. The object of the battle was not to prove the validity of one's own ideology and the falsity of that of one's opponent but to implement an ideology with the view to achieving the desired social effect. It is in this sense, as Lenin noted, that economic interests are decisive in the class struggle, for they are the real object of the ideological confrontation, not ideology itself.[10]

Ideologies are generally based upon some objective truths about the real world. The fundamental weakness of many ideologies is their inability to consider these truths in a societal context. Also they are often unable to perceive the real significance of their role in history. Thus they may be blinded both by self-righteousness, which stresses the internal validity of their doctrines whilst ignoring their correspondence to reality and, more specifically, to the interests of social groups, and by self-consciousness, which exaggerates their importance in affecting social development. For the Polish philosopher Rainko, the superiority of Marxism as an ideology lies not only in the fact that its doctrines concerning the real world are correct but also in the fact that it has no illusions about itself or its function in history.[11] To adapt a well-worn phrase of Marx, whilst other philosophies were (and are) concerned with interpreting the world, the most important role of historical materialism understood as a philosophy is to change it.

This positive role taken upon itself by Marxism distinguished it from the purely 'explanatory' nature of its ideological rivals. Its praxeological thrust meant that Marxism was able to adapt itself and supply impetus to the objective forces it saw as governing historical development. Bourgeois ideologies were perceived as having an appeal in the cognitive sphere only, and even in this respect with major limitations. The Bolshevik Revolution gave Marxism the long-awaited political victory and secure geographical base which it needed in order to diffuse itself further, and up to the late 1920s considerable ideological creativity took place in this first socialist state. With the adoption of a forced industrialisation programme, however, the Soviet Union entered a barren 'doctrinaire' period in which few advances were recorded in furthering historical materialist philosophy. Bourgeois ideologues in the inter-war period were unable to capitalise on the inflexibility and petrification of the Soviet Marxism of the Stalin period: firstly because they, too, could not make their doctrines more fruitful; secondly because the objective conditions they were defending, those produced by capitalism, were marked by a severe economic depression; and thirdly because Marxist thinkers outside the Soviet Union (notably Lukács and Gramsci) proved more adept and constructive in enriching and promulgating historical materialism than anyone else. A relatively short but very intense ideological confrontation took place during the Cold War period; this indeed seemed bound to follow the temporary truce produced by the economic depression in the capitalist world and the industrialisation and collectivism priorities of the USSR in the 1930s, then by the Second World War. Partly as a result of the intensity of this confrontation (and also as a result of many other objective factors), by the late 1950s non-Marxist thinkers turned away from open ideological rivalry and reached for a more subtle 'neutral' doctrine expressing their outlook on the real world. Although many different versions of the doctrine arose in political and economic thought, the main principles of the 'neutral' end-of-ideology thesis were formulated by political sociologists, most prominently by Aron and Bell.[12] This current had its 1970s outgrowths (post-industrial society, technocratic society), and again the theorists of deideologisation were chiefly sociologists. According to the Polish sociologist Morawski, this was because social scientists, and sociologists in particular, now performed a role similar to that played earlier by classical political economists. They supplied information and formulated laws about social development and hoped, with the help of sociotechnics, to affect it.[13]

What follows from this is that much of the ideological debate between Marxists and non-Marxists has been conducted in recent times along a sociological dimension, whereas previously it centred primarily on economic aspects. There are many reasons for this shift of focus. Since Lenin, Marxist models of society have emphasised political and social factors as strongly as economic ones. Marxism's stress on the unity of theory and practice and on its own active role in history has been reflected in the attention paid by socialist states to the question of social engineering, that is to say, to a course which aims at implanting socialist values throughout society. Once again here sociologists must perforce play the leading role. Their importance becomes all the greater after the basic sectors of the economy of a country are transformed and socialised. The main task then becomes to socialise social entities as well, for example, to transform the consciousness of particular classes, to mobilise political support for the new course, and so on. An increasing number of sociologists have also been represented amongst the non-Marxist participants in the ideological debate. Economic attacks on the weaknesses of socialism and legitimations of the strength of the mixed capitalist economy were largely undermined by the actual performances of the rival system. Western sociologists have had to take up the slack and have sought to uncover the social fallibilities of the socialist system or, at the least, to discover the social characteristics both systems supposedly have in common. At the same time in the post-war period sociology as a discipline has generally been a more dynamic and innovative one than economics. It comes as no surprise to find that the most creative and systematic models of historical development constructed in the last two decades are the products of sociologists, especially those who to some degree had have some affiliation with Marxism, for example, the Frankfurt School, the American New Left and the French neo-Marxists. For these reasons, amongst others, it has been sociologists who have carried on the ideological debate dominated initially by political economists and later by philosophers.

The end-of-ideology thesis, like the associated theory of political convergence, belongs now to history.[14] But before becoming outmoded these theories were able to inspire much of later Western sociological thinking on the subject of ideology. The types of assumption contained in the models of post-industrial or technocratic societies derived in part from the end-of-ideology thesis include the views that ideology constitutes a phenomenon (a) which is withering away, having lost much of its historical importance in an increasingly 'rational' world; (b) which has been so greatly transformed by functional imperatives that it cannot be treated as possessing an autonomous existence, though this existence itself is not questioned; (c) which is so quickly and so repeatedly transformed in our technological civilisation that it represents, at most, a passive philosophical product of a society in much the same way as do artistic or literary movements.

Before we proceed to look for an adequate definition and model of ideology which could be applied and operationalised in an examination of a socialist society, it would prove valuable to consider several of the more important models of ideology which have been constructed by Western sociologists in recent years, that is, after the end of the end-of-ideology discussion. The types of assumption they contain, which generally are held to apply to all industrial societies, socialist and capitalist, will be relevant to the analysis of the role of ideology in a socialist state that we will adopt and strive to apply. Likewise their conceptual frameworks and tools of analysis may help us arrive at a suitable research design. We have selected four macro-analyses of ideology representing the main schools of thought in Western sociology in recent years: the Frankfurt School (Habermas), the structuralist current (Althusser), the materialist explanation (Therborn) and the American reflexive sociology approach (Gouldner). Obviously these do not exhaust all the recent thinking on ideology which has taken place in the West, but they do provide an insight into how this thinking has developed and where it is going.

For Habermas science and technology have become the most important variables in social development. They lead a quasi-autonomous existence and are in very great measure responsible for promoting economic growth. In technological societies most people are becoming depoliticised, a pattern which is fully sanctioned by the technocratic ideology. This technocratic ideology has a peculiar quality. On the one hand it is less 'ideological' than all previous ideologies because it does not instil the kind of false consciousness which makes people believe their interests are being pursued when they are not, a principle which governed the great nineteenth-century ideologies. On the other hand it is an ideology which has a more general dimension than previous ones. It is at the same time imperceptible (transparent) and programmatic (fetishism of science). Technocracy is, for Habermas, more than just an ideology: the type of consciousness it generates consists of eliminating the distinction between theory and practice. It reflects the new relationship between the now less-influential traditional institutional framework, composed of the socio-cultural environment which continues to enforce social rules and conventions, and new rational, goal-oriented systems of action which have become autonomous, that is, which apply instrumental or strategic models of action involving rational choice, technical rules based on empirical knowledge, and the like. A technocratic ideology produces, in short, rational and instrumental behaviour whilst diminishing the significance of generally accepted social behaviour.[15]

In addition to possessing these qualities, a technocratic ideology differs from older ideologies in two further respects. Firstly it posits that all class conflict produced by the existence of private capital will be resolved through a process involving compromise and adjustments within the economic system. Unlike older ideologies, it cannot legitimise the use of coercion in settling social strife. Secondly, and related to the first point, technocracy seeks to obtain the loyalty of the masses through a system of allocation of goods and services which ensures that everyone's private needs will be satisfied. That is to say, it wishes to buy the support of the masses by offering them the goods and services they desire. In this respect the achievements of a technological society are measured not by its political performance but by the way in which it succeeds in harmoniously distributing free time and money to its members.

A useful starting-point in a critical appraisal of a model of technological society such as that constructed by Habermas is Morawski's observation that 'due to their elasticity, novel phraseology and weighty subject matter, theories of post-industrial societies constitute an "export" version of capitalist ideology, intended for use in socialist countries amongst others'. This ideology can find particularly fertile ground, Western proponents of the model hold, in those socialist states which are combining a structural with a scientific–technological revolution. The latter is, of course, a policy stressed in party programmes (five-year plans, party Congress resolutions) in socialist countries from the late 1960s onwards. But the major methodological flaw in these theories, Morawski points out, is the way in which the scientific–technological revolution is treated in isolation from the social, economic and political conditions extant in a given country.[16] Furthermore, they assume, as Habermas does, that science and technology will replace such traditional dynamic factors operating in societies as property relations, class structure, ideological conflict, and so on. The latter are considered to play only a secondary role in affecting the social development of technological societies.

The stress on efficiency, competence and scientific knowledge is converted into a new ideal of social justice which, in essence, is regarded by supporters of the technocratic model as neutral in relation to social classes. In practice these values, which represent the central principles of the technocratic ideology, serve only to maintain the existing economic and social order. In heuristically integrating the scientific and political spheres, technocracy assumes that the ruling elite can be treated as an independent variable which need not be affected by the social changes that technology brings. Where it is accepted that the scientific–technological revolution will indeed affect the structure of power in a society, it is in the limited sense that power will be based on knowledge, that is to say, that a meritocratic system of elite recruitment will result. Political conflict will no longer be relevant in such a society, it is argued. But it is obvious that the technocratic ideology seeks only to maintain the mixed capitalist system on the same point of the political continuum as it currently occupies. If Habermas considers depoliticisation to be an important phenomenon of this ideology, it is implicitly to argue that the political status quo will not be challenged. As to the alleged depoliticised nature of this ideology itself, it is held that the rational, fundamentally neutral qualities of scientific reasoning will replace political considerations. But what in fact happens is that science is made to serve political interests, in particular so as to camouflage class contradictions, and not that politics is now to serve scientific interests. One further criticism of technocracy's political character is that advanced by the ecological movements which sprang up in the 1970s: technological progress is a programme the main political priority of which is economic expansion, at the expense of the natural environment and of humanity's place in it. The development of science and technology is no more neutral a policy than are zero growth rate economic programmes or environmental protection. As Larrain points out, the fundamental mistake of the 'technocracy' approach is to see the basis of ideology in scientific rationality. It is itself, therefore, ideological. For 'Science is not in itself ideological, but it may be ideological to claim that it is.'[17]

Even the earlier proponents of the technocratic ideology have begun to express doubts as to its virtues. For example, Daniel Bell stated as long ago as 1971 that the expectations that society would be governed by a type of rationality are diminishing. Increasingly technology is seen as a demonic force pushing humanity towards an inevitable catastrophe, rather than as a solution to the world's social and economic problems.[18] The dangers posed by the technological revolution are reflected in a steadily changing approach to its ideological outgrowth. Rather than accepting technocracy as an ideology which lays claim to political neutrality, some American social scientists have begun to reassert the necessity of confronting Marxism with a more positive and viable alternative ideology. In assessing idealist American thinking on technocratic and post-industrial societies, the Soviet sociologist Kortunow concludes that a tendency to 're-ideologise' issues in social development is emerging. He contends that this is a result of the failures of 'liberal' ideologies, such as technocracy, and of theories of post-industrial society and political convergence successfully to meet the challenge posed by Marxism.[19] If this pattern continues, amplified by the fact that political differences between Marxist and bourgeois ideologies remain much greater than the characteristics that advanced industrial societies have in common, then the models constructed by Habermas, Bell, Brzezinski, Toffler and others who viewed the advance of science and technology in idealist terms seem bound to constitute the false consciousness of that period.[20] Or, as Sohn-Rethel puts it, the technocratic ideology is a contemporary form of alienated consciousness.[21]

Much the same applies to those political actors and social commentators in socialist countries who tended to view the future of technologically advanced socialist states in overly optimistic, uncritical terms. It was argued that the technological and scientific revolution would help break down remaining class barriers in socialist states and would thereby promote the development of a universally accepted, homogeneous, socialist ideology. This view represented a socialist 'end of domestic ideological divergences' thesis. However, as the Czech sociologist Richta has warned, ideological debate is likely to increase rather than to diminish in technologically advanced socialist societies, and this for two very important reasons. Firstly more and more people will have access to vital information and will want to participate in debates on policy. Secondly the choices facing society will be more profound and far-reaching than ever before: they will centre on the type of civilisation and the type of person we are striving to mould. The different options available will necessarily bring about conflict and dissonance along an ideological dimension. The most significant polarisation will involve those supporting the continued use of science and technology to promote social development, and those opposed to it or, at least, wanting to reduce reliance upon it. Richta concluded that what will be at stake in technologically advanced socialist societies will be the humanist value system that has always been so central to socialist ideology.[22] We can suggest, therefore, that in all technologically based societies – capitalist or socialist – the status of ideology and of ideological values is likely to increase rather than to diminish. They seem bound to continue to involve highly partisan political choices.

In contrast to the views which have implied either the end of ideology or its technocratisation, the structuralist approach seeks to prove the social necessity of ideology. Structuralism, Larrain argues, wants to free Marx from a conception of ideology as 'pure speculation' or false consciousness by implying that ideology has a material existence which determines the subject. 'To reject the concept of ideology as false consciousness, it has to do away with the conception of the subject participating in its origin. Ideology is not a false representation of reality because its source is not the subject but the material reality itself.'[23]

The most notable representative in the structuralist school is the French Marxist Louis Althusser. In *Lenin and philosophy* he stressed that ideology remains a crucial element in the 'reproduction of the conditions of production', that is to say, in the maintenance of an existing social formation. Expanding on the classical Marxist standpoint, he has argued that not only do current relations and conditions of production have to be reproduced for the capitalist system to survive, but also a reproduction of the submission of labour power to the rules of the established order has to take place. This involves ' a reproduction of submission to the ruling ideology for the workers, and a reproduction of the ability to manipulate the ruling ideology correctly for the agents of exploitation and repression so that they, too, will provide for the domination of the ruling class "in words"'.

The means by which this is achieved are, for Althusser, the ideological state apparatuses which include the traditional public and private forms of political socialisation (the school, family, mass media, culture, social organisations). No class can hold state power over a long period, he argues, without at the same time exercising its hegemony over and in the state ideological apparatuses. 'The ideology of the ruling class does not become the ruling ideology by the grace of God, nor even by virtue of the seizure of state power alone. It is by the installation of the ideological state apparatuses in which this ideology is realised and realises itself that it becomes the ruling ideology.' Conversely it is ultimately the ruling ideology which is realised in these apparatuses: what unifies the diversity of these social institutions is their functioning within the framework of the ruling ideology. Ideological state apparatuses are not only the stake but also the site of class struggle.

Up to this point Althusser's analysis follows along traditional Marxist lines. He stresses the central importance of ideology in affecting, and being affected by, relations and conditions of production, and the interaction it has with other elements in the political and legal superstructure. Moreover he describes how the school has replaced the church as the dominant contemporary state ideological apparatus, and how it is represented by the ruling bourgeois ideology as a neutral environment purged of all ideological connotations. He refutes all recent attempts to perceive a deideologisation of political life and shows very systematically how even 'private' or semi-autonomous areas of social life are inevitably ideological. Where Althusser begins to depart from classic Marxist thinking on ideology is in his adoption of a view which he describes as 'radically different' from the 'positivist and historicist thesis of *The German ideology*', which holds that ideology has no history because the only existing history is the history of concrete individuals. Althusser imputes to Marx a concept of ideology which is an imaginary assemblage, a 'pure dream, empty and vain, constituted by the "day's residues" from the only full and positive reality, that of the concrete history of concrete material individuals materially producing their existence'. Because Marx stated, and this only very indirectly, that ideology has no history and is therefore an imaginary element (his reference was to metaphysics and ethics, and not to ideology directly), Althusser concludes that *The*

German ideology is not Marxist. For him a correct Marxist approach to the concept is to see ideology as the way in which people express their experience of the material conditions of existence, not simply as the expression of their relation to these material conditions. According to this approach, both objective and experienced relations of existence can be identified; and since ideology is the way in which people express how they actually relate to objective conditions, it therefore involves both types of relations. Departing again from the conventional Marxist view, Althusser suggests that what is represented in ideology is not the system of the real relations which govern the existence of individuals but the imaginary relation of those individuals to the real relations in which they live. A second thesis which he presents is that ideology possesses a material existence: it must always exist in an apparatus and its practices, and this existence must be material. In Althusser's words, 'the existence of the ideas of a subject's belief is material in that his ideas are his material actions inserted into material practices governed by material rituals which are themselves defined by the material ideological apparatus from which derive the ideas of that subject'. What follows on from this and represents Althusser's final proposition is that ideology, being a material phenomenon, has the function of transforming concrete individuals into subjects.[24]

At the core of Althusser's considerations on ideology is the belief that social consciousness or, as he prefers, imagination represents a factor as important as (perhaps even more important than) material conditions in determining the substance of an ideology, this being so because imagination itself has a separate material existence. For him ideology seems to constitute a form of consciousness and materialism simultaneously, although it may be either true or false in relation to material conditions. In claiming that *The German ideology* is not Marxist, he is rejecting, or perhaps ignoring, the exhortation contained in Marx's Preface to the work which says that it is time to free men from the chimeras, ideas, dogmas and other creations which they have brought into existence and which now enslave them. Marx noted ironically that men do not drown because of the thought that they are heavy. Likewise the imaginary relations of individuals to the real relations under which they live carry no weight unless they are accompanied by some kind of praxis, which means that they are real relations after all. Althusser's thesis is correct in so far as ideas and ideologies, as he develops later, take on a proper material existence and become a constituent in real material relations. But this view is neither new nor original, for Gramsci and to a lesser degree Kautsky and Plechanov also described the semi-autonomous existence of ideas and their historical force. An inherent weakness of Althusser's propositions is his belief that the consciousness of a social group may become the major determinant of its ideology, and less so the real relations which affect it. In fact, if we have understood his argument well, this consciousness may be either true or false: its nature will not diminish the influence it exerts on the development of a group's ideology. By introducing the intervening variable of experience of real relations, he proposes a model of ideology which is subject-oriented (although, as we have noted, the structuralist approach sought to diminish the importance of subject) and may theoretically have only a very tenuous relationship to conditions in the material world. Marx, in contrast, made it clear that it is the economic base which makes men adopt the ideas they do: 'Men are the producers of their conceptions, ideas, etc. – real, active men, as they are conditioned by a definite development of their productive forces and of the intercourse corresponding to these, up to its highest forms.'[25]

What Althusser seems to be arguing above all is that ideology, being based on men's subjective experience of material existence, can never be neutral and can never not exist. Material conditions which may seem objective and neutral, such as the legal and educational systems which constitute the foundation of a political framework, or the means of production, increasingly based on scientific and technological values, will not be experienced as objective and neutral by 'concrete individuals'. But Althusser arrives at this result by postulating that ideology is the artefact of human experience and not of material relations and conditions themselves; and for him neither the first nor the second is any more value-free. This is where the main value and 'dilettantism' of his model lie: whilst most other contemporary theorists, Marxists and non-Marxists alike, have tried to describe the link between the evolution of ideological thought and changing material conditions and relations, Althusser has adapted the classic Marxist model and focused on the significance of the relationships between existence and experience and between experience and ideology. It is in this context that he is obliged to polemicise against the 'materialism and positivism' of Marx's *The German ideology*. In doing so he substitutes for Marx's idealism of historicism his own 'transcendental idealism of the eternal ideology'.[26]

The materialist explanation of ideology put forward by Göran Therborn seeks to build on Althusser's structuralist approach. In particular it reintroduces the centrality of materialism in determining ideology, which Althusser had largely abandoned. Therborn disagrees with the proposition that components of the superstructure were fundamentally epiphenomena consisting of forms of illusion and miscognition. Rather, ideologies had to be seen 'as complex social processes of "interpellation" or address, speaking to us'. They included 'both everyday notions and "experience" and elaborate intellectual doctrines, both the "consciousness" of social actors and the institutionalised thought-systems and discourse of a given society'. In this way they resembled more closely 'the cacophony of sounds and signs of a big city street than ... the text serenely communicating with the solitary reader'.

Whilst it is heuristically possible to identify ideologies according to their source, topic, content or interpellated subject, Therborn argues that 'as ongoing processes of interpellation, they have no natural boundaries, no natural criteria distinguishing one ideology from another or one element of an ideology from its totality. Particularly in today's open and complex societies, different ideologies, however defined, not only coexist, compete, and clash, but also overlap, effect and contaminate one another.'

Therborn's major contention is that 'ideologies do not operate as immaterial ideas or interpellations. They are always produced, conveyed and received in particular, materially circumscribed social situations and through special means and practices of communication, the material specificity of which bears upon the efficacy of a given ideology.' This materialist conception is most prominent in a number of propositions which, he argues, govern the structure and generation of ideological systems. For example, he posits that all ideologies operate in a material matrix of affirmations and sanctions, and that ideological change is always dependent upon non-ideological, material change. The dominant mode of production is identified as one important determinant of such change. In contrast, class structuring of ideology is interpreted more flexibly by Therborn than by classic Marxist theory. According to Therborn, class struggle 'in itself does not transcend the mode of exploitation and domination on which it is based and in which it operates'. Moreover, 'it cannot be logically argued that a socialist ideology ... is implicit in working-class existence and therefore forms part of working-class ideology'.

The most that can be said is that there is a strong selective affinity between the two. Rather than adopting the concept of class ideology, Therborn speaks of 'class-specific core themes of discourse that vary enormously in concrete form and degree of elaboration'.

The dialectical nature of ideology is brought out in his ascription to it of the dual functions of subjection and qualification. An ideology helps subject the human being to a particular order, and it assists in giving him qualifications to perform various social roles. The possibility that contradiction between the two may arise is not ruled out: a change may occur in the qualifications which society requires whilst forms of subjection remain constant, or the latter may be modified whilst qualifications stay the same. In the first case we have a potentially revolutionary situation, in the second underperformance and alienation.

Therborn attaches less importance to ideology's role in promoting legitimacy, consensus and class consciousness. This is because these three phenomena assume simplistic, rationalist motivation amongst human beings, which is rarely found. Instead he advances alternative ideological patterns, such as 'ideological drift': this occurs when the discourse of rulers is affected by variations in the number of participants in ideological discussion. An example cited is the realignment of the Swedish peasantry in the 1930s, but a more contemporary case may be the Solidarity period in Poland. The sudden entry of new forces into the political arena, or the withdrawal or suppression of forces hitherto taking part, may cause political confusion, ideological drift and changes in the practices of rulers.

Therborn concludes: 'The power of ideology operates not only in conjunctures of high drama, but in slow, gradual processes as well. Ideologies not only cement systems of power; they may also cause them to crumble and set them drifting like sandbanks, still there though not in the same place and shape.' Explanations for such changes may be found, Therborn suggests, not in analyses of the state of mind of a society at a given time or in the isolated discourse of leaders, but in the materialist basis of society.[27]

The most distinctive feature of Therborn's account of the dynamics of ideological change is the determinism which he assigns to material forces. In many respects it represents a return to the monistic explanations of second-generation Marxists, such as Plechanov and Kautsky. Therborn's 'material matrix' does not produce social formations, but it does produce ideology – the cacophony of the street.

The importance of social consciousness is denigrated, that of social change upgraded. The reaction of Althusser's 'transcendental idealism' is, therefore, centripetal phenomenalism. The process of ideological genesis and transformation is reduced to the classic base–superstructure model which Engels sought to disown in his old age. On the other hand, Therborn puts forth a number of conceptual categories (subjection–qualification, class-specific core themes, ideological drift) which owe little to earlier analyses of ideology, and he refuses to follow well-trodden paths (ideology and legitimacy, consensus, class consciousness). His approach to ideology is both classical and mechanistic, therefore, and innovative and dynamic.

Another school of thought on ideology's position in modern society has been developed by the late American sociologist Alvin Gouldner. In *The dialectic of ideology and technology*, he describes how unfashionable ideology, understood as a belief system about the real world, had become in recent times: it was stigmatised as a 'pathological object', as 'irrational condition', as 'defective discourse', as 'false consciousness' and as 'bad sociology'. For Marx, Gouldner continues, 'ideology was failed science, not authentic science', and for Parsons it acted as sociology's boundary: 'ideology manifests itself as a discrepancy between what is believed and what can be established as scientifically correct'. In defending ideological discourse, Gouldner claims that 'sociology is substantially more ideological and far less scientific than it claims, and ideology is often more rational and even scientific, than sociology conventionally grants'. Not only this: ideologies elude the limits of common sense and the constraining perspective of ordinary language and in this way contribute to rational discourse and rational politics. Whilst ideologies try to synthesise theory and practice by striving both to diagnose reality and to change it, the social sciences claim cognitive superiority on the basis of their rejection of this unity. A further positive attribute of ideology identified by Gouldner lies in its relation to Western society: 'Ideology fosters a politic that may be set off, radically and profoundly, from prosaic bourgeois society with its moral flabbiness, its humdrum acceptance of venality, and its egoism. The conservative ideologist, no less than the radical, is in tension with a bourgeois society that is unashamedly self-seeking and egoistic ... The vulgar venality of the bourgeois thus finds its match in the unembarrassed righteousness of the ideologist.'

For Gouldner the main drawback of ideology is its objectivism, that is, its lack of reflexivity about itself. Ideological discourse focuses one-sidedly on the object, for example, social relations, but it occludes the speaking subject and does not make problematic its own grounds. It pretends to be suprahistorical and supracultural, and it 'entails silence about the speaker, about his interests and his desires, and how these are socially situated and structurally maintained'. In spite of its close attention to these aspects and its fundamental self-awareness, Marxism is regarded by Gouldner as guilty of such objectivism: it may focus on specific sources of lack of reflexivity, for example, class interests, but it never takes into account the cognitive consequences of language, desire and interests.[28]

Gouldner does not accept that the growth of technocracy involves the demise of ideology, or at least a decline in its status. But he suggests that even with an increase in technocratic, scientific and rational–pragmatic consciousness in society, as opposed to ideological discourse, the end result may spell less rationalism rather than more amongst the masses. For more and more people will escape from the technocrat's pressure by indulging in the products of the 'consciousness industry' (radio, television and cinema). Gouldner concludes that a growing number of people in advanced industrial societies are incapable of being reached by either rational–pragmatic or ideological appeals, and are insulated from ideological discourse of all persuasions.

For Gouldner, therefore, ideology is a phenomenon (never strictly defined in the book) which, although fulfilling an important function in society, is dismissed and discarded by just about everyone, from social scientists to the masses. Without going into a critique of his methodology, it should be stressed that the most important point which his analysis leaves in doubt is in what way ideological discourse is related to social conditions and social relations. Whilst convincingly pointing out how science and ideology have developed into rivals because both exhibit similar characteristics, and whilst showing the strength provided by ideological discourse in an otherwise feeble and flabby bourgeois society, Gouldner fails to discuss the reciprocal influence exerted by these factors upon ideology. It is as if ideology led a wholly autonomous existence, cut off from the real world. In this light his call for greater reflexivity amongst ideologues camouflages his own over-reflexivity and subjectivism.

An important heuristic distinction which Gouldner draws in his analysis is between ideology and paradigm. The first entails both the depersonalising of one's own interests and the publicising of private interests. Ideology attempts to resolve the problem of how the pursuit of private interests may generate wider support, and it thus involves large, powerful polities. Paradigms, on the other hand, are grounded in group-restricted interests and as such form a less publicly access-ible symbolic system, that is, they constitute a set of beliefs and symbols of restricted communicability. The relationship between ideology and paradigm is, according to Gouldner, a dialectical one: the first requires that persons transcend their paradigms and their narrow interests, whilst the second disposes persons to compromise their ideologies. Ideologies are, as a consequence, always myths: the generalisation of an interest-grounded paradigm into an ideology is the price which a group pays in order to mobilise the wider support required to achieve its own more limited paradigm. But each group will be ready to stop cooperating with others when it has attained its paradigm. The result is, as Gouldner concludes, that ideologies are not accepted solely for the good reasons that the ideologue puts forward but also for other reasons of which he is unaware and which he cannot control.

The tension generated by ideology's mythologising character has important implications for Gouldner's analysis of the relationship between technocracy and a society's hegemonic class. The latter always requires ideological justification for its rule, but at the same time it is wary of other groups, such as technologues, ideologues and the intelligentsia, formulating their own proper paradigms and thus creating power bases for themselves. As far as scientific experts and technicians are concerned, their claim that their work should be judged by standards of efficiency and that they are not interested in any direct gain for themselves does not hide the fact that they are a specific status group with status interests and a specific paradigm. In this way they may encroach upon the functional autonomy of the hegemonic class, which in all other respects gains power from the growth of technocracy. In his concluding considerations Gouldner applies his ideological model to socialist states as well. He suggests that socialist ideology is a critique not only of capitalist but also of socialist societies. Its ideological egalitarianism undermines its own authoritarian structure. As Holubenko puts it: 'The ruling group is saddled with an ideology which teaches the non-legitimacy of its existence.'[29] The most important fact about ideologies is, Gouldner repeats, that they are always myths, in all societies urging projects that the groups subscribing to them do not fully want. Everywhere ideologies undermine what is because they provide a basis for its critique. In a sense, therefore, what Gouldner is implying is that ideologies and paradigms, ideologues and specific interest groups, the hegemonic elite and its potential rivals, all need, but at the same time compete with, each other. Ideology serves, therefore, as both an integrating and a disintegrating social force.

We restrict our assessment of Gouldner's model of ideology to substantive issues, although Szacki's general observation concerning the methodology used by the American sociologist in an earlier study (*The coming of Western sociology*) seems apposite here, too. Szacki notes that Gouldner's approach is characterised by correct and incorrect statements, accurate and inaccurate observations, simplifications of complex relationships and extrapolations from a crude version of Marxism that is otherwise rejected.[30] The main contention in *The dialectic of ideology and technology* is that ideological discourse is indispensable in modern societies in spite of its limitations, the frictions it generates and the profound 'rational–scientific' advances that have taken place in society. Without ideology society would be deprived of a regulatory mechanism and motivating force. Politics would be reduced to a purely technical process in which the supreme value became manipulation of a social collectivity. To this extent Gouldner's thesis is correct. Likewise his view that technocracy is not a new ideology but actually represses the ideological problem seems justified: 'The new technocracy has not become a mass ideology but, rather, for most of the population obedience is conditioned by the gratification it associates with technocracy.' His distinction between ideology and paradigm is useful, although by no means original, and involves what perhaps could be better described as state, or official, ideology and group ideologies. We return to this point below. His analysis becomes less convincing when he claims that ideologies need always be myths. Although it is true that a general ideology requires support from and acceptance by a plurality of social groups if it is to exist at all, it is incorrect to conclude from this, as Gouldner does, that ideology simply constitutes the sum of the parts, these being group paradigms. An ideology is greater than and qualitatively different from the aggregate of all interests subscribing to it. It represents a wider interest, has more long-term goals and is generally more radical in its prescriptions for society than group paradigms.

Finally Gouldner is on his weakest ground when he attempts to apply his model, which is based on Western capitalist societies, to socialist states. He argues that the same phenomena occur in both types of society. In both ideology is rooted in one-sidedness, in the conflict between the whole and the parts. Each social group possesses interests separating it from others and from the whole. And although ideologies ground their discourse in the interests of the whole (Gouldner cites the example of Marxism striving to transcend partisan class interests), in practice they aim continually at denying the legitimacy of partisan interests and even the reality of partisanship. For Gouldner the result is that Marxism, like liberalism, seeks basically to transform the 'I want' into a 'you should'.[31] Accordingly the ideology of socialist states calls for workers' control of the means of production whilst in fact these are actually controlled by the party and the state. Here a methodological inconsistency has to be pointed out. Gouldner defines ideology as a myth because it is a compromise programme arrived at by divergent interest groups seeking to obtain support for their particularistic goals, none of them being concerned primarily with the overall ideology. Subsequently he attempts to show, using socialist states as an example, that practice is inconsistent with the proclaimed ideology. The problem is that, were it to be consistent, ideology would no longer constitute a myth and, according to Gouldner's definition, would no longer be ideology either. For him socialist ideology must be, by definition, at odds with practice. Setting these issues aside, we can say that the questions he raises are considerably more significant than the sketchy and simplified responses he offers. In particular, if we discard his proposition that the parts (paradigms) equate the whole (ideology) and examine this relationship more carefully, then these components in his model may be useful in tackling the question of ideology's status in a socialist state.

We have presented an account of the way in which four leading Western sociologists – Habermas, Althusser, Therborn and Gouldner – have treated the role of ideology in modern society. All wrote in the 1970s, when the various offshoots of the end-of-ideology thesis were discredited and the search was on to rediscover ideology's importance in governing political and social life. Habermas was fascinated with the potential offered by a technocratic ideology diffusing itself in society. Althusser returned to Marx in order to develop an updated model of the relations between man's ideas and their material foundations. Therborn focused on the materialist determination of ideologies, in particular, on social rather than intellectual processes. Gouldner's reflexive sociology stressed the integrating and disintegrating functions played by ideological discourse. The questions which were raised concerning the role of technology and science, rational goal-oriented systems of action, a person's experience of the material conditions of his or her existence, ideological state apparatuses, subjection–qualification, ideological drift, societal and group interests and their interaction – and the influence of these variables on the development of ideological thought – will appear repeatedly in our examination of ideology in a socialist state. In this respect, they provide valuable analytical insights which overshadow the reservations we have expressed concerning other aspects of these models.

2

Approaches to the study of ideology in a socialist state

Let us seek nothing else in these fables but the errors of the human mind.

de Fontenelle, *Origin of fables*

So far we have considered how different schools of thought have approached the question of ideology's status and function in modern society. In trying to arrive at a further delimitation of the nature of ideology, it would be possible to cite a whole gamut of definitions given by Marxist and non-Marxist scholars which might help us construct an analytical framework useful for an empirical study. A comprehensive survey of concepts of ideology appearing in Polish sociological literature was provided by Wiatr in 1968.[1] This indicated that Polish sociology has, by and large, discarded structural definitions, which identified ideology with belief systems characterised by normative outlooks, or with belief systems offering directives for action, or with false, deforming consciousness. Instead, it stresses ideology's functional relationship with the interests and goals of a given group. Hochfeld, for example, regarded ideologies as systems of social symbols which are correlates of social groups and which, when treated as systems, perform a functional role in affecting a particular group's social relations.[2] For Wiatr 'An ideology is a set of opinions and beliefs which serves social classes, political movements, national – and all other – groups as the foundation and substantiation of their activities.' Socialist ideology is the expression of the consciousness of the working class, and it consists of a systematised integration of normative values, interpretations of reality, predictions about the future and directives for action.[3] In order to study ideology in a socialist state on its own terms, we adopt, accordingly, these general definitions given by a leading Polish scholar.

24

Because the concept of ideology is viewed in many different ways, there are numerous methodological approaches to its analysis. The most important difference between these approaches is the level of abstraction at which each treats ideology. At the most general level, it can be analysed as the 'state of mind' of a society, at the most particular level as an individual's system of beliefs. In order to arrive at an analytical framework for the study of ideology, not only is a general definition required: a decision also has to be taken concerning the level of abstraction at which the concept will be operationalised. We look briefly at some of the ways that have been put forward to operationalise the concept.

Perhaps the most illustrious approach is Mannheim's distinction between ideology and Utopia. The first consists of a system of thought which aims at maintaining the social status quo or, conversely, 'fails to take account of the new realities applying to a situation'. The Utopian distortion tries to change reality, for it originates in a mentality which is 'beyond the present'. Mannheim's total conception of ideology concerns 'the characteristics and composition of the total structure of the mind', and that becomes the realm of sociological knowledge. Sociological truth consists, therefore, of a conjunction of these two belief systems of partial truths. He acknowledges the methodological difficulties involved in answering 'the crucial question ... how the totality we call the spirit, "Weltanschauung", of an epoch can be distilled from the various "objectifications" of that epoch'. But he insists that ultimately 'every idea must be tested by its congruency with reality'.[4]

At the other extreme of complexity is the type of approach designed meticulously to quantify data relating to ideology. This current represents the mainstream American methodology, and it may be illustrated by Robert Lane's complex typology consisting of five factors which are neither easily quantifiable nor easily described. It is summarised in the hypothesis: 'For any society: an existential base creating certain common experiences interpreted through certain cultural premises by men with certain personal qualities in the light of certain social conflicts produces certain political ideologies.'[5] Here ideology is viewed as a product of the confluence of variables so diverse and simultaneously so abstract that its heuristic value is negligible. Moreover it is treated in much the same way as Althusser's individualised 'personal experience' schema. Lane's typology is unhelpful precisely because it lacks

those analytical features of a model which allow it to be operationalised.

The methodological approach to ideology which seems well able to
avoid the pitfalls of the universalism latent in the sociology of
knowledge method and the specificity common in positive sociology is
what can best be described as gradational. It retains several levels of
abstraction of the concept and allows for a choice to be made as to
which level will be the subject of a study. Rather than distinguishing
between what is ideological and what is not, this approach seeks to
answer the question: how ideological is a phenomenon? Put another
way, it can be represented on a continuum ranging from long-term
goals to immediate ones. The gradational approach to ideology has
been considered and developed by a number of social scientists, but it
has rarely been applied in systematic, empirical studies dealing with
the concept. Particularly surprising is the fact that although most
writers have recognised the heuristic advantages of this methodology
in examining ideology in the socialist states in particular (in which
goals are more clearly spelled out), they have not treated the concept
in any other way than at the most general level of abstraction. Often
the underlying reason for this has been a polemical one.

The most basic example of the gradational approach is the
dichotomy between general, long-term theoretical objectives and
specific, short-term practical ones. Lenin distinguished in 1911
between 'general fundamental aims which do not change with turns
of history so long as the fundamental relations between classes do not
change' and 'the aims of direct and immediate action [which] have
changed very markedly during this period [the previous six years]'.[6]
Schurmann has shown that the total ideology of the Chinese Communist Party was made up of Marxism–Leninism as its theory (or
pure ideology), and Mao Tse-tung thought as its thought (or practical ideology). As a leading article in the party newspaper stated in
1964, 'the thought of Mao Tse-tung is one which ... united the
universal truths of Marxism–Leninism with the practice of revolution
and construction in China and creatively developed Marxism–
Leninism'.[7] These distinctions correspond generally to what is often
considered to differentiate the concepts of ideology and doctrine or, in
Gouldner's terminology, ideology and group-oriented paradigms: it
is the universality or particularism of the interests represented that
serves as the basis for the dichotomy.

Several analytical frameworks using the gradational approach have been specifically adapted to study ideology in socialist states. Not unexpectedly, much of this research has focused on the Soviet Union. More surprisingly, little of this has been conducted since the late 1960s. The perceived absence of dramatic ideological innovation in the Brezhnev era appears to be the principal reason for scholars' recent lack of interest in the subject. We wish to look briefly at three studies of Soviet ideology – Barrington Moore's classic work, and two recent analytically fruitful approaches.

Moore's *Soviet politics: the dilemma of power*, completed in 1950, remains a landmark study of the role of ideology under socialism. It set out to examine the interaction between Communist ideology and Soviet political practices from the pre-Revolutionary period to high Stalinism. Changes in doctrine were identified by comparing official speeches, articles by prominent officials and changes in legislation over a period of time. A broad spectrum of issue-areas was analysed, extending from the organisation of authority and the bureaucratic state to labour–management relations and the transformation of the peasantry. Moore's conclusion was that 'On the whole, one is likely to be more impressed with the flexibility of Communist doctrine than with its rigidity.'

He also proposed a scheme to trace the evolution of an ideology. Crucial to this framework was the distinction between an organisation's official (or formal) ideology and its leaders' operative (or informal) ideology. The first consisted of 'publicly stated or printed programs and pronouncements of goals and means, phrased in the symbols common to the original doctrine or to its officially sanctioned adaptations'. The second was composed of basic, often unstated, assumptions made by leaders, which represented 'a compromise between means and ends or ... between power considerations and original doctrines'. Moore suggested that 'the operating ideology of the leaders is more sensitive to environmental factors and the influence of success and failure than is an organised system of overtly expressed doctrine'. In addition, shifts in operative ideology were likely, sooner or later, to produce changes in the officially promulgated doctrine.[8]

Zaslavsky's recent account of changes in Soviet ideology distinguishes between the terms 'doctrine' and 'ideology'. The first is identified with Marxism and the second with its current application. Thus he asserts that the most striking characteristic of Marxist doctrine in various periods of Soviet history is the limited and gradual nature of the change which it has undergone. Three reasons are cited for this: (1) 'the exceptional explanatory strength and absorptive capacity of Marxism'; (2) 'its role as the sole official ideology in a single-party system, where Marxism is used to legitimate the distribution of power and the performance of roles'; and (3) 'Marxism, as the dominant ideology of the international communist movement, plays a unifying role which also prevents it from undergoing major rapid changes.'

For Zaslavsky the major modification can be found at the level of the actual use of doctrine, that is, operative ideology. Expounded through private language and word of mouth, this 'tends to describe experience correctly and predict realistically what is happening to a person'. His conclusion is that two processes take place in current Soviet ideology which contradict and yet supplement each other. Firstly there is a widening of the gap between doctrine and operative ideology: a process of ficticisation occurs. 'The Marxist doctrine, transmitted through official public language, seems to be far from the "real state of life" and to be meant "for them" – for opponents and enemies or for those who are uninitiated and unworthy of knowing the truth.' Secondly there is also consolidation of doctrine with operative ideology. This process serves to meet the needs of important social groups (the highly skilled, professionsls, students) which require a rationally defensible ideology. To this end major changes in the central doctrine have been effected, most significantly, replacing the ultimate goal – a Communist society – with the concept of a 'Soviet way of life'. Zaslavsky states: 'The concept of the "Soviet way of life" can successfully serve as a sort of a middle-level theory mediating between the doctrine and the operating ideology of Soviet Marxism. It aids in consolidating both tiers of Soviet Marxism into a consistent and cogent entity, a Soviet world-view acceptable to and convincing for a considerable part of the Soviet new middle-class.' For him the components of this middle-level theory are the leading role of the party and the planned economy, full employment and the welfare state, the necessity to maintain ideological discipline, an absence of individual freedoms, and socio-economic inequalities.[9]

Like many theorists before him, notably Lichtheim[10] and Drucker,[11] Zaslavsky distinguishes between, on the one hand, the philosophy and theory and, on the other hand, the practice and politics of Marxism. This is a perfectly acceptable approach, but once the two have been defined in mutually exclusive terms, it should not be surprising to find, as Zaslavsky does, that they differ in reality as well. He does not compare the aims, principles or values that Soviet doctrine and Soviet operative ideology espouse, but instead falls into a tautology: doctrine is far from the 'real state of life' whilst operative ideology 'describes experience correctly'. In effect his understanding of doctrine and operative ideology corresponds to Joravsky's distinction between 'grand' and 'petty' ideologies in Soviet ideology, the first presenting unverifiable beliefs, the second presenting verifiable but unverified beliefs.[12] Clearly an examination of the unverified beliefs latent in operative ideology is not the way to try to verify the unverifiable beliefs of doctrine. This methodological confusion undermines the credibility of Zaslavsky's conclusions which, again, are based not on systematic, empirical research but rather on speculation and impression. The third category of analysis introduced by Zaslavsky (the theory of the 'Soviet way of life') can, in reality, be subsumed under both doctrine (a philosophical outlook) and operative ideology (political practice). It appears to follow on from his substantive, not methodological, considerations.

Not all that dissimilar a classification is proposed in Amalrik's otherwise polemical article concerning Soviet ideology. He identifies three levels at which ideologies function: (1) superideologies, that is, general social philosophies (Marxism, liberalism, nationalism); (2) real ideologies, that is, political doctrines (totalitarian ones, such as neo-Stalinist Marxism or nationalism; and pluralist ones, such as liberal democracy or liberal Marxism); and (3) subideologies, that is, what he calls 'political emotions' (the reformism of the middle class, the egalitarianism of the masses).[13] The proposition that ideologies differ according to the extent of their universalism or particularism is commonplace, as we have seen, and there can be no quarrel with Amalrik on this point. On the other hand, his failure to explain the relationship between each ideological level and social variables cannot be justified. Nor can his inability to tell us what produces superideologies, real ideologies and subideologies.

Amalrik makes the important point that the ideology of a group whilst it is in opposition tends to differ from that of the same group when it seizes power. This view is shared by a Polish *émigré* writer: for Hertz, ideology runs into a crisis the moment the movement which it encompasses takes power and is able to implement its belief system. The ideology then undergoes a 'practical verification', being confronted with the reality it seeks to change. Each ideology is inevitably put to this test, and the way in which it responds determines the course of history.[14]

When we turn to studies of ideology in East European states, we discover that their number is very limited. It is commonly assumed that the ideology dominant in the Soviet Union at a given time is simply transferred to these client states; hence analyses of their ideologies would be largely redundant. This view persists in spite of general recognition of the specificities of the Polish road to socialism, of Hungary's 'goulash communism', of Czechoslovakia's doctrinaire restoration and of Yugoslavia's long-standing dilettantism. Nevertheless, several important works have been published, and we look briefly at their analytical approaches and general conclusions.

The most systematic study of ideology in an East European state is Ross Johnson's description of the transformation of Yugoslavia's official ideology between 1945 and 1953. He accepts Brzezinski and Huntington's conception of ideology as officially proclaimed texts having a systematic nature and being institutionalised through the Communist party. Political ideas can be appraised at three levels: (1) general philosophical assumptions; (2) doctrinal elements; and (3) action programmes, which are often indistinguishable from policy courses. For Brzezinski 'Doctrine is thus the politically crucial link between dogmatic assumptions and pragmatic action.'[15] Doctrine, action programmes and concrete political developments directly relevant to ideological change form the core of Johnson's study.

Johnson, then, compares Soviet and Yugoslav doctrine on a number of selected issues. At the most general level, Stalinist and Titoist interpretations of the notion of a people's democracy are contrasted. At a more specific level, their respective views on theories of the state, self-management, socialisation of the countryside, leading role of the party and foreign policy are juxtaposed. The evolution of Titoist ideology is traced using Plenum and Congress reports on the then Communist Party of Yugoslavia. Johnson concludes that ideological change in Yugoslavia was largely reactive, synthetic and derivative in this period, and marked a return to Marx and Lenin rather than an extension of post-Leninist thought.[16]

The most significant study undertaken of ideology in Hungary is that of Laszlo. He is less concerned with gradual evolution in leadership ideology than with overt ideological campaigns launched by the party after 1945 and with debates over issues that had been 'declassified' from Communist dogma. By 'campaigns' he understands periodic but intensive efforts made to propagate classics of Marxism–Leninism, in other words, agitprop work. By 'debates' is meant not 'pseudo-debates' but genuine confrontation of views on carefully screened topics, for example, socialist realism, the role of the church and national culture. Laszlo identifies four distinct periods in the ideological development of the Hungarian Communist leadership: (1) the transitional phase (1945–8), characterised by little ideological cogency; (2) *Gleichschaltung* (1949–56), when ideology always had an 'administratively determined ending'; (3) reorientation (1957–60), when in public ideology was 'vulgarised' but otherwise diversity flourished; and (4) liberalisation (from 1961), when the dominant principle governing ideological debate was that 'Marxism must be turned and twisted until the truth is wrung from it.'

Laszlo uses textbooks, pamphlets and articles of the period to quantify the extensiveness and intensiveness of ideological discussion, but he discards reports of formal party meetings. As a result, although his conclusions are persuasive, the official ideology of the leadership is not as clear as the importance of an issue at a given time. In part, he refutes this criticism by dismissing the importance of official ideology: 'the ground is not yet ready for the large-scale implementation of Communist ideology'.[17]

Studies of ideological developments in the German Democratic Republic have focused on the Ulbricht period, during which the official ideology of the SED leadership was often more innovative and unorthodox than that adopted anywhere else in Eastern Europe. McCauley's analysis of Marxism–Leninism in the GDR contains an incisive account of the new concepts propounded by Ulbricht in the 1960s, for example, the economic system of socialism, developed social system of socialism and socialist human community.[18] More recently, Baylis has examined orthodoxy and innovation in GDR ideology in terms of a fivefold classification of the 'ideological phenomenon'. The first category he identifies is 'ritualistic orthodoxy', the exhortative writings found in party journals 'primarily intended to transmit the current official party wisdom to the cadres, enabling them, in turn, to market it among the general population'. The second, 'corrective orthodoxy', consists of 'the proclamation of a new "line" (often only a new slogan restating familiar assertions) previously agreed to by the Politburo, sometimes including the criticism of past error'. A third category is 'adaptive orthodoxy', that is, usually minor departures from existing dogma, most often found in debates in specialised periodicals. 'Institutional revisionism' is the fourth category: this term refers to publication and discussion of more comprehensive ideological departures from previous dogma. Such ideological 'trial balloons' are eventually dropped, but they do contribute to the emergence of later adaptive orthodoxy. Finally, 'ideological revisionism' signifies both 'left' and 'right' deviations which pose threats to the authority of the party leadership. In his study, Baylis concentrates on the officially sanctioned institutional revisionism of the Ulbricht period and on both adaptive orthodoxy and dissident-led revisionism under Honecker. He concludes that the static ideology which has evolved in the 1970s will be difficult to sustain in the harsher economic climate of the 1980s.[19]

It is surprising that no comprehensive studies exist of ideology in Eastern Europe's largest state – Poland – or its historically most democratic one – Czechoslovakia. In the latter case, considerable attention has been given to ideological developments up to the time of the 1968 Warsaw Pact invasion.[20] In the case of Poland, the lack of such research is perplexing and can only be explained by the concern of scholars to keep up to date with dramatically changing political developments since 1968. The study of ideology appears to have been assigned secondary importance during this stormy political period. Polish scholars themselves have offered few ideas on how to study ideology, in spite of the crucial importance that has been attached to this issue by the political leadership during recent crises. For example, no explicit reference to the study of ideology is contained in an otherwise wide-ranging collection of methodological essays written by Polish scholars and published in the West.[21] The more conventional approach to ideology in Poland is exegesis of Marx's writings on the subject.[22]

The political scientist Wiatr does provide some analytical proposals for the study of ideology. He has argued that a socialist ideology is characterised by a dialectical, or 'affirmative–critical', attitude to the reality it confronts, neither completely accepting nor completely rejecting this. Since it is locked in a dialectical relationship with reality, two types of regress may occur in its further development. Firstly ideological deformation may take place, which is not solely the result of errors committed by individual political leaders. Secondly ideological change may be retarded, even in a socialist society, compared to the material changes taking place.[23] Implicit in these observations is the distinction between the ideology of a group or class in opposition and its adaptation to the conditions of rule or power. Wiatr's analysis suggests that the distinction may be extended one step further to ideological changes occurring as a result of the consolidation or institutionalisation of a group in power. With the passage of time, new problems may arise and old solutions may prove inadequate, forcing ideological principles to be modified and made generally more pragmatic. But the danger remains that ideology may be so radically modified as to cease to have any meta-practical significance at all. Or it may not be modified sufficiently to reflect the changes taking place in material conditions. As Hertz argues, the process of the institutionalisation of an ideology may lead to its alienation from the real issues of social life. Ideology becomes transformed into a formal credo which, in practice, is not taken very seriously.[24]

That these dangers are recognised not only by social scientists but also by political leaders may be reflected in the statement made by Brezhnev at the VI Congress of the Polish United Workers' Party (PUWP), held in 1971, in which he observed that errors and mistakes committed in socialist states 'do not originate in the nature of socialism as a social system nor in its goals and principles but, quite the contrary, they should be brought to light in those cases where these principles are unheeded or in some way violated'.[25] We see again the stress that is placed on ideology's dialectical relationship with reality: it must both undergo practical verification and serve as a criterion to evaluate the correctness of practice.

A second Polish analytical framework for the study of ideology is that provided by the sociologist Kwiatkowska. For her, ideology at a general level takes the form of a set of fundamental principles which influence political practice but are themselves relatively autonomous with regard to it. Ideology's relative independence from the course of events promotes conditions in which long-term political goals and programmes can be drawn up. It may also influence the attitudes and behaviour of the public without becoming unduly subjected to their effect, and its content is, as a result, more stable. In contrast, a lower tier in the ideological construct is made up of operational values, that is, the application of a system's fundamental principles to the existing social and political reality. This level of values is not universal enough to be regarded as ideology and is called 'political practice', or 'policy', by Kwiatkowska. The two levels of ideology are rarely found in a state of equilibrium: values governing the adoption and conduct of political policy are very often inconsistent with the fundamental principles of the official ideology. The nature of the relationship between the two reveals what ideological change has taken place. The optimal situation is when the two are not in conflict, and the most dysfunctional case is when the two stand in contradiction to each other.[26] We see, therefore, that the conventional gradational approach is not without exponents in Poland, although again we must refer to the failure to apply the model in empirical research.

Each of these analytical frameworks for the study of ideology in socialist states possesses qualities which are, individually, very useful. The most developed model, however, and the one which appears most susceptible to operationalisation, is that expounded in the works of Martin Seliger. This, too, is based on the now familiar gradational approach:

all political argumentation normally bifurcates into two interacting and intersecting dimensions: the dimensions of fundamental and of operative ideology, as I call them. To the first dimension belong the principles which determine the evaluation of an existing order, and hence the final goals of the movement or party. These principles also include the broadly conceived ways and means in and by which the goals will be realised. The principles which actually underlie the politics and policy recommendations of parties or, as in political and social philosophies in particular, simply reflect more than do other principles the concern with practical and pressing exigencies, constitute the operative dimension.

Seliger thus furnishes a framework within which fundamental and operative ideology can be related: the principles which are contained in fundamental and operative ideology are comparable in that they must interact with each other. But he warns that these principles are not necessarily identical:

Purists and diehards are normally bothered by dissonance between cherished and applied principles, and, in return, they worry the leadership with their rather articulate misgivings – which at least part of the leadership may share but choose to ignore.

Taking Marxism as a case-study, Seliger contends that:

The writings of Marx and Engels already show inconsistencies stemming from the failure to reconcile adherence to theoretical fundaments with concessions to the requirements of their operationalisation in party politics. Almost from the outset Marxists were bedevilled by the erosion of their dogmas by the political opportunities to alleviate the plight of the working classes within the capitalist system.

That is to say, out of practical necessity operative principles began to deviate from fundamental principles.

Seliger recognises, however, that although such gradational comparisons of levels in Marxist ideology can be drawn, they are beset by complexities stemming from certain 'horizontal' anomalies:

The Marxian and Marxist alternation between the insistence on historical inevitability and the plea for purposive action is due, I suggest, to the interference with fundamental principles of the more or less realistic assessment of requirements normally met in terms of operative ideology. The asymmetric profile of an ideology, or of a belief system which combines, like Marxism, philosophy, social science and ideology, is likewise explained by the advantages which the asymmetry between the fundamentals themselves affords for the propagation and preservation of the ideology in question ... The alternating retreat from and resort to socio-economic determination, as well as the highly variegated results ascribed to it, illustrate the impossibility of upholding the identification of ideology with false consciousness.

The implication is that fundamental principles of Marxism differ as a function of treating Marxism as a philosophy, social science or ideology. We have discussed how Marxists themselves do not see inconsistencies between these various approaches. At the basis of Marxism is the contention that it is able in fact to integrate philosophy, science and ideology in a dialectical way. Its fundamental principles do not themselves change according to the perspective taken because Marxism is not reducible in this way. In this context Seliger's charge of asymmetry in Marxism's profile seems to be unfounded. This does not invalidate his basic tenet that dissonance does occur in the vertical dimension between fundamental principles and operative ideology.

The same writer points out what the objective limitations of an ideology are: it is delimited by material conditions in the sense that it has to cope with certain material conditions and not others. Similarly an ideology is limited by the existing configurations of beliefs and disbeliefs, which affect the propagation of an ideology's objectives. Seliger concludes: 'The fate of Marxism furnishes a singularly instructive confirmation of this rule.' That is to say, Marxism like other 'grand' ideologies is ineluctably interrelated with the 'realities' of the time. But he concedes that it would be wrong to distinguish between a pure and a practical ideology of Marxism: for Marxism is based on praxis, which means it serves as a tool for changing history and as a criterion for historical evaluation. Moreover, 'the direct awareness in Marxist ideology of two-dimensional argumentation' mitigates any gap that may arise.

To examine the nature of any ideology, Marxism included, Seliger proposes a dichotomy based on the relationship between its fundamental principles (F) and its operative ideology (OI). He reiterates that 'ideology applied in action inevitably bifurcates into two dimensions of argumentation: that of fundamental principles, which determine the final goals and the grand vistas in which they will be realised, and which are set above the second dimension, that of the principles which actually underlie policies and are invoked to justify them'. He provides a schematic exemplification of an ideal-type situation in which fundamental principles are related both to their counterparts in another dimension, that of operative ideology, and to each other along the same dimension:

$$F \quad (p_1 \longleftrightarrow p_2 \longleftrightarrow p_3 \longleftrightarrow p_n)$$
$$\updownarrow \qquad \updownarrow \qquad \updownarrow \qquad \updownarrow$$
$$OI \quad (p_1 \longleftrightarrow p_2 \longleftrightarrow p_3 \longleftrightarrow p_n)$$

Obviously divergencies between principles in both vertical and horizontal directions are unavoidable in the ideology of any party holding power or having a chance to do so. The necessity of making operational decisions generates conflict both between a fundamental principle and its counterpart in the other dimension and among principles in the same dimension. The diagram below, found in Seliger's work, illustrates a case in which, for reasons of expediency, the unforeseen results of the attempted realisation of p_1 of F leads to the replacement of OIp_1 by p_1a:

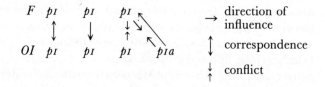

As an example, Seliger describes how Marxism aims at the abolition of private ownership (Fp_1). In practice, however, a corollary of this principle in the operative dimension – fairly equal wages (OIp_1) – becomes displaced by renewed wage differentials (OIp_1a). The initial conflict between Fp_1 and OIp_1a is reconciled, in this case, by a further adaptation of the former, although theoretically, of course, the two need not necessarily be in correspondence with each other. For there are, according to Seliger, two possible directions of adaptation: a return to F or an acceptance of OI. The latter would mean retaining the change of principles in OI (from p_I to p_{Ia}) and, accordingly, changing the corresponding F principle from p_I to p_{Ia}.[27]

This analytical framework, centring on the relationship between fundamental principles and operative ideology on the one hand, and on the relationship between principles within each dimension on the other, seems to be most constructive and susceptible to operationalisation in an examination of ideological continuity and change in a socialist state. It seems to us, however, that one other very important concept, which Seliger did not consider in detail, has to be clarified and put into context. This concerns the question of policy. According to Rose: 'Policy-making is, unfortunately, an ambiguous phrase. It can refer to the intentions of politicians as well as to the outcomes of their activities. Usually it refers to intentions rather than consequences ... In the language of politics, any set of recommendations about what ought to be done or what will be done when power changes hands constitutes a policy.'[28] According to Rose and Wiatr: 'Scholars use the term with a very wide variety of meanings, some overlapping and some mutually exclusive ... The term can be used to refer to a set of expectations and intentions of governors, to a series of actions, to the consequences of a policy or to all these together.' [29] Seliger himself does not define policy but stresses generally that 'to whatever degree policies conform with fundamental principles, "operative ideology" denotes the argumentation in favour of the policies actually adopted by a party. It is "ideology" because it devises, explains and justifies action. It is "operative" inasmuch as it is predicated on what is actually done or recommended for immediate action.' This proclivity towards 'two-dimensional argumentation' in political discourse is a product of ideology's confrontation with reality. Scalapino, cited by Seliger, noted 'the rebound of policies upon long-standing ideological commitments, and also that policies, apart from mirroring change, cause inconsistencies between basic and practical commitments'.[30] Seliger adds that 'ideologies must change with policies, or rather in some manner reflect their change', although 'we cannot simply infer actual policy from the dimension of final goals and fundamental principles – or vice versa'.[31] From the interaction that takes place between ideology (at whichever level of argumentation) and policy, it is clear that in examining ideological change we cannot ignore policy issues. Nevertheless it is just as important to circumscribe the attention we give to policy if our study is not to become unmanageable. Our approach to this concept is grounded, therefore, in the incorporation of the 'expectations and intentions of governors', and the argumentation used to support them, into the notion of operative ideology. It is the actions of rulers (policy formulation such as decrees and legislation) and the consequences (policy implementation) of these that we understand as policy. These are considered in our study only in so far as operative ideology has something to say about them. This distinction is of central importance to our analytical framework, for our objective is to conduct not a policy analysis but a content analysis of ideological declarations made by leaders.

Elsewhere we have set out the Marxist view of the interplay between the economic base and the political and ideological superstructure.[32] The classic Marxist approach is to ascribe primacy to economic relations in determining social development, although this is still far from claiming that all remaining factors play a subsidiary role. Within this general framework we have adopted a somewhat different approach: to examine the effect that one element in the superstructure (political leaders) has on another element (ideology), and vice versa. Whilst promulgating ideological values, political leaders are faced with practical constraints in the conduct of policy, for example, those imposed by the need for system maintenance, consensus building and conflict management. Likewise ideology, whilst at the higher dimension propagating fundamental principles, may undergo modification (as Seliger has described) as the society in which it functions changes. The two are related to the economic base but, simultaneously, to each other as well.

We examine ideological change in terms of the relationship between fundamental principles and 'official' or operative ideology by which rulers justify particular policy courses. It might be expected that the first will remain more or less independent of changes occurring in the second. We consider this question in detail in our final chapter. We also wish to investigate the changes occurring in operative ideology, which is recognised as being the more volatile 'ideologising' level. To do this, we examine the declarations and statements made by political leaders and ideologues during a twenty-seven-year period (1956–83) in the history of People's Poland. Our content analysis is not based on any precise quantitative methods. For in dealing with political declarations we are concerned with the realm of what is sometimes called 'official discourse'. No methodology has yet been devised which would be able accurately to transform selected aspects of discourse analysis into quantifiable variables. Seliger's own attempts to introduce quantification into his model are all too obviously characterised by arbitrariness. The most constructive approach appears to be, therefore, as Burton and Carlen argue, to attempt to analyse the texts of official discourse in terms of their own modes of signification. The discourse's conditions of existence are created by the functioning of the state apparatus, but the internal form of its signification is the product of discursive relations. That is, discourse possesses its own form of logic and meaning independent of external phenomena, and any analysis of it should focus on this internal logic and meaning.[33] As Foucault observes:

The object of a discourse is established through a positive group of relations; these relations are established between institutions, economic and social processes, behavioural patterns, systems of norms, techniques, types of classification – but these relations are not present in the object, they do not define the internal constitution but only what enables it to appear, to be placed in a field of exteriority.[34]

Communist discourse provided a clear illustration of Foucault's point. As Armstrong observes, the connotation of Communist terminology 'is often quite different from the real meaning of the terms – sometimes designedly so, for Communists are skilled in using words to convey one meaning to the unaware outsider, another to the initiated'.[35] Discourse in socialist countries may, then, produce one impression when viewed from an exterior perspective and a different one when seen from an insider's perspective. The central task of a scholar becomes to recognise and decipher rulers' use of Aesopian language.

Our study is concerned with identifying the internal signification of discourse, that is, the real meaning of statements. The initial external conditions which cause them to appear, such as political institutions and socio-economic processes, are not considered in the search for this meaning. Once some signification has been imputed to a discourse and a real meaning has been identified, however, it then becomes possible to relate it to external conditions – for example, to establish its importance in the general political context. Only by proceeding in this order can we ensure that a comparison between an operative principle contained in, say, a 1956 discourse and one found in a 1983 discourse will prove significant.

The study is limited to an examination of declarations and pronouncements made at party Congresses, National Conferences, all Central Committee Plenum meetings and articles published in the party theoretical journal, *Nowe Drogi*. We also include statements made at certain specially convened party study sessions on given topics. On the other hand we do not systematically treat declarations issued in the form of Politburo resolutions; nor do we consider those made in the governmental arena, for example, addresses to and deliberations of the Sejm, and the resolutions and statutes adopted by it. We felt that in these cases we would in reality be dealing less with the declared intentions of the leadership than with policies that were being formulated by it. It is clearly unrealistic to treat this distinction as legitimate and binding at all times: the demarcation line between ideology and policy is often fuzzy, and in fact we do refer occasionally to statements emanating from the governmental arena. Nevertheless we have opted not to conduct any systematic examination of the proceedings and legislative activity of governmental institutions. We hope that any shortcomings resulting from this choice will be compensated for by having avoided an incursion into the policy-making process. We also did not examine speeches made by party leaders to meetings of mass organisations: there were simply too many of these and the volume of official discourse we would have had to analyse would have become unwieldy. Again there are exceptions to this rule: for example, important declarations made at trade union Congresses have been included. Finally, we decided to exclude from our study the analysis of propaganda texts intended for popular use. Initial examination showed these to contribute little to our understanding of ideology because of their superficial and polemical nature.

A few words should be said about sources used during the extraordinary events of 1980–2. The emergence of Solidarity meant, amongst many other things, that discussion of major issues was 'flushed' into the open and was no longer limited to meetings of party organs. As a result, public statements of political leaders reported by the press now possessed ideological significance equal to those made at a party forum. In turn, under martial law, the suspension of all debate, including that within the party, meant that other channels (official communiqués, stage-managed press conferences, selective interviews conducted with leaders) were utilised to convey ideological statements. In both cases we supplemented our usual sources with those new ones appropriate to the changed political circumstances.

Brief mention should be made of the problem of weighting the statements making up official discourse. For the question naturally arises: how do we attempt to resolve the discrepancy between, say, the importance of a declaration on cultural goals made by the party first secretary to a party Congress and that of a view put forward by a social scientist writing in the party theoretical journal? The answer, very simply, is that we give considerably more attention in our analysis to the former than to the latter pronouncement. We report the declaration more fully and explore its possible signification more comprehensively. We believe that such 'invisible' weighting has much the same merit as any quantitative weighting. That is, the illustrative effect is very similar. It could be argued that the problem might have been avoided by including in our analysis only those statements made by given high party officials. Two points can be made here. Firstly the weight of a political leader's remark is also subject to mutability, depending on his or her political standing at any particular time. Moreover we would have to undertake a separate study of the composition of the 'power elite' and of the distribution of influence within it in order to overcome the shortcomings that arise when official discourse is conceived in this way. This we are not in a position to do. Secondly there are many advantages in including the viewpoints of party ideologues, social scientists and other contributors to the party journal in our examination, not least of which is that the 'declarative' dimension of top political leaders' statements finds an echo in the more profound, scientific and ideologising analyses presented in *Nowe Drogi* articles. For the concerns expressed in the pronouncements of party leaders very often become the subject of more thorough elaboration in these articles.

It would have been useful to look more closely at the editorial policy of the journal so as to determine the criteria used to commission some articles, to agree to publish certain unsolicited contributions and to reject other material. In our study we considered all articles published in *Nowe Drogi* between 1956 and 1983, and we can say, at the very least, that the vast majority amplified the general views propagated by political leaders. *Nowe Drogi* was not intended to be, after all, a journal of dissent. We did encounter views put forward by some social scientists which appeared less representative of the official line, perhaps more critical than was usual, such as some published in the late 1970s. In such cases we have signalled this fact in our study. Likewise, statements made by leading politicians which differed from the official line, if only in a minor way, and corresponded to Baylis's category of 'adaptive orthodoxy', are singled out whenever they appeared in an official party organ. It is noteworthy, however, that up to 1980 political and ideological departures of this kind were infrequently published in the official accounts of Central Committee Plena. As a result of adherence to the principle of democratic centralism (interpreted at the top echelon of the party as a principle of 'collective responsibility' along the lines of British Cabinet practice), disagreement with the official line could be reported only when it occurred at another party forum, for example, at a meeting of a Politburo member with his 'constituents', which might be the party committee of a particular region he represented, an industrial enterprise, or a mass organisation. Apart from the period 1980–1, official party documents did not carry competing views, which makes it very difficult to describe on the basis of such documents an alternative 'Gierek' operative ideology in 1968–70, or a 'Kania' or even 'Olszowski' operative ideology in 1976–80. It would be necessary to trace the statements which such leaders made at meetings with their constituencies in order to arrive at a comprehensive picture of their ideologies. Not only did we not dispose of the resources to carry out such a study; we also wished to confine our analysis to the official ideology of the entrenched party leadership.

For similar reasons we did not examine the voluminous opposition literature which appeared in Poland, especially after 1976. This does not mean we consider it unimportant: in fact, the need to reconstruct the ideology of KOR (Committee for the Defence of Workers) and of Solidarity is more urgent than ever. Our study has a more limited objective – to describe how the leadership of the Polish United Workers' Party (PUWP) has perceived its immediate world.

The period under consideration is October 1956 to December 1983. Its length enables one to compare the ideologising discourse of different rulers at different times. The periodisation corresponds to the most significant junctures in the political life of Poland since 1956. Chapter 3 looks at the short-lived 'national road to socialism' period, which began with Gomułka's rise to power in October 1956 and ended with the III Congress of the PUWP in March 1959. Chapter 4 describes the 1960s 'little stabilisation' period. Chapter 5 subsumes the 'period of prosperity', from Gierek's take-over of power in December 1970 to the VII Congress in 1975. Chapter 6 examines 'decadence and opposition', both of which steadily grew in the last five years of Gierek's rule. Chapter 7 deals with the sixteen-month 'Solidarity' period, extending from September 1980 to December 1981. Chapter 8 concerns Poland's year of martial law, suspended at the end of 1982. Finally, Chapter 9 discusses ideological developments during 1983, especially after martial law was completely lifted in July.

The issue-areas we look at emerged naturally from the structure of official discourse: the major political problem-areas covered in Central Committee reports and speeches of the party leader to the Congresses are those we examine. These include: *the status of the party* (subdivided into three aspects: intraparty democracy, leading role in society, ideological functioning); the question of *industrial democracy*, that is, workers' participation and influence in the running of industrial enterprises through such organisations as workers' councils, self-management organs and trade unions; the issue of *church–state relations*; the role of *science* (including technology and the social sciences) *and culture* in society and the political socialisation work they are expected to perform; and the general question of *prescriptive societal values* to be promulgated in society, which serves as a conclusion to each chapter. These issues, however, represent only a selection of the problem-areas covered in Congress keynote addresses. The most notable issues excluded are economic (including agricultural) and foreign policy. It would be impossible to avoid all reference to these subjects, since they do bear on the problem-areas we focus on, and they are considered therefore, incidentally. We believe, however, that economic and foreign policy are such wide-ranging, far-reaching questions that they merit separate attention.

It could be argued that each of the subjects with which we do deal warrants separate treatment too. Such a criticism would be fully justified were we to be conducting an examination of policy on these questions. Clearly that is not what we are doing. We are looking at operative ideology, that is, the explanation and justification of policy. Adoption of such a research framework means that we are constantly encountering the same or quite similar discourse over long periods of time. For example, policy on intraparty democracy, which may have involved institutional reforms, did change, but shifts in operative ideology were confined largely to differing interpretations of the principle of democratic centralism. Likewise the leading role of the party may have signified many things in practice but fewer things at the ideological level. That is why a study of five primary problem-areas (the party, industrial democracy, church–state relations, culture and science, and societal values) is viable. A leading article published in the party theoretical journal of 1964 may be cited to indicate the magnitude of changes in official discourse on particular issues:

It is true that many postulates put forward at the IV Congress can be found in the directives to the previous Congress. Often these sound the same and touch on the same problems. But in the new period they signify something else, they are weighted differently, they originate in new domestic and international conditions and are related to the significantly higher developmental level that has been attained. There are also new postulates and problems which could not appear at all in an earlier period or appeared in an indiscernible shape.[36]

Some observers would go so far as to claim that what was said at the IX Congress, held in 1981, was similar or identical to what was said at much earlier Congresses, even the two preceding the 1956 changes. Such views are obviously a gross exaggeration, but if the assumption is that official discourse has changed very little over the years, then we stand to be accused of not selecting enough subject matter to be able to arrive at meaningful conclusions concerning operative ideology. The object of our study is to demonstrate that, though not as concrete and revealing as policy analysis, a study of operative ideology on selected issues does tell us much about political change.

Our selection of problem-areas was also guided by the extent to which they directly involved ideological questions, in particular, the propagation of political values throughout society. The party organisation, workers' institutions, the church and the cultural and scientific intelligentsia are all central agents for such propagation. In one sense, therefore, we are dealing with the leadership's operative ideology on, its legitimisation of and the qualifications which it placed upon the propagation of socio-political values by these structures.

In another sense, we are concerned with the contrasting interpretations given by political leaders to phenomena in the real world. In the twenty-seven-year period which we cover, different policy courses were pursued and structural reforms were implemented. We cannot ignore the various reforms effected in, for example, workers' self-management. But in the final analysis it is the rulers' declared values and goals which constitute the core of our study; it is upon their statements in favour of these reforms or in support of the status quo, when no reforms were enacted, that our study focuses.

Finally, in a study of this kind we are dealing not solely with statements, values, goals, institutions and reforms, but also with individuals. We are looking, therefore, at the relationship between political leaders and their world outlook. Marxist principles govern this relationship in a socialist state no less than elsewhere. As one distinguished Polish intellectual, Strzelecki, has observed:

Marxism is not a vehicle which it is possible to get out of at any time. This means that the famous principle 'social existence determines thought' applies equally to socialists and Marxists, and does not exclude those who occupy leading posts in the state and economic apparatus. It is theoretically possible that one's social outlook changes on taking power. Other concerns begin to preoccupy one's mind, and previous matters are seen in a different light from a different position in the social hierarchy and in the course of carrying out new responsibilities.[37]

Ideas and ideologies are the products of 'concrete' human beings. They do not lead a separate existence; nor do they reproduce autonomously. They are relevant only in so far as they reveal something about the persons, social groups and society to which they owe their existence. A study of ideological change will necessarily indicate how society has changed, and a focus on changes in operative ideology will point out how the ruling group propounding it has changed, if it has changed at all.

3

The Polish road: fact and fable, 1956–59

Let us imagine for a moment, comrades, that a film has been made in which somebody has shown how socialist Poland became industrialised during those years, how the socialist structure grew, how employment increased. And now let us imagine that we are screening that film in reverse, that Zeran vanishes from the outskirts of Warsaw and the Nowa Huta iron and steel works from the fields on the outskirts of Kraków; that Wierzbica, Kedzierzyn, Jaworzno and Skawina disappear; that the Bierut steel works in Czestochowa shrink to its pre-war size and that the blast furnaces built in Silesia fade away as do the chemical works at Oswiecim; that the coke works are erased and the shipyards shrivel; that millions of peasants employed in the course of the industrialisation return to their villages around Warsaw and Cracow; that the towns become crowded with unemployed; that the number of colleges and vocational schools decreases; that the many thousands of peasant sons and daughters – now among the educated intelligentsia – retreat to the villages and remain on their farms; that millions of illiterates await that their descendants, begotten in backwardness, be taught to read and write in the year 2,000, as promised by the pre-war Polish government which might as well not keep its promise; that the amount of published books diminishes, while more and more people crawl on their knees in pilgrimages so that God might reward them for their cruel fate on this earth.

> Józef Cyrankiewicz, III Congress of the PUWP, March 1959

If the question was posed: in which post-war period did Poland undergo greatest economic, social and political change? we would find it extremely difficult to decide on an answer. Poland seems to have been transformed radically and dramatically at regular intervals in the forty years since it became a socialist state in 1944. The period of political upheaval between 1944 and 1948 resulted in the establishment of a dictatorship of the proletariat which eliminated groups opposed to a workers' state and altered relations of power between social classes in an unprecedented way. The economic transformation of the country, most clearly set out in the six-year economic plan (1950–5), the results of which were described by Premier Cyrankiewicz in his speech to the party's III Congress, laid the foundations of a modern industrial society, which the country did not approach in the inter-war years. Between 1954 and 1959 the political system was affected by the process of destalinisation and the October events, and it was never again to be an unassailable monolith impervious to various reform movements. Crises in subsequent years (1968, 1970–1, 1976, 1980–2) were founded on the October precedent, but only in the last case did important structural change occur, similar in scope and magnitude to that of the destalinisation period.

In this chapter we look at the period 1956–9, when the concept of a Polish road to socialism still had some credibility. Gomułka, reappointed as first secretary of the PUWP in October 1956, had defended this principle nine years earlier, at the founding meeting of the Cominform (the short-lived post-war Communist International) held in Poland in September 1947. For his defiance of Stalin, he was removed from the leadership and eventually imprisoned. But the Stalinist regime in Poland was not as ruthless as elsewhere in Eastern Europe and Gomułka was able to escape the fate of 'Titoists' and 'traitors' in Hungary, Bulgaria, Albania, Romania and Czechoslovakia. It was a cruel irony that those convicted on such trumped-up charges were executed (Rajk, Kostov, Xoxe, Patrascanu, Slansky); Gomułka, who had openly opposed Stalin on the Cominform and on collectivisation, was to return as party leader.[1]

It should be emphasised that destalinisation began in Poland well before Gomułka's return to power in 1956. An important Plenum meeting of the Central Committee took place in November 1954, at which 'a very critical attitude was adopted toward the activities of the Politburo and party leadership'. As Karpinski notes, this was a landmark event because party functionaries now obtained certain freedoms in being able to criticise their superiors.[2] Within a month, Gomułka was released and criticisms of the security apparatus began to multiply. Simultaneously the first attempts were made to decentralise the state administration and economic structure.

Khrushchev's denunciation of Stalinism at the XX Congress of the CPSU in February 1956, the failure of Poland's six-year plan, and factional fighting within the party leadership after Bierut's death in

March 1956 exacerbated general social unrest in the country and helped bring about the workers' strikes and demonstrations in Poznań in June 1956. These were quelled with the use of force, but the new leadership under Ochab, in spite of a declared commitment to demo-cratisation, did not have the popular appeal that the by now charis-matic Gomułka possessed. In October a trial of strength took place in which pro-Gomułka forces organised mass demonstrations and the Soviet rulers, suspicious of him, suddenly arrived in Warsaw to con-front the emerging leader. Following the VIII Plenum, Gomułka was formally given back his post as party first secretary. At the same time in Hungary, Nagy, a leader the Soviets had hand-picked to serve as premier in 1953 and who appeared more trustworthy than Gomułka, was about to take a genuinely independent line and to precipitate the Hungarian Revolution of 1956.

The change in Poland's party leadership at the VIII Plenum trig-gered off adjustments in the ruling group's operative ideology. The Plenum identified three types of institutional reform which were designed to speed up the process of socialist construction: (1) the establishment of workers' councils; (2) the delegation of greater powers to local authorities; and (3) the setting up of peasants' self-government. In addition, reform within the party was considered to be indispensable. Operative ideology, designed to explain and justify new policy courses and to elicit support, became a crucial factor in the reform process. We begin by examining the rulers' operative ideology on the party up to the III Congress.

THE CASE OF THE PARTY

Prior to the crisis of 1956 the nature of the relationship between *Gegen-wartsarbeit* (activity in the here and now) and *Endziel* (final goal) did not pose a major problem for Poland's political leaders. The immedi-ate tasks that were being undertaken were in line with the long-term goals of the socialist system: the industrialisation of the country and, accompanying this, the process of urbanisation; a programme to educate and acculturise the masses; and a campaign to secularise society. All sections of the socialist leadership were committed to engaging in these activities in order to reach the final goal – socialism. Upon this they did not disagree. In his speech to the III Congress (quoted in part at the outset of this chapter), Poland's premier emphasised the differences between the fundamental principles and

operative ideology held by the inter-war 'bourgeois' governments
and those espoused by the post-war socialist government. At the same
time, however, he sounded a warning to those 'revisionist elements' in
the party which appeared in the wake of the 1956 crisis and which
called for a 'second stage of the Polish October', that is the establishment of integral democracy, political pluralism and greater liberalisation in all aspects of social life:

This picture of Poland shown in reverse, this picture of Poland as it would
have been, were it not socialist and industrialised, ought to be dedicated to all
those who during the party's difficult period, particularly in 1956 and part of
1957, wanted to identify the errors committed in socialist construction with
socialism itself, with the gist of socialism, who wanted to throw out the baby
with the dirty bath water.[3]

The premier was thus equating the revisionist challenge within the
party with the principles and ideology of the inter-war governments.
In the process he acknowledged that with 1956 an alternative set of
fundamental principles and, consequently, a different operative
ideology were put forward by a faction in the party. The unity of
Gegenwartsarbeit and *Endziel* was shattered. And although the party
was able to wage a successful struggle against revisionism in the
following years, it could not altogether eliminate the influence of the
alternative ideology that had arisen. Significantly, its origins had lain
in the destalinisation process, especially in the resolutions of the XX
Congress of the CPSU, and were given further impetus by the events
of the Polish October. How, then, did destalinisation affect the state of
intraparty democracy?

1. Intraparty democracy

In the period following the death of Stalin but preceding the events of
1956, a general awareness arose within the Polish leadership that
some reforms had to be carried out in the political system, but that
they could not take on systemic proportions. The 'cult of personality'
had had considerable repercussions in Poland, and the chief task
facing the Polish rulers was to find a way of eliminating these without
calling into question the foundations of the political system, based on
the dictatorship of the proletariat. An important analysis of the
problem was presented in an article in *Nowe Drogi* by a leading
philosopher, Adam Schaff. He began with two overriding assumptions. Firstly the principle of the leading role of the party in society

could not be called into question. Secondly democratic centralism
had to remain the operative concept governing intraparty democracy:
lower tiers in the party structure were bound by the decisions of the
upper tiers, just as minority groups were bound by the resolutions of
the majority. Where the effect of the personality cult had been most
harmful was on the principle of collective leadership, understood as
influence on and responsibility for decision-making by both the party
leadership and its rank-and-file membership. Schaff argued how the
concept could be revived: (1) party activists and the rank-and-file
should be encouraged to take part in Plenum meetings, Conferences
and Congresses which dealt with the important issues of the day; (2)
openness, not secrecy, should characterise party life, and it could be
achieved through the regular reporting of each party committee's
work; (3) a sense of responsibility should be instilled in each committee, and criticism from outside, as well as self-criticism, should
constitute integral elements in this process; and (4) the unity of theory
and practice, word and action, should be respected, ensuring that any
errors committed in the implementation of a given policy would be
understood as errors, not as a deliberate deviation from accepted
policy.[4]

The article was very representative of the nature of the operative
ideology dominant between 1954 and 1956. No concessions were
offered to lower tiers in the party which might give them wider
autonomy. A call was made simply for broader participation and,
related to it, for increased responsibility. Wider participation did not
imply, however, a process which could lead at some point in the future
to a more broadly based form of democracy. For no structural
changes were envisaged by Schaff. Wider participation meant simply
that more people were to take part in the meetings of existing
institutions. Moreover they were still to be bound by the principle of
democratic centralism, interpreted in a very rigorous way. These
conclusions, drawn from the article, suggested an operative ideology
on intraparty democracy which, although encouraging greater participation in party affairs than had been the rule in the past, interpreted the concept of democratic centralism in much the same way as
during the Stalin era.

The VIII Plenum, whilst deciding on a change of leadership, also
stated its categorical opposition to the existence of factions or groups
within the party. In an immediate response to the call for 'integral
democracy' made by elements in the party who were soon to be

labelled 'revisionists', the new leadership asserted that such substantive reforms were not on the agenda, and that intraparty democracy would continue to rest on the principle of democratic centralism. In fact the Plenum refused even to distinguish between those who had been 'responsible' for the political line of the party that had led to the events of 1956 and those who had not been 'responsible': no division of any kind which might split party ranks was to be permitted. What the Plenum did recommend was greater openness in party life and 'above all an ongoing process of informing party members about leaders' standpoints on current aspects of party policy'. And although differences of views amongst members were 'permissible and unavoidable', the Plenum stressed that 'In practical activity they absolutely have to carry out party resolutions.'[5] Given this rigorous adherence to the principle of democratic centralism, therefore, it would be inaccurate to attribute to the new leadership in 1956 an ideology on intraparty democracy which differed markedly from that adopted during the later years of Gomułka's rule. Broader participation and more openness in party affairs were proclaimed, but they were not to be equated with political pluralism.

The dominant themes at the IX and X Plena were, firstly, party unity and, secondly, restoration of links between party leaders and the masses. As far as the first concept was concerned, the IX Plenum declared that the democratic and centralist aspects of the principle of democratic centralism could not be separated. In particular, any attacks on the centralist concept undermined the unity of the party. And although revisionism was mainly responsible for attacking this concept, dogmatism was equally condemned. Advocates of the 'second stage in the Polish October' were criticised as forcefully as the Stalinist reaction. Both wings, Gomułka stated, had to be liquidated: the party had to become politically consolidated, homogeneous and cohesive at all levels, even if it meant reducing overall membership.[6] From the X Plenum onwards, however, political unity increasingly became identified with the elimination of revisionism from the party. It was accused of fermenting a power struggle between factions and of undermining the authority of the party in society. Its representatives (especially Kłosiewicz and Kołakowski) were described as advocates of a 'no programme' which would nullify Poland's democratic achievements and restore a system of bourgeois democracy. There was to be no going back on the Polish October, a leading *Nowe Drogi* article stated, but neither was there to be a second stage. 'Only those

who either consciously treated October as a "first stage" preceding a
second one – a stage which would restore authority to exploiting
strata and bourgeois movements in the country – or did not realise the
objectives contained in the slogans put forward by elements
consciously striving for such a second stage, can talk of a retreat from
October.'[7] The struggle against the 'second stagers' resulted in a
wholesale purge of party ranks: at the XI Plenum Gomułka reported
that the verification campaign in the party had reduced membership
by 200,000 and that political unity had, as a result, been reinforced.
In explaining this campaign, the party journal declared: 'People want
a return to order and authority.'[8] It was not to be the last time this
slogan was propagated.

Struggles for power in Communist parties everywhere are most
often interpreted officially in terms of factional in-fighting between on
the one hand dogmatists or sectarians and on the other revisionists or
liberals. The leader who can successfully attack both deviations and
claim the central ground usually emerges victorious in such struggles.
Gomułka's efforts between 1956 and 1959 to outmanoeuvre his rivals
were no exception. But the international situation also had a major
impact on his approach to party democracy at this time. In June 1957
Khrushchev scored a victory over an 'anti-party' group composed of
hard-liners. The occasion was used by the entrenched rulers of
Romania, Bulgaria and Hungary to expel both revisionist and dogmatist opponents from positions of power. At the international
conference of Communist party leaders held in Moscow in November
1957, the balance finally shifted against revisionism. The failure of the
Soviet–Yugoslav *rapprochement*, the outflanking on the left of Khrushchev by Mao abroad and Suslov at home, and the need for solid
ideological rearmament following the 1956 crises in Hungary and
Poland, led to a more one-sided emphasis on the drive against
revisionism.[9] Gomułka gave way, and only Kadar continued to insist
on a 'battle on two fronts' against both deviations.

In Poland in this period, in addition to political unity within the
party, a second aspect of intraparty democracy was forging closer
links between leaders and the rank-and-file. Two factors promoting
closer links were identified: the struggle against bureaucracy and the
call for greater initiative (or activeness) by local party committees.
The battle against 'bureaucratic soullessness' was launched at the III
Plenum in January 1955 and was aimed at preventing administrative
processes from interfering with the contacts between upper and lower

tiers of the party apparatus. The bureaucratic ethos also tended to attract careerist, opportunist elements which 'dammed up the revolutionary activity of the party'.[10] The result was the emergence of cliques and cliquishness, which weakened intraparty democracy and generated 'moral depravity' of members.[11]

The exhortation to increased initiative by local committees in carrying out their responsibilities was first made at the VII Plenum in July 1956. It was intended to make the lower levels of the apparatus more responsive to the views of non-party members and to transform the latter, in turn, into transmitters of information for the ruling group. Greater activeness would encourage committees, it was argued, to become more open and democratic.

By the time of the party's III Congress in March 1959, revisionism came to be identified as the single greatest threat to intraparty democracy. Whereas at the VIII Plenum both dogmatic and revisionist tendencies 'could have transformed themselves into a severe and dangerous political crisis ... at the present stage revisionism is the main danger for the party, not because of the number of revisionists, but because of the objective association of revisionism with the tendencies of anti-socialist, bourgeois social forces both internal and external'. The aims of revisionism, Gomułka alleged, were to destroy ideological unity within the party, to undermine the principles of the party's leading role in society and the dictatorship of the proletariat and to establish a system of social democracy allowing for a 'free play of social forces'. But the party had offered 'successful resistance' to revisionism, it had 'repudiated and condemned attempts to pave the way to political legality for bourgeois forces' and it had repeated its assertion, first made in 1944, that 'there is no freedom for the enemies of freedom'.[12]

At the same time it was recognised that revisionism had not been completely defeated. In his concluding speech to the Congress, Gomułka observed: 'Why can we consider the latter, i.e. dogmatism, to be no longer dangerous to the party today, and present revisionism as the main danger? ... Dogmatism cannot find for itself a mass basis of support, while revisionism still has considerable possibilities in this field.'[13] The implication was that revisionists could potentially develop a mass basis of support, that is, although they were not numerous at that time, they could become so in the future. But the party could not allow that to happen because 'its watchword is democracy for the working people, for the supporters of socialism', and revisionism stood outside the boundaries of democracy, so defined.

This view of intraparty democracy was reflected in the amendments to the party statutes adopted by the Congress. A number of these were 'devoted to guaranteeing the principles of centralism', for example, the modification contained in Paragraph 22: 'Inner-party democracy cannot be misused for purposes contrary to the interests of the party; in particular, membership in the party cannot be reconciled with any sort of activities of a factional character, with any kind of activities directed against the ideology of the party, its general political line and the unity of its ranks.'[14] The slip in the translation is revealing: 'inner-party democracy' suggested that the democratic process would be limited to the ruling inner circle, in contrast to 'intraparty democracy', which had broader implications. The report on party statutes added: 'only in conditions of party unity can inner-party democracy develop correctly and consistently'. The fact that the term 'democracy' usually implies diversity, not unity, of views suggested that in this context the concept was being used to signify democratic centralism, which was a different idea altogether. Further qualifications of the term were contained in the discussion on a party member's right to maintain a divergent opinion within the general line and ideology of the party. Paragraph 21 now guaranteed his right to engage in 'unhampered and constructive criticism' and 'free and practical discussion of party policy'. But the Congress went no further and refused to adopt recommendations of local party committees calling for additional guarantees. These would have protected members from persecution when they expressed criticism and would have obliged the party to eradicate the suppression of criticism whenever it occurred. The reason given for this omission was that recent 'grave experiences where the resolutions of the VIII Plenum were abused in order to make a general attack on the Party line' necessitated restricting guarantees on the right to criticise.[15]

If party unity continued to be underscored at the III Congress, the importance of forging closer elite–mass links was played down. In particular, local committees were now encouraged to display initiative not in relation to higher party tiers but in relation to their social environment. Gomułka noted with pride how lower party organs 'were given incomparably greater possibilities for action and decision in matters affecting their respective areas', and how factory committees had 'obtained new jurisdiction in carrying out political control over the administration and overall economic activity of the enterprise'.[16] Broader powers for party committees meant a concurrent diminution of the influence of workers' councils (as we see in the next section), and in this way local party initiative was now related less to intraparty democracy than to the principle of the leading role in society.

Let us try to trace a pattern in official discourse on intraparty democracy between 1956 and 1959. The two principal concerns were political unity and elite–mass relations. The view of unity changed from an attack on all factions threatening the leadership to, by the III Congress, condemnation of revisionism first and foremost. Gomułka's statements in this period consistently emphasised the importance of the principle of democratic centralism. Power-sharing by the leadership with representatives of various factions was never on the agenda. In turn, the ruling elite's relations with the party rank-and-file were ascribed considerable importance shortly after Gomułka took power. Local committees were encouraged to take a greater part in decision-making. But again, by the time of the Congress, this participatory value was dropped and instead committees were asked to perform more thoroughly a controlling function in society. From this we may conclude that operative ideology on intraparty democracy was initially ambivalent after October: unity was stressed, but so were closer links between lower levels in the apparatus and the ruling circle. The III Congress formalised the leadership's more doctrinaire conception of intraparty democracy. Advocates of greater pluralism were singled out for harshest criticism and a more centralist view of the exercise of power within the party was taken. Intraparty democracy was effectively removed from Gomułka's list of priorities within two years of his appointment as party leader.

2. *The leading role of the party*

A question even more pressing for the leadership than intraparty democracy was the need for the party to restore its authority throughout society, which had been undermined by the 1956 events. An examination of ideological declarations made at Plenum meetings at this time shows that the rulers used a double-edged sword to resolve the issue. Political unity was paramount, and any form of power-sharing with groups opposed to the official line was anathema and detrimental to such unity. Disposition of political authority was to remain firmly in the hands of the few – the vanguard of the proletarian party – even though this might adversely affect the leadership's relations with the masses. At the same time, the leading role of the party was reaffirmed. For example, the proposal that the party should not put forward detailed plans on matters which lay within the jurisdiction of workers' councils (such as distribution of the wage fund) was bluntly rejected in a *Nowe Drogi* article: 'The suggestion that the party should abnegate its right to present its position on key matters affecting a factory is unacceptable.'[17] Industrial democracy could not imply a reduced role for the party in economic enterprises – quite the contrary (as we see later). Likewise party committees were called upon to exert more influence upon intellectual circles, where 'political apathy, timorous ideological attitudes and remoteness from political organisations are particularly rampant'.[18] In sum, the party had everywhere 'to break from resignation and paralysis'.[19]

Whilst the masses were expected to take a more active role in the political system, their real influence was in no way enhanced: 'systemic changes are an important factor in transforming the consciousness of the masses in a socialist spirit, but the main motor force in this process can only be the party'.[20] Participatory values were advocated, but the structure of power remained unchanged. As with intraparty democracy, therefore, the simultaneous propagation of participatory attitudes and practice of central control reflected the rulers' noncommittal attitude to reform after 1956.

The III Congress repeated the call for a more assertive posture by the party in society: 'Consolidation of the leading influence of our party in all spheres of life is the primary condition of socialist democratisation.' Otherwise party organisations would 'let the steering wheel of social life slip from their hands' and a 'field of activity for hostile anti-socialist elements' would be opened.[21] It was true, Cyrankiewicz acknowledged, that the party had had to 'fight for apparently unpopular issues', such as 'the fight against unjustified surpassing of the wage fund, against excessive employment, and for order in work enterprises, for greater discipline, increased labour productivity as the decisive factors for improving our living standards today and tomorrow'. Since the 1959–65 economic plan did not envisage major improvements in living standards, tomorrow was still a long way off. But if 'contact was established with the masses, with matters put in their true light', party policy would be 'determinedly supported by the working class'.

Finally, it was the view of Poland's premier that the party had never stopped performing its leading role in society anyway: 'Not for a moment, not even at the time of greatest turmoil, did the party surrender its leading role either to the philatelist union, pigeon-fanciers or to any other association or club whatsoever full of political and economic wisdom, of course, and which knew better than the party in which direction Poland should move.'[22] The principle of the party's leading role was considered, therefore, to be imperishable.

3. The party and ideology

In addition to the leadership's operative ideology on intraparty democracy and on its role in society, we look at a third aspect concerning the party – its ideological status. Its ability (or inability) to propagate the fundamental principles of Marxism–Leninism was considered by the rulers to be crucial to its overall prestige and influence in society. In this section we describe how policies related to the party's ideological and agitprop work were explained and justified by political leaders.

Following the October changes, it was publicly admitted that an ideological vacuum had been created. 'In the first instance the party must overcome the ideological waywardness and political disorientation found amongst activists', the IX Plenum declared.[23] Party members, one writer noted, should avoid falling into a state of 'internal emigration', which stemmed from a sense of hopelessness at being unable to eliminate 'apolitical riff-raff' from the party ranks.[24]

The III Congress made no mention of ideological drift, but it did admit that 'the party's ideological activity lags behind its activities in the economic field'. One Politburo member, Kliszko, noted how 'during the last three years we have observed even among some of our comrades, among others, in intellectual circles, something like a lapse into illiteracy in the field of Marxism–Leninism. They have forgotten the basic tenets of the Marxist–Leninist theory of the state, or they have consciously rejected it, not always willing to admit this openly.'[25]

Thus ideological monopoly by the ruling group in the pre-1956 period was followed by the perception of a drift after the October events. Exhortations to greater ideological commitment at the X

Plenum were transformed into a call for a return to Marxist–Leninist fundamentals at the Congress. In this way, the place of the party and its ideology in society was, by 1959, described in much the same way as before the Polish October. The dogmatist tendency in the party had, for all practical purposes, emerged triumphant.

INDUSTRIAL DEMOCRACY

According to a leading article published in a special issue of *Nowe Drogi* shortly after the October events, the main error committed in earlier years was that representatives of the working class had begun to govern in the name of the working class. 'The most important achievement of the VIII Plenum was to outline how to transfer systematically to the working class the task of directly managing industry and influencing policy.'[26] The working class was now to dispose of the already socialised means of production by way of workers' councils, which had recently been set up in economic enterprises.

From the outset, however, ambiguity arose concerning the nature and functions of these new councils. At the IX Plenum Gomułka delimited their spheres of competence: 'workers' councils are neither institutions of political authority for the working class, nor are they tiers in the administrative apparatus; they are organs by which the working class directly participates in the management of the national economy ... This does not signify that factories can be handed over to particular work-forces and placed under their collective ownership.'[27]

This equivocal statement did not help clarify what precisely workers' councils were; it only made clear what they were not: they were neither political nor administrative bodies. From Gomułka's description it appeared that workers' councils were there simply to be participated in by the working class: that was to be their *raison d'être*. If they did have another function, it was to constitute an organ in the system of management of the national economy, but nothing more specific was added. It remained unclear whether they were to have some disposition over the means of production, that is, their factories. It was obvious that they were not being given ownership of them.

Even this limited conception of the role of workers' councils came under attack in subsequent years. For example, one writer described how in certain factories in Łódź: 'An incorrectly understood view of democratisation of social life, as well as freedom in expressing critical thoughts and observations, are frequently exploited by hostile forces to attack the basic principles of the party and of party activists.'[28] The implication was that this kind of freedom was not envisaged by those who had approved the establishment of workers' councils. The resolutions of both the XI Plenum and the IV Congress of trade unions stressed that the spirit of workers' democracy was linked inextricably to the Leninist concept of the leading role of the party in society. The new councils could never not be subordinated to the party; in fact they were expected to work closely with party committees and trade union branches in the factory.[29]

At the same time surveys conducted amongst workers on their view of the new councils showed growing dissatisfaction with their performance during the period 1956–68. The most prevalent opinion expressed was that the councils had become removed from the work-force and that they did not pay attention to its views.[30] Workers' self-management committees, set up in December 1958 to harmonise and coordinate the activities of all workers' organisations in the factory (the councils, trade union branches and party committees), were accused of formalism in their methods of operation.[31] Supporters of the 1958 legislation claimed that self-management organs had practically the same jurisdiction as that given to workers' councils by the November 1956 act. But no longer were they described as institutions concerned with management matters; rather they were considered 'co-management' bodies working closely with trade union and party committees in each factory. For their part the workers 'co-participated in co-management'.[32] The operative words describing the functions of workers' self-management organs became exercise of 'control' and 'supervision' over management.

Even in these respects their freedom was restricted. A provision in the new law stated that 'workers' self-management committees ought to ensure a proper relationship between the interests of the work-force and national interests'. Thus the new 'co-management organs' could not exclusively defend the interests of their members when exercising control and supervision; they had also to take into account and defend the common good. If there had been a shift away from giving greater authority and autonomy to workers' self-management institutions, then it had been induced by the councils themselves, it was claimed. For 'the first months of 1958 had shown the prematurity and incapacity to overcome the tendency for councils to isolate themselves from the work-force. The latter's inability to exercise control over the councils demonstrated that it was not yet ready to play this role.'[33] The workers' consciousness and their cultural level had to be raised substantially, and they had to understand and respect societal interests better before they could engage in such activity.[34]

From October 1956, when workers' councils were set up, to December 1958, when an act was passed specifying the rights and obligations of workers' self-management committees, statements explaining and justifying the policies pursued changed radically. The most notable modification of the operative ideology lay in the terminology itself. 'Councils' were associated with a more direct form of democracy; they implied election or selection of delegates by the workers to deal with a wide sphere of competence. Inevitably they conjured up the picture of soviets formed during the Bolshevik Revolution. Self-management committees, on the other hand, had no revolutionary connotations. They were generally associated with the performance of administrative tasks, and the method of recruitment was, as in the case of most types of committee, indirect – for instance, by appointment from above. Similarly the shift in emphasis from participation by the work-force in management to co-participation with other factory committees (trade unions, party) in co-management marked a departure from the original conception of workers' councils. Finally the increasing use of the concept of societal interests served to underline the diminishing importance of group (i.e., employees') interests, the representation of which had been the original purpose of creating the councils as a direct form of proletarian democracy.

The ideological outlook on workers' self-management was most concisely presented at the PUWP's III Congress. In his opening address the party first secretary reported: 'Although a well-functioning workers' self-management is not yet a general phenomenon, nevertheless it shows a growing concern for increased productivity and for the attainment of better economic results.' He cited how the new bodies had helped bring about a more economic use of resources, the disposal of surplus stocks, the liquidation of excess employment, improvements in work organisation and in the system of norms and wages, the reduction of production costs, concern for better quality of products, and other measures which, in effect, served management. Gomułka referred to the social and educational role that self-management played within the work-force. As examples he gave the creation of an atmosphere in which breaches of work discipline were socially condemned, work emulation was revived and the like. He stressed that it was necessary to ensure the freedom and effectiveness of workers' criticism of the administrative apparatus. But, he added: 'The broad powers of the workers' self-management cannot in practice collide with the authority and responsibilities of the directors, based on the principle of one-man management. The director is obliged to carry out the decisions of the workers' self-management and the instructions of the higher authorities, but he alone runs the enterprise directly.'[35]

Workers' self-management was considered to be, therefore, first and foremost an aid to management in the performance of its duties. As an institution responsible for co-management in the factory it could not by definition serve to defend employees' interests. Gomułka did not refer to the representativeness of self-management committees or to the idea of encouraging broad participation in them. It was indicated, however, that their membership was to be drawn from workers' councils, party committees, trade union branches and, from 1959 onwards, the Socialist Youth Union and the Association of Engineers and Technicians (NOT). And whilst it was said that their decisions were binding on enterprise directors, it was simultaneously stressed that they could not conflict with directors' powers and responsibilities. The latter alone ran their enterprises. Thus the concept of co-management was itself equivocal.

The resolutions adopted by the Congress said even less about the powers of workers' self-management committees. Control over the administration was mentioned as an important activity, but such control 'can and should become a means for improving the work of the administration of the enterprises, and for large sections of workers – a great school of thrifty management of socialist enterprises'. Not once did the Congress note, in the way that the VIII Plenum did, that these institutions were intended to transfer direct management of industry to the working class. The new role assigned to these committees was most clearly described in the short statement delivered to the Congress by the leader of the Trade Union Federation (CRZZ): they should combat all sorts of abuses, wastage and breaches of social discipline in the factory, and they should strive for greater productivity, work emulation and technical progress.[36]

At the same time, in the discussion on workers' self-management another political value was stressed which effectively negated its co-management function and role as aggregator of working-class interests. Namely, workers' interests had always to be subordinated to the interests of society. Included in the resolutions adopted by the III Congress was the statement:

In order to overcome the contradictions that arise between the narrowly conceived interests of the enterprise and its workers and the interests of society, it is imperative, apart from economic incentives, to spread among the workers and management the conviction that no lasting improvement can be made in the living conditions of the workers without carrying out successfully the tasks connected with the national plan.[37]

The most important value in the factory was supposed to be, therefore, fulfilment of the plan: all other interests were more narrowly conceived and of secondary rank.

This examination of declarations made on the subject of workers' self-management between 1956 and 1959 has indicated how the operative ideology justifying policy courses on industrial democracy shifted in this short period. At first workers' councils were construed to be bodies set up to allow for broad participation by workers in the process of economic management. Subsequently the concept of broad participation was dropped, and attention was focused on the perceived difficulties arising in the relations between the work-force and the councils. When the leading role of the party in society, including the factory, began once again to be emphasised, the councils' influence started to wane. This tendency was followed by a further ideological reinterpretation of industrial democracy: newly formed self-management committees were to constitute co-management bodies exercising control and supervision over management. By the III Congress the official ideology stressed the socio-educational functions of self-management, which were of benefit to the work-force, and the rationalisation of the use of resources, which mainly benefited management. Throughout this evolution of ideology, the argument was increasingly advanced that what served the interests of the enterprise, and of society generally, also served the interests of the workers. At the Congress it was claimed that it was in everyone's best interest to fulfil the goals of the economic plan. This was to constitute the dominant outlook of the leadership on industrial democracy until the outbreak of Poland's next political crisis in 1968.

THE CHURCH

Before the October crisis the operative ideology of the then leadership on the church–state question was one of peaceful coexistence and ideological competition. A fundamental principle of Marxism–Leninism was often repeated: the long-term aim of the state was to create a society governed by a materialist philosophy of the world. But the operative ideology was based more on the principle of 'Render unto Caesar'. An uneasy truce was achieved with the church: the latter could continue to promulgate its doctrine amongst its followers, but the state would carry on its programme for a secularist transformation of society. The two principles were bound to collide.

Soon after taking power Gomułka declared his intention to reach some kind of understanding with the church. 'The former conflict with the church opposed millions of believers to popular authority, made their participation in our development difficult, pushed them away from socialism.' He acknowledged: 'For a long time still, believers and non-believers, the church and socialism, popular authority and the church hierarchy will exist alongside each other.' But the party leader also sounded a warning: 'From this we ought to draw conclusions – not only we but the church as well.'[38]

Nevertheless the October crisis turned ideological competition between church and state into an overt struggle for political power. Neither side was content to engage simply in rhetoric. Just as revisionism threatened the party's monopoly of power from within, so the church attacked it from without. In this struggle action took the place of words, policy lines replaced operative ideology. In fact the latter was not always discernible amidst the party's primarily politico-economic counter-attack against the church (a tax levy on church property, restrictions on church building, etc.). We do not intend to examine the policies pursued by the ruling group during this period – that is not the focus of our study. Rather we look at the declarations made on church–state relations at the III Congress. Here a more considered and systematic operative ideology emerged than had existed hitherto.

In his opening address Gomułka reiterated the long-standing principle that 'in no case does our party draw a political line of division in the community according to attitudes to religion. It appraises the attitude of its citizens exclusively according to their relation toward socialism in practice.' Implied in this statement was the view that a citizen's respect for the socialist system had always to take precedence over his religious convictions in situations where the two collided. Religious practices were declared to be the private concern of each citizen because they involved the accepted principle of freedom of conscience. But religion was one thing, the church was another. The latter was a broadly based institution and, as such, its status presented greater problems. In particular, its activity affecting the social and political spheres had to be resolved. Gomułka continued: 'The church is separated from the state, it can operate freely only on the principle of the recognition of the social system existing in Poland and by acting in keeping with the *raison d'état* of the Polish People's Republic.' That is, the church enjoyed freedom so long as it accepted the existing political system. Further, 'in matters connected with the interest and the policy of the state, the church and the clergy must be guided by the laws of our state. They must therefore take an attitude of complete loyalty to the People's government.' These declarations implied that in fact the church was to express a political orientation, one of support for the existing system. Thus it followed that 'we shall not tolerate any reactionary political activity on the part of the church'. Any type of pro-state political activity was, it could be inferred, permitted. And Gomułka duly lavished praise on those Catholic circles which had declared themselves in a decided manner for socialism.

The church's political role was immediately circumscribed by another series of statements made by Gomułka. 'We treat the church as a religious institution called upon to minister to the needs of believers.' Its 'religious functions can in no case be exploited for political purposes'. To sum up, 'the church must be only the church, it must confine itself to matters of religion and remain in church'.[39] This implied that the church was not to get involved in politics after all.

The seeming ambiguity of Gomułka's declarations on church–state relations, which formed the basis of the resolutions officially adopted by the Congress, cannot be treated as an internal contradiction. It represents, rather, opposite sides of the same ideological coin. On the one hand a politicised church supporting the political and social system was acceptable. On the other, if it could not accept this stipulation, the church had to become depoliticised. Apolitical it could not become, because the very act of depoliticisation would be of a highly political nature. The church was, therefore, assigned a political function: 'if you cannot be for us, do not be against us'. In this way, at least in respect to one major social institution in Poland, the Gomułka ideology anticipated Kadar's more generally applicable directive, issued in 1962, that 'whoever is not against us is with us'.

SCIENCE AND CULTURE

Up until the VIII Plenum the leading role of the party in society was interpreted very rigorously. Not only were the scientific and cultural intelligentsia required to submit to the party line on political matters; they also had to contend with party involvement in their own spheres of activity. Science had to serve the needs of socialism, not the socialist system the needs of science. The social sciences in particular were required to adopt a correct ideological outlook. The influence of Western scientific thought on scientific developments in Poland was severely limited until 1956. Likewise in the cultural sphere the principle of socialist realism was viewed in very narrow terms. Its application to creative work was carefully monitored, and imitation of Western currents was strongly discouraged. Literary and artistic output had to be characterised by optimism stemming from the prospect of a better tomorrow. The operative ideology on these activities did not allow much scope for independence from these general lines.

1. Science

The decisions taken by the III Congress did not alter this ideology to any great extent. The resolutions proclaimed: 'The aim of the party's activity in the field of science is to ensure full victory of Marxism–Leninism as the methodological foundation of the whole of Polish learning.' For that reason it 'lends its widest support to the development of scientific research carried on from Marxist positions'. This approach would help 'in the development of an offensive of Marxist ideas against bourgeois theories, in the undertaking of scientific research and the formation of new, young Marxist cadres in all fields of science and learning'. But although such an approach was a desideratum, it need not be the only one taken by scientists. Like the church, they were free to act in their respective areas of jurisdiction, so long as this autonomy was not misused for political purposes: 'The party stands for free scientific discussion and the solution of scientific controversies by the scientists themselves; it also ensures proper conditions for work of non-Marxist scientists. But it will not tolerate anti-socialist attitudes or the use of didactic activity and scientific publications for attacking the party's policy and the socialist system.'[40] Again we observe the formula governing group autonomy: system support or political passivity.

2. Social science

The social sciences were given special attention at the Congress for two reasons. Firstly, they 'occupy a special place among scientific subjects owing to their close links with ideology and politics, and thus with the fight for the victory of socialism being waged in our country'. Secondly, 'despite their achievements they are the most backward sector of the scientific front'. For these reasons 'the party cannot be indifferent to what philosophical, sociological, economic, pedagogic views are disseminated in the community'. Gomułka's speech elaborated further on the subject. The party was engaged in a struggle against bourgeois views which had made themselves felt in the social sciences in recent years. This trend indicated not the real strength of bourgeois views but the weak resistance offered them by social scientists influenced by revisionist standpoints. Much had 'been recently done to overcome the traces of conservatism and dogmatism in the social sciences'. Contacts with scholars in other parts of the world had increased; an atmosphere of discussion and creativity had developed. Such innovations 'should be continued and developed'. However, the party's policy had involved mistakes, most importantly 'the underestimation of the role of the social sciences in the class struggle and in the struggle for the socialist transformation of the social consciousness, which are being waged in our country'. The first secretary concluded that this close link between the social sciences and the ideological and class struggles explained why 'we must differently shape our cultural policy in such ideological sciences as philosophy, sociology, economics and to a great extent, also pedagogy, jurisprudence, history, etc.'.[41]

These declarations indicated that the party would not interfere in the realm of science so long as the latter either did not tackle political issues or at least refrained from doing so in an anti-socialist way. More was demanded of the social sciences. They should not only not follow an anti-socialist course; they should also reject outright bourgeois views and adopt Marxist ones so as to be better equipped to engage in the ideological war with capitalism. One other condition was placed on scientific activity of any kind: 'all scientists should thoroughly acquaint themselves with the lines of development of the economic and cultural life of the country, as mapped out by the party, and try to link their research to the greatest possible extent with the needs of this life'. Here the operative concept was technological progress aimed at accelerating the economic development of the country.

3. Culture

Pronouncements concerned with cultural matters revealed a similar operative ideology. 'The present cultural policy, free of dogmatic errors, ensures to all artists and writers every opportunity for development, state economic help, freedom of artistic search, without administrative interference in matters of creative work.' Artistically worthy works written by past and contemporary authors could be published if, though not Marxist, they served the cause of man's liberation. This was the extent of autonomy allowed the cultural intelligentsia. But the limitations placed upon it were once again political and ideological. Gomułka referred to recently published works which had been influenced by revisionist and liberal–bourgeois tendencies:

Black literature was born proclaiming man's despair and helplessness in the face of evil, man's immanent cruelty and the futility of his social endeavours. Works were created which denigrate socialism and idealise its enemies. We refuse and shall continue to refuse publication of such works for they are not works of art but instruments of the political propaganda of anti-socialist forces.

Thus if cultural activity was seen as promulgating such values, it had to be suppressed. No autonomy could be permitted which was 'misused' in this way. On the other hand the values most highly acclaimed in artistic work were those 'broadening man's mental horizons, shaping his moral character and sense of beauty', those 'which serve to strengthen the socialist consciousness of the masses, to broaden their cultural horizons, to overcome ignorance, superstition, the bourgeois and clerical heritage', those 'which would be accessible, intelligible and near the working people and would express their socialist aspirations'. Works of art infused with these values deserved party support and 'were worthy of the widest popularisation'.[42] The stress laid on the values of realism and socialism remained, but these other types of value were now given equal rank. In this way the cultural intelligentsia was allowed greater autonomy in pursuing creative work than had been the case in the past.

4. Socialisation

Congress and Plenum resolutions dealing with culture usually included consideration of a related subject – *wychowanie*, or socialisation. The Polish term has a broad meaning and subsumes also the concepts of upbringing and education. In short, it refers to the inculcation of a cultural value system in the young person. At the III Congress, the declared purpose of socialisation was 'to form in young people a conscious discipline, orderliness in work, a sense of responsibility for each task received'. In addition; 'The cardinal task of schools should be preparation for productive and socially useful work.'[43] The utilitarian quality of these objectives is clear, and it is congruent with similar goals propounded by the leadership in the other spheres we have described – the use of science to accelerate economic development and the function of art as promulgation of work-related values. Destalinisation in operative ideology took the form, therefore, of a replacement of political rules governing action by economic utility ones.

POLITICAL VALUES AND SOCIETY

So far we have examined the operative ideology of the political leadership on the role of particular institutions and groups in Polish society during the period 1956–9. In this final section we consider the more universalist societal values contained in declarations on the construction of a socialist system. In addition we consider what principal factors were identified by the operative ideology as either promoting or retarding progress towards this goal.

The most important political value propagated in this period was socialist legality. Gomułka's address to the III Congress stressed the fundamental importance for socialist democracy of 'correct mutual relations between organs of state power and the citizens, observance of law and order by the state organs and observance of law and social discipline by the citizens'. In the period 1949–54, he acknowledged, 'abuses, distortions and law infringements' had taken place in the work of the organs of security and administration of justice. These had now been overcome: 'The rights of the citizens regarding legal defence and protection during investigation are at present observed as never before . . . In our country no innocent person can be punished or persecuted, the rights of every citizen are guaranteed.' But if abuses had been committed in the past which had adversely affected the development of socialist democracy, nevertheless the opposite error of unwarranted leniency also had to be avoided in the new social conditions produced by the October events. Thus 'The People's authority must always act according to law, it must be severe in relation to the enemies of socialism and in relation to all types of offenders.' Moreover 'The struggle to strengthen socialist justice and rule of law also calls for a speedy overcoming of excessive liberalism which expresses itself in lightly treating the activities against the People's state, in the renunciation by some courts of a class attitude towards the administration of justice, and in a tolerant attitude to abuses and looting of property.'

The importance of these twin dangers – excessive severity and excessive leniency shown by the judicial branch towards 'all types of offenders' – lay in the effects they could have on the social order. On the one hand corruption and thieving had constantly to be combated and measures for the protection of socialist property reinforced. For, according to Gomułka: 'Rooted deeply in a considerable section of the population is the conviction, inherited from capitalism, that the violation of socialised property is a lesser offence than the violation of private property.' On the other hand, the administration of justice should not lead to 'any suppression of conscientious criticism, any persecution of persons who expose abuses, fight cliques and watch over justice'.[44]

Two important issues were involved in Gomułka's statements on socialist legality; firstly, the observance by the state of legal regulations; and, secondly, the observance by society of social discipline. In the past the first principle had been violated, but following October the second was being threatened. By declaring that the state now intended to guarantee the rights of citizens, Gomułka was hoping to elicit in return wider support for the system. This was the beginning of the 'social compact' between the rulers and social groups which Pravda has described: workers' support for the system becomes conditional on its provision of welfare benefits and its respect for citizens' rights.[45] In the late 1950s, following the excesses of the Stalin era, fulfilment of the latter condition alone was a step forward and provided the regime with limited new support. A decade later, however, such a quid pro quo required compliance with the other condition – provision of welfare and material benefits. Gomułka was unable to fulfil his part of the bargain and was replaced by someone who, for a short while, did.

The problem of the conflicting needs of state (law and order, social discipline) and individuals (freedom to criticise, protection from harassment) did not only involve the judicial sphere. The rulers' overall view of the relationship between state and society was one-sidedly skewed in favour of the first. Gomułka asserted that his government could not promise 'castles in the air' and that the population could not expect 'manna from heaven'. Rather it was necessary 'to raise the consciousness of the masses, to develop among the working people a sense of inseparable unity between their personal fate and that of society, between the interests of individual groups and those of the nation'.[46] Group interests had always to be subordinated to the interests of society as a whole, and societal interests had in turn to be subordinated to the interests of socialist construction. This was, in short, the key societal value prescribed in that period. In later years a similar value was also propagated, but the concept of subordination was treated differently. Between 1956 and 1959 it was interpreted literally. Group autonomy was a function of political attitudes adopted, and society was regarded primarily as an agent of economic development.

The Polish October caused many to believe that the operative ideology of the new leadership would break radically with that of the past. For most people recognised that its fundamental principles could not be modified. In fact operative ideology did not change much either. Where autonomy was demanded the rulers spoke of decentralisation. Where a more democratic system was called for, the leadership reasserted the principle of the party's leading role in society. Where new and different societal goals were formulated, the ruling group announced that such revisionism constituted a threat to the political order and would not be tolerated. In this way the operative ideology of the early Gomułka years did not bear the marks of some distinctive Polish road to socialism, as some have claimed. It was conditioned above all by political expediency – by Gomułka's desire to consolidate his position at the top of the party, and by the party's need to reassert its leading role in society.

In his speech to the III Congress, Politburo member Zawadzki stated: 'Opinions are voiced that people are now living through a period of disappointment, that party matters and its policy are treated with indifference, that this policy represents an abandonment of the policy inaugurated by October 1956, and the like.'[47] The implication was that disillusionment had grown as the new rulers' operative ideology crystallised after 1956. An examination of the official discourse of that period shows that there had been no firm ground for assuming that operative ideology would differ substantially from that of the 1954–6 period. Only the adoption of the concepts of greater decentralisation, increased participation and socialist legality lent support to the view that political values were changing. Even these notions had been put forward before Gomułka's accession to power. Disillusionment appeared to be unjustified, therefore, for the hopes that were raised by the Polish October were founded almost exclusively on changes taking place in the top party leadership, not as some appreciable turn in ideology. Hopes attached to a more nationalist course – a Polish road to socialism – were also unwarranted, for this road referred primarily to relations between socialist states, not to internal power relations in Poland.

There were elements in the operative ideology, of course, which bred optimism amongst those advocating political change. The case of workers' councils furnishes the best example. The conditional autonomy granted to these, as well as to other groups, especially the cultural and scientific intelligentsia, may have been more than simply a short-term political ploy aimed at 'repressive tolerance', to employ Marcuse's term. But when the rulers found that group autonomy was incompatible with their rigorous interpretation of the party's leading role, the latter took precedence. For it was perceived to be more inextricably linked with the fundamental objective of socialist construction than group autonomy. We can suggest that operative ideology throughout that period was marked by conservatism and at no time envisaged substantive reforms in the political system. Its exposition at the III Congress left little room for subsequent doubt.

4

Little stabilisation and great upheaval, 1960–70

During the entire twenty-year period, we have listened to feeble abuse and slander levelled by imperialist broadcasting services, bankrupt elements thrown overboard, representatives of the old reactionary regime, and common traitors who sold themselves to foreign intelligence. If all the efforts of the enemies of socialism, of People's Poland, have ended up in a crushing fiasco, it is because the social and political base on which they could rest in their struggle against our people's state and authority has diminished from year to year. Today we are creating a society of working people without the old divisions into exploiters and exploited, without class antagonisms – a society regenerated in its composition and social structure.

> Władysław Gomułka, 20th anniversary of the
> founding of People's Poland, July 1964

Apologists for the Gomułka leadership have characterised the 1960s as a period of political and economic consolidation – a so-called little stabilisation period. Critics describe it as one of political and economic stagnation, eventual upheavals and disintegration. Both assume uninterrupted linear development leading either to a series of minor achievements or to failures. Yet the distinctive feature of that decade was the frequent political turns or 'zigzags' (as the rulers described them) that took place. The most important political cleavages were the conflict with intellectuals over Polish culture in 1964, the controversy between church and state over the celebration of the Millennium of Poland, which fell in 1966, the student demonstrations of March 1968, and the disturbances on the Baltic coast in December 1970, which toppled the Gomułka administration. In each case the rulers affirmed that enemies of socialism, both within and outside the country, sought to undermine the achievements of People's Poland and to restore a 'bankrupt' and 'reactionary' *ancien régime*. If this was so, then Gomułka's statement that the social and political base upon

72

which hostile forces could rest was diminishing seemed unfounded. If it were not enemies of socialism who were responsible for political instability but more general social discontent with the policies of the leadership, then it was difficult to speak of a regenerated society of working people devoid of socio-economic divisions and class antagonisms.

The Central Committee's report to the V Congress, held in November 1968, included a section entitled 'The social and political situation in the country'. Untypically, the resolutions finally adopted did not contain either this title or the Central Committee's lengthy introduction to this section. The introduction described the problems that the party had encountered in the 1960s: firstly, with 'representatives of the liberal–bourgeois, revisionist and cosmopolitan current' in literary circles who, in 1964, supported by Radio Free Europe, attacked the party using as their pretext the 'defence of the national culture'; secondly, with 'a part of the church hierarchy and the forces of clerical reaction' which, in 1965–6, launched a frontal attack on the People's state and its foreign policy; and, thirdly, with 'revisionist elements' and, aligning themselves alongside these, 'Zionist elements' which had penetrated the academic community and had instigated the 1968 student riots.[1] This was the official explanation for the series of disturbances which occurred during the inappropriately named little stabilisation period. How did the operative ideology promulgated in the 1960s reflect this political instability (if it did so at all)? What values were propagated in the issue-areas we have selected in order to resolve political cleavage? We now turn to an examination of these questions.

THE CASE OF THE PARTY

In the previous chapter we identified two main components in operative ideology on intraparty democracy: (1) political unity and (2) elite–mass links. In turn intraparty democracy was held to influence the extent of democracy within the whole political system, based on the implementation of the principle of the party's leading role in society. The more democratic, assertive and integrated the party, the more democratic the political system was thought to be. By 1959 the key concept in the rulers' operative ideology on intraparty democracy was political unity, and on system democracy it was party involvement in all spheres of society. What ideological modifications (if any) were effected by the Gomułka leadership in the period of zigzags?

1. Intraparty democracy

Political unity within the party, a factor strongly emphasised after Gomułka took power, became less prominent in the operative ideology of the 1960s. The reason for this was clear; as one writer observed: 'After a period of stormy discussion in which the thought of the party became crystallised, after years of struggle with incorrect views and tendencies, consolidation of party ranks has been achieved. With it the party's influence has increased as well.'[2] The years immediately following the III Congress had, it was claimed, strengthened ideological and political unity within the party. The rapid growth in membership meant, however, that considerable efforts had still to be undertaken in this area. For the 'chase after numbers' was often accompanied by diminished concern for the quality of new members, some of whom were dishonest, decadent and without ideals. Tolerance shown towards such people and towards 'all types of cliques, of schemers, of suppressors of criticism and of squabblers harms the party, disturbs its links with its environment, and undermines its social authority. And yet instances of such detrimental and unpardonable tolerance are not at all rare.'[3]

Thus the specific problem of political unity within the party took on secondary importance in the early 1960s and instead the characteristics and calibre of new recruits were given greater attention. The threat posed by revisionism, identified by the III Congress as the most dangerous phenomenon affecting unity, was not altogether dismissed, however. Certain aspects of the revisionist ideology were still reflected, it was argued, in media reporting, such as the propensity towards 'sterile negation' and 'fruitless criticism' of some aspects of social life, and snobbish imitation of Western life-styles and culture.[4] Likewise in the social sciences revisionist views, though now rarer, had not been completely eradicated.[5] We look at these issues in more detail in the section on culture and science; here we may note simply that revisionism was identified as located outside the party apparatus: within the party the revisionist faction was considered to have been eliminated.

Gomułka's address to the IV Congress of the PUWP, held in

June 1964, contained only very brief attacks on dogmatism and revisionism, in contrast to his lengthy diatribe at the preceding Congress. Moreover, having consolidated a centrist position, he balanced criticism of left and right factions within the party: dogmatists 'see the central problem of Marxism not in its evolution and links with real life, but in its scholastic observation of the purity of theses which arose in a different epoch and in different historical conditions'; revisionism 'is knuckling under the pressure stemming from bourgeois ideology, propagating slogans for freedom for anti-socialist forces and anti-Marxist currents, questioning the leading role of the party in the social and cultural life of the country'. The strongest statement on party unity came in the first secretary's closing remarks to the Congress. Party strength was based firstly on its correct general line and secondly on unity and discipline within its ranks, he said. 'We must watch over party unity like over the apple of one's eye. There is no place in party ranks for squabblers, careerists or persons ideologically alien to our party.'[6]

We may suggest, therefore, that the leadership's operative ideology on party unity between 1959 and 1964 was concerned more with the dangers posed by the growth in numbers and the potential deterioration in the moral fibre of its ranks than with political threats posed by the existence of factions or groups. Although never specifically stating it, the Congress seemed to acknowledge that these had now been eliminated.

If the operative ideology contained fewer references to the dangers of revisionism, it did not necessarily follow that a more 'open' process of policy-making within the party was recommended. Few statements stressed the importance of the right to express criticism freely within the party. In his IV Congress speech Gomułka did emphasise the democratic aspect of the principle of democratic centralism in governing intraparty activity. But 'ensuring conditions for free frank discussion and exchange of opinions, for the development of criticism' was placed alongside other democratic mechanisms, such as holding regular general meetings in the party's basic committees and increasing the importance of collegial methods of activity. The party leader simply reiterated long-standing principles without adding new emphasis to them.

In the preceding chapter we noted how at the time of the III Congress basic committees were urged to become more active in party life and how improved elite–mass relations became an often-declared goal of the leadership so as to overcome its previous estrangement from the masses. Between 1959 and 1964 these values were rarely identified. Instead the concerns most frequently expressed in official discourse included the call for individual members to exhibit high moral and ideological qualities and the need for basic committees to ensure that resolutions of higher-level committees were being carried out. Operative ideology, therefore, now focused less on elite–mass relations than on the role of basic committees as moral guardians and executive watchdogs for the entire party. It is true that the IV Congress resolutions called for 'an increase in the activeness and role of the party's basic committees and of the status of the general caucus in basic committees'. But again this could be seen as a *Minimalprogramm*: the absence of such a declaration would have been more unusual than its formal inclusion. What did represent a novel proposal at the Congress was the call for basic committees to inculcate social and political activeness in individual members and to assign them specific tasks to carry out.[7] For even in the party's ranks, it was admitted, socialist consciousness did not arise automatically in step with socialist construction. It did not consist simply of an affirmation of socialist values; it also involved active participation in their application.[8]

Thus, whereas operative ideology after 1956 stressed relations between different tiers in the party apparatus as a means of increasing intraparty democracy, its counterpart in the early 1960s highlighted relations between basic committees and their members. In each case participation and assertiveness were deemed to be the key values which should characterise these relations. Such 'atomisation' of party life may be interpreted as a shift away from simple relaxation of the centralist principle towards positive emphasis by 1964 on the democratic aspect. It may also be viewed as continued concern for the calibre of recruits to the party in the early 1960s. But the neglect of relations between upper and lower tiers in this period may have implied above all *de facto* reassertion of centralist dominance in the apparatus. Elite–mass links may have become an expendable value once political unity and leadership consolidation had been achieved.

In the mid 1960s political unity within the party continued to be accepted as given and did not figure prominently in official discourse. This was in spite of the controversies that took place in this period. Firstly, in March 1964, thirty-four Polish intellectuals signed a letter criticising excessive censorship and describing it as a threat to Polish culture, soon to celebrate its Millennium. Then, later that year, two Warsaw University teachers, Kuroń and Modzelewski, wrote 'An open letter to the party', condemning the central political bureaucracy that was said to run the country. In 1965 the Catholic church embarked on a 'Great Novena', marking the religious basis of the country's approaching thousandth anniversary. At the same time Polish bishops addressed a letter to the German episcopate suggesting, amongst other things, Poland's position as the easternmost bastion of Christianity. The political rulers treated these challenges as isolated incidents. They were not perceived as likely to have any impact on political unity within the party. As a result, this subject remained a non-issue throughout this period.

Organisational considerations, in particular elite–mass relations, were also neglected by the leadership in the mid 1960s. At the II Plenum held in December 1964, the Katowice first secretary, Gierek, disclosed how his provincial committee had received some 21,000 'opinions' from lower levels of the apparatus.[9] The electoral campaign staged by the party in 1965 had, it was claimed, shown an increase in the 'autonomous activity' of local committees.[10] Such indicators of initiative could only mean that intraparty democracy was functioning as it should. From the 1959 PUWP Congress to the May 1967 VIII Plenum, intraparty democracy constituted an insignificant aspect of the leadership's operative ideology.

In 1967 references began to be made not only to the existence of reactionary elements abroad but also to 'liberal–bourgeois' and, eventually, 'revisionist' tendencies found within certain groups of intellectuals and social scientists in Poland. Criticism was directed particularly at those who subscribed to a so-called technocratic view of society, in which the gulf between rulers and ruled, specialists and laymen, was regarded as bound to widen.[11] At the VIII Plenum, the party ideologue Kliszko condemned those who viewed with sympathy the liberal–bourgeois democratic model which permitted a free play of political forces. In socialist conditions, he argued, political liberty had to be limited so as not to allow reactionary elements to abuse it. The Plenum accordingly passed a resolution declaring that the party opposed both those who displayed so little confidence in the masses as to urge a return to a more centrally directed system of government and those who 'in the name of integrally conceived abstract democracy wish to weaken the leading role of the party and the working class in our society and demand a free play of political forces'.[12] The phraseology began to resemble that used at the III Congress, which had launched a scathing attack on revisionist elements in the party.

This identification of liberal–bourgeois tendencies came shortly after calls, originating within the party, were made for greater freedom in expressing criticism. By this time in neighbouring Czechoslovakia, pressure for reform of the political structure had mounted to the point where even Novotny's position could be assailed. Jurists were calling for the establishment of a 'civic society', philosophers for 'authentic Marxism', writers for 'limitless realism' and political scientists for a 'return to Europe'.[13] Economic reforms were being implemented in Czechoslovakia, as well as in the German Democratic Republic, Hungary and Bulgaria. But in Poland the Gomułka administration stood unmoved in the face of pressure for socio-economic reform. The idea of criticism within the party was, therefore, very quickly countered. The trade union leader, Loga-Sowiński, declared that 'criticism and its scope have to be evaluated according to very specific criteria'.[14] The VIII Plenum made clear that whilst constructive criticism was welcome, destructive, demagogic criticism dealing only with negative features of society had to be vigorously opposed.[15] Here, too, the tone of declarations was similar to that at the III Congress.

As a result the principle of democratic centralism, which in the early 1960s was infrequently invoked, now began to be asserted again. The VIII Plenum employed it to place conditions on free discussion in the party. Gomułka's earlier thesis that 'only a system of the dictatorship of the proletariat can proclaim the principle of restrictions on freedom in the name of freedom' was reiterated.[16] And when he addressed party activists in Warsaw in the midst of the March disturbances, he repeated that the concepts of democracy and liberty were not abstract and had clearly delineated parameters.[17]

The 1968 disturbances were triggered off by the closing of a controversial production of Mickiewicz's *Forefathers' Eve*, which contains certain anti-Russian passages. Students staged demonstrations to protest against the closure, and the Warsaw branch of the Polish Writers' Union lent its support to the call for greater cultural freedom. The events were used by rival factions in the party to consolidate their respective positions. Thus the security chief, Moczar, instigated a campaign against alleged Zionist elements in intellectual circles. Many Jews lost their jobs and were forced to leave Poland. Students were beaten and some expelled from university.

Gomułka was obliged to adopt hard-line tactics in order to maintain his centrist position in the ruling elite, but at the same time he dissociated himself from the more extreme aspects of Moczar's campaign. The March disturbances produced battles in the streets and open conflict in the party.

Not surprisingly, therefore, the XII Plenum, which was held shortly after the events, underscored the importance of political unity within the party. Party rulers had even greater reason to close ranks, for by the spring of 1968 the Czechoslovak Communist Party appeared to have lost both internal cohesion and its leading role in society. Where the 'Action Programme' of the Czechoslovak Communist Party now emphasised the need for genuine intraparty democracy, speeches delivered by Gomułka and Gierek at the XII Plenum singled out the importance of unity and democratic centralism. Gierek even argued bravely that party unity 'had been strengthened in its struggle with reaction' during the March disturbances.[18] In reality, however, jockeying for position in the inner ruling circle had increased in intensity.

At the V Congress – Gomułka's last – intraparty democracy was given greater attention than at the previous one. The reason was outlined in the first secretary's opening speech: 'Historical experience demonstrates that a Marxist–Leninist party can successfully perform its leading role in society if it systematically applies the Leninist principle of democratic centralism in its internal life.' Gomułka put forward a balanced view of the concept: one-sided emphasis on centralism in party activity often led to the undermining of intraparty debate and democracy, which was a sectarian deviation; in turn, dropping the principle of centralism and one-sidedly applying the right to discuss and criticise constituted a revisionist deformation which generated factionalism and incapacitated the party's attempts to construct socialism.[19]

Not only political unity was underlined at the time of the March events, however. Relations between tiers in the party apparatus were also now given more attention. Already during the 1967 electoral campaign, Babiuch declared: 'It is a fact that because we are absorbed with problems of the country's economic and social development, we talk more about what party committees should be doing in this sphere and less about what the party itself is like, how its internal life is evolving, how the various tiers are functioning and improving.' He concluded that much remained to be done to improve the work of basic committees, especially with regard to the caucus (or general meeting) at this level.[20] Likewise the VIII Plenum asserted that the caucus was the seat of authority in the party and that the tendency to have the executive committee make decisions on matters affecting the whole organisation was erroneous. The basic committees' general interest in economic and production problems and neglect of broader political issues was condemned.[21] Thus, in a very cryptic way, Gomułka's statement at the 1964 Congress that the economic front should be the chief concern of party committees was by 1967 coming under attack.

Criticism of the party's organisational weaknesses increased after the March events. The role of the caucus remained a purely formal one, it was claimed.[22] In November 1970, one month before the strikes and demonstrations on the coast, Grudzień, a close political ally of Gierek, condemned the inadequate provision of information to party members: 'Sterility of information can bring about serious harm and deprivation. Without candid and objective information, there can be no creative or inspired criticism, which is the mainspring of progress and development.'[23] Gomułka's imminent successors were thus advocating an alternative operative ideology to that in place up to the December crisis.

A certain complacency can be detected in the Gomułka administration's operative ideology on intraparty democracy in the 1960s. For most of the decade, satisfaction was expressed with the state of party unity. It was believed that reaction and revisionism were located outside the party and, for a long time, outside the country. The concern of the leadership was with the calibre of party members rather than with the general functioning of the party apparatus, and with economic functions of the party rather than political ones. Despite repeated challenges to its authority, the leadership never considered overhauling intraparty life, and its one venture into reform – a limited campaign to encourage criticism within lower levels of the apparatus – was curtailed in the wake of the March events and the Prague spring. It is possible, therefore, to speak of a misleading assessment of intraparty democracy by Gomułka. In much the same way as the rulers congratulated themselves on having prevented the working class from allying with the intellectuals during the 1968 troubles (which we examine in some detail below), only to be swept from power by that same working class two years later, so too its operative ideology asserting political unity was camouflage for a quite different reality. Gomułka was alerted to the threat posed to his leadership by Moczar as a result of the March street-fighting and party infighting, but he simultaneously underestimated the threat to his idea of political unity posed by the technocrat faction (Gierek, Grudzień, Babiuch). Failure to look more critically at intraparty democracy in the late 1960s, in terms both of the degree of political unity amongst the ruling elite and of the kind of relations prevailing between upper and lower tiers of the apparatus, contributed to the adoption of the ill-conceived policies which precipitated the workers' protests and led to Gomułka's speedy downfall.

2. The leading role of the party

In the late 1950s operative ideology placed greater emphasis on the party's leading role: as intraparty unity increased, the whole apparatus was expected to adopt a more assertive role in society. In the 1960s economic development became the most important issue for the leadership, and it was in this sphere that the party was supposed to carry out its leading role. As Gomułka made clear to the IV Congress, 'the main front of activity of all party committees is the national economy'. Specific responsibilities included the need to ensure that work discipline was maximised, that the interests of economic enterprises were congruent with societal interests, that a socialist form of interpersonal relations was established, that the competence of management was regularly evaluated and that the economic decisions of party and government were carried out.[24]

At the same time, a qualification was placed on the party's performance of the leading role. Already in late 1963, at the XIV Plenum, Gomułka put forward the thesis that 'the party and its Central Committee cannot duplicate the work of the government and administration'. A precise delineation of responsibilities between the two structures had to be drawn.[25] At the IV Congress he added that the party's role was 'to inspire and coordinate the activity of these bodies, not to become a substitute for them'.[26] The over-zealous conduct attributed to the party and the need to moderate its exercise of the leading role stand in sharp contrast to the immediate post-October period when its ability to carry out its function appeared to be in doubt. The problem of overlap in the activities of party and state organs, caused by a more assertive posture taken by the party, was to bedevil the leadership throughout the 1960s. Under Gierek efforts were made to separate party and state jurisdiction, but it is important to stress that very early on Gomułka, too, became aware of the dangers posed by overlap.

In the mid 1960s the leadership continued to be preoccupied with the party's performance of the leading role. Whilst the economic sector took precedence, other social spheres had also to be penetrated by the party. We say more on this later in this chapter. At this time operative ideology also showed concern with international problems that had a bearing on the party's position. Radio Free Europe and the Polish-language Paris publishing house Kultura were identified as the principal 'reactionary enemies of Poland abroad'. Gomułka's speech, delivered on the twentieth anniversary of the founding of People's Poland (cited at the outset of this chapter), was character-istic of this ideological campaign. Thus, whilst intraparty democracy was taken for granted, the leadership focused attention on economic problems at home and political threats from abroad.

A change in this pattern occurred in the late 1960s. If the 1964 PUWP Congress had urged the party to exert influence in all spheres of society and problem-areas, and had underscored its leading role in such specific areas as the economy, the plan, the work enterprise and self-management, then between 1967 and 1970 greater prominence was given to its role in macro-politics. In particular, the party's relation to three key system variables was highlighted: (1) links with the masses, especially the working class; (2) relations with the state administration; and (3) relevance to the system of socialist democ-racy. We look at each in turn.

Relations between the party and the masses were considered to be inadequate even before the March disturbances. At the VIII Plenum, held in mid 1967, Kliszko chided lower levels of the apparatus for displaying greater initiative and competence during national cam-paigns (such as at election time) than in their day-to-day political activity. One of the results was that attempts to transform the political consciousness of the masses lagged far behind the process of implementing specific policies.[27] Later that year he noted the impor-tance of achieving national unity through the exercise of the party's leading role in society.[28]

In his important speech to party activists in Warsaw at the time of the March troubles, Gomułka concentrated on the positive aspects of the party's performance and, most significantly, its relations with the working class:

There, in the factories, amongst the workers and working people, our party receives its main support; there is found the vital spirit and source of our political power. The focus of our attention and activity should be strengthening and deepening the party's links with the working class. The posture taken by the working class, and the intelligentsia working closely with it, during these March days confirms that no force of reaction can undermine the basis of our socialist system.[29]

After March Cyrankiewicz took a more sombre look at the events. The premier acknowledged that they had 'brought into the open many of the failings, bureaucratic deviations, and even abuses of positions and authority, instances of extravagance, and contempt for societal interests' within the party.[30] But by the time of the Congress in November 1968, a more upbeat interpretation of the troubles was presented again:

The March events showed very clearly once again that the working class performs the leading role in the nation, it constitutes the decisive political force in the country, it represents the mainstay of popular authority. Thanks to the support of the working class, our party is able to resolve bitter class strife with the forces of the social right in favour of socialism.[31]

The most successful example of the implementation of the party's leading role, therefore, and its single greatest political achievement, was held to be its relationship with the working class.

The V Congress also emphasised the mass character of the party: this demonstrated 'the measure of its influence in society, testifying to the broad support of the working class as well as the intelligentsia and peasants for its policies'. The size of the party, therefore, seemed to be equated with the extent of its influence in society. Such a risky proposition may have represented a further misleading diagnosis of the Polish polity given by the rulers in the late 1960s.

From the 1967 VIII Plenum onwards, a second major aspect of the party's leading role was its relationship with administrative organs. Directives for the V Congress stated that the party apparatus should not become a replacement for state administration in the management of the economy. The ambiguous division of jurisdiction between party and state structures had brought about 'the widespread and harmful phenomenon of obliteration of personal responsibility' in various spheres of activity. The Central Committee's report to the Congress went further: it declared that the party's leading role was weakened and deformed whenever it acted as a substitute for the state administration. Lines of responsibility

were effaced and party committees became bureaucratised.[32] Late
in 1970 it was still claimed that party committees were carrying out
the responsibilities of administrative bodies.[33] It would be erroneous to conclude, therefore, that the Gomułka leadership was
oblivious to the problems engendered by duplication of the work of
state organs by the party and that it took Gierek to expose these difficulties in full. It was at the level of practice that Gomułka failed,
not at the ideological level. The classic case of the immovability of
the middle-level party apparatus seems to be illustrated in
Gomułka's failure.

The third relationship stressed in operative ideology on the leading
role in this period was that between the party and the development of
socialist democracy in the country. Naturally the party had always
been seen as the institutionalisation of the idea of socialist democracy,
but in the late 1960s this was highlighted as never before. Politburo
member Spychalski noted the dialectical nature of the relationship:
the political maturity of the party determined the extent of socialist
democracy, whilst the universality of democratic practices affected
the party's ability to introduce appropriate structural changes.[34]
Another writer asserted that those who opposed the party's leading
role were in fact opposing the development of socialist democracy.[35]
Finally, Grudzień, in his article published on the eve of the 1970
upheavals, described the significance of the party's role in socialist
development: a system of checks on the party apparatus at all levels 'is
an effective instrument promoting socio-economic activity, and it
permits us to be wiser not after the damage is done but when the
threat of such damage first appears'.[36]

To summarise, the principle of the leading role of the party in society
was, in contrast to intraparty democracy, stressed throughout the
1960s. At first a more economist interpretation was propounded, but
after 1967 the more orthodox political view was taken. Some of the
concepts more often associated with the Gierek period, such as the
separation of party and state functions and the party's links with the
masses, were operative under Gomułka towards the end of his rule. It
appears that he was not as blind to the political circumstances around
him as is often made out, and that he recognised the need for a more
dynamic operative ideology on the party's role in society so as to
respond to the country's accumulating social, economic and political
problems.

3. The party and ideology

A final aspect of the leadership's views on the party concerned its performance of ideological and agitprop work. The 1959 Congress noted, we recall, that something resembling a lapse into illiteracy had taken place in members' knowledge of Marxism–Leninism. Official discourse of the 1960s referred less to illiteracy in fundamental principles than to lack of commitment at the level of operative ideology. At the 1963 XIII Plenum, devoted exclusively to ideology, Gomułka explained the reasons for this new focus: 'Attitudes to such fundamental questions as socialisation of the means of production outside agriculture, democratic people's authority, Poland's membership in the socialist camp, and our struggle for peace – in a word – to the fundamental principles of the system, have been definitively resolved in social consciousness.' But socialist construction also involved the application of socialist ethics in interpersonal relations, the inculcation of new attitudes to the state, work and public property, and the formation of a new socialist national culture. In these areas, Gomułka contended, the party had not shown sufficient initiative.[37]

The 1964 Congress stressed the significance of carrying out ideological work in society, but added that the party's main task was to intensify the 'pulse' of ideological discourse within its own structure. Growth in membership made this even more urgent. The party's ideological work and socialisation 'had to be more specific, more imbued with solid scientific argumentation than in the past, and it should be more closely related to the practical needs of society'.

In contrast to the 1956–9 period, there were now no explicit references to an ideological vacuum or waywardness. Official pronouncements continued to pinpoint the importance of ideological activity by the party, but with the threat of revisionism regarded as non-existent in the apparatus, ideology was increasingly identified with political socialisation. The party had to inculcate specific, often practical, values in society, most importantly, a work ethic. At this level much remained to be done. But the party could carry out such work in its day-to-day activity by adopting a more 'offensive' stance and by overseeing the moral and political pedigree of its cadres. Official discourse on ideological indoctrination reflected the general assumption that stabilisation had been achieved, for the important task of instilling the fundamental principles of the system throughout society has been 'definitively resolved'. The contradictory conclusions were drawn that the ideological vacuum had disappeared, and that only the specifics had to be filled in throughout society. The party had successfully propagated its fundamental principles, official discourse claimed, and at the same time it had failed to show ideological thrust. As a result we can speak of the emergence of an ideological hiatus during most of the decade.

A shift in the rulers' approach to ideological and agitprop work occurred in 1967. During the election campaign it was pointed out that concern with economic issues had led the party to underestimate the importance of ideology. The widespread belief that 'everything that is obvious to me must be obvious to others' had given rise to self-satisfaction and ideological inertia in some quarters.[38] The Politburo's report to the VIII Plenum recommended that the party's economic and ideological activities should be integrated.[39] Inadequacies in ideological indoctrination had brought about a proliferation of particularist interests.[40] The lack of ideological resoluteness in local committees and individual party members was especially worrying,[41] and at the 1968 XII Plenum Gomułka concluded:

During the entire period that our party has existed, since the liberation of the country and the establishment of People's Poland, we have always displayed certain weaknesses in our ideological work ... The answer to the question – wherein lie the sources of our ideological laxity – may be found in the quite distant past. To a large extent it is the result of our national tradition, of the specific history of the Polish nation.

The March events had not really constituted a threat to socialism, but they had revealed the ideological frailty of the young generation.[42]

The V Congress concurred with Gomułka's analysis. The party's ideological work remained one of its weakest links, and the entire apparatus, from the Central Committee to basic committees, was to blame. So long as capitalism remained superior to socialism in certain economic spheres, 'there will always be people amongst us who will compare our country's level of development with that of advanced capitalist states, and they will harbour doubts as to the superiority of socialism'. Revisionism throve in such conditions, and ideological work had, consequently, to be stepped up.[43]

Yet after the Congress little more was said on ideology. Effective propagation of the rulers' operative ideology was again shelved. The 1967–8 campaign to raise the status of ideological work in the party had petered out. But as we see in subsequent chapters, this was not the last campaign of this kind to be abandoned.

In the last chapter we described the way in which operative ideology on industrial democracy oscillated between 1956 and 1959. An initially participatory ideology gave way to one stressing bureaucratic goals, and this was reflected in practice by the incorporation of workers' councils into self-management committees. The declared functions of the committees centred increasingly on production targets, planning norms and other economic interests of the enterprise, which were claimed to coincide with the material interests of the work-force. Gradually self-management had less to do with management of the enterprise than with mobilisation of the workers.

This trend to have workers' self-management serve management interests continued into the 1960s. Whenever economic difficulties arose, self-management bodies were exhorted to play a greater part in helping resolve them. For example, in the period 1959–62, the III Plenum stressed the importance of strengthening work discipline and productivity in the factory and noted how self-management committees could assist;[44] the V Plenum referred to their role in bringing about savings in the level of investment;[45] the IX Plenum described their importance in overcoming economic problems in 1962;[46] and the X Plenum related technological advances registered by enterprises to the analyses carried out by self-management committees.[47] Only at the XIV Plenum, held late in 1963, did attention shift from the economic interests of the enterprise to the workers' interests: the Plenum urged party committees to ensure that the rights of the work-force were respected, that manifestations of bureaucracy and insensitivity to workers' proposals were countered, and that all forms of cliquishness and collusion between self-management leaders and factory directors were combated.[48] The way out of such difficulties was, predictably, considered to be economist. As the V Trade Union Congress, held in November 1962, put it, 'the authority of self-management committees will grow the more they concentrate on an improvement in the enterprise's economic performance'.[49]

At this time the role of trade unions in the system of industrial democracy was given greater attention. According to one writer: 'The resolutions of the October 1959 Plenum initiated the process of broadening trade union powers and, with it, increased participation of the working masses in management.'[50] Gomułka told the Trade Union Congress that it was the union movement which was primarily responsible for overseeing improvements in work efficiency and reductions in production costs. Congress resolutions urged trade union committees at all levels to 'consider the needs and feelings of the masses, undertake frank discussions with them, confront difficult issues openly, and make the right deductions from workers' criticism'.[51]

The rise in importance of the trade union movement was formalised at the 1964 party Congress. It was placed alongside the National Unity Front (which coordinated the work of the three political parties) and self-management as a cornerstone of the system of socialist democracy. Gomułka's keynote address made only passing reference to self-management and instead concentrated on the role and functions of trade unions. It was true that these functions were, like those of management, mainly economic – improvements in methods of management, exploitation of the full potential of factories, supervision of the system of economic incentives, and evaluations of the distribution of the wage fund. The traditional social, cultural and educational functions of trade unions were also identified.[52] Nevertheless the declared importance of unions now surpassed that of workers' self-management, which was the first time this had occurred since 1956.

Another innovation in operative ideology on industrial democracy came after the IV Congress. The II Plenum expressed its disapproval of the bureaucratic methods used to formulate economic plans, arguing that they imposed decisions on countless economic enterprises from above, thereby stifling their initiative. The actual blueprint for the plan should, the Plenum recommended, be shaped by the factory work-force.[53] Moreover, a climate of unhindered criticism could help overcome many of the problems resulting from bureaucratic practices and ineffective planning and management.[54] As one writer noted: 'Opinions, proposals and criticism are to a greater extent becoming a method of direct social involvement in the country's political process and, to a lesser extent, represent alarm signals pointing to failures and shortcomings.'[55] At the 1967 VIII Plenum, Kliszko concluded that 'criticism from below' had revealed the incompetence of many administrative organs.[56] Directives for the V PUWP Congress recommended an increase in free discussion and criticism throughout the system of socialist democracy, economic enterprises included. No new institutions were required to improve the existing system, the directives argued, if present ones took full advantage of the powers they possessed.[57] Thus, in the mid 1960s, criticism from below became an important component in the rulers' ideology on industrial democracy, as it had been in their ideology on intraparty democracy.

The VI Trade Union Congress, held in 1967, further corroborated the growing importance of the movement in the system of socialist democracy. The slogan of the Congress was: 'Production and self-management are the practical schools of co-management.' Trade unions were identified as the principal institutions promoting both production and self-management, and their functions included linking higher living standards to growth in production. Self-management committees, on the other hand, were ascribed such menial tasks as quality control and work emulation.[58]

The steady decline in the importance of the self-management committee as an institution was reflected in the attempt to broaden the concept of self-management. In a sense this represented Gomułka's 'second stage' in lowering the status of industrial democracy in operative ideology: the first had been the broadening of workers' councils into self-management committees in 1959. As one article published in *Nowe Drogi* in 1967 put it: 'At present we can say that in a broad sense workers' self-management does not simply consist of workers' councils and self-management committees; it includes all organisations of the working class in existence in the factory, above all party and trade union committees.'[59] The status of self-management committees in the mid 1960s went the way, therefore, of that of workers' councils in 1958. The conceptual revision described could only be considered as an attempt to give meaning to the notion of workers' self-management. It was too important an ideological concept to be entirely dropped from official discourse. Nevertheless industrial democracy lost much of its substance with this theoretical revision, which formalised a process that had begun at the III Congress and was given impetus by the IV Congress.

Just before the V Congress, an article appeared in the party theoretical journal which attempted to present a balance sheet of the achievements and failures of workers' self-management during its twelve-year existence. The institution, it was said, had often been ignored by factory management; it had never fully taken advantage of

the legislative powers it had been given in order to control management; and it had frequently been characterised by inertia and lack of
initiative in the factory. On the other hand, workers' self-
management had, it was claimed, proved its indispensability in the
economic life of the country, and the idea of co-management had
especially taken root in the consciousness of the working class.[60]

Yet in the late 1960s another zigzag took place in Gomułka's
operative ideology. At the 1968 party Congress, self-management was
suddenly given more prominence than at any time since 1956. Three
factors appear to have been responsible for this about-turn. The first
was the leadership's perception of the attitude of the working class
during the March disturbances. Interpreting the Kadar thesis *sensu
stricto*, the leadership concluded that since the workers did not join the
intellectuals in challenging the government, they had in effect come
out for the government. As a reward, Gomułka decided to expand the
role of self-management committees. The second factor was the
Warsaw Pact invasion of Czechoslovakia in August 1968. Some
measure had to be taken to win popular support for the regime at a
time when the vast majority of Poles condemned the country's
participation in the invasion. Gomułka had to demonstrate that in
principle he was not against reform, even though the Czechoslovak
experiment had been cut short. A new-found commitment to workers'
self-management could be projected as reform-mindedness in an
otherwise conservative political system. The third factor was the
desire of the leadership to avoid a crisis in the near future. Economic
data spoke for themselves: in 1969, growth in national income was
limited to only 3.5%, whilst real wages increased by only half that. A
cautious programme of economic reform, based on a system of
material incentives, was introduced at that time. But in order to
forestall the workers' immediate economic grievances, an ideological
concession was offered – more responsive and responsible self-
management bodies. This strategy of crisis management was
designed to bolster Gomułka's authority in the one section of society
he considered decisive – the working class.

At the V Congress, therefore, Gomułka lauded the recent functioning of self-management: its influence in economic enterprises had
expanded and, with it, the participation of the working class in
economic management. Weaknesses remained, for example, the tendency of self-management committees to accept uncritically proposals put forward by management. But the responsibilities they

possessed ensured them, argued Gomułka, great stature in the factory.[61]

The Congress also reiterated the importance of criticism from below. As the Central Committee report stressed, 'we should systematically counter attempts of persons in managerial positions to suppress or ignore criticism'. Self-management committees had a crucial role to play in the articulation of 'social criticism'. This concept was to remain operative up to the end of the Gomułka administration.

After a brief period in the mid 1960s, when trade unions received greater prominence in operative ideology on industrial democracy, the 1968 Congress signalled a return to the pre-eminence of self-management committees. After believing earlier on that unions could take up the slack created by increasingly quiescent self-management organs in mobilising workers for greater productivity, the rulers became disillusioned and reverted to these bodies, especially when political cleavage increased. An article published in *Nowe Drogi* in 1970 reviewed the changing fortunes of workers' self-management. In its first phase, immediately after 1958, it concentrated on such issues as production, planning and management. In the second, in the 1960s, it was concerned with improvements in work conditions, the introduction of technology, and so on. In the phase now beginning, the article said, self-management was to focus on more general matters, such as economic growth in enterprises and throughout society, and improvements in management methods. Throughout its history, however, self-management had never been accorded the respect due to it by management. Self-management committees had not been provided with the conditions necessary in order to carry out their functions; nor were their recommendations always treated seriously.[62] Perhaps the most succinct description of the role envisaged for self-management at the end of the decade was that given by the leader of the trade unions to the V Plenum: it had to make it clear to all workers that 'you will have nothing to divide up unless you first produce it'.[63]

This concludes our survey of official discourse in the 1960s on industrial democracy. Whereas during the brief 1956–9 period the idea of industrial democracy was the subject of controversy and differing interpretations, throughout the next decade it became less contentious. Moreover there was greater consensus on its nature. For example, the statement that only production created income was similar to the declaration made at the III Congress that the standard of living would improve if the targets of the economic plan were attained. In each case the propagation of this tenet amongst the work-force was considered to be the most important function of self-management bodies. From 1959 onwards all workers' organisations in existence at the factory level – self-management, trade union and party committees – were urged to concentrate on the 'economic front'. Even the three-phase evolutionary process of self-management described could be reduced to a single stage since production, cost reductions and management efficiency represented a common theme running throughout this period.

But closer analysis indicates that operative ideology on industrial democracy underwent a series of zigzags between 1959 and 1970. Although the IX and X Plena held in 1961–2 reaffirmed the significance of workers' self-management as a concept, the institution of the self-management committee was allocated minor functions. Simultaneously the trade union organisation was declared to have responsibility for the important matters of productivity and efficiency. The IV Congress appeared to confirm the trend towards abandoning self-management committees as the key element in industrial democracy and towards concentrating instead on trade union activity as a way to help boost economic results. Congress resolutions suggested that self-management committees could only succeed in performing their co-management role if trade unions lent them their support. In between Congresses, official statements on self-management, now almost synonymous with all workers' organisations in the factory, stressed its role in improving production, management and technological progress. The importance of 'criticism from below', first put forward at the 1961 IX Plenum, then later of 'social control', increased, largely so as to serve as a check on the growing bureaucratisation, cliquishness and corruption (this term was not used but all its symptoms were described) within management. The co-management function of self-management was rarely identified, however. The V Congress restored its earlier, more elevated status in the system of industrial democracy, largely as a result of the March disturbances, the Czechoslovak events and the concern with avoiding a future crisis. The inconsistency with which the ruling elite approached self-management throughout the decade gave workers little reason for optimism when Gomułka belatedly reaffirmed interest in this institution. His credibility had been undermined by this time, and the propagation of the concept of self-management may only have strengthened the resolve of the working class to achieve it by itself.

THE CHURCH

Between 1956 and 1959 operative ideology on church–state relations reinforced the traditional view of the separation of the two institutions. The state had the right to pursue its long-term goals of secularisation of society and inculcation of a materialist consciousness in individuals, whilst the church could take part in politics only so as to express support for the existing political system. In general, official discourse in that period took second place to action, and implementation of policy courses was more common than official statements on the role of the church.

In the 1960s confrontation between church and state rarely took an ideological form, despite the usual belief that it was precisely on this plane that conflict arose. In fact the 'battle for men's minds' was waged primarily in an institutional setting, above all in schools, and it involved specific issues, such as the place of religious teaching. The state never went so far as officially to identify the church as its ideological opponent. Consequently, it did not engage in ideological confrontation during this period, apart from during the exceptional circumstances of 1964–6. If part of the church hierarchy did consider the socialist state as its ideological opponent, a detailed analysis of the uniformity and representativeness of 'ecclesiastical discourse' in People's Poland would have to be conducted before any categorical conclusions could be reached.

At the beginning of the 1960s, operative ideology on the role of the church appeared to be conciliatory. For a start, non-Marxists were now regarded not only as neither class enemies nor opponents of socialism, but in certain domains as potential allies, for example, in the struggle for world peace.[64] The 1963 XIII Plenum on ideology did not even reiterate the ground rules by which believers generally and the church in particular had to abide. It simply stated that the aim of the party was to 'condition social consciousness in the spirit of socialism, which means promulgation of Marxist–Leninist ideology and socialist ethical and moral principles'.[65] A resolution adopted by the IV Congress declared that 'we judge individuals not according to their religious attitudes but according to their attitude to the tasks involved in socialist construction and to the norms of community life'.

The party wanted to strengthen unity in society, and it opposed any 'artificial division of working people into believers and non-believers'. In his speech to the Congress, Gomułka referred to the question of religious teaching in schools: the latter were secular institutions which aimed at inculcating a rationalist, scientific world outlook in youth. But the state would not get in the way of religious teaching in catechetic centres, which could be established whenever parents wanted their children to receive such teaching.[66] As late as the 1965 III Plenum Gomułka declared: 'The vast majority of believers does not tie its religious faith to political beliefs' and thus there was a permanent place for laic Catholic groups in the National Unity Front.[67] At the same time it was also pointed out that 'there are people ... who are attempting artificially to incite discord between believers and non-believers'.[68]

Only after the publication of the letter of the Polish bishops to their German counterparts in 1965 did the state launch a frontal ideological attack on the church. Very briefly, the letter concerned the state of Polish–German relations and the view that Poland represented the easternmost bastion of Christianity and of Western culture.[69] Its main significance for the government, however, lay in the general context in which it was published, that is, the impending celebrations marking the Millennium of Poland in 1966. A leading article in *Nowe Drogi* described how the church intended to carry out a 'Great Novena' on the occasion, 'which is supposed to end with the rendering of all Poland to the bondage of the Mother of God'. The article considered the 'Great Novena' as 'a programme of general clericalisation of the social and spiritual life of the country, an attempt to return Poland to the darkness of middle-age obscurantism, and to give the church a role it never previously had in the life of our nation, and which it does not today have in any country anywhere, whether socialist or capitalist'. The article cited some of the recent statements made by the church hierarchy to demonstrate its reactionary position: 'Poland will show the world how to deal with Communism, and the whole world will be grateful to her for it' (Cardinal Wyszyński); 'Modern man is in greater need of love and freedom than of factories, machines, enormous corporations' (the episcopate); abortion represented 'the murder of Poles in the womb of their mothers' (unattributed); the separation of church and state was 'an anachronistic, outworn nineteenth-century principle' which should be replaced by 'the universal presence of the church' (Cardinal Wyszyński); and,

'The primate is accused, if one can call it an accusation, of having fought against Communism, that he was always against Communism. This can only be considered as praise, indeed it is perhaps only an understanding of the church's function' (secretary to the episcopate).

The article argued that such statements revealed no appreciation of realities in Poland, of its political system, constitution and laws. Nor did they have anything in common, it was claimed, with religious faith, the cure of souls, or the ministering to the spiritual needs of Catholics. Gomułka was quoted at length:

> The state and party do not in any way hinder religious freedom, but we will strongly oppose all political activity, overt or covert, which is aimed against the interests of People's Poland and of the Polish nation. We seek no pretexts for attacking the church. Let the church carry on its activity and perform the functions that belong to it. What we demand is that if it does insist on taking part in politics, let it show loyalty to the state.[70]

Later, in 1966, Gomułka repeated his view: 'The very thought of waging a battle with the church and religion is alien to the government of People's Poland ... What we combat and will continue to combat is only the exploitation of religious feelings for political purposes detrimental to Poland's interests.'[71]

The 1967 VIII Plenum considered church–state relations and positively assessed the efforts made by the Catholic church since Pope John XXIII to modernise doctrine. It also described how certain elements in the Polish ecclesiastical hierarchy were out of step both with realities in the country and with Vatican reforms. It noted: 'Support for forces hostile to socialism in the country is given by the reactionary part of the church hierarchy.' The Plenum went one step further, however, in enlisting the support of Polish Catholics: in its recruitment of new candidates the party did not require an appropriate attitude to religion, only a favourable attitude to the Marxist–Leninist political programme.[72] The Central Committee report to the V Congress declared that 'the party does not divide society into believers and non-believers but assesses a citizen on the basis of his attitude to state interests and the tasks of socialist construction'. All citizens, regardless of their religious convictions, could find scope for their political views within the existing political framework. Laic Catholic groups participated in the National Unity Front, and, the report noted: 'The attitude of our party to these groups depends on their standpoint on socialism and the Polish *raison d'état*.' At the same time the party would counter all attempts 'to exploit religious and church institutions for hostile, anti-socialist political activity by certain elements in the episcopate'.[73]

What is striking about official discourse on church–state relations in the 1960s is how little of it there actually was. As we have suggested, much of the conflict between the two institutions took place over specific issues and did not involve discursive confrontation. Moreover, the fragile *modus vivendi* established and maintained by party and church leaders did not permit sweeping ideological declarations on the state of their relations to be repeated: the issue was too sensitive to allow for anything but occasional restatements of known principles. The controversy in 1964–6 was exceptional, and even here we observe considerable moderation in the leadership's propagated ideology on the church's role. No statements of a repressive nature were made: the leadership only called for a return to the status quo ante. Likewise no suggestion of the church's part in the 1968 troubles was contained in official discourse. The most that was said was that a certain part of the hierarchy provided a source of support for reactionary elements.

It may be argued that the admission by the leadership after the March 1968 events that the state of social consciousness had revealed the party's failures in carrying on ideological and socialisation work could be construed as an indirect attack on the widespread existence in society of religious rather than materialist beliefs. But although there was mention of 'outmoded customs, habits and traditions' in social consciousness, religious faith was never specifically identified.

It would be inaccurate, therefore, to consider the operative ideology of the 1960s on the role of the church to be restrictive or hostile. It continued, as in 1959, to preclude political activity by the church which was not in conformity with the *raison d'état* and the socialist principles of the Polish state. That there were grounds for presuming the church guilty of just such political activity in the mid 1960s did not lead to the adoption by the rulers of a more virulent or repressive ideology. If anything, official discourse propagated more participatory values than before: both the IV and V Congresses declared that, in the interests of achieving national unity, a 'permanent place' was reserved for Catholics within the existing institutional framework. Such unity remained more of a desideratum, however, than a reality.

SCIENCE AND CULTURE

The 1959 party Congress, we recall, expressed support for two seemingly contradictory principles governing scientific endeavour –

'free scientific discussion' and 'development of scientific research carried on from Marxist positions'. The social sciences were the object of special attention: in view of their inherent ideological content they were called on to participate in the struggle against bourgeois and revisionist views. As for culture, greater autonomy was propounded after 1956, though submission to Western influence was criticised. We now look at rulers' outlooks on these questions in the 1960s.

1. Science

The importance of science, and especially technology, in the economic development of socialist states grew by leaps and bounds in all Soviet-bloc countries in the 1960s. Ideological impetus was provided by the XXII congress of the CPSU, held in 1961: science was categorised as a force of production which formed part of a society's economic base. As a result, Western scientific advances could be adopted by socialist states without fear of ideological slackness. This idea had greatest appeal, predictably, to the Germans. In the mid 1960s Ulbricht and his economic secretary Mittag launched the New Economic System, followed by the Economic System of Socialism, both of which stressed the centrality of the scientific–technological revolution (STR) to the development of the German Democratic Republic. The concept was quickly picked up by Czechoslovak reformers.

In Poland, the importance attached to the STR was reflected in the number of Plenum meetings devoted to it. Both the 1960 IV Plenum and 1962 X Plenum considered the question of accelerating technological progress in society, but it was the XI Plenum of December 1962 which dealt with the issue in depth. According to a Plenum resolution, 'The development of science and higher education must be inseparably linked to the socialist industrialisation of the country.'[74] A series of articles was published in *Nowe Drogi* which discussed the need for closer ties between scientific and research institutes on the one hand and factories and economic concerns on the other. As one author pointed out, it was essential that science be gradually transformed into a force of production, that its experiments and findings be applied to production.[75] Another wrote that subjects of research should be determined by their potential usefulness in solving the country's economic, social and cultural problems: thus the Polish Academy of Sciences should concentrate almost exclusively on applied research related to the country's economic needs.[76]

The IV Congress devoted considerable attention to science, and in particular to the organisation and functions of scientific and research institutes and the development and appointment of qualified cadres. 'Of decisive significance', it declared, 'is the rational and more effective exploitation of existing research potential, for facts indicated that the economy received less from science than it had reason to expect, that results often incurred excessive costs and lagged behind practical needs.' There was no mention now of the need to apply Marxist–Leninist methodology in scientific pursuits. The party was to ensure only that research and polemics were carried on with 'viewpoints ideologically and methodologically alien to Marxism in the fields of scientific creativity and pedagogical practice'.[77] Two years later, however, it was reported that in spite of the Congress resolutions 'no breakthrough has up to now been recorded which would have diverted the attention of central research institutes to solving the key scientific problems bringing about progress and modernisation in the sphere of production'.[78]

In the period following the March disturbances, operative ideology on science placed greater stress on the political qualities of scientific cadres. The basic responsibilities of each academic and scientist included proper socialisation of his or her students, influencing public opinion and rejecting apolitical characterisations of scientific results.[79] The V Congress urged both party committees and the university administration to ensure that cadres possessed both high academic qualifications and 'moral and ideological virtues'. They had also to take care that 'freedom of research and scientific discussion is not abused for the propagation of political views and social theories contrary to socialism'.[80] After this Congress too, however, progress in linking scientific research to the economic needs of the country was not considered satisfactory.[81]

The operative ideology on science throughout the 1960s underscored its importance to the economy of the country. Although as a result of the 1968 student disturbances added prominence was given to certain political factors in the scientific and academic communities, throughout this decade science itself was largely treated in an apolitical fashion. We can say, therefore, that after the politically unstable 1956–9 period, when the party sought to exert its influence on scientific cadres, operative ideology in the 'little stabilisation' period markedly increased group autonomy in the scientific community. Now it was neither the party nor Marxism–Leninism which was primarily to determine the nature of scientific pursuits. Rather it was to be the 'economic needs of the country'.

2. *Social science*

If the operative ideology of the leadership became more restrictive in any sphere during the 1960s, then it had to be in the social sciences. The III Congress had given impetus to the campaign to make the social sciences not only less hostile to socialist principles but also more positively committed to them. They were viewed as having a special ideological function to perform in society: if neutrality or depoliticisation were in the main acceptable in the pure sciences, they were not sufficient in the social sciences. It was true that the resolutions of the III Congress still represented an increase in the autonomy of the social sciences compared to the pre-October period. But their 'special' role in advancing Marxist theory could never allow them to be 'a-Marxist'.

The report by a member of the party secretariat to the 1962 XI Plenum stated that revisionist views were now seldom voiced. But 'an attitude of ideological neutralism taken by some academics has not been overcome, and it manifests itself in an unwillingness to consider the most ideologically demanding topics, in an inclination to deal with subjects far removed from ideological and political problems, in an avoidance of polemics with bourgeois and revisionist views'. An 'absolutely objective', 'a-class' social science was a myth, it was argued, and unqualified acceptance of the methodological approaches of bourgeois sociology (for example, questionnaires) was to be opposed.[82] On the other hand, it would also be a mistake 'to turn the social sciences into an apologia for current policies or to replace scientific analysis of reality with a collection of tenets based on doctrinaire, voluntarist conceptions'.[83]

Sociology, in particular, which was closely related to the political and ideological spheres, could only be based on Marxist principles, one author wrote. Current theoretical approaches, such as the end-of-ideology thesis, so-called sociological objectivity and academicism and the division of Marxism into institutional and intellectual schools had all to be combated. Even today revisionist views in this discipline still made themselves heard, it was claimed.[84] Likewise the XIII Plenum asserted the need for 'the complete victory of Marxism–Leninism in the social sciences'. Some academics continued to believe in the inherent objectivity and scientificity of the social sciences and in their depoliticisation and independence from ideological struggle. 'The departure from the Marxist theory of class and its replacement with stratification theory can eventually lead to the advancement of anti-socialist theories', Gomułka declared. 'Social science has to be governed by Marxism–Leninism, devoid of bourgeois attributes and revisionist wavering.'[85] The Plenum recommended the introduction of political science into the curriculum of higher education so as to increase knowledge about Marxism–Leninism. But criticism of bourgeois and revisionist vestiges in the social sciences increased after the Plenum. The main focus of attack was the view put forward by some social scientists that their discipline should strive for objectivity and should attempt to become 'pure science'.

The IV Congress reaffirmed that 'revisionism remains the principal obstacle to the successful and creative development' of the social sciences. 'The uncritical introduction into Marxist science of elements borrowed from bourgeois social thought led to the divestment of Marxist thought of its most essential class and revolutionary aspects' and had to be overcome. The social sciences had to be indissolubly linked, the Congress declared, to the ideology and goals of the party.[86]

Discussion on Schaff's book, *Marxism and the individual*, provided another forum for attack on the ideological position of the social sciences. Their seeming reluctance to refute Djilas's theory of a new privileged class under socialism, and the related theory of a power elite, was especially condemned. A party ideologue argued that social science did not hold a monopoly of the development of Marxist theory (an ironic observation since not much earlier the person criticised, Schaff, had stated that the party did not hold a monopoly of the development of Marxist theory); nor could it remain impervious to party influence.[87] The 1967 VIII Plenum reaffirmed the need for greater political action by the party in academic circles and, simultaneously, expressed its dissatisfaction with the results of courses offered in institutions of higher learning on political science, political economy, philosophy and the Marxist theory of social development.[88]

Official discourse directly linked the March 1968 troubles to the social sciences. Both social science and social scientists were criticised for their generally feeble ideological commitment. The events were declared to be the 'fruit of years of political activity carried on by a certain group of people within the academic community and student

body of Warsaw University'. In particular, they were the result of
the lack of resistance offered by the social sciences to revisionist
views.[89]

Summing up the status of the social sciences, the 1968 party
Congress noted that 'under present conditions they remain one of the
most sensitive and, at the same time, weakest links on the ideological
front'. The critical campaign continued after the Congress: social
science was termed 'too abstract, overphilosophical, and unrelated
to Poland's problems', and it could not boast of having made any
contribution to resolving basic social problems.[90] Thus it is possible
to detect a consistently critical attitude to this branch of science from
the 1959 party Congress to the very end of Gomułka's rule.
Throughout this period the party had been unable to eliminate
revisionist and bourgeois elements.

To be sure, operative ideology on social science did change subtly.
Its emphasis shifted gradually from the elimination of revisionists to
active promulgation of Marxist ideology. By the end of the 1960s,
and especially after 1968, social science was expected to disseminate
not only fundamental Marxist principles but also the political line of
the party. The group autonomy of social scientists was continually
reduced. If the natural sciences were constrained only by criteria of
economic utility, the social sciences were expected to be both
economically and politically productive. It is not an exaggeration to
state that Gomułka's main nemesis in his nearly fifteen years in
power were social scientists.

3. Culture

The 1959 Congress gave the cultural intelligentsia wider scope for
creativity than had been the case before October 1956. Works could
be published which, though not adopting a Marxist position, served
the cause of human liberation. Administrative interference in the
creative process was now rejected. In exchange the cultural intelligentsia had to meet one stipulation – that it accept the social function
of art and its part in conditioning social consciousness.

The 1963 XIII Plenum considered the question of 'The struggle
for a socialist direction of Polish culture'. It contended that manifestations of ideological and moral nihilism, and even rejection of
Marxism, continued to be in evidence in some artistic milieux. The
Plenum declared its particular opposition to the implanting from the

West of a philosophy of despair and human solitude, and added that the spectre of revisionism remained.[91]

The 1964 Congress reaffirmed that the party 'could not be either indifferent or neutral towards the ideological and moral content of cultural creativity'. In Poland 'the function of artistic creation is best performed when it lends support to the general direction of the country's development, set out by the party, and its social and moral criticism is directed against the vestiges of the past'.[92] Later that year Gomułka elaborated on his ideology on culture in an address to the Writers' Union Congress:

We do not intend to oversimplify or vulgarise the duties and role of writers and the social function of literature. We do not wish to reduce it to the tasks of political propaganda. We are aware that such literature is no longer art; nor is it good propaganda. The party does not require compliments or a glossing over of reality ... What we desire is a literature which inspires people with faith and hope, not despair, doubt and resignation in the face of supposedly blind fate; that it eradicate evil inherited from the past or engendered by present conflicts, not that it propagate an anarchic philosophy which curses all authority.

The first secretary emphasised the party's resolve not to get involved in matters relating strictly to the literary process, and he acknowledged that 'relations between the party and certain literary circles are abnormal and characterised by conflict and mutual mis-understandings'. Gomułka concluded:

We are interested above all in the ideological content of your works, their social and moral meaning ... We evaluate literary worth according to its contribution to the creation of a new socialist consciousness in the nation.[93]

In 1966 the party's specialist on cultural affairs, Krasko, reiterated the unsatisfactory state of affairs, in the party's view, in certain literary circles: 'Various types of spectres are perceived: the spectre of frenzied censorship, the spectre of rigid dogmatism, the spectre of a languid bureaucracy which misunderstands and hates art.' Obviously artists would prefer no restrictions of any kind to be placed on art but, Krasko affirmed, this was out of the question.[94] Thus, even before the March disturbances which involved sections of the cultural intelligentsia, the leadership was aware of opposition to its policies within this milieu.

Accordingly, the March events were regarded as the logical product of these long-standing difficulties. The V Congress reported that the 1964 campaign of intellectuals for 'the cultural defence of the nation' had been initiated by liberal–bourgeois, revisionist and cosmopolitan elements in the Writers' Union (especially the Warsaw chapter), aided and abetted by Radio Free Europe. The 1968 troubles had forced the party's hand, and it would now vigorously counter all efforts to exploit artistic liberty for anti-socialist ends. Now the party would give 'special support to that kind of creative quest which best serves the socialist ideals and needs of the broadest sections of society'.[95]

A domain of culture which received considerable attention in official discourse during the 1960s was the mass media. According to one high-ranking politician, the cultural content of radio and television had displayed the clearest influence of *petit bourgeois* values and snobbish imitation of Western life-styles.[96] The rulers' dissatisfaction with the media was also articulated at the 1963 XIII Plenum and the 1967 VIII Plenum. After purges carried out in the media following the March events, however, no further criticism of this kind was voiced under Gomułka.

To conclude, operative ideology on culture in the 1960s permitted a considerable degree of freedom of expression, experimentation with form and style, and treatment of various topics. The principle of socialist realism, invoked at the 1959 Congress, was discreetly dropped. In spite of repeated admissions of strained relations between the cultural intelligentsia and the party in the mid 1960s, operative ideology did not take a more dogmatic turn. Complete freedom of expression was not possible, a political threshold did exist, it was declared, but otherwise, a relatively liberal approach to culture was taken throughout the decade.

4. Socialisation

Many of the negative tendencies identified in the spheres of social science and culture were also found, official discourse claimed, amongst young people. As a result, political socialisation was given considerable attention in the 1960s. At the 1962 XI Plenum the party's education spokesman referred to 'sad-faced, bearded types' who were full of disillusion and cynicism and to egoistic, self-seeking university graduates whose only goal was to get ahead in life.[97] The 1963 XIII Plenum referred to the crude, snobbish imitation by the young of all things Western and to their complacent, *petit bourgeois* mentality,[98] whilst the IV Congress singled out their existential nihilism, ideological indifference and fascination with capitalist culture.[99]

Four years later, at the V Congress, the tendencies which were most strongly condemned included hooliganism, anti-social behaviour and consumerist values. Prescribed qualities included socialist patriotism and morality, a work ethic, a sense of personal responsibility and a collective outlook.[100] After the 1969 Congress of the Polish Students' Association, its head, Ciosek, argued that identification of the present stage of socialist construction with socialism's final goals had caused many young people to oppose socialism. The importance of political socialisation was, in such conditions, paramount.[101]

Operative ideology on socialisation identified similar objectives at the end of the 1960s as at the beginning. Industry, discipline, responsibility and collectivism were the qualities most strongly emphasised. In contrast, if in the early part of the decade existentialism was regarded as the force most likely to lead youth astray, by the end of the decade explicitly anti-socialist attitudes were specified. This strongly suggested that socialisation work had proved a failure. In large part the blame could be ascribed to the nature of operative ideology. For example, the work ethic was stressed, but the operative ideology, instead of making clear how work could lead to human fulfilment, showed only how it could increase living standards and the national income. The leadership placed more emphasis on youth's adherence to operative ideology than to fundamental principles. Such goal displacement involved a more general issue – the displacement of Marxist values by 'industrial society' ones. The leadership opted for a value system more directly related to the immediate functional imperatives of the country. The vicious dialectic of ideological drift within the leadership and ideological illiteracy within much of society was sharpened by this choice.

POLITICAL VALUES AND SOCIETY

Until the March disturbances, the individual in the socialist state was seen primarily as an economic unit, as a producer of economic value. A majority of Plenum meetings held before and after the IV Congress dealt with economic matters, and the role of the individual was generally defined in terms of economic utility. This was the first major societal value propagated in the 1960s. It was closely related to the work ethic. As the XIII Plenum put it, 'Work is the most important school of life and thought', and a person's attitude to work was the most important criterion determining his or her moral worth.[102]

The dominance of economic values in social life was also reflected in the attention given to material incentives and income differentiation. A view not unrepresentative of early 1960s operative ideology was that a system of purely material incentives could not become a panacea for the country's economic problems.[103] In 1966 a party ideologue reaffirmed that social consciousness, not economic incentives, remained the most crucial factor in socialist construction.[104] But by 1970 this order had been reversed; as Gomułka told the V Plenum: 'Neither economic leaders nor party activists can today avoid using economic criteria' to evaluate social progress.[105] Likewise calls for wage differentiation increased in the 1960s. Initially wages were to be based on the classic principle 'to each according to his work'.[106] The XIII Plenum specified that the operative principle should be 'to each according to the quantity and quality of work',[107] whilst the IV Congress called for increases in material incentives for 'the most socially useful production'.[108] The 1968 Congress officially sanctioned wage differentiation: 'Further systematic differentiation of workers' wages is indispensable and should be based on an individual's input, level of qualifications and degree of responsibility.[109] One writer defended the trend towards enlarging wage differentials in this way: 'It is not the principle of wage differentiation which offends one's sense of social justice, but rather the existence of unjustified, unfair differentiations, or those resulting from abuses.'[110]

The evolution of operative ideology in the 1960s began, therefore, with a view of the individual as primarily an economic unit receiving few material incentives for any additional efforts, and ended with the promulgation of a system of widening wage differentials based on an ever-larger number of factors whilst stressing the importance of the individual's political and moral qualities. This seemingly contradictory evolution is in fact extremely logical. For the principle of wage differentiation displaced that of work as a value in itself in the exhortations contained in official discourse. If the work ethic continued to be cited, it was because of its material importance to an individual and not due to the imperative that everyone make a contribution to socialist construction. The political system's 'economist' view of the individual in the early part of the decade was replaced by the operative ideology's encouragement of the individual to take an 'economist' view of the system in the late 1960s. This shift represented the final attempt, as it turned out, made by the Gomułka administration to forestall the imminent political crisis which it diagnosed. Likewise it constituted a departure from fundamental principles: the principle 'to each according to his work', invoked in the early 1960s to justify wage differentiation, was replaced by ever more nebulous concepts as the decade wore on. The fact that material incentives and wage differentiation proved inefficacious did not prevent a similar operative ideology from being expounded in the 1970s, as we see in Chapters 5 and 6.

In what way, then, could such a significant turn in the operative ideology be explained and justified? How could an increase in the scope for individual economic initiative be reconciled with the ultimate goal of socialist construction? Official discourse appealed once again to a concept prominent during the late 1950s: the indissoluble unity of individual and societal interests under socialism. At the 1962 XI Plenum it was stated: 'No longer do social conditions exist which would ineluctably bring about antinomy between aspirations for personal success and the struggle for a better life for the nation and society.'[111] It was stressed that 'Marxists do not treat the interests of the socialist state as an absolute; they do not see it as something autonomous, but rather as an indispensable way of bringing about individual freedom in a society free of exploitation.'[112] The V Congress declared: 'As a result of the changes made in the economic and social structure of our country, a society has been created in which the fundamental objectives and interests of social classes and strata are in harmony with each other.' It added that economic policies should have as their goal the integration of individual and group interests on the one hand and societal interests on the other. A system of material incentives could serve both individual and societal interests, it was claimed. This represented the essence of socialist democracy, as opposed to bourgeois democracy, which only served the interests of the ruling economic class.[113]

Balancing individual with societal interests was interpreted by operative ideology in different ways at different times. Whereas the 1959 and 1964 Congresses saw these interests reconciled through the subordination of individual (and group) interests to societal ones, the 1968 Congress regarded integration of such interests as following on from the pursuit of individual ambitions and objectives which, along the way, would also serve the common good. This ideological line had already become official before Gierek took power. He extended it much further but, we should note, he did not initiate it. The fact that under Gomułka this ideological shift was not accompanied by the provision of real opportunities to pursue individual interests became a source of further dissonance in society. Increasingly, operative ideology began to become inoperative: not only did it fail to relate to the system's fundamental principles; it was also inconsistent with the policies being pursued. The leadership was aware of the social and economic problems which the country was facing in the late 1960s, and it recommended such remedial measures as grass roots politics in the party, increased socialisation efforts throughout society, greater autonomy for most social groups (social scientists and students constituting notable exceptions), and political and economic reforms for the benefit of the working class. But this operative ideology was plagued by the same ills which affected the party's general ideological activity – superficiality, vacuousness and reification. In a broader context, propagation of participatory values and subsystem auton-omy by Gomułka in the late 1960s marked an indispensable tran-sitional stage before the emergence of the free-wheeling, patronising operative ideology of the 1970s.

5

Prosperity and political style in the second Poland, 1971–75

This is a modern state: powerful as a result of its social consciousness, authoritative and just. There is no struggle between conflicting interests and tendencies, there is no rule by a propertied minority over a labouring majority which could antagonise the nation ... No divisions arise based on party, occupational or religious affiliation. A citizen's position in and the respect due to him by society are and should be determined exclusively by work, patriotic commitment and active service for the socialist fatherland. This can be the only standard used and must apply equally to everyone.

Edward Gierek, 30th anniversary of the founding of People's Poland, July 1974

The concern for greater democracy within the party, for freer discussion, more extensive social control and criticism from below – manifested in Gomułka's operative ideology of the late 1960s – can be regarded, as we have suggested, as the logical response of the rulers to the increasing political and economic stagnation affecting society at that time. Not only did official discourse confirm the leadership's awareness of the crisis implications of this stagnation; it also identified the front on which the crisis could be resolved. It was the working class which played 'the decisive role' in the socialist system; its posture at the time of the March 1968 disturbances had brought about the sound defeat of reactionary, liberal–bourgeois and revisionist elements within the country. And, in the end, its actions in the shipyards on the Baltic coast in December 1970 finally doomed the Gomułka administration.

The workers' strikes were triggered off by the announcement shortly before Christmas of an increase in the price of food. As in Poznań fourteen years earlier, the authorities' first reaction was to use force to suppress the demonstrations. Premier Cyrankiewicz was again assigned the task of telling the nation that anti-socialist activities would be ruthlessly crushed. Much of the responsibility for the shootings of workers lay with the local party head, Kociołek, a member of the hard-line party faction who wielded considerable power in his fiefdom. Gomułka's exact role in the Baltic events is not clear. At the VII Plenum, held in the midst of the crisis, the ageing leader was outmanoeuvred and replaced by the Katowice party secretary, Gierek. Exploiting the Poles' popular image of Silesians to the full, he projected himself as a believer in rational goal-oriented systems of action and in a superior technocratic ideology (as Habermas has used these concepts). But another series of strikes followed in January and February 1971, firstly in Szczecin where the organisation, leadership and political demands of the strike committee foreshadowed those of August 1980, then in Łódź, where textile workers delivered the *coup de grâce* to the price increases. Gierek's meetings with striking workers augured a new political style, and his popularity steadily grew during his first four years in office.

What reasons were given in the official declarations of the new leadership for the 1970 crisis? Up to 1980, socialist states seldom explicitly admitted that political crises were engendered by structural factors within the system. Crises could be brought on by the work of reactionary and revisionist elements at home or imperialist enemies abroad. They could be caused by personal defects in individual leaders. To discover the 'secondary' causes of conflict, it is necessary to proceed by inference: in those areas where official discourse called for a 'strengthening', 'deepening' or 'multiplying' of party efforts, there sources of conflict also resided. As the immediate threats posed by a crisis diminished, the number of such areas identified tended to increase by increments so that, in the end, a wholesale reform programme could be put forward by the new rulers without requiring their admission that the crisis had had such broad ramifications. This was essentially the procedure followed by Gierek after 1970.

But the sources of political crisis can be distinguished not only according to the horizontal sweep of the socio-political spheres involved but also by their vertical impact, by the degree of their profundity – that is, by the extent to which systemic fundaments are affected. An incisive analysis of Poland's major political crises was presented by the sociologist Narojek in his *Społeczeństwo planujące* (*The planning society*), published in 1973.[1] Examining the declarations made at Plenum meetings, the author concluded that political crises were officially explained as being the product of one of two general types of cause: class contradictions or political errors. In 1948 the persistence of a strong private sector in the country's economy was held to be responsible for the 'rightist and nationalist deviation' in the party, which led to the expulsion and imprisonment of reformists such as Gomułka. A 1948 Plenum meeting made what Narojek termed the 'macro-sociological diagnosis' that:

Capitalist forces want to 'freeze' the existing balance in class forces, they desire 'stabilisation' based on a preservation of capitalist elements in the present structure of popular democracy, counting on capitalism's resilience, on its growth from a small producers' economy, and eventually on support from outside. The working class, on the other hand, wants a further increase in the socialist character at the expense of capitalist elements.[2]

Class antagonisms were also considered responsible for the 1968 troubles. As we saw in the previous chapter, the existence of liberal–bourgeois social consciousness in literary and intellectual circles, aided and abetted by reactionary forces abroad, was thought to have led to the March events. The working class was again perceived by the rulers to side with forces of socialism.

According to Narojek, the crises of both 1956 and 1970 were officially treated as the products of micro-sociological factors located principally in the structure of power. Incorrect political decisions were taken and they, in turn, brought about mass social discontent. The causes of the 'errors and distortions' committed in the Stalin period were to be found in the organisational and methodological shortcomings in the party and state apparatus. More specifically, the cult of personality was produced, the 1956 VIII Plenum declared, by the hierarchical structure of authority which required conformist behaviour by lower levels. People were convinced that 'every attempt to express one's thoughts publicly not only would not change anything, but also would lead to dire consequences for those concerned'.[3] As Narojek argued, it was the category of psychological conception that was emphasised in 1956 explanations of the sources of the October crisis; sociological interest constituted only a secondary category.

The official explanations for the crises of 1956 and 1970 were strikingly similar. According to the 1971 VIII Plenum, although 'difficulties, mistakes and developmental retardations have appeared in the process of socialist construction in Poland up to now, a generally correct political line of the party has dominated'. In fact 'All the sources of and reason for the recent events can be reduced to deviations from the correct political line of the party and from the Leninist norms governing its functioning.'[4] The resolutions of the V Congress were not incorrect, for example, but subsequent political practice was often contrary to their objectives. Increasing economic difficulties and deepening social tensions followed and, in turn, contributed to the 1970 political crisis.[5] But there had never been any question of an attack on the socialist foundations of the political system: 'The demands of the demonstrating workers were exclusively socialist in character.'[6] Thus official discourse primarily stressed micro-sociological factors for the historic 1970 events, just as it had done in 1956.

Another reason for the December crisis given by the VIII Plenum was the estrangement of the leadership from the masses. 'It is quite obvious that the causes of the December crisis cannot be attributed solely to embitterment caused by the price increase and the way it was introduced. The crisis had been brewing for a number of years and had more profound origins.' As was stated at the VII Plenum, its main source was 'the weakening and finally deep breach in the links between the party leadership and the working class and other strata of working people, links which are so basic to our system'.[7] We examine this question in detail later in this chapter; here we wish to point out that as in 1956, the new leadership stressed organisational and methodological shortcomings of the party under the previous rulers and called for a strengthening of the party's role as the leading force throughout society. Above all, a new style of party activity was recommended. Again the level of explanation employed by official discourse was primarily micro-sociological.

The most explicit and comprehensive explanation for the 1970 crisis focused, however, on what Narojek termed 'characterological' considerations.[8] That is, as in 1956, certain harmful psychological mechanisms related to the structure of power under the previous leadership were described. Thus at the VIII Plenum much of the criticism expressed was levelled at the former party first secretary personally. According to Moczar: 'Comrade Wiesław ... was an autocrat. He could not stand independent people around him ... As a result Wiesław simply shut himself up in his office and avoided contact with the people.' According to Cyrankiewicz: 'In the leadership of the party ... there was an almost complete decline of the principle of collectivity ... It was not possible to present one's views at the meetings of the Politburo for it only aroused the egotistic sensitivity of Comrade

Gomułka, and assailed his sense of authority ... In the last few years
... Gomułka was losing his temper almost daily.' According to
Kępa: 'Comrade Gomułka's characteristics: his intolerance of
opinions different from his own, his suspiciousness toward many
people ... to a very large extent were responsible for the negative
phenomenon in the party'. According to Łukaszewicz: 'The members
of the inner leadership lived in their own imaginary world.' According
to Werblan: 'We were faced with the situation in the party where the
top political leaders remained too long – until their intellectual
potentialities were totally exhausted; they were unable to deal with
new problems, and were more and more inclined to make irrational
decisions.'[9] And the Central Committee report to the VI Congress
added that in the last years of his leadership the subjects considered at
Plenum meetings were determined more and more frequently by
Gomułka's personal interests and conceptions, and important decisions were increasingly taken by the party leader and his closest
followers.[10]

There is a wealth of evidence to support the view put forward by
Narojek that official explanations of the causes of the 1956 and 1970
political crises concentrated exclusively on micro-sociological and
psychological factors. The importance of this to operative ideology is
crucial. For what this type of explanation enabled the new leadership
to do in each case was to continue not only to propagate the same
fundamental principles of the system which, it was meticulously
stressed, had not been questioned during the crisis, but also to utilise
many of the concepts and values contained in the operative ideology
of the preceding leadership. Put another way, it was claimed that the
correctness of the party's political line was not challenged by the
crisis, but the structure and organisation of power, the methods used
to implement policy, the psychological motivations of the leadership,
and part of its operative ideology were discredited when the previous
leadership fell from power. All these elements had to be overhauled by
the incoming rulers so as to restore general confidence in their
operation. At the same time modifications could not be so drastic as to
beg the question: if the power structure, political style and some
elements of operative ideology have been altered, why not some of the
fundamental principles as well?

In some respects the need to maintain continuity in operative
ideology was in 1970 as important as remaining faithful to fundamental principles. Firstly the latter were not brought into question

during the December disturbances and, consequently, did not have to be reasserted in the crisis resolution period that followed. Secondly it was at the levels of operative ideology and policy that the main challenge to the old leadership was made. It was incumbent upon the new rulers, therefore, to adopt an operative ideology and policy course which, on the one hand, seemed to represent a break with the past and, on the other hand, was sufficiently continuous to avoid isolating fundamental principles as the only remaining link with the previous rule. Thirdly, and related to these points, the operative ideology of the leadership had, by and large, displaced fundamental principles as the most important 'ideologising' factor in the political system, even if it had the lesser impact on social consciousness. As noted in the last chapter, positive attitudes to the most fundamental questions of socialism were considered to have been successfully inculcated. Any wholesale departure from the previous leadership's operative ideology might therefore undermine or reduce its role as a buffer between fundamental principles and social consciousness. A void between the two could arise, and society, whilst awaiting the promulgation and entrenchment of a new operative ideology, might find it justifiable to call for the replacement of some fundamental principles as well. Thus, in adopting an operative ideology, the new leadership was constrained by dual imperatives to guarantee both change and continuity. A final point was that operative ideology had taken on extraordinary significance in the political system during the 1960s. As political consolidation following October was reinforced, so the emphasis shifted from the propagation of long-term political goals to the dissemination of short-term economic ones. The function of operative ideology was to explain and justify both this economist turn and the nature of the infrastructure which had to accompany it. The new leadership did not have the choice whether to maintain operative ideology as a central constituent in the political system or to reduce its role: given the continued priority – in fact, the greater emphasis – attached by the leadership to economic goals, operative ideology had of necessity to remain the principal 'ideologising' justification for this state of affairs. In 1970, therefore, just as attention focused on the question of political style, not political system, so the ideological focus was on stylistic aspects of operative ideology, not on the place of operative ideology within the political system. The result of the concern with style meant not only that the propagation of fundamental principles continued to be neglected but also that the development of the new leadership's own operative ideology was stunted.

In this introduction to the Gierek period, we have looked briefly at some of the purported causes of the December 1970 crisis as they were perceived in official discourse. We have suggested that the identification of micro-sociological factors as the causes of the December events was associated with the need to maintain continuity in operative ideology. Because the latter had in the 1960s replaced fundamental principles as the most important ideologising factor in the political system, we may even speak of the emergence of an operative ideology of the political system rather than, as hitherto, of a particular set of rulers. It consisted of certain components which rarely underwent change (e.g., party activeness in society, workers' self-management, social control, the work ethic, integration of societal and individual interests, and income differentiation). At the same time the new administration had to project an image of change as well. Under Gierek, stylistic reformulations constituted the main ideologising modification, and it often appeared that operative ideology had been replaced by sloganeering: for example, 'the party directs and the government governs', 'socialism for people by people', 'thinking in state categories', 'the right person in the right job', 'people of good work' and, the most classic, 'we are building a second Poland'.

This is not to suggest that discontinuities in operative ideology did not take place after 1970. Industrial democracy became a far less prominent feature of 1970s operative ideology than of that of Gomułka's last years, contrary to the popular assumption that it had been resurrected so as to respond to workers' militancy in 1970–1. On the other hand, intraparty democracy was stressed more than ever before. Political values emphasising individual well-being were now more forcefully propagated. We begin our survey of Gierek's operative ideology with an analysis of attitudes towards the party.

THE CASE OF THE PARTY

Following the 1968 troubles, intraparty democracy again became an important aspect of the leadership's operative ideology. The atomisation in party life that had occurred in the early part of the decade, involving one-sided emphasis on the calibre of members rather than on the calibre of basic committees, was partially alleviated by the effort to elevate the importance of the caucus as a decision-making forum. Likewise the party's leading role came to be interpreted less dogmatically: withdrawal from administrative sectors and the forging of closer links with the working class were stressed. How did the Gierek leadership approach these aspects of party work?

1. Intraparty democracy

In his radio and television address to the nation shortly after assuming power, Gierek stated that respect for the collective principle governing intraparty democracy constituted an iron law of the new leadership.[11] At the party's VI Congress, held in December 1971, the first secretary further stressed the importance of collective decision-making, and party statutes were even amended so as to incorporate the principle. At the same time it was pointed out that the collegial process did not signify relaxation of individual responsibility for decisions.[12] Four years later, at the VII Congress, collective decision-making was again affirmed as the basic principle governing the functioning of the Central Committee.[13] The concept was introduced and remained operative so as to eradicate the autocratic tendencies which had arisen under Gomułka.

The collegial principle did not, however, represent a concession offered to advocates of the view that a more pluralist political system should be introduced. Political unity remained of the utmost significance to the new leadership, and democratic centralism remained the method by which it could be achieved. At the VIII Plenum Gierek made it clear that: 'Our democracy has nothing and cannot have anything in common with the bourgeois–liberal system of a free play of political forces.'[14] At the IX Plenum he stated that equally detrimental to the party was 'anarchistic laxity representing a parody of bureaucracy, and bureaucratic centralism hindering the development of initiative and activeness in Communists'.[15]

Numerous references were made at the VI Congress to party unity: democratic centralism was affirmed as the basic organisational principle of political activity, and the party was described as 'a union of brothers'. Political unity and intraparty democracy were closely interrelated, Gierek asserted: 'In party life, internal democracy creates conditions promoting its unity, whilst party unity allows for its democratic functioning. Following Lenin's teachings in this regard ensures that socialist development will continue properly, without serious errors or shocks.'[16] References to Leninist principles increased in frequency: the rulers' new political style was to be coupled with old and tried methods.

The invocation of Leninist norms was related to a new development in party life: for the first time since the 1964 Congress, the leadership admitted the existence of dogmatist and revisionist elements within the party. Both were strongly attacked at the VI Congress: 'We must overcome dogmatic petrification and subjectivism, which consist of a lack of faith in the strength of the working class and in the creative abilities of the nation.' Simultaneously, the party 'is engaged in an uncompromising struggle with revisionism, which attacks the fundamental principles of our ideology and undermines the achievements registered by our policies'. Nevertheless, a hopeful sign was seen in 'the use of pseudo-socialist slogans by opponents of socialism', which 'testify to the strength and popularity of socialist ideas'.[17]

But by mid 1974 the party ideologue Szydlak claimed that 'the basis of neo-Marxism and other branches of revisionism, which served as apologias for the central features of contemporary capitalism, has been counteracted'.[18] And at the 1975 XVI Plenum Gierek no longer identified opposition within the party but only outside it: 'We still have class opponents, people who do not accept the principles of socialism, and transgress them in their actions. But the social base for the opponents of socialism is continually diminishing.'[19] Gomułka, we recall, had said much the same thing in 1964, once he was certain that his position had been consolidated. At the 1975 VII Congress this belief in the political unity of the party reached its culmination. The Central Committee report noted that the verification campaign conducted within the party between Congresses had produced greater consolidation of party ranks. Gierek did stress that 'democracy is indivisibly linked to discipline', but he did not refer to any threats to party unity, and his only reference to revisionism was in an international context.[20]

In many respects there is similarity in the evolution of leadership attitudes to party unity between the post-1956 and post-1970 periods. In each case the danger of revisionism and dogmatism was stressed immediately after the accession to power of a new team. Later the existence of such tendencies within the party was denied, and revisionism was said to persist only in certain social milieux. Democratic centralism was underscored at all times, but under Gierek various stylistic modifications were introduced, for example, the centrality of Leninist principles, solidarity within party ranks, collegial decision-making, individual responsibility and unity of rights and duties throughout the party structure. References to pseudo-socialist rhetoric, neo-Marxism and left-wing revisionist ideologies suggested a new preoccupation with *gauchisme*, an import from abroad, and not with Gomułka's menaces – 'integral democracy', 'the free play of political forces' and the 'second stage'.

Relations between the ruling elite and the party rank-and-file constituted a second aspect of intraparty democracy. Here Gierek easily outdid his predecessor. Emphasis was placed on a gamut of mechanisms designed to strengthen these links. Concern with the calibre of cadres, with the right to express criticism and with the role of the caucus represented direct extensions of Gomułka's operative ideology. But the novel feature was the new rulers' extensive and intensive interest in catchwords and concepts hitherto propagated only on special occasions (party Congresses, post-crisis explications): consultation, discussion, exchange of information, social control, criticism from below. These were, in particular, connected with improving the functioning of basic committees. Directives for the VI Congress described these terms in detail, and the party subsequently incorporated them into a revised set of statutes.[21] The point to be made here is that cybernetics-inspired concepts became the quintessence of the new political style promoted by Gierek both inside the party and in its relationship to society.

Certain structural factors were also stressed by the Gierek administration in its approach to elite–mass relations. We have already referred to the upgrading of the caucus and of basic committees within the party apparatus. Calls were also made for the Central Committee itself to show more dynamism, and for leadership cadres to be rejuvenated. No specific formal conditions had to be introduced, one author noted, but concern for the stability of cadres should not preclude the influx of new recruits. The length of tenure of political leaders should now be judged on the basis of merit.[22] The guidelines for the VI Congress cited the need to raise the status of elected party organs, 'starting with the Central Committee', and the Congress itself resolved that the role of collegial bodies should also be strengthened.[23] The executive organs of the party at all levels had, therefore, to be more accountable to the general membership.

However, at the I National Party Conference, held in 1973, Gierek took a more generalised view of relations between the inner circle and the membership at large. He simply urged closer ties between the Central Committee and lower party tiers.[24] And at the 1975 Congress there was no mention of intraparty democracy – not to speak of elite–mass relations – in the party leader's speech. Not only that: for the first time, the role of the party did not merit a separate section in Congress documents but was subsumed under a more general heading ('Problems of the state, social life, ideology and the party'). This suggested a decline in the importance attached to intraparty democracy by the Gierek leadership. Moreover, given the fact that the position of the ruling cadres and their relations with the rank-and-file were now ignored (in contrast to the 1971 Congress), it is difficult to lend credence to rumours that Gierek had intended to resign at the VII Congress, in keeping with his belief in the desirability of leadership turnover. There was not the slightest hint in official reports that Gierek still remained committed to this aspect of intraparty democracy, let alone that he intended to act on it. In fact the general popularity that the first secretary had achieved by 1975 might easily have misled him into believing that it was he who was indispensable to the future success of the party, not intraparty democracy.

2. The leading role of the party

Following the 1970 political crisis, the new rulers quickly affirmed their commitment to the leading role of the party in society. The special relationship between the party and the working class was underscored, as it had been by Gomułka after 1968. In his radio and television address to the nation on becoming leader, Gierek declared that the basis of 'our overall policy should always be the taking into account of reality, and broad consultation with the working class'.[25] In his speech to the Sejm in December 1970 he stated that the main task facing the party was 'to reforge and strengthen this indispensable link that binds us with the working class and with all working people, a link without which it is impossible to govern in a socialist state'.[26] In the past, an article in *Nowe Drogi* asserted, 'decisions of major importance to the working class were taken without discussions with the working class'.[27] Simultaneously calls were made to increase the number of workers in the party. This campaign had originally begun in the wake of the 1968 troubles in Poland and Czechoslovakia, which Communist rulers attributed to intelligentsia-led movements. By the early 1970s most East European states had followed suit and sought to 'reproletarianise' the party.

As after the October events, the leadership urged the party to exercise its leading role in all sectors of society. However, this was not interpreted as dogmatically as before. Gierek told a conference of party activists: 'We are now reaching a higher stage of socialist construction. At present we can and should perform the dialectically related tasks of . . . raising the party's leading role to a higher level and broadening participation of the non-party masses in the governing of the country.'[28] The new rulers vigorously propagated this formula of the party's bonds with the working class and all working people. The peasants, intelligentsia and non-party people were also cited, but invariably after the working class.

The 1971 party Congress decided that the principle of the leading role should be incorporated into the new constitution of the Republic, when this was drawn up. The 1960 Czechoslovak constitution had already embodied this principle, and the new Soviet version, first suggested by Brezhnev in 1966, discussed between 1971 and 1976, and approved in 1977, also specifically mentioned this principle. Oddly, the previous 'Stalinist' constitutions had failed to cite the party's leading role. In Poland the process of approving a new constitution proved to be lengthy and arduous, too, and it was only in 1976 that the question was resolved. We return to this issue in the next chapter.

Some of the concepts operative at the VI Congress could be summed up in two slogans propagated by Gierek soon after taking power. One was 'construction of socialism for the people through the people'; the other was 'the party directs and the government governs'. 'Realism' also became a watchword frequently employed in official discourse: it referred to Gierek's 'no-nonsense', goal-directed style which did not avoid broaching contentious issues. The overall objective of the new administration was crystallised in a third slogan promulgated at that time: 'We are building a second Poland.'[29]

Between the VI and VII Congresses the party's links with 'all working people', with 'all of society' and with 'the whole nation' were forcefully underlined. The party had, on the one hand, to make full use of the skills and qualifications abounding in society and, on the other, to encourage everyone to show responsibility for 'his sector of

work'. At the National Party Conference, Gierek launched the drive
to recruit non-party support for his policies. He elaborated:

As a result of profound changes in social consciousness, the role of non-party
people in political life and in productive and social activity is increasing
during the current phase of socialist construction. Non-party people constitute the majority of the population. They give support to the party's policies,
identify with it, and participate in its realisation. The party works in close
contact with non-party people and considers its duty to be continually to
reinforce these ties. The whole party apparatus should treat non-party
workers, peasants and the intelligentsia with respect, allow them scope for
initiative and activeness, and put them forward to positions of authority and
responsibility in social organisations and elsewhere.[30]

As the VII Congress drew near, the slogan 'socialism for the people'
came increasingly to be used. One author even modified the formula
to include the view that socialism was not only 'for the people' but also
'due to the people'.[31] But the clearest summary of the new political
style adopted by Gierek was contained in the Central Committee
report to the 1975 Congress. The party had been consulting with
working people and broadening discussion on key issues. Its links
with the working class, peasants and intelligentsia were more firmly
grounded. Workers had played 'the leading role, most fully reflecting
the unity of socialist ideology with social and scientific–technological
progress'. The proportion of workers in the party had grown. More
rigorous criteria for admission to the party had helped increase its
authority amongst the non-party masses, whilst 'in party life a style
and method of work was initiated and propagated which effectively
ensures the maintenance of a permanent link with non-party people'.
This procedure permitted the party to make a more accurate
appraisal of 'the real situation' and 'the social climate'. In conclusion,
the Central Committee reported that 'the leading role of the party, as
well as its authority in the state, have expanded'.[32]

Gierek's address to the Congress outlined the concept of an
advanced (or developed) socialist society, recently introduced into
official discourse in Poland and throughout Soviet-bloc states. It
signified 'the gradual surpassing of the state of the dictatorship of the
proletariat and emergence of a national state which, under the
direction of the working class, will harmonise the desires and interests
of the entire nation'. In it the role of the intelligentsia was to increase:
according to Gierek, 'the main condition necessary to achieve the
historic objective of integrating the scientific–technological revolution with socialism is the alliance between the working class and the

intelligentsia'. But the principal axis along which the establishment of the national state was to take place was 'a consolidation of the unity of non-party people with the party'.[33]

The adoption of the concept of an advanced socialist society was not exclusive to Poland. As Terry has shown, its origins can also be traced back to Czechoslovakia in 1960. At this time a Plenum meeting referred to the new stage of 'developed socialism' which resulted from the successful collectivisation programme. The 1961 XXII Congress of the CPSU and the 1962 XII Congress of the Czechoslovak Communist Party spoke of an 'all-people's state', and the Bulgarian, Hungarian and East German parties also adopted the term. According to Terry, developed socialism initially had no reformist connotations, only 'a perfunctory, almost ritualistic quality'. By 1968, however, it had become a notion closely associated with reform movements in Hungary and Czechoslovakia. Advanced socialism presented the Soviet leadership with both a challenge and an opportunity, the same author has argued. It was now outwardly reformist but at the same time was a way of confirming the legitimacy of the existing power structure. Following the 1971 XXIV Congress of the CPSU, Soviet ideologues redefined the term, stressing its legitimising dimension. All East European states followed the Soviet example and began to propagate the concept. Poland, Terry claimed, was the last in line, in 1974, because of the existence of its private agricultural sector. This date can be disputed, as Gierek explicitly invoked the concept at the 1971 PUWP Congress.[34] In all the countries considerable efforts were made by academics and party ideologues alike to give precision to the term. But it always contained a degree of vagueness that was exemplified in Gierek's description at the VII Congress.

By the mid 1970s advanced socialism had become an integral part of Gierek's operative ideology. It subsumed the party's new relationship with society and its different political style. Translated into macro-politological terms, it involved such values as national integration, social mobilisation, mass participation and political pragmatism. To be sure, these values had also constituted the immediate, short-term response by Gierek to the political crisis of 1970. But five years later, at the VII Congress, they became codified into the concept of advanced socialism.

In contrast to the approach of the previous leadership, the party's leading role was no longer interpreted as primarily the exercise of unlimited authority in all social spheres – a concept most accurately summed up by the term 'leading role' (in Polish, *kierownicza rola*). Instead it now signified a process by which consensus on and support for the political system could be aggregated. This corresponded more to a 'directive role' for the party(*przewodnia rola*). Under Gierek this second term was in fact used more often. There was also increased use of the terms 'links' and 'bonds' to depict the party's relationship with social classes and strata. Finally these links with classes and strata were new: under Gomułka, the party had ties with more narrowly conceived groups or structures in society, such as economic enterprises, self-management bodies, or literary circles. Of course official discourse still referred to the need for the party to exert greater influence in the work-place, in local government, within the cultural intelligentsia and so on, but in general class alliances were now of primary importance. In a way, therefore, the slogan 'the party directs and the government governs' could be adapted to apply to the party's relations with classes and strata, for example, 'the party directs and the working class works', 'the party directs and management manages', 'the party directs and writers write'. Such an approach was not as appropriate to describe the party's social role under Gomułka.

This subtle change in conceptualisation of the party's role should not obscure the fact that, in the end, its overall control over Polish society was not being relinquished. The party was to continue to monitor and, when necessary, to intervene in all sectors of social life. Within the party, the leading role fell to the working class. Its strongly emphasised 'decisive' role – empirically confirmed by the 1968 and 1970 events – remained a pillar of system operative ideology from the 1968 Congress onwards.

3. The party and ideology

At the 1968 PUWP Congress Gomułka acknowledged that ideology remained the weak link in the party's activity. In the months following the 1970 political crisis, the most important questions the new leadership addressed were performance of the party's leading role in society and intraparty democracy. The ideological dimension was only given detailed attention at the XI Plenum, held in October 1971. It noted: 'In the transitional period between capitalism and socialism, archaic ideas alien to socialism do not vanish automatically. Quite the contrary – under certain conditions they may be activated, finding nourishment in the backward consciousness of some social groups, in imperialist ideology and propaganda emitted by foreign mass media, and also in mistakes in our own policies.' Accordingly 'We have to be more profoundly concerned with Marxist–Leninist theory, we have more forcefully to propagate the policy and programme of the party.'[35] As a leading sociologist, Wesołowski, argued, it was necessary to create 'a state of ideological tension', that is, permanent ideological vitality.[36] At the same time an important theme running through official discourse in the early 1970s was the integral unity of politics, economics and ideology. It was claimed that 'economic, socio-political and ideological-socialisation tasks confronting the party are dialectically related'.[37]

At the VI Congress Gierek referred to the history of the party's inattentiveness to ideology: 'In the past the proposition of developing socialist ideology and undertaking a socialisation offensive was made many times. In practice, however, the life and activity of the party apparatus were shaped by the powerful influence of strict economic pragmatism ... We know that where the ideological front is anaemic and shaky, there the opponent will squeeze in and attempt to deform social consciousness.' Gierek recommended that interrelating party ideology and its socio-economic policy could help exert more efficacious influence on all of society, in particular, on the young.[38]

It is interesting to note the equal importance attached by the party leader to popularisation of both fundamental principles and operative ideology. It lends support to the thesis (elaborated in the last chapter) that the latter had risen in status so as to become at least of equal ideologising rank to that of fundamental principles. Persuasive explanation and justification of policies was held to be of no less significance in transforming social consciousness than inculcation of Marxism–Leninism. The economic pragmatism dominant in 1960s ideology was replaced by ideological pragmatism, which consisted of, first and foremost, selling society the leadership's policy programme.

This tendency was confirmed by the declarations made by party ideologues. Szydlak told the conference of party activists in 1972 that socio-economic programmes had to be more closely integrated with the growth of socialism in the 'socio-psychological' sphere.[39] Łukaszewicz stated that the goal of propaganda was 'the inculcation in social consciousness of belief that the more productive people are, the sooner their material and cultural standards of life will be raised'.[40] At the National Party Conference Gierek declared: 'We are building socialism on two fronts simultaneously – the socio-economic and the ideological. Our dynamic socio-economic programme forms the basis of the Marxist–Leninist ideological offensive, whilst the consolidation and propagation of socialist ideology has a direct bearing on socio-economic development and enriches the ideological motivations of human endeavour.'[41] Finally, the 1974 XIII Plenum underlined the theme of unity of ideological, political and economic objectives. As Gierek put it: 'If we wish to see Poland make progress, each and every Pole has to be transformed ... and has to adjust his or her ideological stance in line with the tasks facing the nation.'[42] Thus, not only were productivity and economic results the core of operative ideology (as in the 1960s); they were now regarded as a function of the successful inculcation of operative ideology. Here again we see how the Gierek administration countenanced ideological pragmatism.

To sum up, official discourse on ideology between 1971 and 1975 condemned economist tendencies and proclaimed the integral unity of ideology with other spheres of party work. Ideological questions were broadened in scope so as to include the party programme. Henceforth operative ideology was classified together with fundamental principles as requiring widespread propagation in society. The state of social consciousness remained a source of concern, and the term 'propaganda' appeared more frequently in official statements than it had done in the 1960s. The realism stressed in the operative ideology on the party's relationship to society was reflected in the ideological pragmatism that was advocated by the mid 1970s: ideology was to be used as a mechanism to help spur economic development. As Gierek stated, that system would win out which generated higher work efficiency, and ideology had a central part to play in this sphere. The *petit bourgeois*, materialistic values ingrained in certain sectors of society had to be liquidated, it was declared, but simultaneously material rewards for 'people of good work' were stressed. The proclaimed inseparability of material and moral motivations was reflected by the end of the decade in the effects of material differentiation on the moral order. Moreover the stress in official discourse on the moral and ideological standards of party members appeared inversely related to their actual moral standards and motivations. What could not be denied was the importance which the leadership attached to ideology's role: two Congresses, the National Party Conference, conferences of party activists, economic leaders and social scientists, and a number of Plenum meetings (especially

the VII, XIII, XVI and XVIII following the VI Congress) were
devoted to the issue. So much significance was attributed to ideology
'under present conditions', in fact, that it was to be expected that
contradictions, inconsistencies and anomalies in leadership declarations would arise: the blanket coverage given to the question had its
price.

INDUSTRIAL DEMOCRACY

Much of the initial scepticism concerning the real worth of ideological
declarations made by the Gierek leadership shortly after its accession
to power was based on their alleged similarity to prouncements issued
by the Gomułka leadership after the October events. Within Poland
there was reference to the 'conditional confidence' initially lent to the
new team by the population,[43] whilst in the West it was suggested
that Poles were wary of placing faith in the same kind of promises that
were made in October but not kept.[44]

The formulation and explanation of policies after the 1956 VIII
Plenum had kindled hopes that the new rulers would institute
genuine political and social reforms. As a result Gomułka's popularity was at its highest immediately after he took office. The same
could not be said of Gierek. Even without access to the results of
opinion polls, one can safely say that his popularity peaked approxi-
mately two or three years after he became leader.

The reserve which greeted the Gierek administration and its
assurances was to a large extent based on the ill-fated experience of
workers' democracy after 1956. Had Gomułka not wooed the workers
in October, and had he not promised, in return for their support, a
system of true industrial democracy? And had he not, in later years,
'gone back' on the Polish October? Had not his patronising praise of
the stance taken by the working class in March 1968 proved to be vain
flattery? Now, after the tragic events on the Baltic coast in December
1970, was not a new party leader reiterating worn, empty phrases in
speaking of the working class as 'the main social force of socialism'
and of the necessity of always 'consulting' with the working class?
Workers' distrust of rulers' promises seemed to be justifiable and
firmly founded.

In examining official discourse on the party's leading role in society
during the years 1956-9, we concluded that so-called revisionist
elements had had in fact no grounds for believing that the party would

surrender its monopoly of power and share it in pluralist fashion with various groups in society. Neither Gomułka nor any other leading political actors of the time ever officially stated their intention to create a more pluralist political system: the party's leading role was at all times asserted, and a model of integral democracy was consistently condemned. Analogously it is possible to hold that industrial democracy – which did constitute an important element in the operative ideology under Gomułka at the outset – was never declared to be of fundamental importance under Gierek, either immediately after his take-over of power or in the ten years that followed. It would be inaccurate to claim that the Gierek leadership made far-reaching promises to the working class regarding industrial democracy that were never kept. It would be truer to say that few such promises were made, in which case it would be very difficult to speak of justified or understandable disillusionment with subsequent policies pursued. We now examine how central industrial democracy really was to operative ideology under Gierek.

Industrial democracy, as we have used the concept thus far, refers to workers' participation in factory management. We have seen that in 1956 workers' councils constituted the chief mechanism through which such participation was channelled, that in 1959 workers' self-management committees became the most important institution in workers' 'co-management' of economic enterprises, that by the mid 1960s the trade union organisation was deemed to be the most appropriate agent through which workers exerted influence, and that by the late 1960s 'workers' self-management' became a more abstract (though no less emphasised) concept which referred to a conglomerate of workers' institutions through which they might participate, largely, it seemed, for participation's sake.

The most striking feature of official discourse on industrial democracy, broadly defined, during the early years of the Gierek leadership is how little of it there actually was. Appeals were constantly made to the working class for help and support, but no specific political concessions were offered in return. What was promised may have ranked much higher on the workers' list of priorities: economic benefits in the form of improved living standards, higher wages, more services and consumer goods. A Politburo report as early as 1971 considered the question of industrial democracy in economic enterprises, but it simply transferred to local party committees the responsibilities which had earlier belonged to self-management: they were to stimulate productivity, to socialise the consciousness of the work-force and to harmonise factory interests with national ones. Self-management committees, on the other hand, were to evaluate the results of the plan, to ensure proper distribution of bonuses and awards and to help improve work and safety conditions.[45] In turn Gierek outlined the traditional responsibilities of trade unions: 'concern with working conditions, social welfare and interpersonal relations in the factory', and 'promoting more efficient work and greater productivity'.[46]

Official documentation of previous party Congresses dealt with self-management in a separate section, but at the 1971 gathering only three paragraphs were devoted to it. Moreover the references were ambiguous and fragmentary. This suggested that the new administration still had an unschematic, makeshift conception of industrial democracy at the end of 1971.

The 1973 IX Plenum was held to fill this lacuna in the rulers' operative ideology. Whilst self-management was not mentioned, trade unions figured prominently at the session. Most importantly, they were exhorted to help transform social consciousness, to mobilise the masses to strive for national goals and to struggle for the improvement of living standards. Defence of workers' interests was not cited.[47] Likewise at the National Party Conference Gierek referred to the mobilisation functions of trade unions and ignored the general concept of workers' self-management. Finally, at the 1975 Congress, Gierek duly noted that the party sought a trade union movement that had 'close ties with the masses', but only one paragraph in official documents dealt with the status of the unions.[48]

From this survey of official discourse on industrial democracy during the period 1971–5, it is not difficult to conclude that the Gierek team attached far less importance to the concept than did Gomułka between 1956 and 1959. The term 'workers' self-management' was employed infrequently, the institution of the self-management committees was all but ignored, and the role assigned to trade unions was almost exclusively economic and social. Responsibilities which were previously allocated to self-management bodies were now transferred to the party's factory committees. By the VII Congress, even management was given certain functions which had previously belonged to self-management committees, for example, combating bureaucracy and formalism. In this way management, not workers' institutions, was to provide a check on its own operation. The very concept of self-management, which by the mid 1960s had been broadened considerably, was now further diluted. The operative terminology of the mid 1970s was democratic 'self-government' (*samorządność*), which was never strictly defined, but which embraced not only all workers' organisations in the factory but also all 'social organisations'. This concept, like advanced socialism, was limited to the level of rhetoric, conveniently used by the Gierek leadership to project only an image of change.

THE CHURCH

Perhaps Gierek's greatest achievement was normalisation of relations between church and state in the 1970s. A meeting between Premier Jaroszewicz and Cardinal Wyszyński, held soon after the new leadership was installed, set the tone for the relationship that was to follow. The state desisted from taking repressive measures against the church, as had occurred on the issues of taxation of ecclesiastical property and teaching of religion in schools under Gomułka. The new rulers no longer issued warnings to the church not to interfere in politics; nor did they delineate what it could or could not do. In turn the church did not embark upon any 'Great Novenas'; nor did it commit any actions which, like the 1964 letter of the Polish to the German bishops, might be regarded as tampering with foreign policy.

We have seen that the new party head appealed to the entire nation, to party and non-party sectors of the population, to believers and non-believers, to work for the economic development of the country. Changes in the composition of the National Unity Front had led, it was argued, to an increase in the influence of Catholic representatives and to 'the mobilisation of all of society, believers and non-believers, based on their common interests and social and national aspirations for social construction'.[49] The party's theses on 'The active participation of the young generation in the construction of socialist Poland' did not, uncharacteristically, mention the desirability of implanting a materialist or even secular philosophical outlook in young people, as had always been the case before. In fact there was no reference at all to the church. The only oblique hint of secularist objectives was contained in Gierek's statement that the socialist state could not be neutral towards the world-view and ideological attitudes adopted by youth.[50] At the National Party Conference the first secretary pointed to the 'useful part played by

Catholic organisations' in the National Unity Front, but otherwise religion was not referred to.[51]

Only in mid 1973 was the first critical remark by a leading party figure published in *Nowe Drogi*: the Minister of the Interior renewed the attack on 'the reactionary section of the church hierarchy' which, he contended, remained the main organised centre of opposition to Marxism.[52] A year later the party's chief ideologue, Szydlak, also noted that 'the experience of recent years had once again shown that a particular centre uniting all currents opposed to the system is the reactionary part of the episcopate'.[53] And the directives for the VII Congress included the declaration which, significantly, was not incorporated in the resolutions subsequently adopted by the Congress, that: 'The state required that all levels of the Catholic Church and other religious denominations acknowledge loyalty to the socialist socio-economic system and to the basic principles of the state's domestic and foreign policy as a permanent structural feature of development of Poland.'[54] In spite of these pronouncements, which implied some strain in church–state relations during the mid 1970s, stress on the unity of the nation was the main aspect of operative ideology at the Congress, and its resolutions specified only that an individual's religious beliefs did not affect such unity.[55]

Thus official declarations on religion and church–state relations corroborate the thesis that under Gierek normalisation of relations between the two institutions was successfully carried out. It is worth citing the observation made by a Polish Catholic historian on the implications of this *détente*. Writing in the early 1970s, Dembiński claimed:

> In past years the official ideology has undergone serious transformation amounting to (what is publicly never admitted, but is evident nevertheless) a growing gap between the official political and socio-economic policy and the philosophical doctrines of Marxism–Leninism. This provides the basis for a certain philosophical pluralism, which admits the existence of various motivations for the acceptance of the socialist society, although the goal of socialism itself cannot be questioned.[56]

Our survey of official discourse on the subject suggests two things. Firstly, it is indeed possible to speak of various motives underlying acceptance of the socialist system. Chief among these were, however, economic – not philosophical – motives, which naturally cut right across society, regardless of social background, party affiliation or religious convictions. Secondly, it seems more risky to venture the hypothesis that philosophical pluralism was now accepted. Although it is true that the goal of secularisation of society, of the inculcation of a materialist world outlook, was now conspicuously absent, non-theless the most one could conclude from this is that an uneasy coexistence between differing world outlooks had been arrived at, not that outright acceptance, much less approval, of philosophical plur-alism had been given. The basis for this coexistence lay in the essentially pragmatic approach adopted by the Gierek leadership to a whole range of issues.

SCIENCE AND CULTURE

In the previous chapter we described how in the 1960s science generally and the social sciences in particular received considerable attention in official discourse. The STR was regarded as a crucial factor bringing about acceleration in the country's economic develop-ment, whilst social science was perceived as a factor no less critical in promoting ideological transformation in society. In the cultural sphere, on the other hand, substantial autonomy in artistic and literary endeavours was sanctioned by the leadership's operative ideology, and integration of creative output with imperatives stem-ming from socialist construction was less forcefully expounded. We look at the operative ideology of the Gierek leadership on these issues.

1. Science

Directives for the VI Congress made clear the role and significance attached to science by the new rulers: 'The party will create con-ditions for science and research to become a more important motor force for national economic and cultural development. Science, research, and their effective integration with the socio-economic development programme will determine the rate at which our country will enter the advanced stage of the scientific–technological revolution.'[57] The only reference to non-economic criteria in the Congress resolutions was the declaration that it was important to influence the ethical and ideological values of scientists. Otherwise politics was not seen as a factor relevant to this particular domain.

A more comprehensive outline of Gierek's approach to science was given in his address to the II Congress of Polish Science, held in mid 1973. He stated: 'In our time the mission of socialism has become to develop a model of civilisation in which dynamic productivity, accelerated scientific and technological progress, and solidly based prosperity are linked with people's general activity and humanist aspirations.' In addition, the scientific Congress had 'demonstrated the deep bond between Polish scientists and socialist ideology, patriotism, the line taken at the VI Congress and the policies of the Central Committee'.[58] The statement was descriptive rather than, as in the past, prescriptive: the relationship was regarded as a *fait accompli* which required no improvement.

From then on, up to the VII Congress, science was related exclusively to the socio-economic goals of the state. The party gathering gave science considerable attention within this framework, and the main call was for greater specialisation. In this way operative ideology on science was largely an extension and intensification of the values propagated in the 1960s: science had to be governed by one overriding consideration – accelerating the country's socio-economic development. The 1975 Congress marked the high point of the rulers' interest in the STR. And although no restrictions, provisions or qualifications of a political nature were imposed on scientific activity, we may be justified in questioning whether, by being forced to pursue the party's socio-economic goals, science enjoyed in effect as little real autonomy as the social sciences, where political criteria were vigorously advocated.

2. *Social science*

In contrast to the pure sciences, the activity of social science was continuously regulated by political and ideological norms under both Gomułka and Gierek. Directives for the 1971 Congress outlined the traditional approach taken by the new rulers: 'The social sciences must perform the educational and socialisation functions of moulding social consciousness, and they should more systematically than in the past carry out ideological and political tasks so as to maintain a constant ideological offensive against anti-Marxist views and socio-political doctrines.' Accordingly it was necessary to adopt more modern research methods 'based on the theory and methodology of Marxism–Leninism and on the achievements of individual disciplines'. Congress resolutions added that empirical social research had also to make use of 'the theoretical implications of the experience of socialist construction'.[59] Social science had to be governed, therefore,

both by fundamental principles (Marxism–Leninism) and by operative ideology (the experience of socialist construction).

Early in 1973 the party convened a special conference on the social
sciences and humanities. One participant argued that 'the cognitive
function of the social sciences and humanities cannot be separated
from their ideological and philosophical functions'. Social science still
displayed numerous weaknesses, such as the use of eclectic
methodologies and a tendency towards ideological compromises. On
the other hand revisionist influence only occasionally made itself felt
now, usually on theoretical issues.[60]

Another conference paper concurred: 'dramatic manifestations of
outright revisionism of Marxism' had, on the whole, not been in
evidence in recent years. The main weakness of social science was,
instead, its slowness in responding to anti-Marxist philosophical,
social and politological conceptions permeating from the West. In the
past it had reacted belatedly to such currents as existentialism,
structural-functionalism, Marcusism, convergence theory and structuralism. At present the same was true in relation to neo-Marxism
and related historiophilosophical standpoints.[61]

The general discussion between party social scientists touched on a
variety of issues. Criticism was expressed of 'the unreflexive fascination with everything from the West' (Białokozowicz); the urgent need
for integration of social science research was underlined (Fritzhand;
in contrast, in the early 1960s, a call had been made for integration of
the disciplines themselves); the desirability of propagating greater
philosophical reflectiveness throughout society was noted (Jaroszewski); the acceptability of only rational, non-bourgeois methods
was put forward (Melich); an admission was made that 'we cannot
boast of a surplus of Marxist strength in the social sciences' (Rybicki);
it was argued that 'socialist societies cannot be content with adopting
capitalist solutions and experiences in all important areas of life'
(Werblan); and the need to combat vestiges of neopositivism in
sociology was identified (Wesołowski). The debate was summarised
in this way: social science had three main functions to perform:
cognitive, ideological and instrumental. 'The bond between science
and political and social activity', it was added, 'belongs to the best
traditions of Marxism–Leninism.'[62] Several months later, following
the Congress of Polish Science, one Central Committee member
wrote optimistically that the 'inferiority complex' which had for long
beset social science had at last been eradicated.[63]

The Central Committee report to the VII Congress described the positive achievements recorded by social science in the previous four years. The teaching of political economy, Marxist philosophy, sociology and political science in institutions of higher learning had helped instil a socialist consciousness in youth. The establishment in 1974 of the Institute of Fundamental Problems of Marxism–Leninism, together with broadening the scope of the party's Higher School of Social Science, had upgraded the status of social science. But new tasks lay ahead for this branch of science: as Gierek observed, it had in future to 'cultivate a scientific view of the world, propagate a socialist value system, structure the nation's knowledge of its own past and present history, open new intellectual horizons, and satisfy the growing cognitive, intellectual and ideological needs of our society'.[64]

At the party conference on social science and the humanities, a leading sociologist, Wesołowski, observed: 'Marxism is the connecting link between the social sciences and practice not only in a general sense ... but also in many specific areas.'[65] Gierek's declaration to the VII Congress suggested that it was in fact social science which served as the intermediary between Marxism and society. The distinction is very important: in each case the relationship between Marxism and social science, Marxism and society, and social science and practice is depicted differently. For Wesołowski, Marxism was seen primarily in terms of praxis, whilst for the party leader social science was conceived largely in terms of its function as social engineering. In the first case social science was viewed in relatively autonomous fashion, leading a mainly independent existence; in the second it was regarded as a means and instrument by which a desired end could be achieved.

Throughout the early 1970s operative ideology on the pure and social sciences was dominated by a utilitarian approach. But whilst the natural sciences were required to engineer the material infrastructure of socialism, the social sciences were expected to engineer its superstructural character. If under Gomułka constraints on the social sciences were imposed mainly for political reasons, under Gierek they also involved pragmatic considerations: thus the autonomy of social science was circumscribed by the dictates of social engineering. In each case social science had to submit to functional imperatives, and we may again raise the question: what real measure of autonomy did this branch of science enjoy if its objectives were formulated and imposed from without?

3. Culture

The VI Congress directives contained the conventional platitude that: 'The party will provide conditions conducive to cultural creativity and innovatory artistic exploration. Support will be given first of all to those activities and fields which combine high artistic values with content that sensitises public awareness to the humanist spirit of socialist ideals.' Both 'ideological tendencies alien to socialism' appearing in cultural activity and 'limitations obstructing cultural life' had to be opposed. The Central Committee report concluded that since the previous Congress 'the situation in culture was differentiated: progress and development were dominant, but difficulties and stagnation also took place in certain spheres of cultural activity'. In particular 'Attempts to reduce the criteria for evaluating the development and promulgation of culture to economic indices were incorrect and detrimental to culture.' The most important standard suggested was the social and artistic value of a work or, as Gierek put it, its 'ideological, social and artistic value, its input into the reinforcement of the patriotic unity of the nation, its internal force and its international status'.[66]

After the Congress it was agreed that dialogue had now been established between the party and the cultural intelligentsia. At the same time, complete eradication of revisionism and non-socialist views in this milieu had not been achieved. One leading ideologue of the Gierek administration, Łukaszewicz, referred to the uncritical acceptance and dissemination of bourgeois values in art and literature, and he condemned the fascination with capitalism and Western life-styles which made itself felt in cultural output.[67] A specialist on cultural matters, Kossak, noted that, although 'our culture is open to everything which is progressive and related to humanism in the art of the capitalist world', selection of such work had to be more carefully screened than in the past.[68] As in the past, therefore, external influences were blamed for incorrect currents in Polish art.

At the party conference on the social sciences and humanities, one participant described the political threshold that the cultural intelligentsia could not exceed: 'Non-Marxist tendencies can be tolerated, but only on the margin of the main current in the humanities, and only on condition that opinions and views disseminated conform with the *raison d'état* and with the requirements of civic loyalty, and that the general political and structural principles of our state are not brought into question.'[69] The 1974 XIII Plenum underscored the patriotic, national values with which culture should be imbued: 'the main trend in creativity should propagate a consciousness of the historic fate of the Polish nation, it should promote better models of living and interpersonal relations, and it should depict the broad possibilities offered by the socialist development of the country'.[70] Another article succinctly described the position of art: 'A socialist society cannot not have socialist art. What this entails is not ideological verbiage but a demonstration in works of art of the laws by which we are governed, an explanation of the facts that make up our life.'[71] The XVI Plenum reiterated the overriding criterion by which art had to be judged: 'enrichment of the socialist content of the life of the nation'.[72] Finally, at the VII Congress Gierek stressed: 'We shall support creativity of high artistic value which enhances the socialist and patriotic content of Polish culture.' One limitation on cultural activity was identified in Congress resolutions: 'We should oppose attempts to transpose on our ground all creativity founded on values or ideals which are alien to our national culture and to the socialist content and life-style of the overwhelming majority of the nation.'[73]

Operative ideology on culture in the early 1970s was, therefore, to a great extent similar to that of the 1960s: considerable autonomy was prescribed for artistic endeavours. Under Gierek operative ideology emphasised the desirability of imbuing cultural output with national values and, simultaneously, condemned the fascination with Western value systems and life-styles. Cultural and creative activity was less closely linked than scientific pursuits to instrumental roles. It had a part to play in political socialisation and it was interrelated with socio-economic development, but these were treated as secondary considerations. For, above all, high artistic values and humanist ideals were to govern the character of cultural output.

4. Socialisation

The exhortation made by the new leadership to broaden the party's ideological front was accompanied by greater prominence given to political socialisation. In this section we conduct a brief survey of social values: those which were identified as dysfunctional in a socialist state, and those which were prescribed for a socialist state. An examination of negative social values, in particular, throws light, firstly, on why political socialisation was now deemed to be of such vital interest and, secondly, on what the social consequences of the mistakes committed under Gomułka were thought to be. The fact that social values received unprecedented attention in this period is itself significant: on the one hand it indicated a positive and self-critical concern with the very bases of a socialist order, and on the other it revealed the extent to which this subject had hitherto been regarded as taboo, and the grave effects of this on the party and society.

The most frequently identified 'negative social phenomena' included parasitic life-styles, speculation and corruption (referred to euphemistically in Polish as 'abuse').[74] Passivity, complacency, smugness, indiscipline, lack of respect for work and selfishness were listed as social problems in VI Congress directives, and at the Congress Gierek referred to wastage and destruction of socialised property, alcoholism and decadence (*demoralizacja*). Congress resolutions added hooliganism, vandalism and violence.[75] Values to be combated in socialising youth included bourgeois acquisitiveness, egoism, mercenariness, insensitivity to others, careerism and consumerist life-styles.[76] Lack of idealism and *petit bourgeois* life-styles were condemned in another article,[77] and one writer, in describing consumerist tendencies, observed that 'material values should be a measure to enrich life, not its goal and index of social position'.[78] A party ideologue referred to lack of concern for societal interests, and egoistic attitudes to socialised property and distribution of wealth in society.[79] At the National Party Conference a Central Committee member identified bribery and theft as further problems,[80] whilst the XIII Plenum added nationalism, cosmopolitanism and social indifference.[81] A concise depiction of the main social problems was provided by Szydlak:

> The influence of *petit bourgeois* ideology considerably surpasses the limits of social groups whose economic position could justify their inclusion in this category. We encounter selfishness and egoism, conceptions of life and career centred on maximum material gain and minimum work input, and the whole system of cunning that goes with it, on quite a large scale, not excluding the peripheries of our mass party.[82]

The XIV Plenum cited instances of demoralisation in youth,[83] whilst Szydlak also noted the harmfulness, wherever they arose, of mediocrity, anti-social attitudes and self-satisfaction.[84] Bureaucratic insensitivity and the use of official positions to obtain personal gain were evils occurring in upper social spheres,[85] whilst ideological confusion, pessimistic gossip-mongering and general incompetence had to be countered wherever they appeared in society. Consumerist life-styles continued to be the most frequently cited social evil, however.[86] The most important social problems mentioned at the VII Congress were lack of conscientiousness, irresponsibility, extravagance, social parasitism, alcoholism, violence and decadence amongst people on the margins of society.[87]

During this period the most important prescriptive value contained in operative ideology remained the work ethic. As the directives for the VI Congress put it: 'Work which is socially useful is in our system the supreme measure of a person's worth.' Or as Gierek told the Congress: 'What we should value most highly is solid work. This is the highest value, the main instrument of progress.'[88] Youth was to be brought up through and for work, for it was the fundamental 'right and moral obligation of every Pole'.[89] At the VII Congress the first secretary reiterated that 'the most valuable attribute of a socialist man is his profound respect for work'.[90]

Other values promulgated in official discourse were 'socialist patriotism' and, closely related to this, 'internationalism'. Patriotic exhortations permeated the vast majority of official statements issued in the 1970s, and it is important to recognise the instrumental quality of this value for the rulers: whatever had to be done was to be done for the good of the nation, of the fatherland, of Poland. Patriotism was, therefore, less of a value in itself than for itself, around which all social endeavours could be organised.[91]

Directives for the VI Congress cited moral sensitivity, humanism and social discipline as other important values to be propagated. To this list Gierek added 'the ability to think in state categories', 'cooperativeness within collectivities' and thriftiness, whilst in relation to youth the values of discipline, idealism, initiative, innovation and self-dependence had to be fostered.[92] The VII Plenum on youth stressed participation in social life as an ideal to be striven for, [93] whilst expertise, now juxtaposed to mediocrity, became an operative concept.[94] Individual responsibility and order were underlined at the National Party Conference, and one speaker summarised the attributes that were desirable in young people: 'a generation open to progress, determined and uncompromising, prepared to fight on the front line whenever socialist ideals require it, thinking in categories of country and socialism, well educated, working reliably, healthy morally, brought up in the revolutionary traditions of the working class'.[95] The XIII Plenum extolled integrity, dependability, honesty, loyalty and altruism in individuals,[96] whilst, finally, the VII Congress added the qualities of enthusiasm and energy.[97]

The agents of political socialisation that were identified included the school, the work-place and mass social organisations. The media were also assigned a special position. But an agent and, simultaneously, a goal of socialisation which did not figure in the operative ideology of the previous leadership was the family. From the beginning Gierek's socio-economic development programme was centred on the family.[98] Above all it was viewed in terms of demographic utility in helping establish 'a nation of forty million' by the year 2000, a major long-range goal set by the rulers. For similar reasons women were given special attention in the operative ideology of the 1970s: increasingly they began to be seen as mothers rather than as working people.[99] This question merits separate detailed study.

To a great extent, therefore, the value system propagated in this period, stressing idealism, work, the common good and the family, was very traditional – a curious hybrid of Catholic morality and Protestant ethic. What was distinctive was the unparalleled importance attached to socialisation by the Gierek administration. In a society in which material expectations were rising at an astounding pace even the materialistically minded rulers realised that some kind of axiological infrastructure had to be promulgated. In the second half of the decade, as we see in the next chapter, this concern with the social value system increased as its basis in society withered.

POLITICAL VALUES AND SOCIETY

This brings us to the question of general societal values propagated during the early 1970s. For the most part these were economic: 'good work' was stressed, and this included such related concepts as work efficiency, quality of work, discipline and responsibility. Strikes, or 'work stoppages' as official discourse called them, continued to be staged for several months after the December 1970 crisis, and order became a watchword during the first year of the new leadership. On the other hand living standards, wages, services and consumer goods received much greater prominence in official discourse than ever before. The role of planning was upgraded, and the importance of cadres was dramatised through the promulgation of the principle 'the right person in the right job'. Income differentiation continued to be a dominant principle, and it resulted in all kinds of sophistry: for example, the theories that inequality in income led eventually to its equalisation and that the responsibilities of socialism did not include the attempt to compensate for the inequalities produced amongst humans by nature but 'quite the contrary – its obligation is to create the best climate and conditions for the appearance and flowering of talent'. As for equal division of power: 'This socialism never promised, for it would be nonsense to allocate an equal "portion" of power to all citizens. At most it is possible to ensure that all citizens have equal opportunities to participate in government.'[100]

The author of these views also invoked the well-known slogan, coined by Lenin in a different epoch and under different circumstances, that 'one who does not work should not eat'. In the Poland of the mid 1970s a growing stratum of society was eating very well without doing much productive work, and it did not consist exclusively of the now well-publicised cases of high-ranking officials embezzling funds and commodities. Others who prospered in Gierek's *laissez-faire* economy, or who took part in quasi-legal or illegal activities to get ahead, included small-scale capitalists with large-scale incomes engaged in services, handicrafts and market gardening; employees in the retail trade, state administration and the professions who would only provide state-subsidised services and goods in exchange for an attractive bribe; *Gastarbeiters* working 'on the black' in Sweden, Austria, West Germany and England whose foreign earnings were multiplied at least fivefold on their return to Poland: time thieves employed in all sectors of the economy who moonlighted in second jobs; and the classic black marketeers, speculators, hustlers and foreign currency dealers. Not all of those involved in such operations had to have *protekcja* in the party or government apparatus: the nature of the economic system itself provided the necessary loopholes for the enterprising individual. When we speak of the economic boom, the 'period of prosperity' of the early 1970s, therefore, some qualifications must be made. Between 1971 and 1975 national income may have increased by 12%, investment by 19% (mostly financed by foreign banks), household income by 14% and currency and savings deposits by 21% (a more accurate indicator of real, as opposed to official, income), but their distribution within society was sharply skewed by the above tendencies. As a result there was considerable dissonance between the fundamental principle of 'to each according to his work', the operative ideology based on it (for example, the call for close interdependence between the results of work and the size of earnings), the actual policies pursued, and the interpretations given them by economic managers. In fact the general theme in operative ideology that progress in all social spheres was interrelated with economic growth appeared to be disproved in practice.

A closely related tenet of Gierek's operative ideology was the unity of economic, social, cultural and ideological spheres. The leadership fully accepted this proposition but was also aware that disparity did exist between the various components. As Gierek told the VII Congress, in many areas 'we are accomplishing tasks characteristic of the new stage', that is, construction of advanced socialism. 'In others we are in the process of resolving the problems of the preceding phase. For the developmental stages of socialist society are not separated by strict boundaries.'[101] The argument could be taken further: it appeared that the state of social relations, morality and social consciousness was, in the 1970s, regressing to a pre-socialist stage of development as economic growth increased. The workers formed an exception to this rule: as they benefited marginally from the new prosperity, their morality and consciousness advanced beyond 'economic socialism', as events in the 1980s were to show. In any case the values inherent in the 'new stage' (such as those identified in the citation at the beginning of this chapter) seemed far more remote and unrealistic than the economic targets set by the leadership. Not only that: they also appeared to be more remote and unrealistic in 1975 than they were before Gierek took power. In this respect the pragmatism and realism of the new rulers had, ironically, boomeranged.

A certain inconsistency in and vagueness about the leadership's perception of the exact nature of the relationship between economic and non-economic processes was accentuated by its view of the interdependence between societal, group and individual interests. It is true that the unity of such interests was propagated by the previous leadership too, but uncritical acceptance of this principle was fraught with greater dangers and pitfalls when a policy course was pursued the central variable of which was individual well-being. Manifestations of the atomisation of society, to which this policy led, were condemned by the operative ideology (the criticism of consumerist and *petit bourgeois* life-styles, egoism, selfishness and so on). A rift occurred, therefore, between policy and operative ideology, whereas under Gomułka the two were for the most part oriented to the viewpoint that what served societal interests was bound to serve group and individual interests as well.

The consequence of the Gomułka leadership's holistic approach was the micro-sociological character of the 1970 political crisis. The consequence of a policy emphasising individual prosperity, and its disparity with operative ideology, was the macro-sociological, structural nature of the 1980 political crisis. We say more about the roots of this crisis in the next chapter. Here we suggest that miscalculations concerning the degree of unity of societal and particularistic interests, together with an inversion of their rank in the policies pursued, not only demonstrated theoretical confusion on the part of the leadership but also had serious practical consequences.

As had been the case on so many issues that we have examined, the implications of the problem were recognised and the leadership was alerted. As one writer noted, conflict between societal and individual interests could occur: 'It is important that activity which sanctioned the pursuit of justifiable individual interests did not produce an apotheosis of all individual interests, especially those rife with *petit bourgeois* values ... It is important that this type of pursuit of individual interests did not receive social acceptance.'[102] Operative ideology began to stress limitations on such pursuits; Gierek argued that: 'The essence of our democracy cannot be reconciled either with anarchic underestimation of state interests, or with rivalry between particularist interests, which can undermine the unity of the nation.' At the VII Congress he stated: 'Our policy course would be very shallow if it linked a person's well-being exclusively with material affluence.'[103] But in many respects that is what it did do, and rivalry between particularist, individual interests did increase. Ideological declarations helped further reveal the rift between operative ideology (let alone fundamental principles) and policy. The basic assumption that under socialism societal and individual interests went hand in hand resulted in the leadership responding to the threats of 'anarchic underestimation of state interests' and 'apotheosis of individual interests' with mere declarations. It could be argued that the long-standing formalist, superficial treatment given to Marxist fundamental principles and methodology had now borne fruit in the shape of theoretical confusion and practical harm. For rather than assuming the unity of societal and individual interests and of economic and non-economic processes, a more correct Marxist approach would have been to stress the dialectical relationship between these elements. Correlation between them did exist, but it was not invariably positive. Some of the pitfalls into which the leadership fell appeared to stem from this basic misconception concerning the nature of the dialectic.

6

Propaganda of success and prognoses of failure, 1976–80

A category of people still exists whose main concern is simply to take, giving of themselves as little as possible. We continue to observe manifestations of ideological confusion and defeatist gossip. Also harmful are symptoms of conservatism, ordinary incompetence and organisational chaos which undermine the discipline required in a country embarking upon the road to modern development. We have not fully uprooted the proclivity towards smugness, the resting on one's laurels, the depreciation of one's obligations, and particularist viewpoints. We have not eliminated inclinations towards showiness, towards 'success for appearance's sake'. We still encounter unpardonable examples of disregard for the ever more important value of time. We have limited the influence of mediocrity and trivialisation. But we cannot claim that we have fully exploited all the opportunities available for publicising the best results, for propagating and adopting the breakthroughs recorded by the truly leading forces in society, for continuously levelling upwards towards the best.

Nowe Drogi, October 1975

If the primary programmatic concern of the Gierek leadership during the first half of the 1970s was to improve the general living standards of the population, then during the second half of the decade it was with 'deepening the moral and political unity of the nation' (as the Politburo report to the II National Party Conference was entitled), with the socialist integration of society, with the proper development of the 'subjective factor' which helped determine the quality of the society in which people lived. Social justice, a socialist way of life, socialist morality and improved interpersonal relations became the key concepts in the operative ideology of the late 1970s. The relationship between the programmatic concerns of the first and second halves of the decade was very direct. The stress on material well-

143

being, together with the policies pursued to attain this end, unleashed a tide of rising expectations which, once set in motion, could not easily be contained. Social injustices, non-socialist life-styles and morality, and rapidly deteriorating interpersonal relations ensued. Only at a late stage did the leadership recognise the fragmentation and atomisation of society, and the superficial nature of the nation's moral and political unity, and it did too little about it. It would be a gross error to conclude that the rulers were totally unaware of and oblivious to what was taking place: as we shall see in this chapter, official discourse constantly returned to these issues, recognised the dangers posed by them, and tried to explain and justify a new policy course which slowed economic growth, thereby necessitating a slowing down in expectations as well. But this came too late in the day, when the social malaise had already reached epidemic proportions, and when an antidotal operative ideology and policy course seemed only to exacerbate the illness.

One thing was certain: whether it was during a period of austerity, such as under Gomułka throughout most of the 1960s, or during a period of relative affluence, such as under Gierek in the first half of the 1970s, the ability of operative ideology fully to penetrate and condition social consciousness encountered stubborn resistance. At the level of fundamental principles the socialist idea had long ago received acquiescence, if not quite enthusiastic acceptance. The important battleground now involved propagation of the secondary principles of socialism, those rooted in the operative ideology which the leadership adopted. Increasingly it was this level which would determine whether the country would enter the stage of an advanced socialist society. As one party academic put it:

In the sphere of the social consciousness of our nation, the attitude to fundamental social issues and systemic principles has been resolved once and for all. But social consciousness cannot be reduced simply to an acceptance of the bases of the system ... It is imperative that Marxist–Leninist ideology and socialist ethical and moral principles governing interpersonal relations be inculcated, that new attitudes to the state, to work and to socialised property be instilled, and that a new socialist type of culture be developed.[1]

On this secondary 'ideologising' front few such values had taken root in social consciousness. To the credit of the Gierek leadership, therefore, a concerted propagandistic effort was undertaken in the late 1970s to make such constituents of operative ideology better known in and more readily acceptable by society. The basic contradiction which affected the success of this campaign lay not between fundamental principles and operative ideology, which were by and large consistent with each other and mutually complementary, but between operative ideology and policy or, even more specifically, between operative ideology and the interpretation and implementation of policy guidelines carried out by the entrenched party and state administrative machinery. In a word, secondary principles would never take root so long as the bureaucracy continued to dilute or otherwise undermine them.

At the same time the propaganda effort also represented a departure from the mainly stylistic, sloganeering modifications of operative ideology undertaken by the leadership shortly after taking power in 1970, towards more general revampment of its content. Elements seemingly endemic to the system, for example, workers' self-management, social control, differentiated incomes and the work ethic, went unchanged. But new aspects were introduced suggesting the evolution of an operative ideology specific to the period and to this leadership, for example, the unprecedented stress on national unity, morality and justice. It is ironic that the harshest accusation levelled at the rulers once they had fallen into disgrace was their contravention of the last two principles.

Much has been made of the 1970s 'propaganda of success', initiated by Gierek and engineered by his television overlord Szczepański. Media reporting bloated domestic economic results and political accomplishments and glowingly described the party leader's close contacts with foreign heads of state. Never had Poland's stature in the international community been so great, propaganda repeated. Less well known is the limited 'campaign of foreboding' conducted chiefly within the ruling circle in this same period. Various reports to the Central Committee, together with studies done by party academics and ideologues, were highly critical of failures in the effort to transform social consciousness – and especially of the way in which *petit bourgeois* values had been allowed to develop in society. In the last chapter we noted intensification of a socialisation drive to overcome the emergent materialist mentality; in the second half of the decade operative ideology stressed antidotal values (such as national unity) even more forcefully. The identification of failings in the party's work had a precedent in Hungary: the New Economic Mechanism (NEM) which came into force in 1968 had created similar social problems. Attempts were made early on, as Gati points out, to counter them:

'Since 1972, ramifications of the so-called *petit-bourgeois* mentality have filled the pages of every newspaper, weekly and monthly in the country. Promoted as a grand national debate, it is more a condemnation of the very attitudes the regime's own policies have fostered.'[2] The campaign was similar in tone to that later conducted in Poland. According to the party newspaper: 'We must confront calmly but determinedly the fact that the philosophy of individualism and egoism is, under the ostensible veneer of socialism, spreading through not negligible strata of our society.'[3]

The Hungarian leadership, however, unlike the Polish, converted the attack on materialist values into a national debate. Moreover Kadar, demonstrating acute responsiveness to social developments very uncharacteristic of a leader of a socialist state, quickly tightened the reins: at the 1975 XI Congress of the Hungarian Socialist Workers' Party, political and economic control was recentralised. In parallel fashion, Tito embarked on a similar course following factional and nationalist difficulties in Yugoslavia. Poland entered the second half of the 1970s with socio-economic ills resembling Hungary's, but without either a NEM or a set of new political mechanisms designed to counter the social malaise. This was in spite of the prognoses of failure within the spheres of ideology and social consciousness submitted to the top rulers. Polish leaders remained complacent that such problems were more of a nuisance than *nuisant*.

In the last years of Gierek's rule two political crises of differing ramifications occurred. As in 1956 and 1970, the working class was the main protagonist. Its reaction to price increases imposed in 1976 was considered by the leadership to be spontaneous and localised in character. Opposition to policy, differences of views, opinions and postulates were 'a natural thing in the face of complex problems and tasks'. This was why the party had placed such emphasis on consultation, 'a permanent form of political life ... an important, innovative method of actualising the principles of socialist democracy'.[4] But disruption of work, the conduct of hooligan elements, and other excesses committed in Radom went far beyond the norms of community life and socialist democracy.[5] Nine months after the events Gierek wrote: 'The June incidents were only an episode on our path. However centres hostile to Poland and to socialism are trying to make capital out of them. Unfortunately they find not numerous, admittedly, but active supporters and allies amongst the opponents of socialism in our country, amongst disillusioned politicisers alienated from the nation.'[6] The causes given by the leadership for the crisis were micro-sociological, but its consequences took on certain macro-sociological features, especially when linked to the activity of dissident groups in the country, to which official discourse made regular, if oblique, references throughout the late 1970s.

The final crisis which deposed Gierek was outwardly macro-sociological in character: the fate of socialism in Poland was at stake, as the VI Plenum held in 1980 underlined. The authorities' reaction to the strikes of the summer of 1980, their final acceptance of the Gdańsk, Szczecin and Jastrzębie documents, and their views on the birth and evolution of the independent trade union Solidarity are described in the next chapter.

One final point to be made in this introduction to the analysis of operative ideology between 1976 and 1980 is that a number of articles published in the party theoretical journal in this period, and especially during Gierek's final year in power, contained critical assessments of the leadership's and party's general style and performance. Naturally much of this criticism was veiled and disguised, but its addressee was quite clearly identifiable – the ruling group. As a result we must be careful in treating the views presented in such articles as representative of official discourse. They are not typical of the mainstream, official position of the rulers, but they do represent 'alternative' standpoints put forward by members of the political leadership and their spokespersons who could not wholly reconcile themselves to the course taken by Gierek and his closest followers. Such dissent was particularly marked with regard to the question of party functioning. Without entering into a discussion of political rivalry within the leadership, we can say that divergences of opinion, reflected in articles published in *Nowe Drogi*, were precipitated by certain shuffles carried out in the composition of the Politburo during the years 1979–80. 'Alternative' views may have differed from the 'official' ones of the ruling group, but as 'adaptive orthodoxy', they nevertheless formed part of the official discourse of the political leadership, conceived broadly. We shall consider them in our survey of declarations relating to intraparty and socialist democracy, taking care to distinguish them from 'official' standpoints.

THE CASE OF THE PARTY

In the previous chapter we described the way in which the Gierek leadership expected to bring about greater democratisation in intraparty life and throughout society. The main concepts advanced were consultation, discussion, information flow, criticism and social control. We pointed out that even at the VII Congress, long after the political crisis of 1970–1 had been resolved, the rulers continued to employ these ideas as part of operative ideology on the party. Attention to structural features of party democracy focused on an upgrading in the roles of the basic committee and its caucus. The party's leading role in society was interpreted largely as a directive one: the main task of the party was to integrate the nation around its policies. At the same time an ideological drive was undertaken to transform social consciousness: several Plenum meetings were devoted to this issue.

There were few discontinuities in this general pattern in the late 1970s. The leadership felt, quite justifiably in certain respects, that it had arrived at the right formula in its operative ideology on the party. The view of the party as an aggregator and adjudicator of all interests flowing from 'below', in society generally, as an articulator of the concerns of the entire nation, appeared to be preferable to the concept of an omnipresent formulator and implementor of general interests determined a priori and in higher circles which was operative in the Gomułka era. We also noted that once the 1970–1 political crisis was overcome, attention given to the question of intraparty democracy lapsed. The same pattern had occurred after the Gomułka leadership had consolidated its position. We look more closely now at the exact content of operative ideology on the party in the late 1970s, and at its responsiveness to the protracted politico-economic crisis of these years.

1. Intraparty democracy

Of the two factors we have identified as having an impact on party democracy, one was virtually ignored in operative ideology during this period. Political unity within the party was treated in official discourse as a non-issue, and no reference was made to the potential existence of revisionist, sectarian or other dissenting elements within the apparatus. At both the II National Party Conference and the VIII Congress, straightforward one-line declarations were made that the political and ideological unity of the party had strengthened. For example: 'Unity of objectives and views characterise our entire 2,700,000-plus party.'[7] This reflected the near-total control and power within the party that the Gierek leadership thought it possessed. It did not perceive any significant rival groups, or if it did, certainly did not deem them serious enough to warrant labelling them as revisionists or dogmatists in public declarations.

The second factor we identified was elite–mass relations, which subsumed such questions as the relationship between upper and lower tiers in the apparatus, the extent of participation and activity by basic committees, activists and members in party life, and other aspects of the principle of democratic centralism (discipline, responsibility, criticism and so on). These topics were regularly broached in official discourse in this period. The 1976 IV Plenum affirmed that 'the more democracy and extensive discussion and consultation there are in the formulation of programmes of action and the taking of major decisions, the more important it is that efficiency and discipline should characterise their implementation'. This necessitated 'strengthening the links between the party's executive bodies and its activists and rank-and-file'.[8] The 1977 VII Plenum called for elevating the role of the caucus so that 'it could become a more effective form of inculcating militant attitudes in members',[9] whilst the 1979 XVI Plenum stressed the need to upgrade the role of basic committees: 'Without very militant, well-organised basic party committees, the party cannot function effectively.'[10] At the VIII Congress, held in February 1980, Gierek concluded that party style had indeed improved in recent years, but 'of greatest value is the continuing lively relationship between the Central Committee and Politburo, and regional party organisations'. In this relationship, 'direct personal contacts in particular facilitate the flow of ideas and information, promote the reliability of evaluations and consultation about objectives, and constitute an important factor in intraparty democracy'.[11] From the party's highest authorities there was no hint that intraparty democracy was anything but satisfactory.

But at the time of the Congress, *Nowe Drogi* published several articles which expressed concern about various aspects of intraparty democracy. One writer contended that the principle of unanimity in views ought not to apply before official deliberations on an issue were held; genuine discussion and consideration of alternative approaches should also be encouraged.[12] Another observer noted that the essential aspect of a Leninist style of activity was not avoiding mistakes but ensuring they were not multiplied.[13] Kruczek, a doyen of the political elite whose fortunes had begun to decline, stressed how important it

was 'to defend resolutely all persons who are victimised and persecuted for expressing justified criticism'.[14] But undoubtedly the bluntest,
most direct attack on the state of intraparty democracy, and on the
rulers' responsibility for it, was articulated by the political scientist
Erazmus immediately before the industrial strife of the summer of
1980. He pointed out that 'style of political work' had become a part of
everyday political vocabulary. But 'In socialist societies, too, despite
the creation of objective conditions for conducting a democratic style
of governing, autocratic and bureaucratic tendencies, formalism and
façade could appear.' Therefore 'It is very important to take into
account the possibility of errors and mistakes occurring during the
implementation of decisions so that deformations can be removed and
their sources identified and eliminated. If some of these are located in
the work of higher bodies, then necessary corrections should be made
there also.' For 'Leaders and central party authorities play a special
role in developing a style of work. This role is a modular one since
their attitudes and activity in large measure influence the climate and
style of party work as a whole. This is a regularity resulting directly
from democratic centralism. There is no place in this general principle for decision-taking of an arbitrary nature.' An excessive number
of conferences, resolutions and rituals only served to by-pass direct
contact with people, with activists. 'A hermetic, phraseological language full of generalities, indices, statistical data and so on serves no
purpose either.' Most importantly, the article stated by way of
analogy that: 'If, for example, a basic party committee does not
control its executive, and it in turn does not control the work of the
first secretary, then this will worsen the style of activity of this
organisation. A departure from the principles of democratic centralism threatens to institutionalise and multiply the errors committed.' Therefore 'The style we indispensably need is to be found in
the rigorous application of principles contained in the ideology,
programme and statutes of the party.'[15]

The publication in the party theoretical journal of this series of
critical articles indicates that public discourse in the party began to
bifurcate into official and alternative versions before the political
crisis of mid 1980. Just as importantly, however, it seems inconceivable that the ruling group was unaware of the imminent political
dangers, as is sometimes claimed. The extent of dissatisfaction with
the party's 'style of governing' is clear even from its own journal. It is
significant that the party style, to which the first secretary had

attached so much importance on his accession to power a decade earlier, now became the issue on which the first serious public accusations were levelled at him. Other charges followed as the crisis took on wider proportions. The point worth underlining is that officially disseminated statements and declarations on intraparty democracy were quite contradictory even before the labour troubles broke out. In this respect it is the first occasion since 1956 on which we encounter such open, fundamental disagreement in public discourse. The question arises, therefore, whether the intraparty dispute served as a catalyst for the appearance of broader social divisions in the early 1980s. Furthermore, were divergent operative ideologies on intraparty democracy carried over to other issues, such as industrial democracy, cultural activity and socio-political value preferences? We return to these questions later in this chapter.

One novel component of operative ideology on intraparty democracy during the period 1976–80 was the stress given to party members' ethical principles. We noted how in the early 1960s Gomułka placed much emphasis on the calibre of party cadres, and especially on their political and professional qualifications. Successive verification campaigns after the 1968 and 1970 crises focused attention on ideological criteria and on socio-occupational background. What was new in the attention given to cadres in the late 1970s was this moral dimension – the personal qualities, style and way of life of members. The 1976 III Plenum found it necessary to warn that: 'For us party members, its leading role never signified or will signify any kind of privileges.'[16] In July 1976 Gierek declared: 'In our party we should mutually demand much of each other.'[17] The VII Plenum theses stated: 'it is impermissible that dishonest, careerist, morally compromised elements lacking respect in their communities should find their way into the party'.[18] Or, as two academics put it: 'There is no way that egoistic attitudes – avidity, striving at all costs to become better off and to distinguish oneself by displaying luxury goods – can be reconciled with membership in a party of working-class origins and popular social orientations.'[19]

Yet a contrary, far more optimistic view was enunciated by Babiuch, a Politburo member who was soon to become premier. He suggested that a quality more commonly found in party members was 'the integration of idealism and high moral standards with knowledge and qualifications; imagination and boldness of action with realistic assessments of capabilities and perseverance in work'.[20] Kruczek, the veteran hard-liner now turned regime critic, disagreed: 'A cause for considerable dissatisfaction is the type of calculating that goes with the construction of private villas, summer cottages, etc.' People were 'enervated by libations organised to mark various kinds of anniversaries, jubilees, etc.'[21] Early in 1980 a leading article in *Nowe Drogi* issued a further warning: 'It is a natural law of our party and of the socialist system that one who is entrusted with directing other people is simultaneously subject to more rigorous demands. There can be no place, therefore, for demagogy, nor for indulgence towards or concealment of dishonesty and decadence.'[22] Disagreement within the ruling elite was emerging into the open, and the central issue concerned Gierek's campaign for greater morality in party members. He was under pressure from, on the one hand, those who believed his campaign had gone too far and wished to curtail it before the elite would indeed have to surrender its privileges and, on the other hand, those who demanded that he act on his words and begin a purge within the top leadership.

As if responding to charges of corruption within the party, its Central Review Commission reported to the VIII Congress that apart from 'not numerous cases of small sums being overdue from treasuries in a small number of basic committees', no other irregularities in party financial operations had been discovered. Gierek reiterated the need 'to make ever greater demands on ourselves, by word and deed demonstrating our party commitment'. But Congress resolutions, in addition to stressing ideological criteria and consistency of word and action amongst party members, noted cryptically: 'The policy on cadres must be based on the principle that the greater the function performed, the greater the demands and responsibilities. This means, amongst other things, removing persons from leading positions whose work does not produce the anticipated results. Particularly strong demands have to be made on party members who perform leading roles.'[23]

This survey of discourse on intraparty democracy between 1976 and 1980 indicates that moral and ethical standards of members were given unprecedented attention. Political unity was a non-issue at a time when it was disintegrating, whilst concern with elite–mass relations was limited to the reiteration of Leninist norms and of the principle of democratic centralism. The consultative process within the party was singled out less and less, though upgrading the role of basic committees continued, as in the early 1970s, to be encouraged.

Alternative discourse appearing in 1980 brought into question the real state of intraparty democracy: it made oblique reference to bureaucratic and autocratic tendencies and arbitrariness, the top echelon not being excluded. In several important respects, therefore, operative ideology now differed from its counterpart in the early 1970s: it placed ethics at the centre of party life, focused on the personal conduct of individual members and was, above all, bifurcated between ritualistic and corrective orthodoxy on the one hand, and adaptive orthodoxy on the other.

2. The leading role of the party

Throughout the entire period examined, in times of crisis and stability, the leading role of the party was, we have seen, never brought into question in official discourse. The last years of Gierek's leadership proved no exception to this rule. But differences did occur in interpretation of this principle, ranging from the call for the party to be everywhere, issued under Gomułka, to the idea that 'the party directs and the government governs', advanced in 1971. The most important relationships the party was expected to foster varied as well: they could be with the economic enterprise, self-management bodies, local government, or with the working class, 'all working people', the peasants, the intelligentsia, the 'non-party millions', the nation. It was in this direction that the focus of party attention shifted. Finally, the mechanisms propagated for the party to carry out its leading role differed: whereas *dirigisme* and control may have been the concepts operative under Gomułka, in the 1970s the stress was on consultation and discussion.

The party's leading role in society became the source of a major controversy in 1975–6, when the authorities finally presented a draft for a new Polish constitution, already promised at the 1971 PUWP Congress. Whilst a number of the other East European states had revised their constitutions by this time, the Polish and Soviet case histories were protracted and, in the first country, divisive. After the 1975 Congress Gierek must have felt confident enough to present the draft: after all, this was the high point of his political fortunes, and he had also brought the country unmatched economic prosperity and some political liberalisation. Three clauses in the draft provoked swift and concerted opposition: (1) enshrinement of the principle of the party's leading role; (2) the statement that the basis of Poland's foreign policy rested in inviolable fraternal ties with the Soviet Union; and (3) the linking of citizens' rights with citizens' duties. In January 1976 a group of leading intellectuals, led by the veteran activist and writer Andrzejewski, addressed a 'letter of the 101' to the Sejm protesting against the proposed changes. Very quickly the first two points were modified to be less dogmatic, whilst the third was effectively dropped. The intervention of the church on the side of the intellectuals played an important part in the outcome. In mid February the revised version was officially enacted. The intellectuals had thus scored an impressive victory over the Gierek government, which followed the partial victory of the coastal workers in 1971. More importantly, the movement of open contestation in Poland had been born with this constitutional controversy. In the next few years it was to mushroom as a result of social discontent at home, the rulers' indecisiveness as to how to counter this and certain inspirational happenings abroad (the Helsinki agreement, the emergence of Euro-communism, the schismatic finale to the 1976 Conference of European Communist Parties, the birth of Charter 77).

As to the party's leading role, if its political meaning had always been unambiguous, its new legal significance was not. As Karpinski asks:

what is meant by the assertion that a certain organisation (e.g., a political party) is entitled to a 'leading role' (guidelines of September 1971)? How does a 'leading force' (guidelines of August 1975) differ from a 'guiding force' (the final version)? One might ask about the difference between 'the guiding ideological force' (the electoral ordinance of January 1976) and 'the guiding political force' (the amendment to the constitution), or whether 'the leading force in the state' (guidelines of 1975) means the same thing as 'the guiding force of society' (the amendment to the constitution).[24]

Ultimately political relations in Poland were not changed by the new constitution, only codified, and that had not proved easy to accomplish. The main effect of this juridical exercise was unintentional: as Karpinski again observes: 'The voices of protest against constitutional revisions demonstrated that the people of Poland (as opposed to the authorities) were prepared to take the law seriously.'[25]

Four months later, in June 1976, Premier Jaroszewicz announced an increase in the retail price of food. In economic terms this measure was justified, for at a time when inflation in the West had skyrocketed, in Poland prices remained pegged at their pre-1970 level. The sudden announcement, however, angered much of the population, especially the industrial workers who felt they were not benefiting from the boom of the early 1970s as much as other sectors of society. Workers in Radom and Ursus organised strikes, street demonstrations and blockage of railway lines. The proposed increase was immediately rescinded and the Gierek administration had suffered another political set-back. But this time reprisals followed: strikers were fired from their jobs and sentenced to stiff prison terms. Very soon afterwards the Committee for the Defence of Workers (KOR), led by Kuroń, was set up to protect the rights of these victims. Within a year almost all those convicted in Radom and Ursus were released. Thus, if the constitutional controversy had sparked open contestation under Gierek, the food price crisis had sealed an 'alliance of the classless', as Starski calls it, between different groups in Polish society.[26] The first showed, symbolically, that the principle of the party's leading role could not be formalised without a challenge being made; the second demonstrated, practically, that the principle could no longer be effectively operationalised by the rulers.

The leadership's response to the June 1976 disturbances was another appeal to the working class for support. Gierek told workers' activists: 'We are above all counting on the Polish working class, on its understanding of the national interest, on its discipline and deep patriotism.' Consultation was the most important aspect of the party's relationship with the working class, and it had become incorporated into the constitution. But, the party leader admonished: 'Refusal to engage in discussions and stoppages in work are not reconcilable with the method of consultation.'[27]

The IV Plenum, held after the disturbances, repeated the importance of the consultative process, adding that 'pressure tactics which incite social tension and create a favourable climate for activity by anti-social elements and forces hostile to Poland' were incompatible with this method.[28] At the 1977 VII Plenum the crucial position of the working class was again spelled out. Gierek stated optimistically: 'We have imperturbable support in the working class.' The Plenum also reintroduced a long-neglected slogan into the rulers' public vocabulary: 'All party members should be agitators. To be an agitator means to know how to persuade working people as to the correctness of party policy, to explain long-term goals and immediate tasks.'[29] By coupling this with emphasis on propaganda, Gierek was putting forward the classic Leninist concept of agitprop work to overcome simmering social tension.

But without doubt the most important component in operative ideology on the leading role in this period was national unity. As Gierek told the Sejm in mid 1980; 'The one road which ensures the security of Poland and its further development is national unity, solid intensive work, day-to-day concern with civic matters, and a sense of responsibility for the fate of the fatherland.'[30] One chapter in the resolutions of the VIII Congress was entitled, significantly, 'The leading role of the party and national unity – guarantees of the socialist development of Poland'.

In the late 1970s the party's leading role continued to be perceived, therefore, in terms of links with various classes, strata and groups (the workers, the intelligentsia, non-party people), but above all with the nation. There were limits on the party's responsiveness to society: industrial strife of June 1976 served to identify what were unacceptable means of applying pressure to the party. During this period official discourse continued to refer to difficulties in the party's efforts to disengage itself from state administrative matters: the 1980 Congress reiterated Gierek's old maxim that the party was to direct and the government to govern. This concept was still more frequently employed in official declarations than that of the party's leading role in society.

If the party was to direct, the government was to govern and society was to be regulated by social processes, to adapt Gierek's formula, then it is not surprising that in the end the political leadership lost control over its direction of society. Only the entire party apparatus, not simply its upper echelons, was capable of exercising directive force throughout society. This could only take place if intraparty democracy throve, and that had not happened under Gierek. Equally the propaganda campaign launched from above prescribing social justice and socialist morality was doomed to failure, for it did not subsume the whole party, including its inner circle. The crisis of the summer of 1980 was an agonising crisis of the party: internal democracy was in a shambles, and the party's directive role was vulnerable to usurpation by other social forces.

3. The party and ideology

Failings in the party's ideological work and the persistence of forms of social consciousness characteristic of earlier non-socialist social formations were, as we have seen, the subject of concern since 1956.

Similar conclusions regarding the inadequacies of ideological activity and social consciousness were reached in 1976 as in 1956: thus the III Plenum asserted how imperative it was to inculcate the view that Poland was and could only be socialist, that love of country was best demonstrated by a correct attitude to the state.[31] Commitment to policy was also important: 'As activists on the ideological front we must realise that eliciting confidence in the party, support for its programme, and belief in the feasibility of accomplishing audacious tasks should be a day-to-day concern.'[32] The 1976 V Plenum blamed 'incorrigible revisionists' for causing ideological disarray: 'Over two decades it has always been the same people who have abused their privileges and democratic freedoms, poisoned national discussions with their demagogy, and attempted to attack the foundations of our political and social system and our foreign policy.'[33] Identifying 'tiny though noisy groups of opponents of socialism', one observer invoked the old adage that 'there can be no freedom for the enemies of freedom'.[34] At the VII Plenum Gierek acknowledged: 'The opponents of Poland and of socialism do not cease in their efforts to create disarray in the consciousness of our nation, to weaken its links with socialism.'[35] In this way official discourse acknowledged the growing activity of KOR and other opposition groups.

Nevertheless the Central Committee report to the VIII Congress concluded optimistically that 'The role and effectiveness of ideological subjects such as political economy, Marxist–Leninist philosophy and sociology, and political science has increased', and that the party had been 'effective in counteracting all demagogy and views hostile to socialism'. Gierek was more cautious:

It would be premature to conclude that cleavages and conflicts of a class character have vanished from our society. Such cleavages still exist, although their scope and forms have changed substantially. The main front in the class struggle lies in the sphere of consciousness and political and social attitudes. A complicated ideological struggle is still taking place in our country with bourgeois mentality, value systems, myths and habits of the old world, constantly fed and stimulated by external influences. We still have to work on uprooting from consciousness conservative political and ideological views, and biases and deformations instilled by the opponents of socialism.[36]

From these declarations we see that some ideological achievements were considered to have been recorded during the period 1976–80 but, simultaneously, many shortcomings – some more serious than others – had to be overcome. What distinguished official discourse in Gierek's last years in power from that of earlier periods was the reference to elements which questioned the very foundations of the system. The existence of external forces hostile to socialism, the activity of revisionists within the country, the persistence of bourgeois mentality and value systems – all these had also been singled out under Gomułka in the late 1950s and mid 1960s. But very rarely had it been admitted that the nature of the system was itself in dispute. Likewise the admission of class struggle in society was now made repeatedly, whereas in the past only isolated statements acknowledged its existence. Most of the attacks on internal opponents of socialism (the harsher label of 'enemies of socialism', employed under Gomułka, was now infrequently used) were directed at the dissident groups which sprung up in Poland in the second half of the decade. The political leadership seemed uncertain as to the exact strength and influence of these groups and the degree of their opposition to the socialist system. Moreover after over thirty years of socialism in the country, it found it difficult to rationalise how it was that enemies of socialism still existed. For these reasons, perhaps, the campaign against anti-socialist elements in the late 1970s was not quite as vitriolic as those initiated under Gomułka. On the other hand the rulers were aware that dissident activity did have fertile ground in the kind of social consciousness existing at this time. The leadership displayed unwitting perspicacity in claiming that the next crisis would be the result of the existence or absence of socialist consciousness. As Gierek told the 1980 Congress, it was in this superstructural sphere that 'the question of people's preparedness to accept and carry out the wide-ranging, complex tasks posed by the present stage [of socialist development] would be decided'.[37]

INDUSTRIAL DEMOCRACY

In Chapter 5 we noted that greater workers' democracy did not constitute a central concept in the incoming leadership's operative ideology, contrary to the popular belief that it had done so. The relationship between the party and the working class was strongly emphasised, material benefits were promised to the workers, but participation in the management of industrial concerns and factories was, if anything, further removed from them than before as a result of the establishment of large economic conglomerates and the application of the principle of one-person management.[38] In the second half of the 1970s, however, a very different tendency arose: operative ideology began once again to stress workers' self-management and, more specifically, the role of self-management committees. We now look more closely at this phenomenon.

A succinct explanation for this new-found concern with an old institution was provided by Gierek at the III Plenum: 'to have means to produce'. The appropriate role of co-management was to assume greater responsibilities and obligations, and both self-management and trade unions had important parts to play in this sphere.[39] In a 1976 address to the Sejm shortly before the announcement of price increases, the premier stated that workers' organisations would be consulted on all questions affecting their standards of living and conditions of work.[40] In practice, as events demonstrated, Jaroszewicz had engaged in empty rhetoric. At a 1977 joint sitting of the Politburo, Council of State, Council of Ministers and Presidium of the Trade Union Congress, Gierek outlined his updated conception of industrial democracy:

> We consider the most important attribute of socialist democracy, and a criterion of its development, to be the active participation of working people, especially the working class, in the government of the state and management of the national economy ... Self-management committees, as representative bodies of the working class and working people, can and should become the most important forum for consultation on the specific problems involved in the development of our country.[41]

The break with the past which this new approach represented was signalled in an article in *Nowe Drogi*: up to the VII Congress (that is, five years into Gierek's term in office), a 'managerial conception of management and planning' and a 'formalist attitude to workers' self-management' had been dominant. Now self-management had matured so as to be able to concern itself with 'the politics of the factory and the generalities of its operation'.[42]

The 1977 IX Plenum on management and the January 1978 II National Party Conference also ascribed considerable importance to upgrading the status of self-management committees. But their reinvigorated role was given greatest emphasis in the period immediately leading up to the 1980 party Congress. A May 1978 Politburo resolution announced the formation of self-management committees in large industrial conglomerates where they had not previously existed.[43] Two months later a Congress of Self-Management Committees was convened by the authorities. Gierek described the main functions they were to perform: 'harmonising growth in productivity with continuous improvement in the working conditions of the labour force'.[44] In the end, there was little new in the 'new' approach: it did not differ significantly from Gomułka's conception of self-management following its reorganisation late in 1958. Workers' participation in management was not, as seemed logical, the *raison d'être* of workers' self-management.

Nonetheless the self-management concept now actively promoted by Gierek continued to expand. The Central Committee report to the VIII Congress asserted that 'self-management committees play an ever greater role in mobilising the work-force, in bringing it into the decision-making process, and in helping resolve key socio-economic problems'. Moreover Gierek told the meeting that he would seek new legislation on workers' self-management which would reflect the different conditions and new tasks arising in the 1980s.[45] In the four months that intervened between the Congress and the first strikes, a national debate was organised around the future of self-management.[46] A representative view of general opinion was contained in one *Nowe Drogi* article: 'Economic democracy will begin to function more effectively when a social approach to economic problems becomes more widely used. An exclusively "economic" approach to the functions and role of self-management and co-management will always be reduced to problems of productivity, growth in work efficiency, and so on.'[47] This was a critique of the conception of industrial democracy which, as we have seen, was propagated from the 1959 Congress onwards.

What the leadership's real intentions were in recommending that a new act on workers' self-management should be drafted cannot be ascertained from official discourse during the short period it remained in power. We do know that the issue became a subject of some controversy in the analyses of the 1980 political crisis that were made at the VI Plenum.[48] But the resurrection of the concept of self-management between 1978 and 1980 resembles Gomułka's sudden interest in it (albeit in a more abstract way) following the 1968 student disturbances. The more practical nature of Gierek's approach can be seen as a response to the industrial strife that occurred in 1976. It may also have been intended to 'neutralise' the industrial workers at a time when intellectual discontent with the system was growing. As had happened in the late 1960s, therefore, the democratising turn in operative ideology on enterprise democracy could be interpreted as an attempt by the rulers to head off a political crisis they saw as imminent. It is more than coincidence that a more participatory-oriented form of self-management, a social as opposed to an economic one, was advocated in the middle of Poland's *Sturm und Drang* period.

Given the multiple causes of workers' grievances in both 1970 and 1980, it seems implausible that the sudden reappearance in each case of more responsive forms of self-management had anything to do with workers' subsequent actions. It could be argued, however, that the propagation of the concept did contribute to stimulating latent expectations in the work-force which had been frustrated in the past. The fact that, having diffused the idea, the Gierek leadership appeared more serious than its predecessor about institutionalising reform in the system of industrial democracy, may also be associated with the greater importance attached by workers in the late 1970s to the need for reform. Rather than assuaging workers' political frustrations, therefore, recourse to the concept of self-management may have helped to aggravate them. Whatever the case, it is ironic that on two separate occasions the idea of workers' self-management became a key element in operative ideology shortly before workers decided to make real, direct interventions in the sphere of political 'co-participation'.

THE CHURCH

In the previous chapter we referred to the normalisation of relations between church and state in the early 1970s. Believers were openly exhorted to take part in the political system, which had not been the case earlier. Much the same line was followed in the second half of the 1970s. As Gierek told the III Plenum: 'In conditions of freedom of conscience and religious practice, the political orientations of the vast majority of Poles, regardless of their religious beliefs, develop on the basis of support for the policies of the state, in accordance with the national and social interests in Poland.'[49] Early in 1976 the premier told the Sejm: 'In recent years the government has done much to improve relations with the Roman Catholic Church.' He referred to the tolerance of religious beliefs which represented a long-standing tradition in the country.[50] At the II National Party Conference the party leader stated that an integral aspect of national unity was 'the establishment of good relations between the state and church, relations based on cooperation in achieving great national goals and the prosperity of the People's Republic'.[51] Following his meetings with the primate of Poland and with Pope Paul VI in 1977, and the election of the Polish pope in October 1978, Gierek claimed: 'There is not and never should be any division of Poles into believers and non-believers on any important national questions.'[52] For the first time since the church's 'Great Novena', organised in 1966, an article in *Nowe Drogi* dealt specifically with church–state relations. Although it was admitted that the two institutions propagated different world out-looks, it was essential that 'this rivalry be based on authentic values and valid arguments, not on confrontation and pressure of a non-ideological nature'. The party itself was not closed to believers, although whenever differences of views arose it was imperative that each person support the party standpoint. Anti-socialist campaigns had often sought moral support amongst church dignitaries: 'It happens that such efforts do indeed find an echo, that the slogans of various dissidents, revisionists, persons striving to break down the socialist model of political life appear more appealing to a small but active group of church representatives than the real unshakeable aspirations of the nation and its leaders for socialism.'[53]

Gierek's initiatives towards the church were not fully backed by all members of the ruling elite. In 1974 Szydlak had attacked the 'reactionary wing of the episcopate'. In 1976 the Minister of Religious Affairs, Kąkol, made clear that 'normalisation of church–state relations did not signify "capitulation"'. In 1978 Grabski, one of the 'enlightened' hard-liners in Olszowski's faction, criticised Gierek precisely on the grounds that he had capitulated to the church.[54] The election of Cardinal Woytyła as pope later that year took the steam out of this anti-clerical movement within the leadership. The result was that Gierek's line continued to dominate. He told the VIII Congress: 'We shall continue to promote cooperation between the church and the socialist state in strengthening the role of the family, combating negative moral phenomena, inculcating the primacy of the common good, and consolidating all of society so as to increase the prosperity of People's Poland.' The party leader also praised John Paul II's efforts on behalf of world peace.[55] In 1980 a leading article in *Nowe Drogi* emphasised cooperation not only between believers and non-believers (as had been the rule between 1971 and 1976) but also between the state and the 'Church' (the word was now capitalised!) 'for the most noble reasons of the fatherland and of peace, for the good of each individual and of the nation'.[56] And in his first speech as premier, Babiuch stressed: 'We are counting on the understanding, goodwill and support of the Church for our objectives.'[57]

Our study has not looked at ecclesiastical policy or discourse, but to put the leadership's operative ideology into perspective it should be noted that 'normalisation' aroused controversy within the church hierarchy too. In 1977 Wyszyński spelled out his reasons for meeting with the party leader: 'I decided after lengthy reflection over several years that in situations which are especially difficult the bishops and primate of Poland must clearly see the demands of Polish *raisons d'état.*' The church, for want of another social force to challenge the party, had been forced to intervene in both the constitutional controversy and the food price riots in 1976, but the establishment of KOR was welcomed by Wyszyński chiefly because it 'set the church free from the role . . . of a para-political opposition'.[58] But some bishops and many priests often preferred to play this latter role, and increasingly they felt that the party leadership was exploiting the church's benevolent attitude towards normalisation. In this way, relations at the summit level were improved dramatically in the 1970s, and the ideology of both the inner party elite and top church leaders sought to justify the policy of *rapprochement*. But sections of the next level in the hierarchies were less enthusiastic about what was viewed in each case as capitulation. Relations between church and state remained precarious, therefore, despite normalisation, and the 1980 political crisis put them to a severe test.

SCIENCE AND CULTURE

The important role of science in socialist society, recognised already under Gomułka but given top priority under Gierek, was conceived principally in instrumental terms, as was noted in the last two chapters. The objectives of scientific endeavour were held to be subordinate to the socio-economic needs of the country. Similarly social science was assigned an instrumental function – to engineer socialist development in the superstructural sphere or, more specifically, to propagate and inculcate socialist values throughout society. Cultural activity was very much left alone, although it was often said that adoption of progressive, humanist values was desirable. Finally the rulers' growing concern with political socialisation betrayed what was seen as the regressive nature of social consciousness. We look now at Gierek's operative ideology on these subjects in the second half of the 1970s.

1. Science

The dominant view remained that 'Socialist society will become more advanced and mature the more it develops and utilises science.'[59] The 1978 XII Plenum focused exclusively on the document 'Further strengthening the role of science in the socio-economic development of the country'. At this Plenum Gierek summarised the dual nature of scientific endeavour:

For science to perform its social function effectively, at least two conditions have to be fulfilled. Firstly science itself has to develop and new cognitive values have to be created. Secondly science is tied to life, to the country's needs, which entails the synchronisation of research areas with directions in the nation's economic and cultural development, a concentration of effort on the most important problems, and an efficiently functioning method of applying research results to economic and social practice.

Scientists themselves could determine their basic research interests, but economic imperatives determined all other research trends. Finally, Gierek called for the development of a technical culture which would make society more responsive to scientific activity and break-throughs, and he added:

The alliance of the working class with the intelligentsia, the links between science and socialism are indissoluble and constitute the basis of all progress.[60]

Repetition of the concepts of earlier years, along with the relatively scant attention given to science at the VIII Congress, suggested that by 1980 Gierek may have become disillusioned with the STR, particularly as it had not apparently helped solve the country's compounding economic difficulties. In turn the almost exclusive, obsessive concern with science's instrumental role in earlier years may also have disillusioned scientists with the political leadership's objectives. As one scientist noted early in 1980: 'Even though the overall balance sheet of Polish science for the 1970s is positive and compares favourably with that of the previous decade, in many areas a decline took place.' The author expressed the hope that in future science would regain priority status.[61]

2. Social science

Following the party's 1973 conference on the social sciences, less attention was directed to this branch in the rulers' operative ideology. One writer interpreted the intention of the VII Congress as 'assuring the domination of Marxism–Leninism in intellectual life and an even closer integration of the social sciences with social practice, with the thought and activity of the party'.[62] The VII Plenum theses listed the main functions of social science: analysis of social phenomena, collection of data on which decisions could be taken, integration of cognitive and intellectual needs, conditioning the nation's knowledge about history and current affairs as well as its attitudes and views, and developing a favourable political culture in society.[63] At the II National Party Conference Gierek stated:

> In the social sciences and humanities, our attention is focused on strengthening the Marxist–Leninist orientation of these sciences and tightening their links with party activity and with its theoretical, political socialisation and ideological work. The party is interested in promoting greater cognitive, ideological and practical activity in the social sciences, and their increased involvement in the confrontation between socialist and bourgeois ideology.[64]

A leading party ideologue, Werblan, added: 'The party opts for a Marxist–Leninist orientation in social science, and for its systematic deepening and strengthening. Only through the use of the principles and methodology of scientific socialism can laws of social life be explained and appropriate solutions proposed.'[65]

Gierek's address to the 1980 party Congress continued the trend towards a more subservient position for social science. He stressed that 'Party direction of social science development should ensure the conditions necessary for it to fulfil its basic cognitive, ideological and practical functions. We expect greater input from social science in enriching national culture, strengthening the ideological and moral unity of the nation, and moulding patriotic, civic attitudes.'[66] The new stress laid on the need for both Marxist–Leninist and party control over social science may, it can be conjectured, have represented a response to the increasing activity of dissident intellectuals in this milieu in the late 1970s. Indeed the adoption of a more restrictive operative ideology at a time of intellectual contestation had precedents in Gomułka's responses to the so-called revisionist challenges of the late 1950s and the late 1960s.

A quite different view of the role of the social sciences was put forward in 1978 by the sociologist Kłoskowska. She polemicised against an idea that had become prevalent that the social scientist should publicise conclusions which might have positive practical consequences even if they were factually inaccurate. 'In reality functional long-term advantages never derive from the acceptance of incorrect views as true.'[67] In this way the propagandistic role more frequently being assigned to social science was repudiated in the party's own theoretical journal. Moreover the long-term effects of the rulers' propaganda of success were seen as being counterproductive. Relations between the party leadership and social scientists appeared to have deteriorated considerably, therefore, by the end of the decade.

3. Culture

Gierek's speech to the III Plenum summarised his operative ideology on culture up to then: 'Never before has scientific and artistic creativity been given such profound respect, never before have conditions for its development been so auspicious as at present. We shall continue the policy of giving broad support for creative activity which inculcates patriotic, humanist and socialist values, and enriches both the nation and the individual.'[68] Theses adopted by the VII Plenum outlined the leadership's approach in more detail: it was important to give 'special care to creativity which describes the lives of working people as well as the historical endeavours of the nation to bring about the socialist transformation of society and civilisation from the founding of People's Poland.' The 'objective function' of culture was to help promote social development; all attempts to minimise the nation's efforts or to depict national moral nihilism had to be combated.[69] Especially after the signing of the Helsinki agreement in 1975, which would promote cultural exchanges between East and West, screening of works from capitalist countries had to be more careful, it was argued.[70] All elitist forms of art had to be rejected; instead culture had to be based on such universal values as patriotism, socialist humanism, morality and progressive traditions.[71]

The Central Committee report to the VIII Congress noted with satisfaction that: 'Literary and artistic works express in a fuller way the realities and problems of the most recent history of the country, which testifies to the ideological commitment of artists.' Nonetheless 'Our party will strengthen its ties with artists, giving special support to everything that enriches the spiritual life of socialist society and strengthens national unity.' Marxist theoretical reflections on culture's role in society were encouraged, but Marxism–Leninism was not directly linked to artistic output in the way it was to dominate social science.[72]

Cultural activity, therefore, remained the sphere in which operative ideology permitted the greatest autonomy and upon which it imposed the fewest conditions of an instrumental or ideological order. This could suggest harmonious relations between the party and the cultural intelligentsia in the late 1970s. More probably, it indicated that so long as it was not oppositionist or otherwise dysfunctional, the contribution which culture could make to constructing an advanced socialist society was regarded as marginal and therefore not worthy of much attention.

4. Socialisation

Failures in political socialisation continued to represent a major problem for the rulers. A wide range of abnormalities were identified in official discourse throughout the 1970s. The main negative components of the social pathology of the second half of the decade included breaches of work discipline, disregard for state interests, abuse of socialised property, inefficiency and wastage. The III Plenum spoke of 'all types of idlers and connivers leading a parasitic life at society's expense',[73] whilst a 1977 Politburo resolution cited 'shoddy work, slyness, disregard for one's duties, ill-conceived tolerance, usurpation of other people's achievements, and egoism'.[74] At the VII Plenum Gierek identified other problems, such as cliquishness, *parvenuism*, dishonesty, hypocrisy and alcoholism,[75] whilst the IX Plenum criticised the use of personal connections and of pull, and 'the chase after money and privileges inconsistent with social and moral principles ... and predispositions towards extravagance and sumptuosity'.[76] On May Day 1979 Gierek described the generally poor climate of interpersonal relations in society. He condemned in particular the haughtiness of those in positions of power and their exploitation of their offices for personal gain.[77] Such indirect attacks on his colleagues were, as we noted in our analysis of intraparty democracy, speedily rebutted and engendered open divisions within the ruling elite.

The most important objective of political socialisation identified in this period was the all-round development of the individual. The economist approach to the citizen taken in the past had now to be discarded. As one writer argued: 'It is imperative to instil in social consciousness the belief that an advanced socialist society is not simply a society of producers and consumers but also one composed of enlightened people possessing broad knowledge and high intellectual, cognitive and cultural aspirations.'[78]

At the II National Party Conference Gierek outlined other important qualities to be inculcated in youth: professionalism, thriftiness, innovation and 'courage in the struggle against evil and against that which hinders progress'.[79] Finally the Central Committee report to the VIII Congress identified patriotism, internationalism and thinking in the categories of the popular state as the most desirable qualities in the young generation, best expressed through 'solid conscientious study and work, and continuous improving of professional qualifications'.[80]

Under the Gierek leadership official discourse on political socialisation was both more comprehensive and more candid than in the past. The work ethic remained of central importance, but by the late 1970s the concept of the well-rounded individual was the ideal which operative ideology most strongly stressed. At the same time its opposite – the materialist-minded, self-centred, cunning stereotype – was most strongly condemned. Such concerns did not figure prominently in the first half of the 1970s, which may have been the most auspicious time to express them, and they were almost totally absent from operative ideology under Gomułka. This socialisation model reflected the economic prosperity that had been recorded between 1971 and 1975, prosperity the distribution of which was not always governed by the principles of social justice, as the leadership freely admitted. Certain social groups benefited more than others, and judging from official declarations we may extrapolate that it was primarily those which held influential 'positions' which gained most. The social malaise appeared, therefore, to be candidly and accurately diagnosed in official discourse. But an element of mistaken identification of patients who had been contaminated by the illness arose. For the contagion seemed to be as widespread amongst the diagnosticians as amongst the diagnosed. This the leadership steadfastly refused to, or could not, act upon. It is ironic, too, that the economism that had been so dominant a part of the operative ideology of both the Gomułka and Gierek leaderships through to 1975 was the social value most vigorously attacked now that it had permeated much of social consciousness and behaviour. Only very late in the day was it realised that the aggregation of individual economic interests did not coincide with the general interests of society. Yet a basic tenet of socialism propagated for a long time was the unity and harmonious development of individual and general interests. A more perceptive approach would have been to view these interests as dialectically opposed to each other. By the late 1970s such an outlook was gaining adherents, as we see in the next section.

POLITICAL VALUES AND SOCIETY

If operative ideology in the first half of the decade placed the individual at the centre of socialist society (which had not been the case in earlier periods), then in the late 1970s relations between individuals received greatest attention. 'Socialism for people through people', the well-being of the individual and his family, gave way to concern with interpersonal relations, social justice, morality and a socialist way of life. Furthermore the supposed unity of politics, economics and ideology was now projected to the dimension of personality, exemplified in the concept of the 'well-rounded individual'. At the most general level, therefore, we detect significant differences between the societal values promulgated in the earlier and later years of Gierek's rule. The importance of the 'subjective factor' (as social consciousness was sometimes called) and the central role to be played by the superstructural sphere in constructing an advanced socialist society were, after thirty years of the existence of People's Poland, finally given due recognition. The first secretary's declaration at the VIII Congress on the primacy of the superstructure in the future resolution of the tasks facing socialism (cited on page 158) officially sanctioned this more 'globalised' view of the individual.

Many values propagated in the first half of the decade also received emphasis in the second. The most important were work (especially the quality of work), patriotism (and, related to it, thinking in state categories), the family, the important status of women in society, effectiveness of management and responsibility. Rational consumption patterns continued to be stressed. As Gierek told the National Party Conference, these had to be more consistent with socialist principles: 'We have decisively to prevent the spread of consumption habits typical of capitalist societies in which material possessions are transformed into prestige symbols which deform consciousness and produce deep, sometimes even extreme, feelings of frustration.'[81]

In attempting to redress social injustices caused by wage differentiation, capitalist consumption patterns and so on, such specific objectives as increasing society's economic and historical knowledge and directing attention to long-term goals were introduced.[82] But at a more fundamental level, we can identify six conceptual categories concerned with the major societal questions of the period. In many ways they interrelate and overlap, since they deal with similar problems confronting society, but the basic values inherent in each are different. These six categories of societal values are: (1) economic egalitarianism; (2) social justice; (3) socialist morality (interpersonal relations, life-styles); (4) psychological development (social consciousness); (5) harmonisation of various interests; and (6) political participation. We now look briefly at each of these.

Since material incentives were first declared to be socially acceptable under Gomułka in the mid 1960s, the question of economic egalitarianism was treated in a number of different ways. In earlier chapters we saw how the principle 'to each according to one's work' was variously interpreted: it could mean input into work, quality of work, the real effects of work, the social utility of work, and so on. Similar inconsistencies can be traced in the late 1970s. The IX Plenum in 1977 and the III Plenum in 1980 declared that wages should be based on people's real input into work, whilst the II National Party Conference said that they should be based on the quantity of work.[83] Another view was that they should relate to the effects of work,[84] whilst even further factors were introduced at the VIII Congress, which referred to the 'quality and complexity of work performed' and to the degree of productivity not just of the individual worker but of the collectivity to which he belonged.[85] And whilst generally greater stress was now placed on the need to reduce variations in income, further differentiation of criteria with which the value of work was to be measured indicated a great deal of irresolution and confusion concerning this question amongst the rulers.

Social justice, as the leadership understood it, signified 'guaranteeing individual rights and equal starts in life whilst ensuring that all society had the ability to satisfy essential needs for subsistence regardless of the size of income'.[86] Gierek referred to the importance of a fair distribution of both income and consumer goods in achieving social justice. As he put it: 'Socialist social justice ... is tested in the distribution of goods to society, which includes both wages and articles found in the shops.'[87] The 1978 XIII Plenum reiterated this point, drawing attention to the political ramifications of 'a just division of certain goods and services, of which there is a relative shortage, consistent with socialist principles'.[88] In 1979, *Nowe Drogi* published an article dealing with poverty which, it was argued, had hitherto been treated as only of marginal importance.[89] In April 1980 Gierek told the Sejm of four possible ways to promote greater social justice in society: (1) reducing unjustifiable, excessive income differentiation; (2) giving special attention to 'social groups and families living in difficult conditions'; (3) equalising life chances; and (4) ensuring fairness in the recruitment and promotion of cadres, in the distribution of social services and in resolving citizens' grievances by public bodies.[90] Resolutions of the VIII Congress spoke of the need to ensure that social justice prevailed in all social relations,[91] whilst one writer drew the following conclusion: 'It is very important that the social structure and hierarchy established in management should not be transposed to political, social and economic life in which people take part and should take part as equal citizens.'[92]

Closely related to the values of egalitarianism and justice was the concept of socialist morality diffused in the last years of the Gierek leadership. It subsumed two main ideas – interpersonal relations and socialist life-style. One observer noted: 'At each stage of socialist development, socialist morality should gradually but inexorably help liquidate the gap existing between ways of life in a socialist society and a socialist way of life.'[93] Gierek told the VII Plenum: 'We have to give considerably greater attention to moulding socialist interpersonal relations ... Political and social relations in our country offer the best proof that overcoming antagonistic class cleavages whilst discarding bourgeois pluralism opens the path towards real democracy.'[94] At both the National Party Conference and the VIII Congress the significance of socialist morality was further underscored. As Gierek told the 1980 meeting, 'ideological and moral values determine the mark of the person of the socialist era'.[95]

The fourth category of societal values disseminated by the rulers in the late 1970s was the psychological development of the individual. More specifically, this concerned the question of stimulating the individual's intellectual, cultural and spiritual needs, and of helping him satisfy them. As one Marxist philosopher wrote:

in the socialist model of the 'affluent society' objects are not an end in themselves but a means of bringing about prosperity, enriching the quality of life, and promoting harmonious, all-round development of personality. In this way the formula, 'to live so as to have', will be replaced by another, 'to have so as to live' – to live in an intellectually stimulating and fruitful way.[96]

Increased recognition of the importance of the subjective factor in attaining developed socialism represented both a key societal and a personal ideological value.

Throughout our study we have seen that harmonisation of individual, group and societal interests constituted an important principle of social development. Usually societal interests were considered as having priority over other ones, although in the early 1970s the idea that what was good for the individual was good for society became common currency. In the late 1970s it was increasingly admitted that individual and particularist interests were not, after all, automatically reconcilable with societal ones. Accordingly the existence of cleavages became an operative concept. We should note, however, that it was largely social scientists, not political leaders, who identified conflicts of interest arising in society. At the time of the June 1976 disturbances, the term used by the leadership to describe collision with state interests was 'differences of views and opinions', not 'cleavages'.[97] The V Plenum and VIII Congress referred to particularistic attitudes in economic management as a problem that had to be overcome but made no mention of conflict of interests.[98]

In 1977, however, a number of social scientists closely connected with the party's research institutes took the lead in developing the social conflict concept. According to Dobieszewski, for example, it was when national income was being divided that a collision of group and individual interests with societal ones 'most often occurs, which may turn at times into very pronounced cleavages between immediate and long-term social interests. The peculiarity of cleavage under socialism is that it occurs not only directly between particular classes and strata but also between these and the state.'[99] Widerszpil pointed out that cleavages between particular social groups and the authorities should not necessarily be regarded as conflicts between anti-socialist and socialist forces, that is, as 'antagonistic conflicts'.[100] Wesołowski and Wiatr concurred: most differences in the interests of social groups were characterised by an economic, non-antagonistic dimension.[101]

But as the events of 1980 were to show, this was largely a spurious argument. Economic conflict between social groups was bound, ultimately, to become both antagonistic and political. Later interpretations of the 1980–1 Polish crisis were actually to emphasise this transformation of economic cleavages into political ones. Moreover cleavages between particular social groups (in fact, classes) and the authorities did not have to involve conflict between anti-socialist and socialist forces for antagonism to arise. The misleading views on the nature of cleavage given by social scientists prominent in the party were grounded in an overly optimistic interpretation of the 1976 conflicts: one-sided emphasis was laid on the fact that Gierek had survived the crises, and the true sources and dimensions of the conflicts were neglected.

In 1980 another series of articles was published in *Nowe Drogi* dealing with cleavage and conflict. One writer referred to 'immanent cleavages' dwelling in the very logic of socialist development, such as cleavages between ethnic, class, group, regional and specialist interests, or between the economy as a whole and its constitutive elements (economic sectors). But cleavage could also arise between the moral and political unity of the nation, on the one hand, and the actual bureaucratic methods used to apply policy, on the other. Citing the Soviet academic Sztraks, the writer concluded: 'The same general dialectical laws which functioned in all other social formations also function at the present stage.'[102] Two other contributors underlined the economic basis of conflict: in their view, structural solutions were necessary in order to reduce the potentiality of conflict.[103] Finally a leading article in *Nowe Drogi* issued this warning: 'We should remember that unity ... is not something that is given for always; it needs to be continually operationalised and reinforced. Likewise it would be premature to suggest the disappearance of cleavages and conflict of a class character from our society, which today takes place in the sphere of consciousness.'[104]

Never before, therefore, was the harmony of societal and particularist interests viewed in such sceptical terms as in the late 1970s. It was now acknowledged that class conflict continued to occur under socialism. Although this was not inconsistent with Marxist thought, it was something which, until then, had not been freely admitted. Moreover the kind of class conflict described was not simply 'horizontal', polarising different groups in society, such as the new bourgeoisie against the proletariat. It was held to be 'vertical' also, pitting the state bureaucracy against social groups or, put more drastically, the rulers against the ruled. The dialectical laws governing capitalist social formation could also apply to the socialist stage, it was suggested. Class struggle in socialist societies could involve, therefore, as one of the protagonists, the ruling class itself.

It is significant that this blunt thesis was advanced by social scientists writing in the party theoretical journal. Firstly, it was a clear warning to the leadership of the gravity of social divisions then in existence. By 1980 Gierek himself was speaking of 'conditions of class conflict', if not of class conflict itself. Secondly, it revealed dissension within the top echelons of the party. The articles that Werblan, a Politburo member and chief editor of *Nowe Drogi*, was allowing to be published demonstrated how an anti-Gierek coalition was able to speak out publicly, within the party forum, against the policies of his administration. And thirdly, it showed the centrality of theory to the political process. The arguments advanced by social scientists were for the most part highly abstract and generalised. Nevertheless they had a direct bearing on the political options available to the rulers. The fact that the theories of class conflict under socialism were, in a number of important respects, proved correct later in 1980 is not insignificant either.

The final category of societal values propounded in the late 1970s concerned political participation. Several Plenum meetings in this period (the V, VII, IX, XIII and XVI) emphasised the importance of participation, consultation, discussion, information flow and criticism – just as in the early part of the decade. In turn the National Party Conference and the VIII Congress dealt with institutional methods of exercising social control over the activity of the state administration. The true significance of this societal value was once again best described by a social scientist, not a political actor:

Ignoring public opinion, avoiding social control, placing one-sided faith in the effectiveness of administrative activity, and the presumptuousness of claiming one's infallibility – attitudes which are not that rarely encountered – are manifestations of the inability to comprehend the fact that in our conditions administrative work and social activeness serve the same goal – the construction of a socialist society – and express the same profound mutual interests.[105]

The diffusion of participatory values throughout society was intended, therefore, to counteract the inflexibility, poor understanding and ethos of infallibility which pervaded the entrenched administrative apparatus.

In conclusion, the diagnosis contained in official discourse of the malaise which befell Polish society in the second half of the 1970s appeared to be substantiated. In fact the analyses, recriminations and harsh criticisms of Polish society, its economy and policy made after the Gierek leadership fell from power are in large measure similar to those found in official discourse of the late 1970s. It was not at the level of operative ideology, which in many of the problem-areas we examined recommended remedial action, that the problem lay. The banal truth was that too many key political and economic actors had too powerful a vested interest in the existing system, however imperfect it was, to want to act on the basic tenets of that operative ideology. As a result not only did political life go on as if the mainly valid operative ideology did not exist at all. The fundamental Marxist principle of praxis – of the unity of word and deed – was also not heeded. Disregard by the leadership for both ideologising levels – fundamental principles and operative ideology – brought about the corresponding danger that not only the rulers but also the system itself were vulnerable to attack.

7

Interlude I: Solidarity, 1980–81

Are there any limits to compromise? No, a hundred times no, neither in the economic sphere nor in the political sphere.

Stanisław Kania, IX Plenum, March 1981

We must make it very clear that there are limits which, if transgressed, would be fatal for the nation and the state. We cannot permit this to occur.

Wojciech Jaruzelski, IX Congress, July 1981

In the summer of the 1980 Gierek was swept from power under circumstances remarkably similar to those of his assumption of power ten years earlier. The government announced an increase in food prices, industrial workers responded with strikes to protest against the decision, and a party leader suddenly taken ill was unable to attend the Central Committee Plenum which ousted him from power. On the surface, little had changed: unpopular policies were still pursued, the working class remained, collectively, the vanguard of society, and the leadership carousel continued to spin whenever energy was applied to it.

In most other respects, however, the crisis of 1980 differed radically from that of a decade earlier. Most importantly, the protests were more widespread and determined. The reasons for this were numerous. The hot summer was conducive to the spread of 'work stoppages', as the authorities initially labelled the strikes. Polish revolutions usually took place during the short murky days of winter, it is true: the uprisings of 1794, 1831, 1863, 1905 and 1970 were cases in point. But in 1980 no insurrection was being planned. The protest movement just mushroomed, first in Mielec in southern Poland, where demands were economic (higher wages), then in the central regions, where demands were socio-economic (better food supplies, improved living conditions), and in the end on the Baltic coast and in Silesia, where strikes took on a political character (expressions of solidarity with other workers, then the twenty-one points). According to official sources 2,000 factories employing 1,200,000 workers had taken part in strikes that summer.[1] The existence of a more civilised and modern political culture contributed to the extensiveness of the strikes. Participants' lives were not on the line as in earlier periods: after all, had Gierek's response to the strikes of 1971 and 1976 and to the first series in 1980 not been primarily one of negotiation and compromise? In turn, had not the politically more mature working class avoided mass street demonstrations and attacks on public buildings, and opted for occupation strikes instead? The emergence of embryonic trade union organisations free from party domination in the late 1970s in Poland, coupled with the existence of KOR since 1976, also helped coordinate the protest movement. Not least, the extent of dissatisfaction with the government's policies was no less than in December 1970: standards of living were admittedly markedly higher now but, simultaneously, Poland was being projected as the tenth industrial power in the world. Economic expectations were concomitantly much higher. The unequal distribution of wealth had hit manual workers most forcefully, and a sense of relative deprivation had become instilled in them. Finally, a feeling of having been deceived and outmanoeuvred in 1970 and, even earlier, in 1956 prompted the workers to stand resolutely together. As a banner at the Gdańsk shipyards put it: 'Workers of all factories, unite.'

The desperation, doggedness and hopes of the Polish August were not confined to the working class. Intellectuals had either given support to the idea of independent trade unions earlier or were now boarding trains for the Baltic ports to aid the nascent movement. The birth and evolution of the self-governing trade union Solidarity was watched with admiration by journalists, scholars and millions of ordinary citizens throughout the world. The sixteen months of its existence were truly a 'hallucinatory experience', as the Polish poet Miłosz observed. A large and varied body of literature has arisen on the period: some works are eye-witness accounts, others present political manifestos, whilst others still offer deeper analyses of the events.[2] Within Poland, academics, writers and journalists published fascinating accounts of all aspects of social life in these sixteen months. It is no exaggeration to say that Solidarity, whatever its political failings, released the creative energies of the entire nation. Even Marxism, a doctrine reduced to petrification after years of neglect, began to revive in the intellectual climate of 1980–1.

In focusing on party ideology, we may be dealing with one of the less innovative spheres of intellectual life in this period. On the other hand, it is interesting to study the changing response of party ideology, because this specifically was being attacked under the new conditions. The way in which the political leadership perceived the events from August 1980 to December 1981 was ultimately the source of the decision to impose martial law. Party ideology is, therefore, of crucial importance to an understanding of this period.

At the outset two important characteristics of the operative ideology of this period have to be underscored: the party leadership was divided over this ideology, and it underwent various mutations and modifications in the sixteen months. Let us look more closely at these aspects.

After Kania had succeeded Gierek it was difficult to speak of a dominant political leader or even of a *primus inter pares*. The nature of the events and the prolongation of the crisis produced a veritable schism within the ruling elite and throughout the party over ideology, policy, strategy and tactics. The fortunes of individual political actors and particular factions ebbed and flowed. The post of party first secretary was no longer synonymous with enlightened despotism, at least not whilst Kania occupied it. He was neither the charismatic leader that Gomułka had been in 1956, when his 1947 defiance of Stalin had taken on mythological proportions, nor the party strongman that Gierek had been in the late 1960s, when his rule over his Silesian fiefdom and over production of King Coal established him as heir apparent. It was Kania's misfortune that the principal base of support he did command – the internal security apparatus – was unwilling to back his centrist 'socialist renewal' programme.

Personal qualities also played an important part in Kania's failure to stamp his authority on the Politburo, Central Committee and party. Immediately after his appointment at the VI Plenum, he made it clear that he did not intend to create a cult around his leadership as his predecessors had done: 'A position does not make a person into a leader. I am not sure anyway that the party needs a leader. I am deeply convinced that my duty is above all to ensure that collective wisdom dominates at this forum and throughout the party.'[3] After being re-elected party chief at the IX Congress in July 1981, Kania reiterated this conception of leadership. Given also the emergence of profound cleavages within the ruling elite any time a Communist system is confronted with a crisis, it is not surprising that power was shared by a number of party officials during the Solidarity period.

To Kania's credit the party did not completely disintegrate during his term, and it may actually have regained vitality shortly before his replacement by Jaruzelski. To have maintained the mass character of the party at a time when one of every three members belonged to Solidarity was an achievement made possible through the use of conciliatory tactics. Jaruzelski's *caudillo* style was more appropriate to a cadre party, and one can only speculate on what would have happened to the PUWP had heavy-handed methods been utilised early on to restore democratic centralism.

Who, then, belonged to the inner ruling circle which ran the party in the Solidarity period? Six individuals have to be included. There was Kania *ex officio*. There was Jaruzelski who, as Minister of Defence and then premier, wielded considerable power before his accession to leadership of the party. The general's right-hand man, Rakowski, became deputy premier and head of the government commission on relations with trade unions; this ensured his influence on decision-making. Barcikowski, the government's chief representative on the Joint Government–Episcopate Commission and later responsible for party organisational matters, had to be included. Two members of the hard-line faction, Olszowski and Grabski, could not be left out: the first was head of the party's ideology section and chairman of the Congress Commission which drafted guidelines for the IX Congress; the second was head of the party commission investigating responsibility for the 1980 crisis. All these persons were Politburo members apart from Rakowski; in addition Grabski was not re-elected to the Politburo by the Congress.

In looking at individuals who shaped party ideology in this period, three members of the Central Committee ought also to be identified, not so much for their political influence as for the constituencies which they represented. These were Fiszbach, first secretary in Gdańsk and a representative of a very liberal grouping in the party which sought close cooperation with Solidarity (not re-elected to the Politburo at the IX Congress); Siwak, representative of the neo-Stalinist working-class wing of the party which gained strength in the autumn of 1981 (elected to the Politburo at the Congress); and

Werblan, long-time editor of *Nowe Drogi* and more recent champion of the horizontalist movement in the party (dismissed from the Politburo in December 1980). The operative ideologies propounded by these leaders encompassed the various views existing within the party and, on occasion, they formed a synthesis which could be termed the party's 'official ideology'.

The second characteristic of operative ideology in this period was its mutability. Attempts have been made to draw up a periodisation of these sixteen months,[4] and a study of the leadership's response to events does suggest trends. At the most general level, a shift took place from initial ambivalence in August and September 1980, to firm commitment to socialist renewal in October (at the second session of the VI Plenum), to negation of Solidarity policies following the reception of the letter from the Central Committee of the CPSU in June, to confrontation following the union's Congress and the almost immediate accession of Jaruzelski in October. The major disadvantage of adopting the thesis of linear development in leadership policy is, however, that it obscures the improvised, *ad hoc*, often inconsistent reactions of the rulers to Solidarity's initiatives throughout most of this period. It also makes light of the persistence of real dissonance within the ruling elite, at least up to Jaruzelski's take-over of power in October 1981. It was precisely the existence of such inconsistencies which induced Solidarity's leaders to believe that the authorities were incapable of taking resolute action. It is important to underscore, therefore, the emergence of a degree of pluralism within the party itself: this was as distinctive a characteristic of the Solidarity period as was Solidarity.

Before we turn to the rulers' operative ideology on specific issues during 1980–1, let us look briefly at the nature and sources of the crisis as identified in official party reports. In Chapter 5 we reviewed how past crises were explained in either macro-sociological or micro-sociological terms. The attacks on Gomułka in both 1948 and 1968 owed their origins, it was held, to the existence of class contradictions. In the first case the survival of a private sector in the national economy was considered to be responsible for the rightist, nationalist deviation in the party leadership. In the second case reactionary sections of the intelligentsia were viewed as having organised the March protests. In contrast, the 1956 and 1970 crises were officially attributed to micro-sociological factors (personality flaws in the rulers, organisational and logistical shortcomings in party work). The fundamental principles of the socialist system were not brought into question, only errors and distortions in their application.

According to one observer, there were three kinds of reaction within the ruling elite to the 1980 crisis. Firstly there were those who simply moralised about the events. No attempt was made to relate the social processes behind the crisis to more general aspects of the political system. Secondly there were those who concluded that nothing exceptional had occurred: economic problems had led simply to dissatisfaction and protest. The one relation held to have importance was between satisfaction of material needs and social consciousness. Thirdly there were those who included many factors in their analysis of the crisis. Some focused on the class basis of society, others on institutional factors producing conflict.[5] As the crisis wore on, only the last two explanations had credibility. Those who adopted the mechanistic, materialist position were in great part the forces of conservatism; those who took the organic view tended to be strong advocates of socialist renewal.

Disparate aetiological interpretations emerged at the IV Plenum in August, when Gierek insisted that micro-sociological factors had caused the industrial strife. Economic difficulties were paramount, of course, but the beleaguered leader added that overcentralisation of trade union and self-management organisations had contributed to workers' unrest. Even after being deposed Gierek maintained that his rule had witnessed 'consolidation of the nation', and he refused to acknowledge any class basis for the conflict.[6] At first Kania, too, cited structural defects as a primary cause of the troubles: workers' protests had not been aimed at the principles of socialism or at the party's leading role but at 'errors and distortions' in party policy. In September, however, he took a graver view: the strikes had represented the protest of a class which felt itself to be 'the ruler of the Republic'. Moreover opponents of the socialist system were actively involved in organising the strikes. By the VII Plenum he spoke openly of 'the continuation of a sharp class struggle' and the appearance of counter-revolutionary forces in society. He noted defensively: 'One may not be a supporter of socialism, one may not like it, but it is dangerous to try to undermine the bases of the system, its class and national foundations. Such people should feel ill at ease in Poland.'[7]

The fullest explanation of the 1980 crisis was given at the party Congress. The official resolutions declared that 'improper mechanisms functioning in the party, the state and society, together with shortcomings and faults in concrete individuals exercising power', had caused the 1980 troubles. But the political system's ills were also traced back to 1948 when an 'abrupt turn in party policy' had, it was argued, led to deformations never subsequently eliminated. The distinctive feature of the most recent crisis was the 'acute ideological and political struggle for power' that was taking place. In Kania's view, it was a 'class struggle for power', one which required a comprehensive analysis of relations between classes. Which classes were struggling for power was never specified. The convenient Marxian explanation, later developed by Stalin, that remnants of the bourgeoisie intensified the class struggle before they were completely liquidated was in fact not employed. But a clear inference was that a configuration of proletarian and intellectual forces had united on the basis of a shared counter-revolutionary design to form a new political class. It was now challenging the old class, made up of party rulers and bureaucrats, who represented the vanguard of the enlightened socialist working class. Continual references to the class basis of party rule and the class character of the enemies of socialism suggested in an indirect way a conflict between rulers and ruled.

Not all elements in the leadership subscribed to the class conflict explanation. Characterological reasons were also advanced, as they had been in 1956 and 1970. At the VI Plenum, for example, Olszowski adopted the well-tried strategy of shifting responsibility to past rulers and their style of governing. An 'administrative, Cabinet-type' rule had been imposed by a handful of Politburo members, he argued. As a result of their behaviour party life had been given a 'theatrical twist'. But a veritable coup performed by Olszowski was in persuading the XII Plenum to approve a resolution ascribing most of the blame for the 1980 crisis to a series of micro-sociological factors. As chairman of the Congress Commission he was able to add an appendage to sources identified for the crisis. These included such characterological features as autocracy, incompetence and short-sightedness on the part of the ruling oligarchy and other subjective aspects such as a misguided sense of loyalty by various members of the ruling circle to the first secretary and the premier.[8]

The characterological explanation was less convincing than ever before. As one writer noted: 'In the history of People's Poland, various types of people, including genuine statesmen, have occupied prominent party and government posts. Nevertheless the sources of social conflict have not been eradicated.'[9] The fact that it was advanced at

all, however, was significant. The interpretation of historical developments was no scholastic debate between over-ardent historians; in the
context of a Marxist-grounded political system it had praxeological
implications as well. If the consensus in the leadership was that cadre
and procedural changes were all that were required to put the system
right, the programme of socialist renewal could indeed be regarded as
the renewal of old methods of governing, as cynical Poles remarked
very early on during the crisis. The party Congress did balance
macro-sociological and micro-sociological explanations for the 1980
protests, but then it was an extraordinary Congress which reflected
the views of rank-and-file party members more than those of the
leadership. Let us look more closely now at the various components of
the official operative ideology of the period – socialist renewal.

THE CASE OF THE PARTY

In the sixteen months of Solidarity's existence, there was more self-
examination on the part of the party than had taken place in the ten
years of Gierek's rule. Of the fifteen Central Committee Plenum meetings between August 1980 and December 1981, only one (the September 1981 III Plenum on self-management) did not have as its main
topic the tasks facing the party in the existing socio-political situation.
The party's self-appraisal can be looked at in terms of the threefold
typology that we have employed so far – the state of intraparty democracy, the party's leading role in society and the nature of its ideology.

1. Intraparty democracy

A major dilemma that Gierek's successors faced after taking power
was to reconcile two conflicting imperatives of intraparty democracy.
On the one hand they had, as always during a crisis, to restore political
unity within the leadership, which had been undermined during the
succession process. Party unity had evolved over time into a functional imperative of the socialist political system. The conventional
approach taken by past rulers was to call for a return to Leninist
norms governing party life, especially the principle of democratic centralism. On the other hand, an *ad hoc* imperative of equal importance
was to give a semblance of going forward, of introducing innovations
in party functioning. The usual tactic adopted by an incoming leadership was to propagate participatory values.

It has become a canon of socialist states that political rulers are judged less according to their ability to innovate in times of crisis than according to their ability to reimpose Leninist norms without bringing about friction. In these terms Kania proved to be a mediocre leader. Very early on he committed himself to party renewal, and he was instrumental in having party statutes redrafted so as to guarantee a greater measure of intraparty democracy. The price paid for this policy was loss of political unity within the party, which eventually led to Kania's downfall. By mid 1981, one of three party members belonged to Solidarity. Structural experimentation had begun in the party, most notably, the emergence of horizontalist organisations which sought to link lower-level committees to each other rather than to superior bodies. The movement had begun in late October 1980 and culminated in a national forum the following April. In short, both political and institutional pluralism had developed within the usually impregnable monolithic party organisation during Kania's first year in power, making him vulnerable to the criticism that he had 'de-Leninised' the party. Let us examine more closely his view of intraparty democracy.

Inconceivable as it may be, at the August 1980 Plenum Gierek proposed the same panacea for improving intraparty life as he had done ten years earlier: the party should change its political style; it should allow for freer expression of criticism; the leadership should strengthen its links with the rank-and-file membership. Rakowski harshly attacked this approach: 'Comrades, we are simply repeating everything. There is absolutely nothing new in what we are saying.'[10] More radical solutions were required to restore intraparty democracy. The new party leader was obliged, therefore, to provide more durable safeguards. These included such structural features as more democratic elections to top party posts, collegial forms of decision-making, clear delineation of the responsibilities of the Politburo, Secretariat and first secretary, and greater accountability of all to the Central Committee. Later Kania also proposed limitations on 'function accumulation', that is, on the number of party and government offices one person could hold, and on the number of terms in office that party leaders could serve. Most of these reforms were subsequently incorporated into the party statutes: for example, the first secretary could now serve only two consecutive terms (ten years).

In the previous chapter we noted how criticism of Gierek's leadership was publicised with increasing frequency in official party publications in the period before the VIII Congress. In the post-August period a principal accusation levelled at Gierek was his disregard for such criticism. As one writer asked: 'Why did the broad leadership of the party, Central Committee members, VIII Congress delegates, not take a more decisive stand? Why did they allow the last Congress to be turned into a stage-managed spectacle? Why were errors in the party and in its top leadership not identified when the premier of that time was being criticised?'[11] What was more, a common view in the party was that the 1980 crisis could have been averted had Gierek heeded the advice proferred during the pre-Congress campaign. As Fiszbach declared, 'most of the demands put forward by the strikers are identical with the proposals put forward in the pre-Congress campaign and during the VIII Congress discussion'.[12] Others went further and claimed that the innate wisdom of the party masses and the ignorance of the Gierek leadership were already apparent after the 1976 disturbances: for example, demands for Jaroszewicz's removal were dismissed, and when he was finally replaced at the 1980 Congress it was in conditions of 'immoral manipulation'.[13]

Kania's institutional reforms were designed to ensure that there would be no recurrence of the obliviousness to criticism that had been manifest before the VIII Congress. But they could not guarantee that political unity would be restored. Kania launched into an 'accountability' campaign which resulted by the end of 1980 in the expulsion of all of Gierek's supporters from positions of influence. He did not transform this process, however, into a wholesale purge of party ranks, and at the VII Plenum he argued that little would be gained from a verification campaign. This marked a departure from the tactics of political consolidation used by incoming leaderships in the past. It also came in the face of a critical situation in the party, which was divided on the programme of socialist renewal. At this Plenum Rakowski stated that 'criticism of the leadership is quite universal', whilst Fiszbach added that 'the moral and political condition of party members following profound disillusionment, frustration and sense of responsibility for the present situation renders appeals to traditional party discipline useless'.[14] At the VIII Plenum the situation in the party was described in even gloomier terms. According to Grabski, 'opportunistic, social-liberal, and even anarchist tendencies, as well as apathetic, capitulating and dogmatic views' had taken root. The loss of nearly 100,000 members between July 1980 and February 1981 was even harder evidence of the disarray in the party.

If the schism between liberal and conservative forces worried the Kania leadership during the winter of 1980–1, then the emergence of the horizontalist movement became the major source of concern in the spring. At the IX Plenum Barcikowski agreed that contacts between lower party committees were useful, but only as a means of exchanging information and ideas. They were not to serve as a substitute for the unity and discipline that the party required, for 'the party cannot simply be a sum total of its organisations'. Kania concurred: the party could not be transformed into a loose functional union of committees free from central control; 'this stage in the history of the workers' movement, the stage of educational circles, has long passed'.[15]

Representatives of the horizontalist movement were barred from participating in the X Plenum even though the Central Committee had earlier officially recognised the national forum of thirteen regional horizontal structures held in Toruń in April. The leadership's ambivalence was sharply attacked by Rakowski and Werblan. The latter observed that 'the balance of political forces in the country has undergone considerable change. But the balance of forces within the central authorities has changed insignificantly.' He called for greater congruence between the two and suggested that the horizontalists ought to play a greater role in central policy-making.[16] The decision to hold openly contested elections of delegates to the party Congress did more to undo the influence of the horizontalists, however, than the ruling elite's equivocalness. As Kolankiewicz has argued: 'In a situation where few delegates knew much about each other, the highly publicised activities of some of the "horizontalists" made them a natural target for "deletion" from ballot sheets.'[17] As a result the threat posed by the movement to Leninist norms waned after the April Plenum.

Kania's centrist policies were also repeatedly challenged by hard-line elements in the leadership. Olszowski, for example, emphasised that 'the party must be a party' and he added: 'reform yes, reformism no'.[18] The Katowice Forum, established in May to serve as a counterweight to the horizontalists, accused Kania of having lost his 'ideological and political compass in the struggle for socialism'. The CPSU letter addressed to the Central Committee in early June claimed that Kania and Jaruzelski had not followed up assurances made to Soviet rulers: their policy of compromise and capitulation had not been corrected in any significant way. The Silesian leader,

Żabiński, cited a remark made by Gomułka in order to demonstrate where the greatest danger lay at present: 'Dogmatism is a flu or cold for the party, but revisionism is a cancer.'[19] His fellow traveller, Grabski, was even blunter and attacked Kania personally at the XI Plenum, claiming he was unfit to lead the country out of the crisis. Press reports in July noted a strengthening of the position of conservative forces in various party organisations, whilst a public opinion poll discovered that 80% of respondents did not detect signs of renewal in political life.[20]

Yet Kania was able to survive the criticism of his leadership and programme. At the XI Plenum he was given a vote of confidence by a margin of eighty-nine to twenty-four, and at the party Congress he was democratically elected over his only rival, Barcikowski, by a vote of 1,311 to 568. The Congress also endorsed his socialist renewal platform. It was not as radical and far-reaching as it was claimed to be, it is true. Kania outlined its main features:

Its essence is restoring the basic values of socialism in the country and the ideological and political principles of Leninism in the party. It aims at profound economic reforms, the development of socialist democracy, respect for law and strengthening of social discipline. Its course is consolidation of the directive role of the party. It reinstates the ideas of social justice and ethical and moral norms, helps shape humanist interpersonal relations, and promotes respect for the dignity of the individual, the worker and the citizen.[21]

Given such a definition, it was not difficult for Poland's subsequent military regime to reaffirm commitment to socialist renewal. Nevertheless Kania's approach to other issues, most significantly, his readiness to negotiate with Solidarity and his view of intraparty democracy, was generally liberal. Horizontal contacts between basic party committees were recognised as useful so long as they were consistent with the party's ideological principles and statutory norms. At the same time the new statutes made clear that 'factional activities, defined as formalised groups within the party which propagate a separate programme, party line and organisational principles and establish a command centre autonomous from the statutory party authorities, are unacceptable'. One important disparity between Congress resolutions and the guidelines drafted at the X Plenum was the omission from the former of the declaration contained in the latter referring to the need to prevent the rise of an individual over and above the party. As later events proved, this was a prophetic decision taken by the extraordinary Congress.

Party unity was less shaky after the Congress than at any time since the crisis broke. Several factors explain this paradoxical shift towards intraparty stability in an otherwise destabilising country. Firstly the horizontalists had been defeated, as we have noted, in the pre-Congress elections. Secondly many key representatives of the party's two warring factions – the liberals (such as Fiszbach and Rakowski) and the dogmatists (such as Grabski and Żabiński) – were kept out of the Politburo, ensuring greater consensus within it. Thirdly the socialist renewal programme had been so diluted that only liberals could object to it. In a situation increasingly polarised between the party and Solidarity, those party members who disagreed with the tameness of socialist renewal either voluntarily left the organisation or were given a gentle push. A Politburo declaration issued after the first session of Solidarity's Congress emphasised that 'one cannot belong concurrently to our party and to another which is its enemy'. In one of Kania's last acts as party chief he reversed his earlier stand and recommended that an exchange of party cards be carried out as part of a general verification campaign. In short, by autumn 1981 there was less disagreement within the leadership on the importance of restoring Leninist norms of intraparty democracy.

When Jaruzelski succeeded Kania at the IV Plenum in October, the attention given to this question declined. A more fundamental issue overshadowed such structural considerations: was national reconciliation or open confrontation to triumph? In contrast to his predecessor, who had managed to survive exclusively as a result of skilful political balancing of conservative, centrist and liberal forces in the party, Jaruzelski actually elicited positive support from each of these groups. The party's political unity may not have been cemented, but agreement on its leadership was now achieved.

In the Solidarity period, approaches to intraparty democracy were so disparate that the issue itself became a major source of political cleavage within the leadership. The July Congress did produce a consensus that led to an unofficial truce being declared on the question. Does this suggest, as some observers have argued, that the party gained strength after July ? There is, on balance, slender evidence to support this hypothesis. The party was now run by the handful of experienced politicians who had survived the Congress elections. This may have facilitated the task of planning the December coup, but it did nothing to revitalise the party.

The results of public opinion polls carried out in May and November 1981 clearly illustrated how the PUWP became increasingly discredited. In the first poll, only 32% of respondents declared confidence in the party. Fourteen other institutions ranked ahead of it: the church was the most trusted institution (94%), followed by Solidarity (90%), the army (89%) and the Sejm (82%). Even the universally ridiculed militia was placed ahead of the PUWP (50%). By early November public confidence in most Polish institutions had waned. The church maintained its 'leading role' (89%), but it was now followed by the army (87%), which had recently been sent to the countryside and then to towns to engage ostensibly in community work (delivering food, repairing roads and the like). The fortunes of both Solidarity and the party fell sharply: only six out of ten respondents now expressed confidence in the independent trade union whilst just one in ten trusted the PUWP. A similar survey conducted by the Solidarity sociological research centre amongst its members in the same month revealed an even greater spread. Not unexpectedly, Solidarity topped the list (95%), closely followed by the church (94%). The army was considerably behind (69%) and the party was a distant last (7%).[22] From these results it was clear, therefore, that as a political institution the party was a spent force. As a conspiratorial organisation, it may actually have gathered strength.

Differences between factions in the PUWP continued to persist up to the declaration of martial law. The VI Plenum was a case in point. But divisiveness was now based on the question of how to deal with Solidarity, not on the more erosive and self-destructive issue of intraparty democracy. What can be asserted is that the resolutions and statutes on intraparty democracy adopted by the Congress put an end to the critical introspection, rancour and infighting which had dissipated the party's strength in the previous twelve months. They prevented disintegration and dismemberment of the PUWP and, accordingly, made immediate Soviet intervention in Poland unnecessary. Their importance in regulating intraparty life in later months was, by comparison, minor.

2. The leading role of the party

More than any other principle, the party's programmatic leading role in society was directly challenged by the emergence of independent, self-governing trade unions in September 1980. Solidarity's refusal to incorporate this concept in its statutes, and a lower court's insistence that it should do so if it wished to become legally registered, pro-voked the first major crisis after September and nearly brought Soviet troops into the country in early December. It is particularly important, therefore, to discover whether the principle was in any substantive way reinterpreted by the party leadership to bring it into line with the new reality existing in Poland following the Gdańsk, Szczecin and Jastrzębie accords.

Shortly after becoming party leader Kania put forward a different form of operationalising the concept. At the September session of the VI Plenum he recommended that the party exercise its leading role indirectly, through the influence exerted by its members on various state and social bodies, such as the Sejm, local councils, self-management committees and youth organisations. Separation of party from state was to be achieved through restrictions on party officials' right to hold government posts, and the new statutes adopted by the July Congress stated that the party discouraged function accumulation. This did not prevent Jaruzelski three months later from concentrating more party and government functions in his person than any leader had done in the history of People's Poland.

The new leadership also extended the government's powers. Two important coordinating commissions were set up – the Joint Government–Episcopate Commission in September and the government commission on relations with trade unions in February. In this way the party retained its leading role whilst avoiding direct responsibility for policies pursued.

A key method of applying the leading role principle was through the one million party members who joined Solidarity after September. Kania urged these members 'to adopt positions promoting the preservation of the socialist character of the union'; adopting intra-party democracy as a model, they were to ensure democratic functioning within the new organisation. Following Solidarity's Congress, however, party members were exhorted to leave the union. At the IV Plenum twelve party officials, including Grzyb, a member of the Politburo, ostentatiously declared that they were leaving Solidarity and encouraged the rank-and-file to do likewise. Also in October a prominent Solidarity leader, Lis, and the head of the Polish Journalists' Union, Bratkowski, who was closely identified with pro-Solidarity forces in the party, were both expelled from the PUWP. This harder line on membership in Solidarity did not represent an abandonment of the party's leading role in the organisation as much as abandonment of Solidarity altogether.

In many respects the fate of the leading role principle was definitively resolved at the XI Plenum in June, which was called to discuss the CPSU letter. The meeting made clear that the leadership 'decisively rejects revisionist views which would eliminate the party's leading role, reducing it to only the ideological and moral spheres and depriving it of instruments of political authority'. The PUWP was not about to follow earlier precedents and change the significance of the concept. The cases which the Soviet leadership probably had in mind were Yugoslavia in 1952 and Czechoslovakia in 1968.

In the first case, the VI Congress of the Yugoslav Communist Party had decided to change both the conception of the leading role and, with it, the party's very name. The newly formed League of Communists was expected to 'act in all organisations, organs and institutions to have its line and positions, or the positions of its members, accepted by means of its political and ideological activity, primarily through persuasion'. Even though Tito returned to a more conventional view of the leading role after Stalin's death – the Brioni Plenum of June 1953 declared that the League continued to have responsibility for developing socialism in the country – the LCY had taken a path different to that of the Soviets. The 'Action Programme' of the Czechoslovak Communist Party, adopted at its April 1968 Plenum, had also modified the leading role principle: it was no longer to be equated with 'monopolistic concentration of power in the hands of party organs' or with a view of the party as 'the universal "manager" of society, binding all organisations and every step in life by its directives'. The free play of political forces that followed proved unacceptable to the Soviet rulers.[23]

The PUWP's IX Congress ratified the approach taken at the XI Plenum. Kania reaffirmed that the party would not be reduced to an ideological discussion club; in fact 'The kind of Poland we will have depends on the kind of party we will have.' Congress resolutions spelt out the specific responsibilities that the leading role entailed: identification of strategic goals and the main directions of national development, control over the work of state institutions, the dominance of working-class interests in party policy and the strengthening of democracy in social and political life.[24] It would be difficult to detect differences between this conceptualisation and that given at the 1980 Congress. Despite a challenge to the leading role principle from both

Solidarity and reformists within the party, it had managed to survive in a fundamentally unaltered way. Some party leaders were willing to concede that the system of democratic socialism could be changed so as to allow for a modicum of political pluralism, but this did not imply forsaking the PUWP's leading role in society. As Rakowski stated: 'If we conclude that it is time to abandon a dogmatic interpretation of the one-party system, this does not signify that we wish to surrender the leading role of our ideology and our position.' For the leading role of socialist ideology could only be guaranteed by giving the party a leading role.[25] After becoming party leader Jaruzelski expanded on this view: 'Without socialism Poland cannot be independent; without the party there can be no socialism.'[26]

Ultimately the leading role of the party was preserved by the imposition of martial law in December 1981. The party hardly occupied a directive position at that time: it was divided, weakened and besieged. Significantly, the carefully orchestrated campaign against Solidarity had as its *tour de force* the accusation made in the autumn that the union had begun to drive party committees out of the factories. Earlier charges of anti-socialist and anti-state activities were, in the final analysis, much less serious than the accusation of anti-party activities. The latter most fully merited the description of 'counter-revolutionary'. Indeed, then, there could be no Poland without socialism, no socialism without the party and no party without its exercise of hegemonic rule over society.

3. The party and ideology

Initially it may appear surprising that official discourse paid relatively little attention to the party's ideological work during 1980–1. The dominant ideology of Marxism–Leninism was, after all, being directly challenged by Solidarity's syndicalist ideology of *au syndicat le pouvoir*. A closer analysis of the rulers' perception of the crisis reveals, however, that it was seen primarily as a power struggle between two rival political forces rather than as a battle for men's minds. At issue was who would run the country, and political tactics counted more in this struggle than ideological successes. Repeated rebuttals of an exclusively ideological role for the party confirmed that the leadership was concerned most with power.

This is not to suggest that ideological activity was completely ignored during this period. Plenum meetings continually referred to the need for party organisations to increase their ideological unity and offensiveness. Moreover several innovations related to party ideology were introduced. In the first place the party Congress passed a special resolution recommending the elaboration of a formal PUWP programme. It was argued that the party had never, throughout its history, possessed a comprehensive document of this kind. A draft of the programme was to be submitted to the next National Party Conference, which was expected to identify 'the goals of socialist construction in Poland, the long-term directions for socio-economic and socialist democratic development, and the tasks of the party in its exercise of a directive role in society'.[27] Previous attempts to draw up such a programme had, according to one writer, either failed or adopted erroneous premises. The 1964 Congress had described the need for such a document, but work was never begun on it. In turn the 1971 Congress platform, 'For further socialist development of People's Poland', was treated as such a programme; in reality it had constituted an incomplete and shorter-term strategy. Only the extraordinary IX Congress, it was claimed, had distinguished between programmatic resolutions and an authentic party programme.[28]

A second innovation was Kania's recommendation, made at the IV Plenum, that regional party organisations should be established whose main activity would focus on ideology. The aim was to counter Solidarity's regional structure. Kania's dismissal as first secretary two days later left this proposal stillborn. His successor's concern was more with logistics than with ideology.

Thirdly at the same Plenum Olszowski, responsible for ideological matters in the party, called for a National Party Conference on Ideology. Such a session could elaborate on the four components of the party's ideology that Olszowski identified: (1) Marxist–Leninist theory; (2) party methods, especially Leninist norms; (3) party policy; and (4) history of People's Poland.[29] The imposition of martial law led to a postponement of this conference until April 1982.

But in spite of such proposed innovations, in spite of the call made at the IV Plenum for a grand ideological offensive, in spite of the 'ideological waywardness' (as the November 1981 Plenum put it) that bedevilled many party organisations, party ideology was accorded secondary importance by the leadership during this period. The Congress had not identified ideological weaknesses as a cause of the 1980 crisis. Instead, as one writer cogently remarked, 'the source of the crisis of the system is not ideology but social relations'.[30] The interdependence between the two was never explicitly outlined, and party leaders' familiarity with the principles of Marxism remained superficial.

INDUSTRIAL DEMOCRACY

To carry out a comprehensive analysis of the rulers' operative ideology on industrial democracy in 1980–1 would require a separate monograph. The party leadership's conflict with Solidarity on the issues of free trade unions and workers self-management was protracted, complex and often legalistic, and we cannot do justice to these questions in our study. In our brief consideration of industrial democracy, we simply sketch the chief orientations that existed within the Politburo. At the same time we examine the rulers' perceptions of Solidarity itself: we wish to indicate what, in their view, an independent trade union could do and what it could not.

Let us look briefly at the first reactions to workers' demands in August 1980. At the IV Plenum Gierek committed two major political blunders. Firstly he laid much of the blame for the crisis on the old trade unions which, he claimed, had become bureaucratised and centralised. Although this was undeniable, his failure to acknowledge the efforts made to reform the unions before the VIII Congress further alienated many rank-and-file union members. Secondly he promised a new law on trade unions which would make only cosmetic changes to the existing structure. His patronising declaration that strike leaders had a good chance of getting elected to the Central Trade Union Congress (CRZZ) in the future caused greater resentment. Not surprisingly Gierek's position was untenable after the signing of the Gdańsk agreement.

At this stage Kania was not prepared to go much further either. On the issue of free trade unions he told the IV Plenum: 'what are needed are better trade unions, closer to workers' concerns, ready to protect their interests and rights, an important cog in socialist democracy'. By the VI Plenum, however, he had performed a volte-face and lent support to the idea of independent trade unions. Two reasons were advanced: (1) 'not a small number of factories' had demanded their creation; (2) their founders declared that the new unions would remain faithful to the Polish constitution, which specified the bases of the socialist system, the party's leading role and the country's international alliance system.

In addition, Kania outlined the leadership's approach to independent unions which dominated party thinking for the next twelve months. Eight key concepts can be identified: (1) the new unions were formed to defend workers' interests; (2) they were to organise workers' participation in factory management; (3) they were to be equal partners with the state administration; (4) accordingly, they were to assume equal responsibility for socio-economic results throughout the country; (5) whilst differentiated organisationally into independent, autonomous and branch unions, the entire movement was to be politically united; (6) as a result, all new unions were to have a socialist character; (7) branch unions were singled out as the rulers' preferred organisational form; and (8) from the outset, anti-socialist forces were identified as wishing to exploit the free trade unions to further their own political interests. Concluding the Plenum Kania declared: 'We are faced with a new situation and we should not consider it as temporary.' In the following months he constantly repeated the need to reach an understanding with Solidarity: as he put it in February, 'we should never run out of patience in our contacts with Solidarity, its organisations, the workers'.[31]

A general assumption that shaped the leadership's thinking during 1980–1 was that Solidarity was founded primarily as a result of the country's economic problems. Certainly workers had justifiable grievances with the economic performance. In 1979 national income fell (by 2%) for the first time in the history of People's Poland. Whilst real wages had risen by 7·2% annually during the period 1971–5, they increased by only 1·3% annually between 1976 and 1979. Income differentiation had compounded economic dissatisfaction: for example, whilst only 6% of directors and managers in administrative political and economic institutions earned less than 4,000 złotys during 1980, 63% of employees, 64% of private farmers and 87% of pensioners were in this bracket.[32] In 1979 one in four workers felt that his income represented a 'social minimum' (defined as 'sufficient wages to purchase only the cheapest food and clothes'), whilst only one in ten members of the intelligentsia stratum fitted this category.[33] As early as 1975 Poland had the worst ratio of minimum to average income in the Comecon bloc: the minimum wage was only 34% of the average, whilst in Romania, the most egalitarian country in this respect, the proportion was 61%. Such disparities had increased further by 1980.[34]

The supposed economic basis of Solidarity's foundation led rulers to overemphasise its economic functions and to play down its socio-political character. At the VI Plenum, for example, Olszowski described the August agreements as a social contract between an employer and an employee based on mutual obligations. Likewise Rakowski recommended that: 'The escalating demands of the new unions should be channelled into assumption of responsibility for running the country.' The call for collective responsibility was the only road open to the new rulers in dealing with Solidarity: they could obviously not delegate any political functions to the independent union, but at the same time they could not buy off the workers (as Gierek had done in 1971) because their demands were not simply economic. After several rounds of classic collective bargaining, during which substantial pay rises were offered, the leadership finally recognised that whilst economic forces may have contributed to the foundation of free unions, they did not generate their subsequent expansion.

The crisis provoked by the registration of Solidarity in late October was, as Kania put it, not over a 'formal matter'. The party was made aware of the meta-economic dimension to Solidarity and soon equated it with the movement's alleged aspirations to 'dual power' in the country. It was at this point that the authorities elaborated on their doctrine of what free trade unions in a socialist system could not be. Resolutions adopted by the December 1980 Plenum illustrated the shift in operative ideology from the party's self-criticism to attacks on Solidarity's encroachment into new spheres of socio-political life: 'The evil caused our country by irresponsible voluntarism cannot be magnified each day by self-seeking autocracy. The arrogance of power that we have condemned cannot be replaced by arrogance of a new kind which disregards the legal order and agreements reached.' At the VIII Plenum Solidarity was explicitly warned to keep to matters involving industrial democracy. Many strikes staged at the beginning of 1981 were, according to the leadership, of a clearly political nature. Solidarity had violated the August accords and was bent on becoming a socio-political movement. The authorities were ideologically and legally bound to negotiate with the new union on issues related to industrial democracy, the Plenum concluded, but negotiations on all other questions were held under duress and could not be justified. At this time Lis, one of Solidarity's leaders, had described the union's attitude to the party: 'We tolerate the party and have nothing against it, but we have no confidence in it.'[35] The approach of most of the party leadership was precisely the same with regard to Solidarity.

In his speech to the Sejm on becoming premier in February, Jaruzelski indicated that his government was prepared to recognise, in part at least, the broader character of Solidarity. He issued an appeal for 'ninety quiet days': 'this will be a time of comprehensive social dialogue . . . We can bring the social agreements up to date.' At the same time he warned that there was no room for 'two authorities within one state' and blamed hostile political activists for generating tension in society.

There was no systematised ideological conception of free unions in the first months of Jaruzelski's stewardship, but there appeared now to be a conscious deployment of what can best be described as 'accede-and-obstruct' tactics. This was illustrated by the government's approach to demands for separate unions by students and private farmers. The Independent Students' Union (NZS) was quickly registered after Jaruzelski became premier in spite of the fact that it had listed fifteen demands of an overtly political nature. These included adoption of new history textbooks, popularisation of Polish *émigré* writers, private ownership of small publishing houses, independence of the judiciary, celebration of Poland's traditional historic anniversaries and accountability for the 1970 and 1976 repressions. Other demands were just as radical: free elections of university governors and institute heads, full independence for all tertiary education institutions in scientific, pedagogical and organisational questions, free choice in studying foreign languages, and abolition of compulsory manual work, rectors' quotas (students accepted to university on the recommendation of the rector) and social origin points (awarded for working-class or peasant background to candidates applying to university).[36] Such demands went beyond the authorities' general view of unions as instruments of self-management. In contrast the registration of Rural Solidarity had to wait ninety days, even though a temporary agreement was signed at Rzeszów in mid February. The demands of private farmers were also radical: in particular they wanted equal treatment with state and collective farmers, control over the government-subsidised agricultural development fund and stabilisation of prices for agricultural services rendered by the agricultural circles. But no open political demands such as those put forward by the students were made. The authorities' procrastination in recognising Rural Solidarity was partially explained by Soviet pressure and ideological constraints: acceptance of the right of private owners to form a union in a socialist system would signal a departure from fundamental principles in a way that simple acquiescence towards a private sector or formal approval of an employees' trade union did not imply. Nevertheless tactical considerations played an important part in obstructing Rural Solidarity's legalisation, as in acceding to NZS demands. The 'two-track strategy', as Ascherson labelled it,[37] was designed to baffle and mystify the social reform movement, to give the leadership time to regroup and to allow the rulers to evade ideological commitment to a self-governing Poland.

The Bydgoszcz events, which many observers have regarded as a turning point in the Solidarity period, caused sharp polarisation within both the party and the union movement. The beating up of local Solidarity leaders by the police marked the first instance of the use of organised violence since the August strikes. Whilst Wałęsa had to use all his political skill to dissuade the union from staging a national strike, and local party organisations throughout the country demanded an explanation of the events, the Politburo issued a statement which was hardly gracious or conciliatory. Public order, it said, had been violated in the first instance by those who had occupied the town hall after an official meeting had ended. Moreover 'This regrettable incident, even before it could be explained, triggered off a new national campaign of an extremely aggressive nature: Solidarity's propaganda machine was immediately set in motion, a warning strike was held, and an ultimatum demanding personnel changes was issued.' The four-hour strike was 'no longer just a form of pressure on the authorities. It is an open struggle against our party, the state authorities and socialism.' Rakowski even argued that Solidarity's actions were pushing all Europe towards a catastrophe, that 'social peace had been broken much earlier than the Bydgoszcz incident'.[38] In this way the rulers diverted attention from the events and blamed the union for all the misfortunes that befell the nation. Solidarity was depicted as more than a trade union or socio-political movement: it represented an inexorable force pushing the country towards an abyss. Wałęsa himself drew a strikingly similar analogy: 'The world is astonished how we have balanced on a tightrope and not fallen.'[39]

The programmatic declaration adopted by the party Congress was more moderate in tone than successive resolutions passed by Plenum meetings. It constituted a deviation from the increasingly firm line that the central authorities had been taking since February and continued to pursue after the Congress. There were two reasons for this. Firstly Congress delegates were more representative of rank-and-file attitudes in the party than was the Politburo. Many shared the values espoused by Solidarity, and the programme of socialist renewal meant to them genuine intraparty democracy and socialist democracy. Secondly there was still no alternative to reaching an understanding with Solidarity. As Rakowski argued; 'The alternative can only be a major conflict between the authorities and most of society, a bloodbath and national tragedy after which all our problems would remain except in a far more dangerous form. Such a conflict would resolve nothing for the nation, the state or Polish Communists.'[40]

The Congress pledged loyalty to the August agreements, declared that the crisis had to be solved through negotiation and reiterated the independence of trade unions from the administrative apparatus. Solidarity was described as a highly differentiated organisation whose functions ranged from trade union affairs to providing a forum for reactionary, extremist political groups. The movement's usurpation of decision-making on appointments of top personnel, its publication of anti-state materials, the support it received from KOR and from extreme right-wing circles in the West, and its concept of transforming socialised ownership of industrial enterprises into group ownership were roundly condemned. Nonetheless unions had a constructive role to play in the country: they were to help co-manage enterprises, and they were to protect workers' interests.[41]

At the beginning of August, government and Solidarity representatives met to work out a joint programme on economic reform, prices, a bill on trade unions and Solidarity's access to radio and television. A conflict arose between Rakowski and Wałęsa and the talks were broken off. Any goodwill that may have followed the Congress decisions was undone. During the remaining three weeks in August, both General Kulikov, Commander-in-Chief of Warsaw Pact forces, and General Yepishev, head of the Main Political Bureau of the Red Army, met with Jaruzelski in Warsaw. In addition Kania and his premier paid a visit to Brezhnev on the Crimea. That month's Plenum accused Solidarity of being responsible for a 'qualitatively new phenomenon': 'the street is no longer quiet'. It declared that the line of reaching an agreement with the union might have to be revised.

Solidarity activists were arrested in Silesia for distributing leaflets, and Wałęsa stated that a confrontation was now inevitable.[42] The atmosphere of a Greek tragedy became inescapable even before the union held its first Congress.

The harder line adopted by the authorities after the party Congress was acknowledged by all sides. Rakowski claimed that the framework established by the August agreements was too rigid for many Solidarity activists and that 'at present the authorities take a more decisive stand in many situations'. In turn the report of Solidarity's National Coordinating Commission noted that the government had given the impression of returning to pre-August 1980 methods of running the country in recent weeks.[43] Bratkowski, head of the Journalists' Union, warned: 'Cursed for ages will be the one who uses force and violence to solve our problems.'[44]

The rulers' view of the September session of the Solidarity Congress was presented in a Politburo declaration. This asserted that the destructive current in the movement had been elevated to the status of the official union programme. The August agreements had been one-sidedly broken and Solidarity had been transformed into a political opposition. The Congress had been a triumph of the extremists and of the union bureaucracy which now employed tens of thousands of people. The government announced, therefore, that it had 'discussed the specific measures which may prove indispensable to the defence of socialism and the basic interests of the Polish state and nation'. Referring to the Congress poster which portrayed a strapping one-year-old waving the Solidarity banner, Rakowski observed: 'I deal in fact with grown-up people, with battle-scarred veterans and not with infants. That infant often wears a beard and moustache, is extremely articulate and – although he is only a year old – visits the antechambers and halls of anti-Communist union head-quarters, and not just union ones.'[45]

The growing intensity of the anti-Solidarity propaganda campaign at the time of the Congress had mixed effects on public opinion. Over 90% of respondents in a mid-September poll said they felt a state of tension and anxiety: 51% blamed this on a lack of food, 25% on the conflict between the government and Solidarity, 17% on incorrect government policies and 9% on Solidarity's incorrect policies. While 53% believed most of the problems would be resolved through negotiation, four of ten respondents thought that force would soon be used. Of these, 56% blamed the authorities, 12% Solidarity and 32%

both. Forty-eight per cent of the sample maintained that the union's goals were appropriate, 23% said they were too radical, and only 4% said they were too moderate. But there was agreement that Solidarity's Congress had led to greater tension than that of the party: 43% asserted that tension had been heightened by the union gathering and 20% said it had decreased. This pattern was the reverse of respondents' views on the party Congress: only 12% claimed it had aroused tension and 54% said it had defused it.[46]

The Central Committee Plenum held after the October session of the Solidarity Congress heaped further abuse on the union. It was described as a 'shelter for the entire Polish reaction, a training ground for counter-revolutionary forces and groups'. The Congress had revealed its totalitarian ambitions, its intolerance, its centralised authority structure, whilst its leaders had demonstrated 'ideological membership in the Western world'. Plenum resolutions concluded: 'Solidarity's leadership has unilaterally broken the social agreement and has usurped the role of a force superior to all others.'

If these accusations had a tactical purpose, designed to maintain tension, rather than a persuasive quality, seeking to influence public opinion, then on the question of strikes the two converged. The one-hour warning strike organised by Solidarity in late October was supported by less than half the respondents (45%), the first time that union action obtained so little support. Just before the strike, two of three respondents polled said that a temporary suspension of the right to strike would be justified and only 23% disagreed. Rakowski's demagogic declaration that 'he who organises strikes at this time is simply an enemy of the nation' was not that unrepresentative of public opinion in November 1981.[47] Neither was Jaruzelski's metaphor that whilst strikers sang the national anthem 'Poland has not yet disappeared', in fact 'Poland is disappearing.'[48]

The Solidarity leadership was aware of the growing opposition to the strike tactic. In late November Wałęsa argued against calling a strike to protest against an increase in the price of vodka: 'This price rise is a crude and simple provocation designed to ridicule us in the eyes of the world ... Let us not be pushed down to such a humiliating moral level. Vodka will not decide the fate of the nation and the country.' The union's National Coordinating Commission acknowledged that 'we are entering a phase which will decide many issues for years to come' and it convoked a special committee charged with resolving strikes and protests.[49] But whilst Jaruzelski was now openly

requesting that legislation be drafted which would furnish his government with emergency powers, Solidarity appeared to make no parallel contingency plans. Its approach remained founded on the
all-or-nothing concept described by Gwiazda, Wałęsa's main
rival on the union executive, at the Congress: if a state of emergency
was declared 'either we answer with a general strike and we lock
ourselves in factories, or we continue to work as if nothing had
happened'.[50] But at the famous Radom meeting of the Solidarity
leadership in December, Wałęsa gave Gwiazda greater credit for
his strategy: 'We differed only in that his approach was to take tanks,
airplanes and other things right away, and he is right of course.' At
the same meeting Modzelewski, a Solidarity adviser and former KOR
member, made what turned out to be an obituary for the movement:
'Our union is weaker than it was, much weaker. Every activist knows
this.'[51]

The final Plenum held before martial law reported that not a day
had passed in the last year when there had not been a strike or the
threat of one. National income had fallen by 15% and had attained its
1974 level. The need for a National Unity Front was more urgent than
ever. What was to be the structure of this Front which Jaruzelski had
actively propagated since becoming party leader? For once Solidarity
might have agreed with Siwak's interpretation: 'I understand this
Front in the way Comrade Jaruzelski described it to the Politburo.
The skeleton, the basis, the structural framework are the three
political parties; ours has the main role. The consultative body
consists of all trade unions, youth organisations and the church. That
is the type of arrangement and balance of forces that I support.'[52] It
also was the arrangement that Solidarity was obliged to turn down.

From this brief survey of official discourse on Solidarity and some of
its leaders' reactions, it becomes clear that the rulers' propaganda
campaign escalated in line with the union's expanding activities. A
surprise element in the martial law declaration lay in the reversal of
roles between the two protagonists. At their December meetings in
Radom and Gdańsk Solidarity leaders concluded that confrontation
was unavoidable but approved no decisive action (apart from the
unrealistic proposition to stage a national referendum on self-
management). In contrast the authorities stopped verbally attacking
Solidarity and finally acted. Perhaps the movement's organisers had
indeed shown resemblance to a one-year-old infant.

A fundamental question remains unanswered: was the party

leadership committed to greater industrial democracy? The difficulty in answering this question lies in the fact that Solidarity was simultaneously the guarantor of industrial democracy, system democracy and even socialist renewal. But for party rulers only the first association could be made. Condemnation of the union was based on its so-called usurpation of the last two functions. Over time this fine distinction became difficult to maintain, and Solidarity's three roles were equally attacked. For a clearer idea of the party's operative ideology on industrial democracy we need to turn to its attitude to workers' self-management.

As early as the VI Plenum Kania recommended the adoption of a new law on self-management. The number of workers' councils had fallen from over 5,000 in 1956 to some 500 in 1978 and to six in 1980. Workers' representation had to be restored, Kania concluded, and a newly termed 'employees' self-management' soon became an important component in the programme of socialist renewal.

Solidarity challenged the authorities' conception in two ways. Firstly, in April 1981, an association of seventeen large enterprises (called 'the Network of Key Factories') was established which began to elaborate a different approach to self-management. Secondly Solidarity itself issued a blueprint for reform immediately before the party Congress which countered the party's piecemeal policy. The enterprise was to become socialised (in the party's view this meant group ownership), and all major decisions, including appointment of directors, were to be taken by self-management organs. The Congress rejected this conception and affirmed the need for societal (in Solidarity's view, nationalised) ownership of the means of production. At the III Plenum the main functions of self-management were spelled out: the 'work-force council', an executive committee of the employees, was to decide on such matters as economic planning, annual investment plans, enterprise statutes and affiliation to associations of several enterprises. Appointment of directors and distribution of enterprise earnings had to be approved by the council but were determined by central or local authorities. The party reform was designed, it was claimed, to integrate group and national interests. The first would be represented by the work-force council, the second by the enterprise director who, as Lenin had noted, 'is above all the representative of the socialist state'. This conception was said to avoid two pitfalls: (1) the technocratic, where experts took all decisions; and (2) the anarchistic, where the work-force had full autonomy.[53]

Solidarity's response was its famous call for the creation of a self-governing Republic. It particularly objected to the appointment of directors by state bodies. In the end an intricate compromise was worked out: in key and newly established enterprises the authorities would make the appointment; in all others the work-force council would decide. A reciprocal veto was given in each case. The new law was passed by the Sejm in September but considerable misgivings remained in the Solidarity leadership, part of which called for a national referendum on the subject. In the wake of Solidarity's subsequent dissolution under martial law, the self-management law represented one of its main legacies.

It is easy to dismiss the rulers' approach to industrial democracy as a series of tactical shifts designed to neutralise Solidarity's initiatives. To be sure, the new union had continually to fight for an autonomous existence. Concessions extracted from the authorities were in many cases obtained by brinkmanship. Nevertheless, given the volatile political circumstances of the time, the party leadership did adopt a logically consistent line on industrial democracy. It was to serve as a key element in the system of socialist democracy; it was to take responsibility for the country's economic results; it was to include co-management of the factory; and it was, above all, to reflect the interests of the workers.

Where the leadership lost its way was in not perceiving the dialectical relationship between the economic and political spheres. Admittedly, when it came to protecting the party's vital interests, the dialectical argument was advanced. In reply to the suggestion that the party should confine its activity to politics and leave economic matters to the government and trade unions, the Politburo report to the III Plenum cited Lenin's thesis that politics was simply a synthetic amalgam of economic issues. The party could not very well withdraw from one sphere and not from the other. Yet this was precisely what Solidarity was expected to do. It was to aggregate the economic interests of the workers but it was not to convert them into political demands. Even if the Leninist thesis was abandoned, the structural nature of the state socialist system, where power is monopolised by a single party, forced Solidarity's entry into the non-economic domain. Its origins may have been economic, its functions were primarily economic but their successful execution required a measure of political power. This the leadership refused to grant. Not surprisingly, therefore, the existence of free trade unions could not be countenanced in terms of either ideology or *realpolitik*.

THE CHURCH

The protracted crisis of 1980–1 demonstrated one thing: the foundation for church–state relations laid in the 1970s was indeed very solid. Despite continuous tension whilst Solidarity existed, despite the liberating, rebellious mood in all social milieux, despite the disappearance in 1980–1 of the founders of the church–state *entente*, Wyszyński and Gierek, relations between leaders of the two institutions were never seriously in jeopardy during this period. On balance, it was the guarded, prudent attitude of the church hierarchy which contributed most to the stability of these relations.

Very early on, even before the signing of the Gdańsk accords, the Polish primate set the tone for the church's role in the crisis. In a homily delivered at Częstochowa on 26 August, he declared that abstention from work struck at the life of the nation, and he urged all Poles to assume responsibility for the fate of the country. Wyszyński spoke of the significance of observing *prudentia gubernativa*, wisdom in governing over the nation, and exhorted: 'Let us defend ourselves through the fulfilment of our duties, for when we perform these we shall have greater title to demand our rights.'[54]

The cardinal's image in the West was tarnished by his apparent readiness to reach compromises with the authorities, but in Poland he remained the object of deep reverence and respect. His behaviour in the days prior to the conclusion of the Gdańsk agreements was not hostile to the strikers, as was made out by both the Polish and the foreign media, but formed part of a long-range programme elaborated by the Catholic church. It was spelled out in late August 1980, well before Kania talked of socialist renewal and Solidarity opted for a self-governing Republic. The Main Council of the Polish Episcopate identified the inalienable rights of the Polish nation: the right to God, to a decent existence, to truth and to a knowledge of the country's history and culture. It declared the right to possess farmland, to have employment, to receive just wages and to associate in representative and responsible trade unions and freely elected self-management institutions.[55] The Gdańsk agreements were still five days away.

In September a joint commission of government and episcopate representatives was established which met each month during the

Solidarity period. Personal meetings between Wyszyński and the party leaders also took place regularly. These helped to defuse a number of crisis situations, for example, the crippling strike in Bielsko-Biała early in 1981. No less stabilising a factor, however, was the judiciousness displayed by Pope John Paul II. During Solidarity's sixteen-month existence he never set foot in Poland, yet his presence was continuously felt. Meetings held in the Vatican with Polish government, Solidarity and even Soviet officials allowed him to play a direct role in Polish politics, and his encyclical on workers' rights, 'Laborem exercens', was also influential. The absence of violence in extraordinarily tempestuous times was in no small way attributable to the moral authority wielded over virtually the entire Polish nation by the head of the Roman Catholic church and his primate in Poland. As Wyszyński appealed in one of his last sermons: 'The crime of Cain must not be repeated in Poland. Brother must not lead brother into the fields so as to murder him. This must not happen in Poland.'

The operative ideology of the party leadership towards the church was, given its policy of moderation and mediation, favourable. In September both the party leader and the premier praised the patriotic and balanced stand taken by church leaders at the time of the strikes. In spite of Wyszyński's uncompromising stand on the need to register Rural Solidarity, his death several weeks after its legalisation was observed with four days of official mourning. Radio and television programmes carried the five-hour funeral service live, and the head of state and deputy leaders of the party and government attended. The official expression of condolences described Wyszyński an 'an outstanding priest and a great patriot', a statesman 'characterised by understanding for historical processes and civic responsibility'. It added that 'his life, thoughts and work created a model for cooperation between the church and a socialist state'.

In early July Glemp was appointed to succeed Wyszyński. The authorities wished him success 'in the service of the church and the nation' and expressed the hope that he would continue 'the task of his great predecessor'. Glemp's first interviews displayed his intention to pursue this line. He urged moderation, begged Solidarity leaders to put an end to strikes and party leaders to act wisely, and concluded: 'The church will never become a tool of either the state or Solidarity. We shall maintain our independence and in this way we shall serve both sides.'[56] The statement was strikingly similar to one made later by Wałęsa, who was also concerned that his movement maintain an independent character: 'So long as I am head of this movement no one other than working people will run it – neither the party, nor KOR, nor the church.'[57] The relationship between the church and Solidarity is outside the analytical bounds of this study, but its crucial importance in affecting political developments in 1980–1 brings out the need for a separate study.

A major ideological innovation during this period was the acceptance by the party Congress of Kania's recommendation that believers be allowed formal admission to the PUWP. The party remained committed to a scientific world outlook, resolutions stated, but believers subscribing to other aspects of the party programme could now join its ranks.[58] During the course of a decade, therefore, the rulers went from appealing for cooperation with believers and then from the church itself to encouraging the enlistment of believers into the party. The party's increasing dependence on and, simultaneously, use of Roman Catholics in gaining legitimacy for itself was clearly brought home by this development.

In late October separate meetings between Glemp, Jaruzelski and Wałęsa were held in an effort to reach agreement on a National Unity Front. This was followed in early November by a historic summit of the three leaders. Whilst these meetings produced no tangible results, they promised certain institutionalisation of existing pluralism. Glemp stated that the summit had demonstrated the need for authority and social order for Poland,[59] but his presence may have helped the leadership mask its own approach to authority and social order, which became known in mid December. Whatever the case, the authorities' desire to keep the church on their side did little to enhance the legitimacy of the party, whilst it elevated the position of the church even further. Successive opinion polls carried out in 1981 (and described earlier in the section on the party) convincingly demonstrated that, of the major institutions, the church enjoyed the greatest public confidence and the PUWP the least. This suggests that it was the church, not the political leadership, which broadened its authority as a result of the *entente*. Not surprisingly, after martial law was declared some of the rulers called for a reappraisal of the church–state nexus.

SCIENCE AND CULTURE

Two weeks after the signing of the Gdańsk accords, Rakowski described the consequences of the Polish August:

Politics now constitutes Poland's life. People hold discussions in trams, at
home, in their place of work. The intelligentsia is on the march and so are
artists' and writers' associations. All kinds of proposals are put forward
suggesting what should be changed in Poland ... Some participants in the
discussions leave the impression that they want to be remembered by
posterity as those who, in the nick of time, jumped on the train heading for the
station named 'renewal' – not merely on the train but into the locomotive.[60]

Indeed the demands put forward by the industrial proletariat had a
domino effect on Polish society. Apart from sections of the political
apparatus, virtually everyone turned out to be a liberal or a 'closet'
liberal in the wake of the Gdańsk agreements. Previously quiescent
scientific and cultural institutions were suddenly transformed into the
vanguard of the renewal movement. The Polish Academy of Sciences
and the writers' and journalists' unions played a major role in
bringing about unprecedented subsystem autonomy for these
spheres. Apart from the issue of censorship, the principal demand
voiced by these organisations during the autumn of 1980 was for the
replacement of the authorities' instrumental approach to science and
culture with spontaneous, intrinsic values.

The general strategy of the political leadership during these sixteen
months was to attempt to contain the intelligentsia within the
framework worked out before August 1980 whilst disassociating itself
from Gierek's discredited approach. At the VI Plenum Kania outlined the modified programme on science: 'less spectacular gestures
towards the world of science, greater concern for its working conditions, more effective implementation of scientific findings in all
spheres of life, including policy-making'. With regard to culture,
Kania promised support for progressive, humanist art but upheld the
right of the artist to hold his or her own world outlook. A more
comprehensive operative ideology was presented in December to the
Writers' Union Congress by Tejchma, Minister of Culture: 'Writers
will be able to create within extremely wide boundaries of freedom. I
use the term "boundary" purposely to show that the question of
literary freedom must be approached realistically ... There will be no
freedom for nihilist or extreme negativist currents or for pseudo-
literary propaganda booklets having no artistic merit whatsoever.'
The basic function of literature, Tejchma concluded, was to serve as
'a barometer of important social issues, a signal of social unrest'.[61]

The IX Congress outlined the roles which science and culture
would play in the process of socialist renewal. The task of science was

to harmonise its two chief functions – theoretical-cognitive and practical-utilitarian. The tasks of social science were to propagate Marxism–Leninism, to mould social consciousness and generally to assist in political socialisation. Both were guaranteed freedom of expression and unhindered access to social, economic and political information. In turn culture was expected to serve the humanist goals of socialism. Within this framework no instrumental functions were added and one ideological innovation was put forward: Polish culture was to develop in conditions of a confrontation between various ideological and philosophical currents. Socialist renewal did augur broader freedom for science and culture, therefore, and it also marked a significant departure from the instrumental approach which dominated the Gierek administration's operative ideology. On the other hand the rulers' commitment to the Congress's renewal programme was questioned by the intelligentsia. The issue of censorship best illustrated its source of concern.

The Gdańsk agreement obliged the government to introduce a draft bill on censorship to the Sejm within three months. When it was presented in mid November, the draft contained only minor modifications to the 1946 censorship law. As a result a group of representatives of the cultural intelligentsia was formed which drafted its own version, but talks with the government were unproductive and a revised draft was presented to the Sejm only in April after sustained protests from various social groups. The government and a Solidarity commission continued to disagree over three points: (1) whether all writings jeopardising Poland's national interests should be banned; (2) which institution was to supervise the work of the Main Censor's Office; and (3) what penalties and rights of appeal were to obtain. After considerable negotiation the law for the control of publications and public performances was approved at the end of July. The compromise agreement stated that speeches in the Sejm and local councils, university scientific and educational publications, all church-approved publications, and internal house publications issued by social organisations which were consistent with their statutes were to be exempt from censorship. The Council of State, which was responsible to the Sejm, was to control the work of the Main Censor's Office. Infringing the censorship law was treated as only a misdemeanour which resulted in fines, whilst appeals against the censor's rulings could be made to the supreme administrative court. Moreover censored passages had to be clearly marked in the published text.

The new law, the first major Solidarity-approved piece of legislation passed by the Sejm, also reversed the principle existing up to then and declared that what was not specifically forbidden could be published. Formal restrictions on state interference in the media were set out. The first and only case of an appeal against government interference produced a ruling in favour of Solidarity in November. The lengthy process required to draft legislation safeguarding the right of Polish culture to exist in pluralist conditions indicated that socialist renewal signified one thing in theory and another in practice. Solidarity's inability to gain access to the media during its existence illustrated this point even more clearly. Not only the cultural milieu had cause to doubt the rulers' sincerity on socialist renewal. In spite of promises to improve conditions for scientists, science's share in the national budget – already the lowest in East Europe – was reduced further in 1981. One final factor which aroused mistrust in the cultural and scientific intelligentsia was that the programme of socialist renewal was not interpreted uniformly by all members of the leadership. In his first speech as premier, Jaruzelski affirmed that the main function of science, culture and education was 'to contribute to the building of socialism, to the patriotic socialist education of young people, and to the good name of Poland in the world'. There was nothing new in this interpretation of socialist renewal.

POLITICAL VALUES AND SOCIETY

The types of value which should dominate in Polish society formed a central issue in the national debate that took place during the Solidarity period. The emerging political pluralism gave rise to a multiplicity of normative conceptions developed by individual movements, organisations and groups. The church, as we have seen, and the Catholic intelligentsia put forward a long-term vision of a socially just Poland. In the spring of 1981 Solidarity published a comprehensive programme which sought to synthesise national traditions, Christian ethics, democratic values and socialist social thought.[62] The most interesting of the intellectual groups which flourished at this time, the Experience and the Future Group, also drafted its conception of a new Poland.[63] To a lesser degree political organisations such as the Confederation for an Independent Poland, the Clubs for a Self-Governing Republic and even the notorious Grunwald Patriotic Union adopted systems of prescriptive values differing sharply from each other.

In contrast the attempts made by party leaders to elaborate an updated normative programme were very modest. The ideological tenet of advanced socialism, which formed the cornerstone of the party's vision during the second half of the 1970s, was now denounced. Poland was far removed from this stage, it was argued, and construction of socialism's foundations had still to be completed. As Simon concluded, 'the developed socialism doctrine was superseded by the politics of "renewal" and "partnership"'.[64] The ideological underpinnings of such politics remained flimsy and it was only under martial law that the rulers' normative vision was formulated in greater detail.

The political values that were propagated by the leadership had a stop-gap, crisis-management character. Chief amongst these were respect for the law and maintenance of social order. Political prudence and realism were emphasised, and in socio-economic questions greater income egalitarianism and social justice were propagated. The IX Congress, for example, declared that in the 1980s the minimum wage should be no less than half the average wage whilst the highest income should not exceed the average by more than three and one-half times. In contrast to earlier periods, when first societal and then individual interests were held to be paramount, it was Poland's national and international interests which now came to the fore. The Yalta agreement was repeatedly invoked to show that Poland's fate had been sealed with Western complicity and that it could not now be altered. Consequently strongest condemnation was made of 'the Herostratos syndrome – those prepared to burn their parental homes in order to draw attention to themselves'.[65] In the autumn of 1981 the importance of national reconciliation was underscored. Invoking the phrase used during the signing of the Gdańsk agreement, the rulers appealed for a return to the method 'to talk as Pole to Pole'. The only alternative to this approach was, as one writer put it, 'to debate as Iranian with Iranian'.[66] Having adopted this contrived dichotomy the rulers opted for martial law.

8

Interlude II: martial law, 1981–82

Was the use of force possible in August 1980? Yes, it was possible. Would it have been possible to introduce martial law at an earlier date? Yes, this too would have been feasible: the authorities disposed of the necessary means then as they do today. Was the dissolution of trade unions possible when martial law was first introduced? Yes, this possibility did exist.

Wojciech Jaruzelski, Sejm, October 1982

When the independent self-governing trade union Solidarity was finally delegalised in October 1982, the authorities might well have felt that they had displayed exceptional magnanimity and tolerance in permitting it to have existed at all, then only to have suspended its activities during the first nine months of martial law. In truth, however, the sudden demise of Solidarity must have exceeded the wildest expectations of the Polish generals and party leaders. What were the principal factors which brought about the dissolution of a ten million member social movement?

At the most general level three factors can be identified: (1) the might of the state security apparatus; (2) the element of surprise produced by the authorities' two-track policy; and (3) the change in the character and tactics of Solidarity.

The most obvious explanation is that Solidarity never possessed either coercive or real political power whilst the authorities did. The imposition of martial law exposed a double failure, as Gitelman has argued: 'The PUWP failed because it had power but little authority. Solidarity failed because in the short time it had, it could not translate authority into sufficient power.'[1] The union had been striving for a measure of coercive and political power: at its Radom and Gdańsk meetings in December, for example, calls were made for both the formation of a workers' guard and the holding of a national referendum on the establishment of a provisional government. Solidarity's pursuit of power caused the authorities to mobilise their half a million strong security forces against it.

The rulers' two-track policy manifested itself in several ways. There were the accede-and-obstruct tactics – giving in to the demands of some social groups and not to those of others. The government was portrayed as amenable to serious negotiation, the PUWP as opposed to all concessions. In late 1981 disorientation tactics also were employed. For example, a Solidarity bulletin issued in September reported Politburo member Siwak's statement to branch trade unionists in Krosno that a six-man Committee of National Salvation, headed by Generals Jaruzelski and Kiszczak, had been formed to plan the suppression of Solidarity in several months' time.[2] *El Generalissimo* himself appealed to the Sejm on several occasions to grant his government emergency powers. Yet three days before martial law was imposed, the party daily noted on its front page: 'The constitution of the Polish People's Republic does not recognise the concept of a state of emergency.'[3] Solidarity was lured, therefore, into a false sense of security.

Finally the change in the movement's nature and tactics contributed to its fall. Not long after the Bydgoszcz events, Solidarity ceased to be a self-limiting revolution. As was noted by Staniszkis, the Polish sociologist who first formulated the concept, the rulers' intransigence and the movement's inability to wrest power forced the latter to discard its initial non-ideological, socially rooted character. By autumn 1981 Solidarity sought to overcome its identity crisis by resorting to 'open conspiracy'.[4] The switch to an 'incremental revolution' of escalating demands facilitated the rulers' ability to misrepresent the union's position.[5] In July 1982 Jaruzelski justified his coup in these graphic terms: 'During the past seven months a veritable river of human blood was spilt in the world . . . We imposed [martial law] here just to prevent Poland from streaming with blood.'[6] Yet the incremental revolution and open conspiracy had nothing in common with blood spilling. As one of Wałęsa's last statements before martial law made clear: 'Confrontation on our part is no threat to society: our most lethal weapon is the strike. The other side has, in contrast, the ability to use the same methods as in December 1970.'[7] The defence of martial law as 'the lesser of evils' was a bogus argument, of course, but Solidarity's transformation lent it some credibility.

The social movement was, in short, outmuscled, outsmarted and outflanked. Successful logistics rather than an effective operative ideology sealed the fate of Solidarity. During the first months of martial law the primacy of logistics was demonstrated further: for the militarisation of society to be achieved a plethora of regulations, decrees and irrational acts was adopted which ensured that no sphere of social life could be regarded any longer as private or sacrosanct. Crude propaganda put out by the media formed part of a psychological war designed to convince the population that both social organisations and rational discourse had been suspended by martial law. There was to be no return to August 1980 when Pole talked as to Pole. Rather than operative ideology, therefore, the military rulers opted for operative logistics – a series of detailed instructions and irrational acts, never explained, justified or amplified by the rulers, the purpose of which was to elicit compliant behaviour.

These logistics were only gradually supplanted by operative ideology as martial law restrictions were eased. In late February 1982 a Central Committee Plenum was finally held which drew up a tentative ideological programme, entitled 'What we are fighting for, where we are heading'. The fact that part of the title was borrowed from the Polish Workers' Party first programmatic appeal to the nation in November 1943 was no coincidence. In each case the party's position was circumscribed by military circumstances, and a promise of the future activisation of ideology was believed to be of crucial importance. By autumn 1982 the leadership had adopted an interim operative ideology. It was that martial law had been effected in true Polish style, having been the most liberal martial law in the world. As Jaruzelski told the October Plenum, whilst 'a sharp class struggle is being waged ... our martial law is exceptionally moderate'.[8] Any attempts to develop a more comprehensive ideology were, however, unsuccessful for some time to come. This was most clearly illustrated in May 1983 on the eve of the pope's visit to Poland. The PUWP leadership had promised that the XII Plenum would adopt a final version of the programme 'What we are fighting for'. Instead of demonstrating ideological consolidation before John Paul II's arrival, however, the Central Committee put off consideration of the document to a later date. PUWP ideology once again proved too fragile to face a challenge.

THE CASE OF THE PARTY

There are two contradictory views on the role of the party in the imposition of martial law: (1) the PUWP had failed so miserably in asserting its leading role during the Solidarity period that the army had to supersede it and declare martial law; (2) the December coup was decided upon by the inner ruling circle of the party which then entrusted the military command with carrying it out. The first view was dominant in the early period of martial law. In order to counter it, Jaruzelski stressed in his 13 December speech that his had not been a military coup; nor was the Military Council of National Salvation (WRON) to replace constitutional organs of power. He also re-affirmed the importance of the party: 'Despite mistakes that have been made and bitter reverses that have been suffered, the party remains an active and creative force in the process of historic change.' Certainly the Politburo was very active in 1982: it met forty-one times, whereas WRON held only thirteen meetings. The militaris-ation of the power structure did not preclude, therefore, a continuing role for top political leaders.

The view that it was in fact the PUWP rulers who had master-minded martial law was advanced later when it became apparent that consolidation of power had been achieved. Barcikowski even argued that the party had always played the leading role in the political process:

We must not draw hasty conclusions from the fact that martial law was introduced during a period of great party weakness. Those who believe that the decision to declare martial law was taken outside the party are wrong ... What happened on 13 December happened by party mandate. Is it a coincidence that Comrade Jaruzelski was elected first secretary at the IV Plenum and that he also assumed leadership of WRON? Only naive people or those who like sowing confusion in our ranks can say that our party was losing its leadership role in the state. The party never watched events from the wings.[9]

The statement was remarkably similar in content to that of Cyran-kiewicz at the 1959 Congress, once the so-called revisionists had been vanquished: 'Not for a moment, not even at the time of greatest turmoil, did the party surrender its leading role.' PUWP leaders appeared to be strong adherents of the view, therefore, that 'all's well that ends well'.

It is now obvious that only a coalition of forces could have produced successful execution of the coup. Party authorities coopted the generals to prepare martial law. In turn some 80% of the officer corps belonged to the party and carried out its instructions. Only by surrendering its leading role to the army could the party hope to regain it. But in effect this represented a Hobbesian choice: reasons of state, not party orders, dictated to the generals that such a course of action was required.

At the beginning real political power was reported to be vested not in WRON but in an octovirate – three generals (Jaruzelski, Kiszczak and Siwicki), three Politburo members (Barcikowski, Czyrek and Olszowski), and two deputy premiers (Obodowski, Rakowski). In this way a representative institutional balance was achieved. Paradoxically the most influential party leaders were the so-called centrists, not hard-liners, even more so after Olszowski's dismissal from the Politburo in July. In short, those who supported socialist renewal during the Solidarity period were those who governed under martial law. The facility with which leaders 'cross the floor' to another political position in state socialist societies is confirmed by this evidence. Let us look now at their approach to key issues affecting party functioning.

1. Intraparty democracy

The primacy of logistics over ideology in the early months of martial law was substantiated by certain unpublicised developments within the party. It was rumoured that just before 13 December the entire Central Committee apparatus was sent out to the provinces in order to forestall infighting within the party once martial law was announced. A secret Politburo instruction entitled 'Party activity under conditions endangering the security of the state' was allegedly circulated which overrode PUWP statutes and centralised authority. Intraparty life was suspended until late January when provincial committees held their first meetings.

As might be expected, the value most strongly stressed at this time was political unity. Jaruzelski told the VII Plenum in February that unanimity of principles and objectives ought to prevail in the party: it was to be neither sect nor discussion club but a disciplined organisation which spoke with one voice.[10] To promote unity the strategy of 'clipping both wings' was initiated in January and led to the removal of the liberal Fiszbach and the hard-liner Żabiński from the Politburo. It was repeated at the provincial level in May with the replacement of Poznań's popular party chief Skrzypczak and Warsaw's reviled boss Kociołek, and it culminated in July with the forced resignations of Łabęcki and Kubiak (accused at the VII Plenum of being an agent of foreign intelligence) on the one hand, and of Olszowski on the other. These changes were only the tip of the iceberg, of course. Early in 1982 a purge was begun amongst the party rank-and-file. Officially this was to be based on the principle set out by Barcikowski, responsible for organisational matters in the party, in January: 'the one sphere integrating the party remains the resolutions of the IX Congress. Who feels uncomfortable in this framework should leave the party, who acts inconsistently with this line must be removed from the party.' In practice a second principle took precedence: 'today the indicator of party-mindedness is the attitude to the decision of 13 December and type of behaviour after this date'.[11]

The main purposes of the purge were to eliminate those members who had become 'lost' during the Solidarity period and had adopted 'opportunist' attitudes, and to reduce overall membership in the party, the uncontrolled expansion of which had 'paralysed the criticism of the old and experienced party cadres'.[12] In this respect the leadership followed the post-1968 Czechoslovak precedent. At least 100,000 members were purged up to May 1982 alone, over half of them for lack of interest in party life or failure to carry out party resolutions. In the first five months of martial law only 3,000 new members were approved. In sum, between February 1980 and February 1983 membership fell by 800,000 or 33%. Entire party committees were disbanded in places and others collapsed when all members returned their party cards.[13] It goes without saying that most who resigned or were removed were members who could not reconcile themselves to the provisions of martial law.

At the VII Plenum Jaruzelski also made clear that there was no going back to methods of governing prevailing before either August 1980 or December 1981. This theme was a throwback to one propagated by Husak in 1969–70, when he abjured a return either to 'Novotny bureaucracy' or to 'Dubcek anarchy'. Jaruzelski added that there was to be no substantive reform of the PUWP: 'Under its present historic name and in its current organisational form the party will find enough strength within itself to be reborn and effectively lead the working class.'[14] Siwak went further and urged the leadership to replace the 'un-Leninist' motto that Kania propagated, 'neither to the left nor right but straight ahead', with the 'courageous working class call "go left"'.[15]

The measures adopted by Jaruzelski to restore Leninist norms of interparty democracy were highly centralist. In March a system of direct contact between central authorities and party committees of the country's 207 largest economic enterprises was instituted. The VIII Plenum extended central supervision by calling on all Politburo and Secretariat members and Central Committee department heads to visit factories each week and explain the rulers' policies. In July the regional centres for party work were added to the dozens of façade institutions created under martial law. The 365 that existed in mid 1982 were to act as executive arms of the forty-nine provincial party committees and to supervise implementation of their resolutions.[16] The IX Plenum recommended that party committees keep better records of resolutions they adopted and ways they were carried out. Under martial law, therefore, democratic centralism was replaced by the bureaucratic centralism that had so recently been condemned.

In spite of this process of party consolidation through concentration of power, the Jaruzelski line was questioned by reformist and conservative forces alike. The political scientist Erazmus, who, as we saw in Chapter 6, published early in 1980 an article highly critical of Gierek's administration in *Nowe Drogi*, now challenged Jaruzelski's approach in the same journal. He argued: 'Unity is not reinforced by resolving ideological problems through political means nor political problems through ideological or, even worse, administrative means.' As a result 'Unanimity of views in party work ought to be a source of concern. Experience shows that unity does not arise from unanimity of views.' Erazmus proposed a different conception of intraparty democracy – 'unity through disagreement, disagreement through unity'.[17] During martial law such reformist conceptions of democracy continued to be articulated in specialised periodicals. Their publication was designed to demonstrate that the spirit of August lived.

A far more serious attack on Jaruzelski's approach was made by Grabski, head of the Stalinist-oriented Rzeczywistość (Reality) Clubs of Socio-Political Knowledge. At the X Plenum he distributed a letter to Central Committee members which criticised Jaruzelski on three counts: (1) counter-revolutionary forces had not been defeated; (2) the party was mired in a state of stagnation and atrophy; and (3) no practical economic programme had been adopted. He urged an even more radical purge of the party, which allegedly remained 'a con-

glomeration of different ideologies' – Marxist–Leninist, social democrat and Christian democrat.[18]

Martial law had not, therefore, overcome political disunity within
the party. The strategy of clipping wings did not succeed in eliminating reformist as well as dogmatist forces. The failure of the rulers
was underscored when one year after martial law was proclaimed the
Politburo was required to pass a resolution ordering the disbanding of
various societies and clubs within the party organisation which were
'dissipating the party's strength'.[19] The drawn out struggle over
drafting the final version of 'What we are fighting for, where we are
heading' symbolised the difficulties which the central leadership was
encountering in imposing its conception of intraparty democracy.

2. *The leading role of the party*

In his martial law speech Jaruzelski asserted the party's right to play
an 'active and creative' role in the historic process. Several weeks later
Barcikowski refuted the view that martial law had created a political
vacuum: 'no one can replace the party in fulfilling its mission'. At the
VII Plenum the party chief emphasised that 'socialism without the
party is not socialism; it is a ship without a rudder or sails'. As in all
post-war Polish crises, therefore, many aspects of the political system
might be questioned but the party's leading role was a fundamental
principle that was upheld at all times and remained the cornerstone of
the system of socialist democracy.

In the draft version of 'What we are fighting for, where we are
heading', the principle was given a broad interpretation: 'The party
can perform its directive and leading role only in alliance with all
social and political forces which respect the constitution of the Polish
People's Republic and the Polish *raison d'état*.' The importance of
reaching a national accord was strongly propagated during the first
months of martial law. Accordingly a concerted effort was made by
the leadership to identify itself with the early Kadar regime and the
draft programme included the principle 'who is not against us can be
with us'.[20]

Throughout 1982 the party was projected as the main instrument
and guarantor of socialist renewal. A profusion of new laws and
institutions was approved by an active but compliant Sejm. Measures
purportedly promoting the system of socialist democracy included
establishment of the constitutional tribunal, a tribunal of state, a

socio-economic council responsible to the Sejm, a consultative
economic council answerable to the Council of Ministers and a
national council of culture. Bills were passed concerning the Polish
Academy of Sciences, the press, higher education, trade unions and
the status of public servants, and a teachers' charter and national
cultural fund were approved. Measures concerned with economic
reform included changes in the system of management and price
structures as well as new laws on private ownership of land, private
crafts and services and the cooperative movement. Finally social
policy legislation included new provisions governing social parasitism, alcoholism, minors and welfare benefits, and the establishment of a national committee for the elderly. The creation of, first,
Citizens' Committees for National Salvation (OKON), then the
Patriotic Movement of National Rebirth (PRON) was portrayed as
having occurred spontaneously, without interference from the party.
They were to give institutional form to the front of national accord
initially proposed by Jaruzelski at the October 1981 Plenum, and the
future role of PRON in particular within the Polish political system
was depicted by the authorities as significant. This barrage of legal
and institutional measures was intended to demonstrate the rulers'
continued commitment to reform and symbolised the broader interpretation now given to the leading role principle.

Here too, however, dissent was apparent. The spirit of August was
recalled in an article advocating a system of 'socialist pluralism' in
which a multiplicity of political forces would coalesce and determine
policy.[21] Wiatr, head of the party's ideological institute, warned: 'The
day we forget what caused August 1980 is the day we set out on the
road to the next August.'[22] Some highly placed observers expected
the PRON movement to take on the role of 'loyal opposition'. Most
importantly the party and military apparatuses began to disagree on
ways of exercising the leading role. According to Staniszkis, the party
bureaucracy criticised Jaruzelski's non-ideological approach and his
lack of class language and of a class-based model of terror. Whilst
some party ideologues repeatedly invoked the class character of the
political system which was based on the worker–peasant alliance, and
called for the use of selective class repression aimed principally at the
intelligentsia, the military's model of repression was non-selective
and economic (dismissals from work, transfers to worse jobs).[23] In
this way the party's leading role was questioned not so much ideologically as in logistical terms. It would be inaccurate to conclude,

therefore, that martial law had led to a restoration of the privileged dominating role which the PUWP had enjoyed before August 1980.

3. *The party and ideology*

In the previous chapter we described how the leadership paid relatively little attention to ideological activity at a time when it was involved in a power struggle with Solidarity. After December 1981 efforts were made to resurrect a class-based ideology. The dialectic between party and ideology was succinctly described by one political commentator: 'The fate of Marxism as an ideology will always reflect the fate of the party: if the party suffers set-backs, so will Marxism as the value system propagated by the party.'[24] The importance of transforming social consciousness was underlined by Jaruzelski: 'The crisis in the realm of social consciousness cannot be overcome using the forces of law and order. Real and enduring political situations are needed. What is significant is not that we have an enemy but that through his demagogy the enemy is getting through to a section of society.'[25]

The party's ideological offensive was spearheaded by Olszowski. Ideological disintegration had, in his view, led to the emergence of anarcho-syndicalist and bourgeois currents in the party which had discarded class criteria in analysing the political situation. The 'theoretical voluntarism' of the Gierek administration had served as the catalyst for such non-Marxist conceptions. At the first National Party Conference on Ideology and Theory, held in April 1982, he presented a report on the PUWP's ideological mistakes that was uncharacteristically sophisticated for an East European Communist leader:

The 1950s theory of a sharpening of the class struggle as socialism developed was profoundly incorrect and harmful. Likewise the other extreme view embodied in the thesis that class struggle completely disappeared with the liquidation of antagonistic classes and construction of socialism was also mistaken. An ideological and political class struggle continues so long as a basis still exists in those active strata of social consciousness which represent the vestiges of earlier formations, and so long as support and inspiration are found externally, amongst imperialist forces, which engage in diversions against socialism.

The aetiology of post-war crises could be traced to 1948, Olszowski argued, when the campaign against the so-called rightist–nationalist deviation led to the negation of Leninist party norms. This thesis became very popular in 1982 as a way of explaining the cyclical pattern of political crises: it permitted the authorities to ascribe responsibility for all of Poland's problems to a distant regime. Opportunities to eradicate structural defects were not exploited in 1956 and 1970, the party ideologue continued. Under Gierek ideological blunders were compounded: Western *petit bourgeois* value systems, condemned by enlightened circles in capitalist countries themselves, were imported into the country along with technology. Marxism–Leninism was treated formalistically and instrumentally. The erroneous tenet of the 'moral and political unity of the Polish nation' and of the imminent creation of an 'all-people's state' obscured the real structure of class forces. The propaganda of success which depicted an idealised reality superseded class analysis which perceived the true social conditions prevailing in the country. In this way the dogmatic ideology of the 1950s was displaced by the ideological opportunism of the 1970s.

Olszowski concluded, therefore, that Solidarity found fertile ground to propagate four appealing but misleading theses: (1) the socialist system was incapable of achieving social justice, equality and democracy; (2) 'socialism without the party' was possible; (3) relations between rights and responsibilities, income and work, and group and national interests were questioned; and (4) patriotism signified chauvinist and anti-Soviet attitudes. In order to revitalise the PUWP's ideology Olszowski recommended extensive research into the actual phase of socialist development that Poland had reached, its class structure, and the type of social consciousness dominant in particular classes and strata.[26]

During Kania's interregnum the 'class origins of political crisis' argument was advanced principally by advocates of socialist renewal to substantiate the need for sweeping reforms. Dogmatists identified only micro-sociological factors behind the emergence of conflict, thereby minimalising the need for structural change. Under martial law the class position was appropriated by hard-liners in order to legitimate the need for a settling of accounts with liberals, revisionists and social democrats who had found their way into the party. Jaruzelski himself kept a safe distance from those who sought a return to class ideology and was therefore vulnerable to charges of a non-ideological (or logistical) approach.

Which classes were locked in struggle was never specified, but the obvious target of the campaign was the intelligentsia which was thought by much of the leadership to have masterminded the Solidarity counter-revolution. As Siwak concisely noted: 'What we can forgive a shipyard worker, a spinner or a miner, we cannot forgive a politician, a professor or an ideologue from a party institute. It is for the latters' mistakes that we are paying so dearly today.'[27] One professor and ideologue was, however, able to turn the class argument around so as to underscore the indispensability of authentic socialist renewal: 'Much as they have tried, the authorities of the people's state have never succeeded in clearing away the problems they started with: the opposition between the "governing" and the "governed".' Political crises were caused by 'alienation of government' from the ruled, and only institutional reform could finally eliminate the roots of such class-based conflict.[28] Ideological orientations constituted, therefore, not only a major difference between social classes; they also distinguished the reformers from the dogmatists within the ruling group in the martial law period.

INDUSTRIAL DEMOCRACY

The clearest case of the precedence of logistics over operative ideology was on the issue of industrial democracy. Whilst self-management institutions in higher education, for example, such as the Conference of University Rectors and the Independent Students' Union, were quickly dissolved after martial law was imposed, the institutions which were to guarantee industrial democracy were ostensibly still to be determined in a national debate. Solidarity's future remained a supposedly open question up to September. The authorities even claimed to have made offers to negotiate with its leaders in both February and April, but these had been turned down by the union. Why, then, was the decision taken in October to ban Solidarity altogether? According to Rakowski:

The following months brought the expansion of the underground structures of the union, the activisation of the struggle against the legal institutions of the state, the organisation of strikes, the publication of leaflets and circulars that were hostile to the PUWP, the security apparatus and the army, as well as moral terror directed against those who not only wished to remain loyal to the state but had had enough of incessant tension and friction.[29]

During the early months of martial law the rulers skilfully manipulated feelings of fear and hope amongst the population. Physical force and irrational acts elicited fear whilst occasional official discourse gave grounds for hope. Two weeks after the declaration of martial law Jaruzelski was still promising that 'there is a place for self-governing and truly independent trade unions in our system – independent from the state employer and independent from the machinations and terror of irresponsible politicians *manqués*'.[30] A commission chaired by Rakowski to study the future of trade unions reported in February that the authorities had 'no intention of imposing any definite concept for the organisational reconstruction of the movement'. It did make clear, however, that regionally based unions were undesirable and that in the open debate 'the opinions of avowed enemies of socialism and advocates of confrontation are no longer needed'.[31] By July, when Rakowski submitted to the Sejm a progress report on the debate, the outcome was obvious. Solidarity members had, he alleged, boycotted the debate. The general consensus amongst actual participants was that there could be no return to either pre-August or pre-December unions. The deputy premier adopted the commonly used tactic of juxtaposing 'extremist' views of supposedly equal weight in order to justify pursuit of a 'middle' course: both the proposals for a reformed Solidarity and those for a three-year ban on all trade unions were 'half-measures' that would satisfy no one. The most logical course was to create entirely new trade union structures which would represent a third chance (after the failures of branch unions and Solidarity) to achieve workers' democracy.[32]

In October this zero option was given legislative form: Solidarity was delegalised and the rudiments of a new union movement established. Rakowski refuted the criticism that the trade union act signified a return to *tabula rasa*: 'The new movement will not be founded in an empty field but on a reinforced construction site.' The provisions of the bill envisaged a spontaneous process of forming unions in individual work-places. By April 1983 it was claimed that over 10,000 such unions had been set up, and by a decision of the Council of State the second stage in the rebirth of trade unions was begun: national structures grouping unions and employees of the same occupation (for example, railwaymen) could be created. The final phase, confederation of national structures, was scheduled for January 1985 but also was likely to be brought forward. Estimates of the number of members the new unions had suggested 4.3 million (or less than 40% of those eligible) in March 1984.

The most detailed statement of the authorities' view of the new unions was given at the X Plenum in October 1982. The resolutions noted: 'Without self-governing trade unions independent of the administration and willing to cooperate with the party in protecting the rights and interests of working people and defending the socialist system, our country's socio-political system would be neither democratic nor effective.' The party's relationship to the unions was spelled out: (1) it was to recognise and protect the independence of trade unions from the state administration; (2) relations between basic party committees and the unions were to be based on cooperation, not on superior–subordinate lines; (3) first secretaries were urged not to take top posts in the unions; and (4) all local party resolutions concerned with trade union activity had to take account of their views.[33] The patronising tone of these directives showed that if unions were to be independent at all, it would only be by the grace of the PUWP.

If the process of creating a union movement in the party's image was drawn out over a year, very early on the authorities promised to reactivate the other major instrument of industrial democracy, workers' self-management. The Politburo report to the April Plenum emphasised the importance of self-management bodies in protecting the spirit of reform against bureaucratic counter-thrusts. But the influence of self-management was reduced in a more indirect way than was the case for trade unions: the overall autonomy of the economic enterprise was curtailed by increased state supervision. Military commissars (responsible for discipline in the factory), operational programme plenipotentiaries (responsible for distribution of resources in fourteen selected areas, such as energy, utilities, machinery and food), newly formed economic associations (loose conglomerates of factories which sprang up after the previous associations, or *zjednoczenia*, were abolished) and the ever-present party first secretaries combined to make a shambles of the decentralising provisions of the economic reform programme. Employees' self-management was also reduced to a façade stature.

Public attitudes to some aspects of industrial democracy appeared to break down along the class lines that the leadership had stressed. In a poll taken in September 1982, 58% of workers allegedly supported the suspension of the right to strike whilst only 28% disagreed. Within the intelligentsia a reverse pattern emerged: only 36% found the suspension justified and 57% said it was unjustified.[34] Such data were used to rationalise the rulers' decision to impose a system of industrial democracy developed by the party of workers, not by groups of intellectuals as purportedly had been the case in the Solidarity period. The authorities' approach to the subject was above all logistical, therefore, and aimed at clawing back the concessions which the working class had obtained in 1980.

THE CHURCH

The imposition of martial law seriously challenged the *entente* established between the church and the state in the 1970s. Conservative elements in both the ecclesiastical and political hierarchies had long been critical of the pragmatism that had helped forge normalisation, and the harsh provisions of martial law presented an opportunity to question the wisdom of cooperating with a suspect rival institution. To be sure, efforts were made at the summit level to maintain the *modus vivendi*: on 13 December Jaruzelski praised 'the patriotic attitude of the church' whilst Glemp called for the 'utmost prudence' and avoidance of blood spilling. The two leaders met in early January, then again in April and November, so as to promote 'calm, social order and honest work', as the communiqué from the last meeting stated. The need for such summits was 'determined by the dramatic nature of our domestic situation rather than by problems of church–state relations', and they were complemented by meetings of the Joint Government–Episcopate Commission which, in the view of the Minister of Religious Affairs, Kuberski, ensured that 'no discrepancy between the state and church arises which cannot be solved nor problem exists which could lead to conflict'. He described the privileged position which the church enjoyed in Poland: it had 7,600 parishes, 20,000 priests, 40,000 other members of religious orders and eighty-nine newspapers. More significantly, it had received 700 licences for church construction between 1971 and 1981 and some 300 additional ones since.[35] Of all social institutions the church had been least affected by martial law: Sunday mass continued to be broadcast over state radio and curfews were even lifted before Christmas and Easter to permit worshippers to attend midnight services. The influence of the Catholic church was so great that in 1980 80% of party members were reportedly believers.[36]

Critics of Glemp claimed he had struck a deal with the military leadership – moral support for the regime in return for further church expansion. His defenders stressed how in December he had appealed to the Sejm not to adopt the emergency powers bill, how he had declared the moral invalidity of the loyalty oaths which the authorities sought to extract from various individuals, how he had stated in a March sermon that 'social agreement must be a compromise, but not with evil', and how he had inspired the April 'Theses of the primate's social council on matters of social reconciliation', which called for the reactivisation of Solidarity. The fact was that the position of the church was circumscribed by both the military might of the authorities and the influence of party hard-liners who questioned the desirability of cooperation with it. In his exposé at the party ideological conference, for example, Olszowski condemned the church's 'misuse of the pulpit for anti-state and anti-socialist activities'. This statement was subsequently dropped from official proceedings of the conference. Several newspaper reports in September, in attacking an outspoken sermon by Bishop Tokarczuk of Przemyśl, warned the church not to evolve into an opposition political party: it ought not to 'regard the government, that is, its partner, as an opponent, thereby repeating the fatal mistake of Solidarity's leadership which had underestimated the power of the state'.[37] Three articles published in *Nowe Drogi* in 1982 sought, to varying degrees, to expose the conservative nature of church doctrine, in particular, its concept of national (as opposed to class) solidarity. One party specialist on church dogma described how it had become both 'agitator' and desirable partner in seeking a way out of the crisis: as a result 'it could count on further benefits and enrich its possessions'. Moreover the entire normalisation policy had led to consolidation of the Catholic world outlook in Poland at the expense of a Marxist one.[38] The campaign to limit the power of the church, backed by the dogmatist faction in the party, was without parallel since Gomułka's attacks in the mid 1960s.

Jaruzelski acknowledged that church–state relations had been a subject of conjecture during the martial law period: not everyone was pleased with the harmonious coexistence of believers and non-believers. In fact:

Inflammatory voices can be heard originating from the darkest pages of counter-reformation. Illegal actions also are undertaken. The advocates of politicising the church support an outlook eradicated long ago. They reflect not the conciliatory spirit of the Second Vatican Council but the evil trends of political clericalism. In Poland there is no room for fanaticism.[39]

The most representative view of the leadership was, however, that set out by Deputy Premier Obodowski early in 1983: 'Relations with Cardinal Glemp are good: he belongs to the category of statesman and it is from this viewpoint that he reasons. Relations with the clergy, the lower clergy, are different: many Catholic circles and some groups in the church hierarchy seek to play a political role.'[40]

Operative ideology on the church was, therefore, challenged in an unprecedented way. Jaruzelski, like Glemp, was under cross-pressure, firstly, to maintain the working relationship established in the 1970s and, secondly, to exhibit a commitment to dogma that some critics saw as lacking in the past. The 1983 papal visit offered incentives to both leaders to consolidate their respective positions. Glemp would be confirmed as a worthy head of Poland's most respected institution, whilst Jaruzelski could display the power of the regime he headed in retaining a right of veto over such a historic event. Above all the authorities desperately needed a modicum of legitimacy in the short term whilst the church was concerned with improving the conditions required to carry out its long-term historic mission. The Jaruzelski–Woytyła meetings strengthened the position of moderate forces in both state and church and ensured that the church–state concordat would remain in effect for the foreseeable future. The belief that a 'deal' had secretly been struck at Wawel Castle was, in contrast, shared by the more conservative elements in each institution which opposed the *entente* established by Gierek and made unpalatable by martial law.

SCIENCE AND CULTURE

On 11 December 1981 the first independent Congress of Polish Culture opened its meetings in Warsaw. Forty-one national associations concerned with various aspects of culture, humanities and the arts gathered for a three-day session to formulate an organisational and ideological blueprint for future development. The slogan of the Congress was 'culture knows no boundaries'. On the first day Szczepański, president of the Writers' Union, observed: 'The view has been put forward that the Congress of Polish Culture will be reminiscent of a concert given by the ship's orchestra on the deck of the *Titanic*.' If the ship still remained afloat, he argued, no small part was played by 'the determination of the orchestra, which did not set aside its instruments and sheet music but continued to play'.[41]

Eighteen months later, even after the dissolution of a number of organisations which took part in the Congress (actors, journalists) and the continued suspension of others (writers, film-makers), the cultural intelligentsia remained determined not to sink. Probably more than any other social group in Polish society, it steadfastly refused to yield to the 'business as usual' exhortations of the authorities.

The key role that intellectuals played in political life was underscored by the fact that Rakowski met with some of their representatives ten days after martial law was imposed. He accused them of having become 'overawed with everything that Solidarity activists did' and rhetorically asked: 'Why did Polish intellectuals remain silent when they should have shouted loudly? Why did many feed on myths and ignore reality? Why did they permit the dismantling of the Polish state?' Another critic noted: 'If young people did not understand anything that was going on, it was because neither their fathers nor their professors nor their favourite writer told them.'[42] The leadership's anti-intellectual attitude was apparent before martial law was declared, but it increased in intensity after that.

At the VII Plenum Jaruzelski described the ideological irresolution and anarchy that had pervaded cultural circles in recent years. At the same time he made it clear that artistic freedom of means of expression and selection of themes was to be preserved. This was to constitute the operative ideology of the rulers under martial law. Attacks on the intelligentsia's vacillation did not signify greater state interference in the cultural realm. The leadership was offering the intelligentsia continued subsystem autonomy in return for political compliance. The same principle was applied to the scientific and academic spheres.

During the first six months of martial law Kubiak, a Kraków sociologist and Politburo member, exerted a strong moderating influence on the state's approach to intellectuals. At the party ideological conference, for example, he advanced a carefully balanced view on the rights and obligations of science and culture. 'Conscientious and competent pursuit of truth in itself performs a positive ideological function benefiting socialism', he argued. In turn cultural freedom had to be delimited only by the imperatives for truth, humanism, progress and internationalism. Invoking the slogan of the Congress of Polish Culture, Kubiak stressed the importance of guaranteeing 'openness of Polish culture and science to the whole world'.[43] In the practical sphere, it was largely as a result of his influence that institutions of higher education resumed classes in early February. As a result, the most drastic variant of suppressing the intellectual community in the propitious early months of martial law was avoided.

In his speech to the Sejm in May, at the time of the passing of a bill establishing a national cultural council and cultural development fund, Rakowski also emphasised the indispensability of creative freedom for science and culture: 'When urging that science serve practice we are aware that this is not the only task of science. The main function is cognitive.' Similarly the chief characteristics of Polish culture were its heterogeneity and openness, which had to be defended. It would continue to 'participate in the dialogue of European and world cultures' and attempts to 'shut it off artificially, to enclose it in an enclave' would be resisted. At the same time, Rakowski added, 'from the standpoint of a socialist state the limits on freedom are the good of the human community, that of the national community, and that of the socialist state which is the only guarantor of this community'.[44]

Under martial law the social sciences were not, as might have been expected, accused of revisionism to the same extent as after the March 1968 disturbances. Kubiak told the ideological conference that the two extreme distortions committed in the past – domination of ideology at the expense of scientific values and complete disappearance of ideological values – had to be avoided. The former Minister of Higher Education, Górski, also exonerated social scientists: their knowledge of contemporary Western economics and sociology was too superficial to accuse them of returning to bourgeois science. Furthermore their major function was critically to analyse existing reality. Approval of the socialist system did not imply the need to accept all social and economic policies of the rulers.[45]

The leadership's approach to culture and science appeared to differ in three principal ways, therefore, from that adopted in the other issue-areas we have examined. Firstly a systematised operative ideology, rather than a series of improvised logistical measures, was formulated early on. Secondly the leadership's approach was considerably more liberal in this than in the other spheres. At the practical level this was reflected in the policy of not conducting a wholesale verification campaign in the universities. Thirdly, in contrast to the class approach grounded in the worker–peasant alliance (in short, excluding intellectuals) that was adopted in other spheres, the leadership recognised that Polish culture and science were created by 'all classes and social groups', as the new Minister of

Culture, Żygulski, declared in October. Nothing and no one was to be excluded.[46] The irony was that none of these characteristics helped break the passive resistance to the martial law rulers undertaken by the cultural and, to a lesser extent, the scientific intelligentsia.

POLITICAL VALUES AND SOCIETY

At the VII Plenum in February 1982, Jaruzelski appealed to the public 'not to fall once again into that very Polish cycle – a straw fire followed by profound depression'. When martial law was finally lifted in December, it appeared that this appeal, like many others of the rulers, had not been heeded. This depression was most clearly visible in economic activity. For the fourth consecutive year net material product had fallen, this time by 8% (compared to 13% in 1981). Whilst nominal wages increased by 51%, inflation ran well over 100%: for example, food prices had officially risen by 238% and other consumer goods by 185%. One study estimated that ten million people in Poland now lived below subsistence level.[47] The allocation of scarce resources took on an increasingly partisan character. At the X Plenum, for example, a hint was given that socio-economic policy would have to reflect the class character of society.[48] The separation of economic from political activity that Solidarity had been ordered to follow was now demonstrably abandoned by the authorities. As one Politburo member told the party ideological conference: 'There is nothing more political than the economy or economic decisions ... Politics cannot be divorced from economics or party policy from economic policy.'[49]

For obvious reasons political socialisation of youth was given high priority in 1982. Solidarity had represented a radical movement of young people, and with half the population under thirty the leadership had to find an effective antidote. The IX Plenum, devoted exclusively to the issue, invoked, predictably, the centrality of class orientations in the process of socialisation. It noted how its precursor Plenum of 1972 had underestimated the importance of the class struggle in influencing the young. Jaruzelski emphasised: 'Youth must become aware of what stream the Polish boat is to sail. It cannot sail upstream of history, nor will our country head for the Western bank.' During the Solidarity period 'youthful romanticism and readiness for sacrifice were abused and exploited for political ends'. The Plenum adopted a 'programme of improvement in life and career opportunities for young people' which stressed such values as social justice, equal opportunity, partnership and reciprocal loyalty between the authorities and youth.[50]

The supreme value that was propagated in the martial law period was, however, the Polish *raison d'état*. Group and individual interests might or might not be embodied in the national interest; that was irrelevant. Poland was depicted as a nation besieged: as Jaruzelski put it at the VIII Plenum, 'an iron curtain is formed again but it is not we who build it'. At the same time Poland was required to accept the realities of the Yalta and Potsdam agreements, which were hammered home by the state propaganda machine. The Military Council projected itself as the saviour of Poland's independence and, simultaneously, as the incarnation of the country's national and class interests. In this way it represented one more clumsy attempt in a long series that has dominated twentieth-century European history to fuse nationalism with socialism.

In his study of the development of national Communism, Zwick suggested reasons for the double failure of party rulers and Solidarity:

The failure of the Gierek and Kania regimes lay in their inability to adjust party policies to national realities, and those national realities exploded in the form of Solidarity. The failure of Wałęsa and Solidarity lay in their inability to adjust their demands to international realities, and those international realities exploded in martial law. What remains is for Poland's leaders to come up with a formula that will satisfy both the Marxist and national imperatives that constitute the current Polish reality.[51]

The failure of the martial law regime lay in the fact that its sole *raison d'être* was to sacrifice both national and socialist values in the interests of the international alliance system. Poland's political reality was used to justify crude *realpolitik*. When in early 1981 the Solidarity underground launched the slogan 'the spring will be ours', Jaruzelski retorted that 'the spring will be Polish and socialist'. Neither that spring nor all of 1982 will be remembered as a time that was particularly Polish or socialist.

9

Operative ideology, fundamental principles and social reality

> People always were and always will be the stupid victims of deceit and self-deceit in politics until they learn to discover the interests of some class behind all moral, religious, political and social phrases, declarations and promises.
>
> V. I. Lenin, 'The three sources and three component parts of Marxism'

Writing in 1977, Evans, a specialist in Soviet affairs, drew the following conclusion: 'Recent changes in Soviet communist ideology have been ignored almost completely by Western scholars. The reason is evident: most observers assume that the Soviet ideology is not changing.' According to Evans: 'The ideology was forgotten by many outsiders, but not Soviet leaders.' They instituted 'explicit revisions in the framework of the official ideology', the most important product being the concept of 'developed socialism'. This concept, designating a further stage along the road to the achievement of Communist society, was new. And although the central values it embodied were closely linked to past experience and long-standing norms (especially the maintenance of authoritative political institutions, the conscious organisation of society, the continuation of industrial growth), it could be generally said, in the view of this scholar, that 'Contemporary Soviet ideology reflects the erosion of utopianism and the strength of "developmentalism" in the Soviet regime', which, in turn, reflects the need 'to identify the ideal with the features of existing institutions'.[1]

A West German Sovietologist, Dahm, stressed the plurality of ideological approaches that had appeared in Soviet ideology in the 1970s. This originated, he claimed, in the very nature of the relationship between Marxism as a body of theory and socialism as a form of practice:

233

the relations between the original (e.g., 'theoretical structures of socialism/ Communism') and its representation (e.g., 'model of socialism') are not isomorphic (reversely unequivocal, true to original, structurally same) but homomorphic (not reversely unequivocal, similar, structurally different). This means that the relation between original and model is not one of identity but one of analogy ... Whence, ideology – even that of Marxism–Leninism – is plural.

Moreover:

'functional aspects' (scientific Communism as the Marxist–Leninist science of politics) gain ascendancy over the 'epistemological aspects' (diamat and histomat as world-view and as scientific last word) ... The readiness to renounce ideology in the name of truth – under pressure from scientific fact – is admissible now not where it does not threaten the stability of the system but only where it contributes to this stability. In all other cases, the truth must give way to ideology.[2]

The view that under socialism ideology does not change requires qualification, therefore. It does change in developmental fashion, often imperceptibly, rarely dramatically, locked as it is in a dialectical relationship with social truth. To discover the extent of change ideology has to be examined over a relatively long timespan and at the heuristically more visible level of abstraction that we have called 'operative ideology'. Whilst we cannot expect a party Congress in a socialist state to discard an ideological principle as fundamental as dictatorship of the proletariat (as did the XXII Congress of the French Communist Party, held in 1976), we can expect concepts at a more functional level to fall quietly into disuse whilst other innovative ones are introduced. The reasons for such modifications are obvious: society evolves, and with it so does ideology. At a certain level ideology is required to fit both current political institutions and social processes, each of which is characterised by evolution and flux. As a result, whether we study socialist ideology under Soviet, Polish or other conditions, we are bound to encounter change.

In this chapter we look at the interaction of operative ideology, as it existed in Poland between 1956 and 1983, with two dimensions immediately 'above' and 'below' it (seen from the perspective of Marx's base–superstructure model in which operative ideology occupies a lower tier of the superstructure): with fundamental principles of Marxism–Leninism, and with 'hard' social reality. We wish to determine to what extent this operative ideology was in alignment with the theoretical framework of socialism as well as with the actual conduct of society. Did the constituent elements of Polish rulers' operative ideology represent an ideological deviation from, or at least revision of, Marxist–Leninist doctrine, and a bending to the exigencies of reality? Or were they simply old wine in new bottles, that is, an updated but faithful extension of fundamental principles manifesting a minimal adjustment to reality?

OPERATIVE IDEOLOGY AND FUNDAMENTAL PRINCIPLES

For some time many Western critics have subscribed to the argument that Marxist ideology and socialist practice, in its Soviet modular form, are at odds with each other.[3] Marxist ideology is treated as the body of theory ensconced in the writings of Marx and Engels. Sometimes the works of Lenin are included in this theoretical framework, but as often as not his contributions, along with those of Stalin, are considered as argumentation in support of socialist practice, hence embodiments of the operative ideologies of those epochs. Western critics are quick to point out the basic inconsistencies within Marxist ideology itself (regardless of whose theoretical considerations are included), but this does not stop them from treating it as a unified or cohesive body of thought when comparing it with deviations and revisions alleged to arise in socialist practice. Few systematic attempts have been made to relate the fundamental principles of Marxist ideology to operative ideology (defined as explanations and justifications of policy formulated but not of policy consequences ensuing) since the time of Stalin. One of the reasons for this has been that, for many Kremlinologists, Stalin was the last ideologising leader the Soviet Union had. Some have approached Khrushchev's XX Congress declarations and his concepts of 'peaceful coexistence' and an 'all-peoples state' as ideological contributions, whilst others have identified the concept of developed socialism along with the Brezhnev doctrine on the socialist community as a form of ideology of the recent leadership. Generally, however, the fact that these rulers did not advance any specific theoretical elaboration of Marxism as such has been interpreted to mean that little or no ideological change has been undertaken.

The 'nothing has changed' thesis suggests that the political leaders of socialist states are doctrinaire and inflexible: their ideological faithfulness to Marxist thought is considered to be a primary cause of failures within the political system. In this way Marxism itself is regarded as a failure and as praxeologically bankrupt. Other Western scholars, however, including many neo-Marxists, subscribe to the view that in socialist states both the policies pursued and the argumentation employed to justify them have been inconsistent with the values, principles and goals spelled out in Marxist theory. Real existing socialism, state capitalism, or degenerate workers' states (as various critics describe Soviet-type systems) have been produced by aberrations in interpretations of Marxism.

The ideological status of Leninism has aroused particular controversy. Its axiological and praxeological consistency with Marxism is frequently questioned. Some Trotskyites see it as the first major theoretical departure from Marxism, whilst at the other extreme ideologues of state socialism resolutely defend the integral whole constituted by Marxism and Leninism. In relating an operative ideology to fundamental principles it is important to specify whether both Marxist and Leninist thought is to be included as representing the latter.

In our comparison it seems only fair to include Leninist norms as part of such principles since, ultimately, this is the way in which the Polish political leadership perceives its parent ideology. What we wish to find out is whether, during the past twenty-seven years, Polish rulers have argued in a manner consistent with the Marxism–Leninism they purportedly cherish. We look, therefore, at the operative ideology which evolved on each of the issue-areas studied and relate it to the central, most representative concepts contained in Marxist–Leninist doctrine. In this way we may be able to answer the question: between 1956 and 1983 were Polish rulers genuinely Marxists–Leninists or not?

1. The case of the party

It was only in Marx's lifetime that the idea and structure of the modern political party arose; hence we do not find in his writings any direct consideration of the internal nature of the mass party. In their 'Address of the Central Committee to the Communist League' Marx and Engels did stress the importance of centralism to this institution: 'the workers' party must act in the most organised, most unanimous and most independent fashion possible if it is not to be exploited and taken in tow again by the bourgeoisie as in 1848'.[4]

It was Lenin, of course, who set forth the doctrine on the party most fully. In his view the party had to consist chiefly of people 'professionally engaged in revolutionary activity'; all functions of the party had to be concentrated 'in the hands of the smallest possible number of professional revolutionaries'; and centralisation of the conspiratorial functions of the organisation had to be combined with the enlistment of the broadest masses within the movement.[5] But such recruitment had to be accompanied by occasional purges: 'The party is a voluntary association which would inevitably disintegrate, first ideologically and then also materially, if it did not rid itself of those members who preach anti-party views.' Therefore those 'not completely Marxist and not altogether correct' had to be removed from the party by 'periodical cleansings'.[6]

Lenin's formulation of the classic principle of democratic centralism permitted 'freedom to criticise, so long as this does not disturb the unity of a definite action; it rules out all criticism that disrupts or makes difficult the unity of an action decided upon by the party'.[7] Later he emphasised the duty of members to bring about 'unity and closing of their ranks'. That is, 'the harmful nature and inadmissibility of the formation of any kind of faction whatsoever' was proclaimed, and the expression of criticism had constantly to take account 'of the position of the party, surrounded as it is by enemies'.[8]

From these citations on intraparty democracy it becomes apparent that the operative ideology of Polish leaders from 1956 to 1983 was to a very large degree congruent with fundamental principles. In the late 1950s the struggle against factionalism was based on the leadership's invocation of democratic centralism: power-sharing was not on the agenda, whilst political unity within the party was at the top of the agenda. Participation by lower committees in general party life was encouraged but it was soon transformed into the related notion of greater assertiveness of such committees in their immediate environments. Their involvement in overall party life gradually became an inoperative concept. Moreover the influence these committees should wield in relation to the Central Committee was conveniently ignored. Between 1960 and 1967 party unity was taken for granted and little attention was paid to either aspect of democratic centralism. It was the question of cadre recruitment and qualifications which received most prominence. Operative ideology on intraparty democracy of this period did represent a deviation from Leninist principles, therefore, in that, if not contradicted outright, they were neglected by the leadership.

By the end of the decade, especially following the 1968 disturb-

ances, structural factors, such as upgrading the role of basic committees and their caucuses, and conceptual considerations, such as
the calls for more discussion and expression of criticism, represented
a shift towards participatory (although not necessarily democratic)
values. The 1970 crisis and the subsequent change in leadership did
not lead to a major shift in operative ideology. Although centralism
was given greater emphasis and party unity was more strongly
underlined, consultation between higher and lower party echelons,
together with information flow, discussion and control from below,
remained the main participatory forms governing intraparty life. In
these respects operative ideology under Gierek merely extended and
amplified the operative ideology promulgated by Gomułka between
1968 and 1970.

The VI Congress referred vaguely to the election procedure for
the Central Committee, to the term of office of leaders, to cadre
turnover and to collective decision-making methods, but these
crucial democratic aspects of the Leninist principle were not
brought up again until the IX Congress. Attention to party unity
diminished in the latter half of the decade, was made inoperative
with the emergence of Solidarity in 1980–1 when the rulers were
required to countenance greater ideological and institutional pluralism in the PUWP, but was reasserted forcefully with the imposition of martial law. Whilst generally remaining committed to the
Leninist concept of democratic centralism, therefore, during the
past twenty-seven years Polish rulers' operative ideology has swung
like a pendulum from one component to the other. Centralism
(party unity) was affirmed at times of political crisis but was otherwise largely ignored, whilst democracy as outlined by Lenin (pluralism of views during discussion, collective decision-making,
election of leaders by lower tiers) was put forward only at the VI
and IX Congresses. At all other junctures it was participatory
values which the leadership had extrapolated from the democratic
concept (and were not, therefore, to be mistaken for it) that were
propagated. We can conclude that Polish rulers may not have
contradicted the letter of the Leninist principle of democratic centralism, but they were rarely willing to propagate the idea of 'just as
much democracy as centralism', which constituted the spirit of the
Leninist norm.

Apart from views on intraparty democracy, we also examined
approaches of the leadership to the leading role of the party in

society. Marx and Engels set out an early theoretical rationalisation of this principle when they wrote:

The Communists are, on the one hand, practically, the most advanced and resolute section of the working-class parties of every country, that section which pushes forward all others; on the other hand, theoretically, they have over the great mass of the proletariat the advantage of clearly understanding the line of march, the conditions, and the ultimate general results of the proletarian movement.[9]

For Lenin, the proletariat's position as the leading force in society signified that its party, too, was empowered to play a leading role. More specifically, a dictatorship of the proletariat, representing political rule by the working class, would only succeed if it were placed under the leadership of the party. It was the party's task 'to direct and organise the new order, to be the teacher, guide, leader of all the toiling and exploited'. For Lenin the dictatorship of the proletariat was a special form of class alliance between the proletariat – the vanguard of the working people – and other strata of society, such as the *petite bourgeoisie*, the small property owners, the peasantry and the intelligentsia.[10] Above all, he stressed the need for the party, in carrying out its leading role in society, to be prepared to make compromises and concessions so as to gain allies, to 'take advantage of any, even the smallest, opportunity of winning a mass ally, even though this ally is temporary, vacillating, unstable, unreliable and conditional'. Thus 'It is necessary to link the strictest devotion to the ideas of Communism with the ability to effect all the necessary practical compromises, tacks, conciliatory manoeuvres, zigzags, retreats, and so on.'[11]

We have seen how Polish rulers interpreted the principle of the party's leading role, and how they singled out various groups or classes as 'most favoured allies' during the period 1956–83. Between 1956 and 1959 there were several zigzags in such conceptions: the initial more liberal approach to the leading role was meant as an antidote to excessive party control over society and the estrangement of the party from the masses which characterised the Stalin period. Later exhortations for renewed party militancy throughout society were a reaction to a popular belief that integral democracy might be implemented. By 1964 the party was urged to become the leading force in all social sectors, above all, in economic matters. The level of democracy in the state was considered to be a function of the party's performance of its leading role. Towards the late 1960s, however, a somewhat different operative ideology was promulgated: the party's special links with the working class were singled out, whilst its overinvolvement in the administrative sphere was condemned. Following the March troubles, socialist democracy – which sub-sumed the party's leading role together with other systemic features such as the importance of representative bodies – became the key concept in operative ideology. After these tacks, a continuation and elaboration of this conception followed in the 1970s. More and more the party's leading role was identified with acquiring new allies: its links with all important groups in society were stressed, the chief ones being the 'non-party millions', the Catholics and the intelligentsia. Significantly the term 'dictatorship of the proletariat' became less frequently employed than before, though it was never abandoned. Directing rather than leading was the idea put forward at this time. By the late 1970s the party's major consideration in exercising its influence in society became national unity. The largest and most powerful potential ally – all of society – was courted so as to overcome growing socio-economic problems. Even when in August 1980 society made it clear that it had no wish to ally itself with a spent force and created a new movement instead, PUWP rulers continued to assert the party's leading role (especially at the XI Plenum). The principle was interpreted in a broad way so as to allow all social forces loyal to the Polish constitution and to the Polish *raison d'état* to take part in a National Unity Front. Suspicion of a party-dominated front led to increasing political conflict and the authorities opted for martial law. Even in 1982, however, the leading role principle was not viewed in a dogmatic way but was supposed to be exercised within the framework of a front of national accord. No other approach was possible given disarray within and discredit outside the party.

We see that the leeway in interpreting the principle allowed for in Lenin's writings was used to the full by Polish rulers between 1956 and 1983. The zigzags from rigorous to broad interpretations con-stituted the manoeuvres necessary for the leadership to gain impor-tant allies at critical junctures. Accordingly it is difficult to speak of congruency or dissonance between operative ideology and funda-mental principles when the latter provided such broad scope for imputations. It suffices to say that the leading role of the party, in whichever way it was perceived and regardless of how many allies were sought to make it workable, remained a central principle invoked in periods of stability, crisis or accumulating tension. It represented the cornerstone of both the ideological superstructure and the political system which, if removed, might cause the entire construction to collapse.

2. Industrial democracy

Although the question of labour was one of the most central issues considered in Marx's analysis of history, he actually said very little about its organisation in a future Communist society. He argued that free labour could only occur 'if (1) it is of a social nature, (2) it has a scientific character and at the same time is general work'. The final goal was the creation of a 'cooperative society based on common ownership of the means of production'.[12] The achievements of the emergent trade unions in all this lay, according to Marx, 'not in the immediate result, but in the ever-expanding union of the workers . . . It was just this contact that was needed to centralise the numerous local struggles, all of the same character, into one national struggle between classes.'[13] But Marx warned:

If they wish to accomplish their task, trade unions ought never to be attached to a political association or place themselves under its tutelage; to do so would be to deal themselves a mortal blow. Trade unions are the schools of socialism. It is in trade unions that workers educate themselves and become socialists because under their eyes and every day the struggle with capital is taking place. Any political party, whatever its nature and without exception, can only hold the enthusiasm of the masses for a short time, momentarily; unions, on the other hand, lay hold on the masses in a more enduring way; they alone are capable of representing a true working-class party and opposing a bulwark to the power of capital.[14]

For Lenin, too, trade unions were 'a school of Communism' and 'a school in the art of managing socialist industry'. They were to express the 'lawful and practicable demands of the masses' and to 'protect the interests of the masses of the working people'.[15] As early as 1907, however, he condemned the idea of neutrality of trade unions and concluded that 'we must work persistently in the trade unions for the purpose of drawing them nearer to the Social-Democratic Party'.[16] By 1921 he stressed even more strongly the subordinate role of trade unions in relation to the party: 'We must combat the syndicalist deviation which will kill the party if it is not completely cured of it', for it 'leads to the fall of the dictatorship of the proletariat'.[17] Not only that: 'If the trade unions, nine-tenths of whose members are non-party workers, appoint the managers of industry, what is the use of

the party?' By this time trade unions were sometimes equated with
realisation of the concepts of workers' control and industrial democracy. Lenin rejected the latter term, put forward by Bukharin, which
he labelled 'a verbal twist', 'a tricky phrase', 'confusing'. For 'Industry is always necessary. Democracy is not always necessary. The term
"industrial democracy" gives rise to a number of utterly false ideas.'
For example 'It might be understood to repudiate dictatorship and
individual [one-person] management.'[18]

At the XI Congress in 1922 Lenin added: 'It is absolutely essential
that all authority in the factories should be concentrated in the hands
of management ... Under these circumstances any direct intervention by the trade unions in the management of enterprises must be
regarded as positively harmful and impermissible.'[19] Instead 'We
must see to it that every member of the trade unions, without
exception, should be interested in production and that he should
remember that only by increasing production and by increasing the
productivity of labour will Soviet Russia be able to succeed.'[20]

The immanent contradiction between the Marxian and Leninist
conceptions of trade unions is evident from this brief survey. In
Poland the operative ideology of the state between 1956 and 1983 was
based on the latter approach and, as is all too obvious, came under
repeated fire from the working class. The purpose of establishing
workers' councils in 1956 was to return to the original Marxian idea of
an independent workers' organisation. But despite initial vacillations
on the part of the leadership, its operative ideology on 'workers'
self-management committees', as they became known in 1958,
reflected the same attitude as to the entrenched trade union movement: they were to be subordinated to the influence of the party.
Co-management and participatory values were replaced by the
'school of socialism' idea. In the 1960s a further function assigned by
Lenin to trade unions was imposed by operative ideology on self-
management: the need to raise productivity. This 'trade-unionising'
of self-management was most clearly exemplified by the oscillations
in operative ideology as to which of these organisations should rank
more highly: after token attention had been given to self-management
committees, by the mid 1960s trade unions re-emerged as the
workers' organisations most highly esteemed by the political leadership. Economic responsibilities (conditions of work, technological
progress and productivity) were considered to be the primary *raison
d'être* of both institutions, although social control functions were also

cited. By 1967 the concept of self-management was broadened in such a way that any mass organisation which included workers was subsumed under it. Following the workers' apparent neutrality during the March 1968 disturbances, self-management became a modish concept once again. But at no point was management's control over the means of production challenged; in this respect, therefore, operative ideology was in line with Leninist norms.

In the years immediately following Gierek's assumption of power, official discourse rarely touched on the idea of industrial democracy. Instead economic carrots were dangled before the working class, whilst one-person management was introduced and industry reorganised. Productivity and living standards were the questions with which trade unions and self-management committees (on the rare occasions they were mentioned) had to be concerned. In the second half of the 1970s, however, quite the opposite tendency arose: self-management was ideologically rehabilitated and, along with it, the concepts of joint decision-making and co-responsibility. The 1976 industrial strife had been the trigger releasing this long-suppressed concept, and from then until the end of Gierek's rule operative ideology continued to underscore the important part to be played by workers' self-management in the political system.

Faced with the massive workers' protests of 1980, Polish rulers had little choice but to agree to independent self-governing trade unions and authentic workers' self-management. The Marxian conception was adopted unwillingly, however, and led finally to martial law which provided the leadership with the means necessary to claw back most of the concessions given to workers. Whilst lip-service continued to be paid to the independence of trade unions, this was a patronising and meaningless act. The Leninist version of industrial democracy was effectively reinstated.

Apart from the sixteen months of Solidarity's existence, therefore, when the socialist renewal programme foresaw relative autonomy of workers' institutions, the rulers' approach to industrial democracy was consistent with Leninist thought. The need for a specific worker-controlled organisation to aggregate their demands and protect their interests, such as that called for by Marx, was not represented in the dominant ideology of this twenty-seven-year period. Instead the dogmatic line taken by Lenin in his polemics against syndicalist critics was appropriated by the leadership to rationalise party hegemony over the working class. It is this line which can lead to an un-Marxist degenerate workers' state.

3. The church

One of Marx's most frequently cited statements is that 'Religion is the sigh of the oppressed creature ... it is the opium of the people.'[21] In the *Communist manifesto* he warned of the threat to socialist doctrine posed by religion: 'Nothing is easier than to give Christian asceticism a socialist tinge. Has not Christianity declaimed against private property, against marriage, against the state? ... Christian Socialism is but the holy water with which the priest consecrates the heart-burnings of the aristocrat.'[22]

It was again left to Lenin to furnish a more precise and practical conception: 'The complete separation of the church from the state – that is the demand which the Socialist proletariat makes of the modern state and the modern church.' Religion was to be a private affair, and 'No distinction whatever between citizens, as regards their rights, depending upon their religious beliefs can be tolerated.' Initially Lenin argued:

we must not under any circumstances fall into the abstract and idealist error of arguing the religious question from the standpoint of 'reason' apart from the class struggle ... That is why we do not and must not proclaim our atheism in our programme; that is why we do not and must not forbid proletarians who still cherish certain relics of the old superstitions to approach our party. We should always preach a scientific outlook, it is essential for us to combat the inconsistency of 'Christians'; but this does not mean that the religious question must be given a prominence which it does not deserve, that we must consent to a division of the forces of the truly revolutionary economic and political struggle for the sake of unimportant opinions or ravings which are rapidly losing all political significance and are being rapidly cast on the scrap heap by the very course of economic development.[23]

Four years later, however, in 1909, Lenin clarified this outlook: 'The Party of the proletariat demands that the state should declare religion a private matter, but does not regard the fight against religious superstition, etc., as a "private matter".' At the same time 'A Marxist must be able to take cognisance of the concrete situation as a whole' and 'puts the fight against religion not abstractly, not on the basis of abstract, purely theoretical, unvarying propaganda, but concretely, on the basis of the class struggle which is going on in practice'.[24]

The operative ideology of the political leadership on church–state relations between 1956 and 1983 was very consistent with these Leninist guidelines. Under Gomułka the doctrine of separation of church and state was regularly proclaimed, whilst at the same time there was commitment to the inculcation of a materialist social consciousness in society. If there was more militancy in this operative ideology up to the late 1960s, in this way more closely resembling Lenin's 1909 principle, then under Gierek the view was taken that there was really no need to create conflict for the sake of this relatively insignificant issue. Consequently, first of all progressive Catholic social groupings, then all Catholic believers, and finally the church establishment itself (which under Gomułka was sometimes labelled 'reactionary') were encouraged to support the party in its socialist construction programme. During the Solidarity period the leadership even managed ideologically to reconcile religiosity with membership in the party and later, in spite of the rigours of martial law and the countervailing pressure of party dogmatists, the official attitude to the church remained grounded in an unofficial concordat, cemented by the 1983 Woytyła–Jaruzelski meetings.

Polish rulers could defend their gradual collaboration with the church by recalling Lenin's admonition not to allow religion to divide progressive forces. It may be asked, however, whether he had actually envisaged as much accommodation for the church as was given in the late 1970s and early 1980s in Poland, and whether the feeble attempts made and meagre successes recorded in moulding a materialist outlook on the world – after nearly forty years of socialism – reflected a wavering commitment to the philosophy of historical materialism. On this question serious doubts arise as to how Marxist–Leninist Polish rulers really were. The inability to inculcate a socialist world outlook in social consciousness contributed to estrangement of the regime. The necessity of compromising continually with the church demonstrated how desperately rulers sought to gain legitimacy. The neutralisation of a Marxist–Leninist operative ideology on the religious issue underscored the strength of traditional Polish values within the population.

4. Science and culture

Initially Marx was very sceptical about the role of science in society. 'Science', he wrote, 'appears, in the machine, as something alien and exterior to workers.' But once 'the mainstay of production and wealth is neither the immediate labour performed by the worker, nor the time that he works – but the appropriation of his general productive force, his understanding of nature and the mystery of it as a special force', then science and technology would afford opportunites for the universal development of the individual.[25] With regard to culture Marx contended that in a future Communist society 'there disappears the subordination of the artist to local and national narrowness, which arises entirely from division of labour ... In a communist society there are no painters but at most people who engage in painting among other activities.'[26]

Lenin's analysis of scientific thought was also firmly grounded on class struggle: 'To expect science to be impartial in a wage-slave society is as silly and naive as to expect impartiality from manufacturers on the question whether workers' wages should be increased by decreasing the profits of capital.'[27] Lenin also considered the specific status of the social sciences: 'there can be no "impartial" social science in a society based on class struggle'.[28] Moreover, 'as long as no other attempt is made to give a scientific explanation of the functioning and development of any social formation ... until then the materialist conception of history will be synonymous with social science. Materialism is not "primarily a scientific conception of history" ... but the only scientific conception of history.'[29]

As for the scientific and cultural achievements of capitalism, Lenin advocated that socialist societies should 'take all that is valuable from capitalism, take all its science and culture'. For 'The task is to bring the victorious proletarian revolution together with bourgeois culture, bourgeois science and technology, which have so far been the attainment of few.' He believed that it was misleading to speak of a national culture – 'Only the clericals and the bourgeoisie can speak of national culture in general' – for it constituted an element in the superstructure of class relationships and had little to do with nations.[30] As for the question of party influence on cultural activity, Lenin put forward his views in his considerations on literature:

it cannot, in fact, be an individual undertaking, independent of the common cause of the proletariat. Down with non-partisan writers! Down with literary supermen! Literature must become part of the common cause of the proletariat, 'a cog and a screw' of one single great Social Democratic mechanism set in motion by the entire politically conscious vanguard of the entire working class. Literature must become a component of organised, planned and integrated Social Democratic party work.[31]

It is important to note Stalin's contribution to the Marxist analysis of culture. By asserting that language did not form part of the superstructure of a given society, he implicitly recognised the autonomous existence of certain national cultural features, ones which transcended the Marxist scheme of historical development.[32]

In our study of operative ideology on science and culture, we observed how the autonomous development of these fields of activity was progressively encouraged by the political leadership. In the late 1950s 'Marxist positions' were still to determine the nature of scientific and cultural output, but apart from such political limitations, no professional interference was to occur. In the 1960s and 1970s science was viewed almost exclusively in utilitarian terms, and its relationship to economic progress was stressed. In a similar way the social sciences were expected to contribute usefully to the spheres of social development and theoretical advancement. Whereas the autonomy of the pure sciences was constrained primarily by the targets set out in the economic plans, the independence of the social sciences was curtailed by class considerations and ideological factors. In contrast, operative ideology on cultural activity gradually shed all restrictions, utilitarian or political. Whilst the nihilist and existentialist currents of the early 1960s were condemned and uncritical imitation of Western art forms discouraged, the rulers propagated in their stead a conception of progressive art which was imbued with humanist values. Under Gierek this overall operative ideology on science and culture was extended: science was to play an instrumental, economic role, the social sciences an ideological one, whilst culture was to disseminate high artistic values and humanist ideals, thereby contributing to socialisation work. In the Solidarity period Polish rulers were compelled to reject both ideological and instrumental approaches to science and culture. So long as the intelligentsia did not use them to purvey anti-socialist views, the two fields 'knew no borders'. Even under martial law the autonomy of science and culture was stressed. More than that: the un-Leninist conceptions of national culture and dialogue between socialist and capitalist cultures were propagated in an attempt to win over the intelligentsia to the new post-Solidarity order.

The Marxian conception of science as a means to human emancipation was reflected only indirectly in an operative ideology stressing its use value for economic growth. The Leninist emphasis on a materialist philosophy and methodology governing the social sciences was manifested in operative ideology underlining ideological commitment of social scientists. The integral autonomy of cultural activity, put forward by operative ideology, especially under Gierek, was based more on the Stalin model of cultural existence outside the superstructure. Leninist norms concerning party literature and culture were, by and large, not vigorously promulgated. In all cases there were no discontinuities in the evolution of operative ideology: progressive freeing of science (though not social science) and culture from political constraints characterised this evolution from the Stalin period through to martial law.

5. *Political values and society*

Our survey of official discourse identified the most important political values that operative ideology disseminated between 1956 and 1983. Some were continuously stressed throughout this period whilst others emerged together with new social conditions. One value which underwent ideological modifications concerned the relationship between general or national interests and particularist or individual ones. According to Lenin: 'If the political power in the state is in the hands of a class the interests of which coincide with the interests of the majority, the administration of that state in accordance with the will of the majority will be possible.'[33] Up to 1970 the leadership believed that state interests should take precedence over group ones because they reflected the will of the majority more accurately. Under Gierek an atomistic view was adopted: individual interests were the more important because their aggregate constituted the majority will. Under Solidarity group interests were stressed by the authorities, and under martial law national and international interests were given absolute primacy. The 'stop–go' orientation of operative ideology on this subject contributed to the public's lack of faith in Polish rulers.

In the late 1950s and early 1980s much attention was given to the question of socialist legality. In each case it contained two stages: the state would respect a new order that had been created (October 1956, August 1980), then the public was exhorted to observe the provisions of the law (1957, 1982). Lenin had made clear that 'the use of violence arises from the need to crush the exploiters, the landowners and capitalists. When this is accomplished we shall renounce all extra-ordinary measures.' Presumably this was the rationale for Gomułka's anti-revisionism campaign and Jaruzelski's martial law. But Lenin had also argued that once conditions were established which pre-cluded 'the subjection of one man to another, and of one section of the population to another . . . people will become accustomed to observ-ing the elementary conditions of social life without force and without subordination'.[34] It appears that People's Poland had not yet created such conditions by 1983.

The most discernible prescriptive societal values were, in the 1960s, the economic utility of all activity, and, in the 1970s, material incentives and income differentiation. These latter were consistent with Leninist thought, as represented by the statements that 'every important branch of the economy must be built on the principle of personal incentive' and that the bonus system 'should become one of the most powerful means of stimulating competition'.[35] Marx's con-siderations also lent support to an ideology of differentiated wages: because of 'unequal individual endowment and thus productive capacity . . . one will in fact receive more than another . . . These defects are inevitable in the first phase of communist society.'[36]

In the early 1970s the fundamental unity of economic, social and ideological activity – representing an inaccurate interpretation of Marx's base–superstructure model – was promulgated so as to overcome the one-sided economism found in operative ideology under Gomułka. Similarly a set of socialist ethical principles (economic egalitarianism, social justice, socialist life-styles) was propagated in the late 1970s and early 1980s in order to try to overcome the socio-economic pyramid which had previously arisen. A basis for this was Marx's view of the unity of ethics and economics, put forward in his *1844 Manuscripts* and in *Grundrisse*.

Societal values promulgated between 1956 and 1983 did not change in any significant way. Traditional socialist values such as work, responsibility, discipline, collectivist outlooks, professional qualifications and respect for socialised property were stressed as much in 1983 as in 1959. Under Gierek patriotism and family values did become more important than earlier, and by the late 1970s the all-round development of the individual was a key prescriptive value. Under martial law the centrality of class consciousness made an ideological come-back: class consciousness was a criterion which was now to determine entry into the party, economic promotion and even eligibility for welfare benefits. How seriously the leadership took this quality remains to be seen. What becomes clear is the constant repetition by Polish rulers of the need to inculcate basic socialist values. No better proof of the failure of political socialisation is available.

From this comparison of Marxist–Leninist fundamental principles with the operative ideology of the Polish leadership between 1956 and 1983, we see that both consonance and dissonance occur. In the more macro-political issue-areas (the status of the party and of industrial democracy), operative ideology had a particularly marked affinity to Leninist norms. On the more parapolitical questions (the role of the church, science, culture, political socialisation) there was often less 'fit' between Marxism–Leninism and Polish rulers' concepts. Given the country's post-war history this pattern is not unexpected: commitment to fundamental principles in the first sphere has permitted the regime to survive (with considerable moral and other support from its eastern neighbour); deviations in the second sphere have ensured that the leadership is regularly faced with crises.

Are Polish rulers, then, Marxists–Leninists? Because of the hybrid operative ideology they have adopted, we cannot give a direct answer to this question. We can gain some insight from a recent study carried out by David Lane on Soviet applications of Leninism. He suggests that Marxism–Leninism as the application and development of Marx's and Lenin's theories has been superseded by a new legitimating value system which he describes as 'Soviet Marxism–Leninism'. It results when 'the conditioning roles of sub-systems "feed back" on the legitimating value system of Marxism–Leninism and modify it', a process that Weber termed 'elective affinity'. Lane concludes: 'The "logic of development" under socialism may be limited by the structural constraints ... but it does not follow from this that there is no choice, that there is only one correct policy for all countries.'[37]

We can suggest, in turn, that a legitimating ideology called 'Leninist Marxism of People's Poland' has emerged since the establishment of state socialism in the country in 1944. Whilst based primarily on Marx's, and especially Lenin's, thought, it has, through the process of elective affinity, added concepts of its own. Thus such traditional socialist principles as democratic centralism, the leading role of the party, socialist democracy and 'school-of-socialism' trade unions exist alongside such operative concepts as the church–state concordat, the autonomy of cultural and scientific activities and the inviolability of private ownership of land. The dominant prescriptive value system is made up of an amalgam of socialist (work, responsibility, discipline), corporatist (the fatherland), Christian (the family) and 'conjunctural' or opportunist values (consumerism). The fierce individualism that is found in the traditional Polish national character is also at least partially accommodated in this amalgam: for example, the relatively tolerant attitude to dissent is consistent with a history of individual free thought in the country. To be sure, Leninist Marxism of People's Poland need not be viewed as a eufunctional development. For whilst more than one form of Marxism–Leninism is indeed possible for a given socialist country, the question is whether Polish Leninist Marxism has been the correct choice for Poland.

OPERATIVE IDEOLOGY AND SOCIAL REALITY

Our survey of official discourse on various problem-areas which, when systematised, gives rise to an operative ideology, revealed a number of seeming ironies and paradoxes in the values that political leaders attempted to propagate in society. A question that some critics would have posed at all critical junctures in the socialist development of the country was: how could rulers speak publicly of the importance of a particular value whilst quite its opposite was dominant in society? How could they talk of workers' councils whilst their powers were gradually being eroded, of the need for good work whilst not offering rewards to those who practised it, of the party members' responsibilities and obligations whilst providing them with special opportunities and privileges, of the necessity of reducing economic inequalities, social injustices and Western-style consumerism whilst allowing a new middle class to prosper and flaunt its wealth? Dissonance between prescriptive values propagated, policy courses pursued and, most importantly, policy consequences resulting was striking for the entire twenty-seven-year period we examined, but probably never more so than in the last years of Gierek's rule. It is as if Poland had two completely separate histories between 1956 and 1983: that described in the discursive statements and reports of political leaders, and that which the population actually lived and experienced. Familiarity solely with one of these histories represents as partial and incomplete an image of Polish socialism as the distortion of reality that was propagated in official discourse.

To much of the population this deformed view of reality constituted as integral a part of the socialist idea as the Hobbesian life situation it encountered. Material hardship and ideological platitudes went hand in hand and, in popular belief, were indispensable to each other. Yet drawing this equation represented the greatest myth of all, the 'myth of socialism', as it could be called. This myth assumed that the dominant productive relations in Polish society in this period and the functioning of the political and ideological institutions which these relations helped determine were an 'ideal-typical' depiction of socialism. Real existing socialism became synonymous with the socialist ideal. Hostility to the state's operative ideology and to the realities of life began to extend to socialism itself.

In this way societal attitudes contributed to the failure of the socialist system in Poland. The interrelationship between public orientations and the fate of socialism was cogently described by Robert Lane:

Marx was quite right: it is a mistake to press socialist institutions upon a society that is not ready for them, but the 'readiness' consists of the personological qualities required to work a democratic socialist system and to protect it from degeneration into poverty, stasis, or the abuse of power.

In contrast to the Marxist–Leninist thesis that collectivist values had to be inculcated throughout society, however, Lane argued the opposite case:

Of all the qualities which seemed most central to the prosperity of the socialist cause, something close to individualism is the most important: the individual's belief that outcomes are contingent upon his own acts, his autonomy from collective pressure and authoritative command, his capacity for independent moral reasoning, his belief in himself and his own powers. Only such 'individualised individuals', generated by complex and nurturant institutions, can work a collectivist system. Further it is affluence and security, not scarcity and threat, which create the possibility of generating such qualities. There may be other roads to socialism ... but they will not be democratic socialisms unless these societies first create the conditions of autonomy, and then the autonomous persons themselves.[38]

It is common currency to perceive Polish political culture as replete with individualist and even anarchist values. The *liberum veto*, elective monarchy, the insurrectionary tradition and political romanticism have formed integral parts of the nation's historic consciousness which, some believe, demonstrate the Poles' fundamental dislike of authority. If this were indeed the case, Poland ought to have been propitious ground for democratic socialism, to follow Lane's argument. It is true that Poland's socialism is more democratic than that of its neighbours. Undoubtedly the nation's political culture played no small part in achieving this modicum of democracy. The fact that it is not more democratic can also be linked to the traditional value system and orientations of the Poles. Empirical data on contemporary Polish attitudes suggest a tendency to value strong government and obedience as well as individual freedom. One study concludes: 'The popular stereotype of the Pole, therefore, as a defender of individualism and liberty needs to be modified. He may well value liberty more than most other qualities, but he may also be attracted to strong government which he regards as security after Poland's experience under the partitions.'[39]

Since 1944 strong government and geopolitical security have been embodied in the Communist regime. As much as the regime is disliked, Poles recognise its limited usefulness and only challenge it when 'strong government' is transformed into absolutism and autocracy, as has happened at regular intervals in post-war history. But Poles never had the affluence or the political self-confidence, nor did they fully become 'individualised individuals', to assure the implementation of democratic socialism. The Solidarity experience marked a caesura in this regard: the social movement cultivated such personological values and was able to establish a provisional form of democratic socialism. But without the requisite affluence, and with a regime which suddenly feigned weakness, thereby bringing into question geopolitical security, Solidarity lacked the conditions needed to consolidate this system. Regular demonstrations in 1982–3 in support of Solidarity show the durability of values and attitudes developed in the sixteen months of the movement's existence.

The antinomy between Polish rulers' ideology and social reality has been described by several prominent Polish social scientists and philosophers living both abroad and in the country. Let us look at some of their views. For Kołakowski the reification of ideology began shortly after the Polish October: 'By pointing out the grotesque contrast between Marxist–Leninist phraseology and the realities of life, the revisionists laid bare the contradictions of the doctrine itself. The ideology became detached, as it were, from the political movement of which it had become a mere façade, and began to live a life of its own.' As a result, at the theoretical level: 'There is probably no part of the civilised world in which Marxism has declined so completely and socialist ideas have become so discredited and turned to ridicule as in the countries of victorious socialism.' In terms of practical effects: 'At present Marxism neither interprets the world nor changes it: it is merely a repertoire of slogans serving to organise various interests, most of them completely remote from those with which Marxism originally identified itself.'[40]

A similar argument was advanced by Bauman: 'This contradiction between the utopian thrust and the recalcitrant "actuality" institutionalising and effectively protecting the former *telos* should be seen as the most embarrassing antinomy of all those which have haunted modern socialism up to the present time.' Thought becomes disarmed in the face of reality and the two become mutually impenetrable. Consequently 'Unless a "third force" is used (e.g., political power) critical thought and the criticised reality will perhaps coexist, with time remaining on the side of reality, as the "hard" partner in the game.'[41]

The interaction between ideology and reality was treated in a more complex manner by Staniszkis. For her the Polish political system

is a system legitimated by mostly a lack of alternatives, where so-called 'ideological' legitimating arguments are most often traps for the ruling group itself, limiting its freedom of manoeuvre, rather than a catalyst for social involvement. The situation described above is the result of the abandonment of a utopian ideal, even for party functionaries themselves. This ideal persists only as a magic system, with symbols used as the instruments of inter-organisational games and the levers of particular interests ... Caught in the trap of its own myths and rationalisations of previous activity, the ruling group is now easily blackmailed by those at executive levels. The latter play the leading role and use the myths and rationalisations to support their own interests, exploiting the lack of content of these 'conjurations'.

The result is 'the self-reproduction of artificial reality in society', that is, all types of institutional concepts and political programmes can be introduced and eventually may become objectivised and even reified. Whenever the ruling group tries to escape from ensnarement in its own legitimacy arguments by refusing to identify itself publicly with its own more pragmatic and liberal actions, society fails to respond. This peculiar association between 'artificial' and 'real' reality leads to a form of society with ritualised, reactive, jerky regulation and a mode of learning by cyclical but more ritualised crisis situations. According to Staniszkis, planning and ritualising crises, in part through ideological recourse, stabilises the current political order and temporarily reduces the level of social tension.[42]

A high-ranking East European official writing under a pseudonym has also examined the dialectic between ideology and reality. For Casals ideology dissolves when confronted with the reality of so-called premature socialism. Actions of rulers are not subordinated to the end; rather the end becomes subordinated to actions. Accordingly, 'the end is no longer the subject of transformation, but its object. Instead, now, of inspiring the conversion of the possible into the actual, it inspires its own involution: from strategic opposition to a pragmatic submission to necessity.' According to Casals, ideology is not threatened with reification so much as with transformation into actuality, into materialism.[43] In the process it loses its autonomous force.

This brief survey of the way in which scholars view the interrelationship between ideology and social reality suggests elements both of disparity and of congruence. The ideals set forth in socialist ideology were a sterile but indispensable ritualisation for Kołakowski, a utopian thrust against recalcitrant actuality for Bauman, a trap and a magic system for Staniszkis, and a reproduction of the actual for Casals. Thus Marxism–Leninism could be reified, yet it could just as easily become materialised. The point on which all scholars agree is the dissolution of the force that ideology possesses under state socialism. Social reality indeed emerges as the harder partner in the game and either turns Marxism–Leninism into 'mummified remains' (in Kołakowski's words) or overwhelms and eventually absorbs it. The power that Habermas assigned to his technocratic ideology, that Althusser thought he located in the ideological state apparatus, and that Gouldner believed could be exerted by ideological discourse was found lacking by these critics. Instead the concept put forward by Therborn of ideological drift, under which ideology resembles 'sandbanks, still there though not in the same place or shape', seems most apposite in depicting ideology under state socialism.

This is not to say that ideology plays no useful function in this system. Its ceremonial quality serves to identify the rulers' team colours. It acts as a set of signals outlining the practical dos and don'ts of the state. It highlights the regime's successes and even failures. It does help explain and justify policy and may create an 'artificial reality' which becomes a half-way house between an unattainable socialist utopia and a grim and stark present-day reality. It can also serve as an exclusive code for the ruling group, pre-empting the emergence of an autonomous political language amongst outsiders.

Nonetheless these functions are a long way from the role which Marx and Lenin ascribed to the ideology of historical materialism: it was not only to undertake scientific analysis of historical development but also to constitute an independent factor playing a part in historical development. At both fundamental and functional levels, the ideology of Polish rulers has proved a failure in three respects: (1) it has contributed to the spread of the myth of socialism; (2) it has been increasingly divorced from social reality; and (3) it has not fulfilled the historic goal expected of it.

Ideological developments in Poland in the first part of 1983 – following first the suspension and then abolition of martial law – have only substantiated these points. The Polish socialism that Jaruzelski invokes has become associated in the public mind with the militarisation of political, social and economic life, even after the Military Council (WRON) and the army commissars officially returned to barracks. Accordingly the use of military means is now commonly identified as an additional trait of the socialist system and has further fed the myth of socialism. Key ideological declarations, above all the additions made to the constitution in July 1983, have remained at odds with social reality. The elevation to constitutional status of the Patriotic Front of National Rebirth (PRON) – the catch-all institution supposedly set up spontaneously during martial law by supporters of the idea of a National Unity Front – has been widely interpreted as confirmation of the façade democracy which the present leadership wishes to construct. The new pronouncement that the Polish People's Republic embodies the aspirations of the working class and broadens its participation in the state is seen as singularly cynical in the light of the political ostracisation of even the most moderate elements in Solidarity. The constitutional guarantee that farmland can be privately owned has not allayed the fears of the Polish peasant who has experienced the application of other forms of pressure in the past. Only the incorporation into the constitution of the right of the Council of State to declare martial law has narrowed the gap between operative ideology and reality: it makes clear that the Council of State did not possess such constitutional power in December 1981.

Ideological developments in the second half of 1983 have demonstrated how the Jaruzelski leadership, despite its unprecedented military dimension, has continued to pursue an ideological line consistent with that of previous administrations. In the first place operative ideology remains chiefly a *post facto* reaction to political circumstances rather than an explanatory programme charting out the country's historical course. The failure of the XII Plenum, held in May, to adopt a final version of the PUWP's document 'What we are fighting for, where we are heading' reflected both the party's unwillingness to take an ideological stand before the papal visit and its deep internal divisions. It considered the findings of the commission investigating the sources of post-war Polish crises but did not publicise them, underscoring again the leadership's equivocalness on major ideological questions. The fact that between October 1982 and October 1983 the rulers called only this one Plenum (if we exclude the unprecedented joint Plenum held with the Peasants' Party in January) further suggests a desire to avoid making ideological decisions. During this period no ideological assistance was lent by the Soviet Union either. For example, at the June conference on ideology held by the CPSU and attended by East European ideologues, neither Andropov nor Chernenko could advance a more profound explanation for the Polish crisis than political backsliding by past PUWP rulers along with Western interference.

In the second place the Jaruzelski operative ideology is very much 'Polish Leninist Marxist' in content. At the XIII Plenum, convened in October, a number of concepts were portrayed as novel when in reality they have constituted the core of the state's ideology since at least 1956. These included the hegemonic role of the party in society, openness of political life, a new style of governing, close consultations with society, the need to combat the twin dangers facing the party of dogmatism and revisionism, the importance of countering the influence of the class enemy (who was found both internally and internationally), and observance of the principle 'from each according to his capabilities, to each according to his work'. Incongruence between base and superstructure was again invoked: the Politburo report to the Plenum spoke of an increasing discrepancy between ideological values and practical solutions in the spheres of politics and economics, whilst Jaruzelski deduced from Marxism that 'Being determines consciousness but without appropriate consciousness it is difficult to determine being.' Only in one respect did this Plenum depart from the established tradition of Polish Leninist Marxism: a strong attack was launched on the alleged growing 'clericalisation' of society and on the 'abuse of pastoral robes or places of religious worship for political activities incompatible with the interests of People's Poland'. It can be argued, of course, that the state–church *entente* has always been the most tenuous component of Polish rulers' operative ideology.

Perhaps the greatest dilemma that has confronted ideology in

Poland during the past forty years has been the legitimacy of the revolution which brought socialism to the country. At the October 1983 Plenum the party's ideological secretary acknowledged this when he stressed: 'The socialist revolution in Poland was born of the national soil.' Views suggesting that the country had been objectively and subjectively immature for revolution and socialism, that the revolution had been imposed, and that the kind of socialism introduced had not been Polish, were refuted by Orzechowski.[44] The fact is that since 1944 the ideology of Polish rulers has been singularly unsuccessful in convincing the public that such views are indeed inaccurate.

The conclusion is, therefore, that the Polish leadership has not come far down the ideological road since it was catapulted into power forty years ago. The stop-gap measures taken at the level of operative ideology do have a logic and adaptive capacity of their own, but they cannot *ipso facto* produce durable results. The waywardness in, and just as often neglect of, ideological matters by the PUWP since 1956 has been a major factor contributing to popular discontent with the socialist system. Leninist Marxism of People's Poland is largely a makeshift and shaky construct. Post-war Polish history can be characterised, therefore, as a protracted and profound ideological crisis interwoven with the cyclical occurrence of political crises. Without definitive resolution of the former, the latter are bound to recur.

Appendix

Central Committee Plenum meetings, Party Congresses and National Party Conferences, 1956–83

Date	Meeting	Main subject(s)
March 1956	VI Plenum	election of new first secretary: Ochab
July 1956	VII Plenum	current political and economic situation
October 1956	VIII Plenum	election of new first secretary: Gomułka
May 1957	IX Plenum	key policy issues of the party
October 1957	X Plenum	situation in the party and in society
February 1958	XI Plenum	economic policy for 1958
October 1958	XII Plenum	guidelines for the 1959–65 development plan
March 1959	III Congress	Central Committee report; Central Committee elections; development plan for 1959–65; changes in party statutes
March 1959	I Plenum	elections to Politburo and Secretariat
June 1959	II Plenum	agricultural development 1959–65
October 1959	III Plenum	current economic situation
January 1960	IV Plenum	technological development
June 1960	V Plenum	investment plans 1961–5
September 1960	VI Plenum	current agricultural situation
January 1961	VII Plenum	reform of educational system
June 1961	VIII Plenum	local government
November 1961	IX Plenum	economic policy for 1962
April 1962	X Plenum	machine industry
December 1962	XI Plenum	science and higher education
February 1963	XII Plenum	agricultural investment and production

Date	Meeting	Main subject(s)
July 1963	XIII Plenum	ideological problems of the party
November 1963	XIV Plenum	economic policy for 1964
March 1964	XV Plenum	guidelines for the IV Congress
June 1964	IV Congress	Central Committee report; Central Committee elections; development plan for 1966–70; changes in party statutes
June 1964	I Plenum	elections to Politburo and Secretariat
November 1964	II Plenum	methods of planning and use of production reserves
March 1965	III Plenum	national and local elections
July 1965	IV Plenum	changes in planning and management for 1966–70
December 1965	V Plenum	foreign trade
April 1966	VI Plenum	investment rationalisation for 1966–70
October 1966	VII Plenum	management and work organisation in industry
May 1967	VIII Plenum	political tasks facing the party
September 1967	IX Plenum	agricultural development 1967–70
November 1967	X Plenum	supply of food and consumer goods
February 1968	XI Plenum	foreign trade
July 1968	XII Plenum	guidelines for the V Congress
November 1968	XIII Plenum	organisational matters
November 1968	V Congress	Central Committee report; Central Committee elections; development of socialist Poland; changes in party statutes
November 1968	I Plenum	elections to Politburo and Secretariat
April 1969	II Plenum	investment and development plan for 1971–5
June 1969	III Plenum	report on International Conference of Communist Parties in Moscow
November 1969	IV Plenum	science, technology and the economy
May 1970	V Plenum	material incentives in the state economy
December 1970	VI Plenum	current economic situation
December 1970	VII Plenum	election of new first secretary: Gierek

Date	Meeting	Main subject(s)
February 1971	VIII Plenum	assessment of the December events
April 1971	IX Plenum	reports of the Politburo and Secretariat
June 1971	X Plenum	socio-economic development 1971–5
September 1971	XI Plenum	guidelines for the VI Congress
November 1971	XII Plenum	report for the period between the V and VI Congresses
December 1971	VI Congress	Central Committee report; Central Committee elections; economic plan for 1971–5
December 1971	I Plenum	elections to Politburo and Secretariat
December 1971	II Plenum	economic policy for 1972
February 1972	III Plenum	national elections
March 1972	IV Plenum	economic plan for 1972–5
May 1972	V Plenum	housing programme; foreign policy
September 1972	VI Plenum	reorganisation of local government
November 1972	VII Plenum	youth
February 1973	VIII Plenum	utilisation of raw materials
June 1973	IX Plenum	the role of the party, state and trade unions; foreign policy
October 1973	X Plenum	socio-economic development in 1971–3
October 1973	I National Party Conference	socio-economic development for 1974–5; role of local government
October 1973	XI Plenum	adoption of National Party Conference proposals
January 1974	XII Plenum	salaries and conditions of work
February 1974	XIII Plenum	ideological and socialisation tasks
June 1974	XIV Plenum	current socio-economic situation
October 1974	XV Plenum	agricultural development and food supplies
January 1975	XVI Plenum	ideological, political and organisational strengthening of the party
May 1975	XVII Plenum	local government; foreign policy
September 1975	XVIII Plenum	guidelines for the VII Congress
November 1975	XIX Plenum	report for the period between the VI and VII Congresses
December 1975	VII Congress	Central Committee report; Central Committee elections;

Date	Meeting	Main subject(s)
		socio-economic plan for 1976–80; changes in party statutes
December 1975	I Plenum	elections to Politburo and Secretariat
January 1976	II Plenum	utilisation of material reserves
February 1976	III Plenum	the role of the party
September 1976	IV Plenum	agricultural development
December 1976	V Plenum	economic efficiency
January 1977	VI Plenum	agricultural development
April 1977	VII Plenum	the party and political socialisation
June 1977	VIII Plenum	housing programme
October 1977	IX Plenum	economic efficiency
January 1978	II National Party Conference	living standards and quality of work; the party and political socialisation
January 1978	X Plenum	adoption of National Party Conference proposals
March 1978	XI Plenum	agricultural development and food supplies
June 1978	XII Plenum	science
December 1978	XIII Plenum	living standards and quality of work
April 1979	XIV Plenum	light industry
June 1979	XV Plenum	agricultural situation
October 1979	XVI Plenum	guidelines for the VIII Congress
January 1980	XVII Plenum	report for the period between the VII and VIII Congress
February 1980	VIII Congress	Central Committee report; Central Committee elections; socio-economic plan for 1981–5
February 1980	I Plenum	elections to Politburo and Secretariat
April 1980	II Plenum	national and local elections
June 1980	III Plenum	health care
August 1980	IV Plenum	current socio-political situation
August 1980	V Plenum	report on Gdańsk and Szczecin postulates
September 1980	VI Plenum	election of new first secretary: Kania
December 1980	VII Plenum	socialist renewal programme

Date	Meeting	Main subject(s)
February 1981	VIII Plenum	the role of trade unions
March 1981	IX Plenum	current socio-political situation
April 1981	X Plenum	guidelines for the IX Congress
June 1981	XI Plenum	current socio-political situation
July 1981	XII Plenum	election of delegates to IX Congress
July 1981	IX Congress	Central Committee report; Central Committee elections; socio-economic and political programme; changes in party statutes
July 1981	I Plenum	elections to Politburo and Secretariat
August 1981	II Plenum	current socio-political situation
September 1981	III Plenum	self-government and economic reform
October 1981	IV Plenum	election of new first secretary: Jaruzelski
October 1981	V Plenum	situation in the party
November 1981	VI Plenum	current socio-political situation; economic reform
February 1982	VII Plenum	the role of the party
April 1982	VIII Plenum	economic reform
July 1982	IX Plenum	youth
October 1982	X Plenum	socio-economic development for 1983–5
January 1983	XI Plenum	agriculture (joint Plenum with Peasants' Party)
May 1983	XII Plenum	ideology
October 1983	XIII Plenum	ideology
November 1983	XIV Plenum	current economic situation

Notes

The author wishes to express his gratitude to Joseph Placek, head of the Slavic division of the Hatcher Graduate Library, University of Michigan, for his assistance in completing these notes. Throughout the notes the theoretical journal of the Polish United Workers' Party, *Nowe Drogi*, is cited as *ND*.

1. THE CONCEPT OF IDEOLOGY AND WESTERN SOCIOLOGY

1 J. Larrain, *The concept of ideology* (London, Hutchinson, 1979), p. 46.
2 F. Engels, Introduction to K. Marx, 'The eighteenth Brumaire of Louis Bonaparte' in Marx and Engels, *Selected works* (Moscow, Progress, 1970), p. 95.
3 G. Gurvitch, *Le Concept des classes sociales de Marx à nos jours* (Paris, Centre de Documentation Universitaire, 1954), pp. 29–30.
4 M. Seliger, *The Marxist conception of ideology* (Cambridge Univ. Press, 1977), p. 26.
5 S. Kozyr-Kowalski and J. Ładosz, *Dialektyka a społeczeństwo*, 2nd edn (Warsaw, Państwowe Wydawn. Naukowe, 1974), p. 475.
6 Larrain, *The concept of ideology*, p. 65.
7 B. Parekh, *Marx's theory of ideology* (Baltimore, Johns Hopkins Univ. Press, 1982), pp. 3, 7, 14, 30.
8 A. Naess, J. A. Christophersen and K. Kvalø, *Democracy, ideology and objectivity* (Oslo Univ. Press, 1956).
9 J. J. Wiatr, *Czy zmierzch ery ideologii?* (Warsaw, Książka i Wiedza, 1968), p. 64.
10 V.I. Lenin, 'What is to be done?' in *Collected works*, 45 vols. (London, Lawrence and Wishart, 1960–6), vol. 5, pp. 390–1fn.
11 S. Rainko, *Świadomość i historia* (Warsaw, Czytelnik, 1978), p. 96.
12 R. Aron, *The opium of the intellectuals* (New York, Norton Co., 1962), pp. 305–24; D. Bell, *The end of ideology* (New York, Free Press of Glencoe, 1960).
13 W. Morawski, 'Marksizm a teorie postindustrialnego społeczeństwa' in W. Wesołowski (ed.), *Marksizm i procesy rozwoju społecznego* (Warsaw, Książka i Wiedza, 1979), p. 677.
14 A recent resurrection of the end-of-ideology thesis was offered by the West

German journalist Peter Bender, *Das Ende des ideologischen Zeitalters* (Berlin, Severin und Siedler, 1981).

15 J. Habermas, *Toward a rational society* (Boston, Beacon Press, 1971), pp. 102–4, 110–13.

16 Morawski, 'Marksizm a teorie postindustrialnego społeczeństwa', p. 655; idem, *Nowe społeczeństwo przemysłowe* (Warsaw, Państwowe Wydawn. Naukowe, 1975), pp. 295–8.

17 Larrain, *The concept of ideology*, p. 211.

18 D. Bell, 'Technocracy and politics', *Survey*, vol. 17, no. 1 (1971), pp. 222–4.

19 W. W. Kortunow, *Ideologia i polityka* (Warsaw, Państwowe Wydawn. Naukowe, 1976), pp. 236–7.

20 Habermas, *Toward a rational society*; D. Bell, *The coming of post-industrial society* (New York, Basic Books, 1973); Z. Brzezinski, *Between two ages* (New York, Viking Press, 1970); A. Toffler, *Future shock* (New York, Random House, 1970). For a dissenting view, see T. Roszak, *The making of a counter culture* (Garden City, NY, Anchor Books, 1969).

21 A. Sohn-Rethel, 'Science as alienated consciousness', *Radical Science Journal*, nos. 2–3 (1975), pp. 65–101.

22 R. Richta, *Cywilizacja na rozdrożu* (Warsaw, Książka i Wiedza, 1971), p. 304.

23 Larrain, *The concept of ideology*, p. 154.

24 L. Althusser, *Lenin and philosophy* (London, New Left Books, 1977), pp. 128, 151, 158, 172; idem, *For Marx* (London, Verso, 1979), pp. 231–6.

25 K. Marx and F. Engels, *The German ideology*, 2nd edn (Moscow, Progress, 1968), p. 37.

26 Larrain, *The concept of ideology*, p. 164.

27 G. Therborn, *The ideology of power and the power of ideology* (London, Verso, 1980), pp. vii, viii, 2, 40–3, 72, 79, 125.

28 A. W. Gouldner, *The dialectic of ideology and technology* (London, Macmillan, 1976), pp. 3, 9–10, 19, 29, 50.

29 M. Holubenko, 'The Soviet working class: discontent and opposition', *Critique*, no. 4 (spring 1975), p. 7.

30 J. Szacki, 'Wstęp' in *Czy kryzys socjologii?* (Warsaw, Czytelnik, 1977), pp. 27–8.

31 Gouldner, *The dialectic of ideology and technology*, pp. 246, 283.

2. APPROACHES TO THE STUDY OF IDEOLOGY IN A SOCIALIST STATE

1 Wiatr, *Czy zmierzch ery ideologii?* pp. 64–92. See also Kozyr-Kowalski and Ładosz, *Dialektyka a społeczeństwo*, pp. 472–86.

2 J. Hochfeld, *Studia o marksowskiej teorii społeczeństwa* (Warsaw, Państwowe Wydawn. Naukowe, 1963), pp. 100–1.

3 J. J. Wiatr, *Ideologia i życie społeczne* (Warsaw, Książka i Wiedza, 1965), p. 7; idem, *Przyczynek do zagadnienia rozwoju społecznego w formacji socjalistycznej* (Warsaw, Książka i Wiedza, 1979), p. 274.

4 K. Mannheim, *Ideology and Utopia* (New York, Harcourt, Brace and

World, 1955), pp. 49–50; *idem, Essays on the sociology of knowledge* (London, Routledge and Kegan Paul, 1968), p. 73.

5 R. E. Lane, *Political ideology* (New York, Free Press of Glencoe, 1962), pp. 415–16.

6 V. I. Lenin, 'Certain features of the historical development of Marxism', *Zvezda* (23 December 1910) in *Collected works*, vol. 17, p. 39.

7 F. Schurmann, *Ideology and organisation in Communist China*, 2nd edn (Berkeley, Univ. of California Press, 1968), pp. 23–7. For another study of Communist ideology in China, see J. C. Hsiung, *Ideology and practice* (New York, Praeger, 1972).

8 B. Moore, Jr, *Soviet politics: the dilemma of power* (New York, Harper Torchbooks, 1965), pp. 416–22.

9 V. Zaslavsky, 'Socioeconomic inequality and changes in Soviet ideology', *Theory and Society*, vol. 9, no. 2 (March 1980), pp. 395, 402.

10 G. Lichtheim, *Marxism: an historical and critical study* (London, Routledge and Kegan Paul, 1961).

11 H. M. Drucker, *The political uses of ideology* (London, Macmillan, 1974).

12 D. Joravsky, 'Soviet ideology', *Soviet Studies*, vol. 18, no. 1 (July 1966), p. 6.

13 A. Amalrik, 'Ideologies in Soviet society', *Survey*, vol. 22, no. 2 (spring 1976), pp. 1–11.

14 A. Hertz, *Szkice o ideologiach* (Paris, Instytut Literacki, 1967), p. 63.

15 Z. Brzezinski and S. Huntington, *Political power: USA/USSR* (New York, Viking Press, 1965), p. 19; Z. Brzezinski, *The Soviet bloc: unity and conflict*, rev. edn (Cambridge, Mass., Harvard Univ. Press, 1967), pp. 489–90.

16 A. R. Johnson, *The transformation of Communist ideology: the Yugoslav case, 1945–53* (Cambridge, Mass., MIT Press, 1972).

17 E. Laszlo, *The Communist ideology in Hungary* (Dordrecht, D. Reidel, 1966), pp. 37, 49.

18 M. McCauley, *Marxism–Leninism in the German Democratic Republic* (London, Macmillan, 1979).

19 T. A. Baylis, 'Orthodoxy and innovation in East German ideology', paper presented at the annual meeting of the American Association for the Advancement of Slavic Studies, Washington, DC, 14–17 October 1982.

20 See especially V. Kusin, *The intellectual origins of the Prague spring* (Cambridge Univ. Press, 1971); G. Golan, *The Czechoslovak reform movement: Communism in crisis, 1962–68* (Cambridge Univ. Press, 1971).

21 J. J. Wiatr (ed.), *Polish essays in the methodology of the social sciences* (Dordrecht, D. Reidel, 1979).

22 See, for example, J. Raciborski, 'Marksowska koncepcja ideologii', *Studia Filozoficzne*, vol. 4 (April 1980), pp. 117–32.

23 Wiatr, *Przyczynek do zagadnienia rozwoju społecznego*, pp. 283, 302.

24 Hertz, *Szkice o ideologiach*, p. 84.

25 VI Zjazd PZPR, Warszawa 6–11 XII 1971 r., stenogram (Warsaw, Książka i Wiedza, 1972), pp. 666–7.

26 T. Kwiatkowska, 'Czas w ideologii i ideologia w czasie', *Studia Nauk Politycznych*, no. 1 (January 1978), pp. 85–6.

27 Seliger, *The Marxist conception of ideology*, pp. 4, 74, 209; *idem, Ideology and politics* (London, Allen and Unwin, 1976), pp. 109, 181–94, 233.
28 R. Rose (ed.), *Policy-making in Britain* (London, Macmillan, 1969), p. ix.
29 J. J. Wiatr and R. Rose (eds.), *Comparing public policies* (Wrocław, Zakład Narodowy im. Ossolińskich, 1977), pp. 14–15.
30 R. A. Scalapino, 'Ideology and modernisation' in D. E. Apter (ed.), *Ideology and discontent* (New York, Free Press of Glencoe, 1964), p. 113.
31 Seliger, *Ideology and politics*, pp. 175, 233.
32 R. Taras, 'Polish sociology and the base–superstructure debate', *Philosophy of the Social Sciences*, vol. 13, no. 3 (September 1983), pp. 307–24.
33 F. Burton and P. Carlen, *Official discourse* (London, Routledge and Kegan Paul, 1979), p. 48.
34 M. Foucault, *The archaeology of knowledge* (London, Tavistock Publications, 1972), p. 45. For a more recent approach to discourse analysis, see M. J. Shapiro, *Language and political understanding* (New Haven, Yale Univ. Press, 1981). A notable example of the use of discourse analysis is G. W. Breslauer, *Khrushchev and Brezhnev as leaders* (London, Allen and Unwin, 1982).
35 J. A. Armstrong, *Ideology, politics and government in the Soviet Union*, 3rd edn (New York, Praeger, 1975), p. 28fn.
36 'W obliczu nowych zadań', *ND*, no. 8 (August 1964), p. 31.
37 J. Strzelecki, *Kontynuacje (2)* (Warsaw, Państwowy Instytut Wydawniczy, 1974), p. 80.

3. THE POLISH ROAD: FACT AND FABLE, 1956–59

1 See N. Bethell, *Gomulka* (Harmondsworth, Penguin, 1972), Chapters 8–12.
2 J. Karpinski, *Countdown* (New York, Karz-Cohl, 1982), p. 32.
3 J. Cyrankiewicz, 'Speech' in *Third Congress of the Polish United Workers' Party, March 10–19, 1959* (Warsaw, Central Committee of the PUWP, 1959), p. 264.
4 A. Schaff, 'Z czym walczymy i do czego dążymy występując przeciwko "kultowi jednostki"', *ND*, no. 4 (April 1956).
5 'Uchwała VIII Plenum: o aktualnych zadaniach politycznych i gospodarczych partii', *ND*, no. 10 (October 1956), p. 4.
6 'Referat W. Gomułki na IX Plenum: węzłowe problemy polityki partii', *ND*, no. 6 (June 1957), pp. 40–1.
7 'W rok po VIII Plenum', *ND*, nos. 10–11 (October-November 1957), p. 32.
8 W. Matwin, 'Ludzie chcą porządku', *ND*, no. 3 (March 1958).
9 For a fuller discussion of this period, see F. Fejtö, *A history of the People's democracies* (Harmondsworth, Penguin, 1974), Chapter 6.
10 J. Jarosławski, 'Socjalizm Marksa', *ND*, no. 3 (March 1958), pp. 76–7.
11 M. Michlewicz and L. Krasucki, 'O klikach i klikowości', *ND*, no. 1 (January 1959), p. 29.
12 W. Gomułka, 'Report of the Central Committee of the PUWP' in *Third Congress*, pp. 95–7.

268 Notes to pp. 53–66

13 W. Gomułka, 'Concluding speech' in *Third Congress*, p. 298.
14 'The statutes of Polish United Workers' Party adopted by the Third Congress of the PUWP' in *Third Congress*, p. 583.
15 R. Zambrowski, 'Changes in the party statutes' in *Third Congress*, pp. 189–90.
16 Gomułka, 'Report' in *Third Congress*, p. 102.
17 'Nie tędy droga', *ND*, no. 7 (July 1958), p. 155. See also J. Wacławek, 'W sprawie koncepcji roli partii w zakładach pracy', *ND*, no. 2 (February 1959), p. 42.
18 Z. Zandarowski, 'Początek już jest', *ND*, no. 8 (August 1958), p. 113.
19 'W przede dniu III Zjazdu partii', *ND*, no. 3 (March 1959), p. 3.
20 'Referat W. Gomułki na IX Plenum', p. 31.
21 Gomułka, 'Report' in *Third Congress*, pp. 67–8.
22 Cyrankiewicz, 'Speech' in *Third Congress*, pp. 265–6.
23 'Uchwała IX Plenum: o sytuacji i najważniejszych zadaniach partii', *ND*, no. 6 (June 1957), p. 146.
24 R. Jurys, 'Spór wokół jednej osoby i dwóch problemów', *ND*, no. 3 (March 1958), p. 103.
25 Z. Kliszko, 'Speech' in *Third Congress*, p. 277.
26 'Suwerenność, demokracja, socjalizm', *ND*, no. 1 (January 1957), p. 23.
27 'Referat W. Gomułki na IX Plenum', pp. 9–10.
28 M. Tatarkówna-Majkowska, 'Prawidłowa struktura partii: warunkiem rozwoju i żywotności organizacji partyjnej', *ND*, no. 3 (March 1958), p. 30.
29 'Praktyka decyduje', *ND*, no. 6 (June 1958), p. 9.
30 J. Kulpińska and M. Rokacz, 'Rada robotnicza w opinii załogi', *ND*, no. 8 (August 1958), pp. 77–83.
31 J. Balcerek and L. Gilejko, 'Aktualne problemy samorządu robotniczego w Polsce', *ND*, no. 9 (September 1958), p. 20.
32 J. Kofman, 'Na marginesie dyskusji nad projektem ustawy o samorządzie robotniczym', *ND*, no. 12 (December 1958), p. 105.
33 Wacławek, 'W sprawie koncepcji roli partii', p. 41.
34 B. Gliński, 'Możliwości i formy rozszerzania udziału załóg pracowniczych w zarządzaniu przemysłem', *ND*, no. 2 (February 1959), p. 54.
35 Gomułka, 'Report' in *Third Congress*, pp. 73–5.
36 'Resolution of the Third PUWP Congress on the key problems of party policy' in *Third Congress*, p. 462. See also I. Loga-Sowiński, 'Speech' in *Third Congress*, p. 241.
37 'Resolution of the Third PUWP Congress on the directives for development of People's Poland during the years 1959–65' in *Third Congress*, p. 536.
38 'Referat W. Gomułki na IX Plenum', pp. 27–8.
39 Gomułka, 'Report' in *Third Congress*, p. 69.
40 'Resolution on the key problems of party policy' in *Third Congress*, p. 466.
41 Gomułka, 'Report' in *Third Congress*, p. 85.

Notes to pp. 67–78

Notes to pp. 67–78

42 'Resolution on the key problems of party policy' in *Third Congress*, p. 466; Gomułka, 'Report' in *Third Congress*, pp. 51, 90.

43 Gomułka, 'Report' in *Third Congress*, p. 82.

44 Gomułka, 'Report' in *Third Congress*, p. 76.

45 A. Pravda, 'Industrial workers: patterns of dissent, opposition and accommodation' in R. L. Tokes (ed.), *Opposition in Eastern Europe* (London, Macmillan, 1979), pp. 209–54. See also A. Pravda, 'East–West interdependence and the social compact in Eastern Europe' in M. Bornstein, Z. Gitelman and W. Zimmerman (eds.), *East–West relations and the future of Eastern Europe* (London, Allen and Unwin, 1981), pp. 162–87.

46 Gomułka, 'Report' in *Third Congress*, pp. 98–9.

47 A. Zawadzki, 'Speech' in *Third Congress*, pp. 228–9.

4. LITTLE STABILISATION AND GREAT UPHEAVAL, 1960–70

1 'Sprawozdanie Komitetu Centralnego oraz zadania partii w dziedzinie umacniania socjalizmu i dalszego rozwoju Polskiej Rzeczypospolitej Ludowej' in *V Zjazd Polskiej Zjednoczonej Partii Robotniczej, 11–16 listopada 1968* (Warsaw, Książka i Wiedza, 1969), pp. 104–5.

2 W. Badura and J. Kapliński, 'Z przebiegu wojewódzkich konferencji partyjnych', *ND*, no. 4 (April 1960), p. 56.

3 R. Zambrowski, 'Na tematy partyjne', *ND*, no. 10 (October 1961), p. 8.

4 A. Starewicz, 'Radio i telewizja', *ND*, no. 5 (May 1960), pp. 69–71.

5 'Przemówienie wprowadzające W. Jarosińskiego wygłoszone 17 grudnia 1962 na XI Plenum', *ND*, no. 1 (January 1963), p. 17.

6 'Sprawozdanie Komitetu Centralnego i wytyczne rozwoju Polskiej Rzeczypospolitej Ludwej w latach 1966–70' in *IV Zjazd Polskiej Zjednoczonej Partii Robotniczej, 15–20 czerwca 1964* (Warsaw, Książka i Wiedza, 1964), pp. 223–4; 'Przemówienie końcowe W. Gomułki' in *IV Zjazd*, p. 377

7 'Uchwała IV Zjazdu Polskiej Zjednoczonej Partii Robotniczej' in *IV Zjazd*, pp. 358–9

8 L. Stasiak, 'Uwagi o ideowo-propagandowej działalności wewnątrzpartyjnej', *ND*, no. 8 (August 1963), p. 62.

9 'Referat E. Gierka na II Plenum: realizacja uchwał IV Zjazdu przez katowicką organizację partyjną', *ND*, no. 12 (December 1964), pp. 3–19.

10 M. Marzec, 'Po sprawozdawczo-wyborczych konferencjach partyjnych', *ND*, no. 2 (February 1965), p. 13.

11 'Dyskusja nad książką Adama Schaffa pt *Marksizm a jednostka ludzka*', *ND*, no. 12 (December 1965), pp. 70, 81, 178; I. Loga-Sowiński, 'Partia na czele narodu w walce o wolność i socjalizm', *ND*, no. 1 (January 1967), p. 10; T. Jaroszewski, 'Perspektywy demokracji socjalistycznej w Polsce', *ND*, no. 8 (August 1967), p. 18.

12 'Referat Z. Kliszki na VIII Plenum: o aktualnych zadaniach w pracy politycznej partii', *ND*, no. 6 (June 1967), p. 29; 'VIII Plenum', *ND*, no. 7 (July 1967), p. 5.

13 See Kusin, *The intellectual origins of the Prague spring*.

14 Loga-Sowiński, 'Partia na czele narodu', p. 13.

15 'Referat Z. Kliszki na VIII Plenum', p. 26.
16 Jaroszewski, 'Perspektywy demokracji socjalistycznej', p. 14.
17 'Przemówienie W. Gomułki na spotkaniu z aktywem warszawskim w dniu 19 marca 1968', *ND*, no. 4 (April 1968), p. 23.
18 'Dyskusja na XII Plenum', *ND*, no. 8 (August 1968), p. 6.
19 'Sprawozdanie Komitetu Centralnego' in *V Zjazd*, pp. 186–90.
20 E. Babiuch, 'Kampania sprawozdawczo-wyborcza,' *ND*, no. 4 (April 1967), pp. 10–13.
21 'Referat Z. Kliszki na VIII Plenum', pp. 32–5.
22 A. Banaszak, 'Wysoka efektywność pracy partyjnej: celem kampanii sprawozdawczo-wyborczej', *ND*, no. 11 (November 1970), p. 112.
23 Z. Grudzień, 'O niektórych problemach praktyki partyjnego kierownictwa', *ND*, no. 11 (November 1970), p. 124.
24 'Sprawozdanie Komitetu Centralnego' in *IV Zjazd*, pp. 231–2.
25 'Przemówienie W. Gomułki wygłoszone na XIV Plenum', *ND*, no. 1 (January 1964), p. 9.
26 'Sprawozdanie Komitetu Centralnego' in *IV Zjazd*, p. 232.
27 'Referat Z. Kliszki na VIII Plenum', p. 23.
28 Z. Kliszko, 'Państwo socjalistyczne: instrument realizacji wielkich idei Rewolucji', *ND*, no. 11 (November 1967), p. 33.
29 'Przemówienie W. Gomułki na spotkaniu z aktywem warszawskim', p. 24.
30 'Naród z partią: przeciwko siłom reakcji', *ND*, no. 5 (May 1968), p. 10.
31 'Sprawozdanie Komitetu Centralnego' in *V Zjazd*, p. 106.
32 'Tezy KC PZPR na V Zjazd partii uchwalone przez XII Plenum', *ND*, no. 8 (August 1968), p. 203; 'Sprawozdanie Komitetu Centralnego' in *V Zjazd*, p. 174.
33 Grudzień, 'O niektórych problemach', p. 126.
34 M. Spychalski, 'Rola partii w kształtowaniu i rozwoju ludowego państwa polskiego', *ND*, no. 7 (July 1969), p. 13.
35 A. Łopatka, 'Kierownicza rola partii marksistowsko–leninowskiej w systemie demokracji socjalistycznej', *ND*, no. 2 (February 1970), p. 26.
36 Grudzień, 'O niektórych problemach', p. 126.
37 'Referat W. Gomułki na XIII Plenum: o aktualnych problemach ideologicznej pracy partii', *ND*, no. 8 (August 1963), pp. 3–5, 38.
38 'Uwagi o polityczno-propagandowej działalności organizacji i instancji partyjnych', *ND*, no. 3 (March 1967), pp. 27–8.
39 'Referat Z. Kliszki na VIII Plenum', pp. 5, 20.
40 Jaroszewski, 'Perspektywy demokracji socjalistycznej', p. 23.
41 'Instancje organizacji młodzieżowych o wydarzeniach marcowych', *ND*, no. 6 (June 1968), p. 146; H. Jankowski, 'Etyka członka partii', *ND*, no. 7 (July 1968), p. 55.
42 'Przemówienie W. Gomułki na XII Plenum', *ND*, no. 8 (August 1968), pp. 129, 132.
43 'Sprawozdanie Komitetu Centralnego' in *V Zjazd*, pp. 178–82.
44 'Uchwała III Plenum o zadaniach wynikających z sytuacji gospodarczej kraju', *ND*, no. 12 (November 1959), pp. 33–41.
45 'Uchwała V Plenum o zadaniach w dziedzinie inwestycji w latach 1961–65', *ND*, no. 8 (August 1960).

46 'Uchwała IX Plenum w sprawie podstawowych problemów gospodarki narodowej w roku 1962', *ND*, no. 12 (December 1961), p. 35.

47 'Po X Plenum: na porządku dnia – postęp techniczny', *ND*, no. 6 (June 1962), p. 9.

48 'Uchwała XIV Plenum', *ND*, no. 1 (January 1964), p. 20.

49 'V Kongres związków zawodowych', *ND*, no. 1 (January 1963), pp. 44–5.

50 T. Jaroszewski, 'Rewolucja techniczna a humanizm', *ND*, no. 2 (February 1960), p. 68.

51 'Przemówienie W. Gomułki na V Kongresie związków zawodowych wygłoszone dnia 26 listopada 1962', *ND*, no. 12 (December 1962), pp. 4–5; 'V Kongres związków zawodowych', p. 48.

52 'Sprawozdanie Komitetu Centralnego' in *IV Zjazd*, pp. 158–63.

53 'Podstawowe wytyczne II Plenum', *ND*, no. 1 (January 1965), pp. 3–8.

54 Marzec, 'Po sprawozdawczo-wyborczych konferencjach', pp. 15–17.

55 A. Banaszak, 'Krytyczne uwagi i wnioski inspiracją twórczego działania', *ND*, no. 2 (February 1967), p. 85.

56 'Referat Z. Kliszki na VIII Plenum', p. 31.

57 'Tezy KC PZPR na V Zjazd', pp. 162–4, 204.

58 'VI Kongres związków zawodowych', *ND*, no. 8 (August 1967), pp. 4–5; T. Lipski, 'W obliczu VI Kongresu związków zawodowych', *ND*, no. 6 (June 1967), p. 109.

59 A. Owieczko and S. Widerszpil, 'Samorząd robotniczy: kilka refleksji', *ND*, no. 9 (September 1967), p. 29.

60 H. Magdziak, 'Samorząd robotniczy: blaski i cienie', *ND*, no. 7 (July 1968), pp. 3–15.

61 'Sprawozdanie Komitetu Centralnego' in *V Zjazd*, pp. 121–4.

62 T. Jaworski and R. Stachulski, 'Samorząd robotniczy na obecnym etapie rozwoju gospodarki', *ND*, no. 7 (July 1970), pp. 559–60.

63 W. Ratyński, 'Udział związków zawodowych w pracach nad nowym systemem bodźców', *ND*, no. 9 (September 1970), p. 113.

64 A. Schaff, 'Aktualne zagadnienia nauk społecznych', *ND*, no. 6 (June 1959), p. 32; 'Pokojowe współzawodnictwo dwóch systemów a walka ideologiczna', *ND*, no. 2 (February 1963), p. 5.

65 'Referat W. Gomułki na XIII Plenum', p. 3.

66 'Sprawozdanie Komitetu Centralnego' in *IV Zjazd*, pp. 141–2.

67 'Referat wprowadzający W. Gomułki na III Plenum', *ND*, no. 4 (April 1965), p. 7.

68 'Front Jedności Narodu', *ND*, no. 6 (June 1965), p. 5.

69 See K. Grzybowski, 'Tysiącletnia historia polskiej kultury', *ND*, no. 2 (February 1966), pp. 41–50.

70 'W sprawie stosunków między państwem a kościołem', *ND*, no. 4 (April 1966), pp. 3–14.

71 'Przemówienie W. Gomułki wygłoszone na uroczystej sesji Sejmu w dniu 21 lipca 1966', *ND*, no. 8 (August 1966), p. 21.

72 'Referat Z. Kliszki na VIII Plenum', pp. 20–2.

73 'Sprawozdanie Komitetu Centralnego' in *V Zjazd*, pp. 115–16.

74 'Uchwała XI Plenum', *ND*, no. 1 (January 1963), p. 31.

75 E. Szyr, 'Działalność naukowo-badawcza a postęp techniczny w gospodarce narodowej', *ND*, no. 5 (May 1963), p. 3.

76 H. Jabłoński, 'Kryteria wyboru kierunków badawczych', *ND*, no. 2 (February 1964), pp. 45–53.

77 'Sprawozdanie Komitetu Centralnego' in *IV Zjazd*, pp. 142–8.

78 Z. Kaczmarek, 'Niektóre problemy współdziałania nauki i gospodarki narodowej', *ND*, no. 11 (November 1966), p. 61.

79 I. Malecki, 'Postawa naukowca w społeczeństwie socjalistycznym', *ND*, no. 8 (August 1968), pp. 217–24.

80 'Sprawozdanie Komitetu Centralnego' in *V Zjazd*, p. 145.

81 Z. Kaczmarek, 'Warunki podwyższenia efektywności badań naukowych', *ND*, no. 11 (November 1969), pp. 3–10; 'Referat Biura Politycznego na IV Plenum: zwiększenie efektywności badań naukowych i postęp techniczno-organizacyjny w gospodarce narodowej', *ND*, no. 12 (December 1969), pp. 7–39.

82 'Przemówienie wprowadzające W. Jarosińskiego', pp. 16–17.

83 'Pokojowe współzawodnictwo', p. 71.

84 A. Werblan, 'O socjologii krytycznej', *ND*, no. 7 (July 1963), pp. 12–24.

85 'Referat W. Gomułki na XIII Plenum', pp. 19–23.

86 'Sprawozdanie Komitetu Centralnego' in *IV Zjazd*, pp. 145–7.

87 'Dyskusja nad książką Adama Schaffa', pp. 57–186.

88 'Referat Z. Kliszki na VIII Plenum', p. 35.

89 'Przemówienie W. Gomułki na spotkaniu z aktywem warszawskim', p. 20; 'Naród z partią', p. 11; H. Jabłoński, 'Zaburzenia studenckie w marcu 1968', *ND*, no. 5 (May 1968), p. 33.

90 B. Pleśniarski, 'Praca ideowo-wychowawcza w szkołach wyższych', *ND*, no. 3 (March 1969), p. 81; C. Madajczyk and W. Markiewicz, 'Nauki społeczne w ostatnim ćwierćwieczu', *ND*, no. 7 (July 1969), p. 132.

91 'Referat W. Gomułki na XIII Plenum', pp. 25–9, 48.

92 'Sprawozdanie Komitetu Centralnego' and 'Uchwała Zjazdu' in *IV Zjazd*, pp. 149–51, 340.

93 'Przemówienie W. Gomułki na XIV Zjeździe Związku Literatów Polskich w Lublinie', *ND*, no. 10 (October 1965), pp. 3–12.

94 W. Krasko, 'Myśl i działanie', *ND*, no. 10 (October 1966), pp. 9–15.

95 'Sprawozdanie Komitetu Centralnego' in *V Zjazd*, pp. 104, 149–50.

96 Starewicz, 'Radio i telewizja', p. 71.

97 'Przemówienie wprowadzające W. Jarosińskiego', p. 7.

98 'Referat W. Gomułki na XIII Plenum', p. 34.

99 'Sprawozdanie Komitetu Centralnego' in *IV Zjazd*, pp. 155–7.

100 'Sprawozdanie Komitetu Centralnego' in *V Zjazd*, pp. 140, 124–33.

101 S. Ciosek, 'Po VII Kongresie Zrzeszenia Studentów Polskich', *ND*, no. 3 (March 1969), p. 37.

102 'Referat W. Gomułki na XIII Plenum', p. 15.

103 S. Jędrychowski, 'O działaniu bodźców ekonomicznych w naszej gospodarce', *ND*, no. 4 (April 1962), p. 3.

104 'Program wszechstronnego rozwoju kraju', *ND*, no. 12 (December 1966), p. 9.

105 'Przemówienie W. Gomułki na V Plenum', *ND*, no. 6 (June 1970), p. 34.
106 J. Rutkowski, 'Socjalistyczna zasada podziału', *ND*, no. 1 (January 1960), p. 43.
107 'Referat W. Gomułki na XIII Plenum', p. 17.
108 'Sprawozdanie Komitetu Centralnego' in *IV Zjazd*, p. 118.
109 'Sprawozdanie Komitetu Centralnego' in *V Zjazd*, p. 91.
110 J. Danecki, 'Uwagi o polityce podziału', *ND*, no. 5 (May 1970), p. 78.
111 'Przemówienie wprowadzające W. Jarosińskiego', p. 7.
112 M. Maneli, 'O zgodności interesów jednostki i społeczeństwa', *ND*, no. 4 (April 1967), p. 91.
113 'Sprawozdanie Komitetu Centralnego' in *V Zjazd*, pp. 42, 114.

5. PROSPERITY AND POLITICAL STYLE IN THE SECOND POLAND, 1971–75

1 W. Narojek, *Społeczeństwo planujące* (Warsaw, Państwowe Wydawn. Naukowe, 1973), pp. 275–81.
2 'Referat na Plenum KC PPR w dniu 31 VIII 1948: o odchyleniu prawicowym i nacjonalistycznym w kierownictwie partii i o sposobach jego przezwyciężania', *ND*, no. 11 (November 1948), p. 28.
3 'Przemówienie W. Gomułki na VIII Plenum w dniach 19–21 października 1956', *ND*, no. 10 (October 1956), p. 40.
4 'Przemówienie E. Gierka na VIII Plenum: program rozwoju socjalistycznej Polski', *Trybuna Ludu*, 28 February 1971.
5 'Sprawozdanie Komitetu Centralnego Polskiej Zjednoczonej Partii Robotniczej za okres między V a VI Zjazdem' in *VI Zjazd Polskiej Zjednoczonej Partii Robotniczej, 6–11 grudnia 1971* (Warsaw, Książka i Wiedza, 1972), p. 65.
6 M. Rakowski, 'December 1970: the turning point' in A. Bromke and J. W. Strong (eds.), *Gierek's Poland* (New York, Praeger, 1973), p. 31.
7 'Przemówienie E. Gierka na VIII Plenum'.
8 Narojek, *Społeczeństwo planujące*, p. 281.
9 See 'The party leaders speak' (appendix) in Bromke and Strong (eds.), *Gierek's Poland*, pp. 216–19. See also 'VIII Plenum', *ND*, special issue (*ca.* May 1971).
10 'Sprawozdanie Komitetu Centralnego' in *VI Zjazd*, p. 69.
11 'Przemówienie radiowo-telewizyjne E. Gierka', *ND*, no. 1 (January 1971), p. 7.
12 'Referat programowy Biura Politycznego wygłoszony przez E. Gierka: zadania partii w dalszym socjalistycznym rozwoju Polskiej Rzeczypospolitej Ludowej' in *VI Zjazd* p. 140; 'W sprawie zmian i uzupełnień w statucie PZPR' in *VI Zjazd*, p. 216.
13 'Sprawozdanie Komitetu Centralnego Polskiej Zjednoczonej Partii Robotniczej za okres od VI do VII Zjazdu' in *VII Zjazd Polskiej Zjednoczonej Partii Robotniczej, 8–12 grudia 1975* (Warsaw, Książka i Wiedza, 1975), p. 54.
14 For an insider's account of the VIII Plenum, see M. Rakowski, *Przesilenie grudniowe* (Warsaw, Państwowy Instytut Wydawn., 1981), pp. 121–99.

15 E. Babiuch, 'O niektórych problemach rozwoju i umacniania partii', *ND*, no, 9 (September 1971), p. 12.

16 'Referat programowy' and 'Sprawozdanie Komitetu Centralnego' in *VI Zjazd*, pp. 141–3, 68, 71, 77.

17 'Referat programowy' and 'Uchwała VI Zjazdu PZPR: o dalszy socjalistyczny rozwój Polskiej Rzeczypospolitej Ludowej w latach 1971–75' in *VI Zjazd*, pp. 105, 262–3.

18 J. Szydlak, 'Aktualne problemy pracy ideologiczno-propagandowej', *ND*, no. 5 (May 1974), p. 20.

19 'Przemówienie E. Gierka na XVI Plenum', *ND*, no. 2 (February 1975), p. 14.

20 'Sprawozdanie Komitetu Centralnego'; 'Uchwała VII Zjazdu PZPR: o dalszy dynamiczny rozwój budownictwa socjalistycznego – o wyższą jakość pracy i warunków życia narodu'; 'Sprawozdanie z prac komisji statutowej'; 'Referat programowy Biura Politycznego wygłoszony przez E. Gierka: o dalszy dynamiczny rozwój budownictwa socjalistycznego – o wyższą jakość pracy i warunków życia narodu'; in *VII Zjazd*, pp. 53–4, 265, 192–3, 118.

21 'Wytyczne KC PZPR na VI Zjazd partii: o dalszy socjalistyczny rozwój Polskiej Rzeczypospolitej Ludowej', *ND*, no. 10 (October 1971), pp. 77–80; 'W sprawie zmian i uzupełnień w statucie' in *VI Zjazd*, pp. 214–16, 222.

22 A. Dobieszewski, 'Węzłowe problemy struktury i zasad działania partii marksistowsko-leninowskiej', *ND*, no. 6 (June 1971), pp. 60–4.

23 'Wytyczne KC PZPR na VI Zjazd', p. 78; 'Uchwała VI Zjazdu' in *VI Zjazd*, p. 285.

24 'Referat Komitetu Centralnego PZPR wygłoszony przez E. Gierka: o konsekwentną realizację uchwały VI Zjazdu, o dalszy wzrost gospodarności' in *I Krajowa Konferencja PZPR, 22–23 października 1973* (Warsaw, Książka i Wiedza, 1973), pp. 44, 53.

25 'Przemówienie radiowo-telewizyjne E. Gierka', p. 7.

26 'Przemówienie E. Gierka na plenarne posiedzenie Sejmu PRL', *ND*, no. 1 (January 1971), p. 13.

27 'Brzemienny czas: doniosłe decyzje', *ND*, no . 1 (January 1971), p. 22.

28 'Dyskusja przedzjazdowa', *ND*, no. 10 (October 1971), p. 113.

29 'Przemówienie E. Gierka na VII Plenum', *ND*, no. 12 (December 1972), p. 11.

30 'Uchwały' in *I Krajowa Konferencja PZPR*, p. 272.

31 M. Fritzhand, 'Budownictwo socjalistyczne a badania nad osobowością', *ND*, no. 12 (December 1974), p. 39.

32 'Sprawozdanie Komitetu Centralnego' in *VII Zjazd*, pp. 3–4, 32–6, 48–9, 52.

33 'Referat programowy' in *VII Zjazd*, pp. 87, 112–21.

34 S. Terry, '"Developed socialism" and the disintegration of the Marxist–Leninist synthesis in Eastern Europe', paper presented at the annual meeting of the American Association for the Advancement of Slavic Studies, Washington, DC, 14–17 October 1982. For Gierek's statement, see 'Referat programowy: VI Zjazd', *ND*, no. 1 (January 1972), p. 72.

35 'Wytyczne KC PZPR na VI Zjazd', pp. 75–6.
36 W. Wesołowski, 'Miejsce i rola naszej klasy robotniczej na obecnym etapie', *ND*, no. 11 (November 1971), p. 28.
37 T. Jaroszewski, 'Kierownicza rola partii w warunkach intensywnego rozwoju', *ND*, no. 3 (March 1971), p. 121.
38 'Referat programowy' in *VI Zjazd*, pp. 143–5.
39 J. Szydlak, 'Główne zadania w pracy ideowo-wychowawczej', *ND*, no. 7 (July 1972), pp. 38–9.
40 J. Łukaszewicz, 'Niektóre problemy frontu ideologicznego partii', *ND*, no. 4 (April 1973), p. 5.
41 'Referat Komitetu Centralnego' in *I Krajowa Konferencja PZPR*, pp. 55–7.
42 'Przemówienie E. Gierka na XIII Plenum', *ND*, no. 3 (March 1974), pp. 13–14.
43 Rakowski, 'December 1970'. See also 'Przemówienie E. Gierka na VIII Plenum'.
44 For example, R. Staar, 'Poland: old wine in new bottles', *Current History*, vol. 64 (May 1973), pp. 197–201.
45 'Sprawozdanie z działalności Biura Politycznego i Sekretariatu KC przedstawione przez E. Babiucha', *ND*, no. 5 (May 1971), pp. 181–3.
46 'Przemówienie E. Gierka na VIII Plenum'.
47 'Podstawowy materiał na IX Plenum: zadania partii, państwa i związków zawodowych w kształtowaniu warunków pełnego zaangażowania twórczych sił narodu dla rozwoju kraju', *ND*, no. 7 (July 1973), pp. 25–67.
48 'Sprawozdanie Komitetu Centralnego'; 'Referat programowy'; 'Uchwała VII Zjazdu'; in *VII Zjazd*, pp. 34, 118, 232, 262.
49 'Sprawozdanie Komitetu Centralnego' and 'Referat programowy' in *VI Zjazd*, pp. 46, 134.
50 'Tezy programowe KC PZPR – o aktywny udział młodego pokolenia w budowie socjalistycznej Polski: zadania partii, państwa i narodu w wychowaniu młodzieży', *ND*, no. 12 (December 1972), pp. 20–54.
51 'Referat Komitetu Centralnego' in *I Krajowa Konferencja PZPR*, p. 51.
52 'Przemówienie F. Szlachcica: o dominacje marksizmu-leninizmu', *ND*, no. 6 (June 1973), p. 16.
53 Szydlak, 'Aktualne problemy', p. 28.
54 'Wytyczne KC PZPR na VII Zjazd partii: o dynamiczny rozwój budownictwa socjalistycznego – o wyższą jakość pracy i warunków życia narodu', *ND*, no. 9 (September 1975), p. 56.
55 'Uchwała VII Zjazdu' in *VII Zjazd*, p. 259.
56 L. Dembiński, 'The Catholics and politics in Poland' in Bromke and Strong (eds.), *Gierek's Poland*, p. 180.
57 'Wytyczne KC PZPR na VI Zjazd', p. 69.
58 R. Jezierski, 'Rozwój nauki a zadania kształceniowe', *ND*, no. 9 (September 1973), p. 36. See also 'Wystąpienie premiera P. Jaroszewicza: o wysoką dynamikę społeczno-ekonomicznego rozwoju Polski w latach 1974–75' and 'Zespoły problemowe' in *I Krajowa Konferencja PZPR*, pp. 96–7, 242–4.
59 'Wytyczne KC PZPR na VI Zjazd', pp. 70–1; 'Uchwała VI Zjazdu' in *VI Zjazd*, p. 274.

60 J. Maciszewski, 'Nauki społeczne i humanistyczne w ideologicznej i politycznej działalności partii, w realizacji programu przyspieszenia społeczno-ekonomicznego rozwoju Polski', *ND*, no. 5 (May 1973), pp. 84–101.

61 W. Markiewicz, 'Stan i perspektywy rozwoju nauk społeczno-humanistycznych', *ND*, no. 5 (May 1973), pp. 102–17.

62 'Partyjna narada nauk społecznych i humanistycznych: wystąpienia w dyskusji', *ND*, no. 6 (June 1973), pp. 19–76.

63 J. Kaczmarek, 'Dorobek II Kongresu Nauki Polskiej i niektóre najbliższe kierunki jego wykorzystania', *ND*, no. 10 (October 1973), p. 65.

64 'Sprawozdanie Komitetu Centralnego' and 'Referat programowy' in *VII Zjazd*, pp. 39–40, 57, 217.

65 'Partyjna narada nauk społecznych i humanistycznych: wystąpienia w dyskusji; p. 70.

66 'Wytyczne KC PZPR na VI Zjazd', pp. 71–3; 'Sprawozdanie Komitetu Centralnego'; 'Referat programowy'; 'Uchwała VI Zjazdu'; in *VI Zjazd*, pp. 56–7, 144, 276–9.

67 Łukaszewicz, 'Niektóre problemy', p. 11.

68 J. Kossak, 'Refleksje o polityce kulturalnej', *ND*, no. 12 (December 1971), pp. 30–47.

69 Maciszewski, 'Nauki społeczne', p. 91.

70 'Trzydziestolecie PRL: tezy KC PZPR', *ND*, no. 3 (March 1974), p. 38.

71 W. Sokorski, 'O ciągłości rozwoju kultury', *ND*, no. 6 (June 1974), pp. 60–1.

72 'Przemówienie E. Gierka na XVI Plenum', p. 17.

73 'Referat programowy' and 'Uchwała VII Zjazdu' in *VII Zjazd*, pp. 126–7, 257.

74 'Sprawozdanie z działalności Biura Politycznego', p. 178.

75 'Wytyczne KC PZPR na VI Zjazd', pp. 61, 74; 'Referat E. Gierka na krajowej naradzie partyjnej w Warszawie', *ND*, no. 10 (October 1971), p. 105; 'Referat programowy' and 'Uchwała VI Zjazdu' in *VI Zjazd*, pp. 137, 265.

76 'Tezy programowe KC PZPR', pp. 25, 32.

77 B. Waligórski, 'O wychowanie pokolenia epoki socjalizmu', *ND*, no. 3 (March 1973), p. 88.

78 S. Ciosek, 'Zadania Federacji Socjalistycznych Związków Młodzieży Polskiej', *ND*, no. 5 (May 1973), p. 44.

79 A. Werblan, 'Niektóre problemy roli klasy robotniczej i jej partii w budowie socjalistycznej Polski', *ND*, no. 7 (July 1973), p. 89.

80 'Dyskusja na obradach plenarnych' in *I Krajowa Konferencja PZPR*, p. 130.

81 'Trzydziestolecie PRL', p. 37.

82 Szydlak, 'Aktualne problemy', p. 28.

83 'Referat E. Babiucha na XIV Plenum: o działalności Biura Politycznego i Sekretariatu KC PZPR', *ND*, no. 7 (July 1974), p. 29.

84 'Na finiszu pięciolatki: osiągniecia i zadania', *ND*, no. 2 (February 1975), p. 28.

85 J. Ładyka, 'Humanizm a rozwój społeczeństwa socjalistycznego', *ND*, no. 3 (March 1975), p. 39.
86 'Kierunek: VII Zjazd PZPR', *ND*, no. 10 (October 1975), p. 7; W. Klimczak, 'Problemy pracy ideowo-wychowawczej', *ND*, no. 12 (December 1975), p. 32.
87 'Sprawozdanie Komitetu Centralnego' in *VII Zjazd*, p. 36.
88 'Wytyczne KC PZPR na VI Zjazd', pp. 60–1; 'Referat programowy' in *VI Zjazd*, p. 145.
89 'Przemówienie E. Gierka na VII Plenum', p. 13; 'Tezy programowe KC PZPR', pp. 33–5.
90 'Referat programowy' in *VII Zjazd*, p. 123.
91 'Tezy programowe KC PZPR', pp. 29–30; 'Referat Komitetu Centralnego' in *I Krajowa Konferencja PZPR*, pp. 57–8.
92 'Wytyczne KC PZPR na VI Zjazd', p. 65; 'Referat programowy' and 'Uchwała VI Zjazdu' in *VI Zjazd*, pp. 134, 145, 269.
93 'Tezy programowe KC PZPR', pp. 34–6.
94 J. Szydlak, 'Wielka siła ideologii socjalistycznej', *ND*, no. 5 (May 1973), p. 11.
95 'Referat Komitetu Centralnego' and 'Dyskusja na obradach plenarnych' in *I Krajowa Konferencja PZPR*, pp. 57, 175.
96 'Przemówienie E. Gierka na XIII Plenum', p. 15.
97 'Referat programowy' and 'Uchwała VII Zjazdu' in *VII Zjazd*, pp. 122–3, 272.
98 Z. Sufin, 'Cele społeczne w programie perspektywicznego rozwoju', *ND*, no. 7 (July 1971), p. 50.
99 'Uchwała VII Zjazdu' in *VII Zjazd*, p. 232.
100 M. Fritzhand, 'Marksizm a idea równości', *ND*, no. 3 (March 1974), pp. 69–93.
101 'Referat programowy' in *VII Zjazd*, p. 113.
102 H. Jankowski, 'Niektóre kwestie etyki marksistowskiej', *ND*, no. 11 (November 1973), p. 143.
103 'Przemówienie E. Gierka wygłoszone na przedwyborczym spotkaniu w Katowicach w dniu 21 lutego 1972', *ND*, no. 3 (March 1972), p. 27; 'Referat programowy' in *VII Zjazd*, p. 110.

6. PROPAGANDA OF SUCCESS AND PROGNOSES OF FAILURE, 1976–80

1 A. Dobieszewski, 'Obiektywne i subiektywne czynniki integracji społeczeństwa polskiego', *ND*, no. 3 (March 1977), p. 131.
2 C. Gati, 'The Kadar mystique', *Problems of Communism*, vol. 23, no. 3 (May–June 1974), pp. 32–3.
3 G. Kállai, *Népszabadság*, 27 June 1976; cited in B. Kovrig, *Communism in Hungary* (Stanford, Hoover Institution Press, 1979), p. 425.
4 'Narada I sekretarzy KZ PZPR największych zakładów produkcyjnych: przemówienie E. Gierka', *ND*, no. 8 (August 1976), pp. 9–10.
5 'W trosce o rozwój kraju i narodu', *ND*, no. 7 (July 1976), p. 54.
6 'List E. Gierka do załogi zakładów im. gen. Waltera w Radomiu', *ND*, no. 3 (March 1977), p. 38.

278   *Notes to pp. 148–55*

7 'Przemówienie końcowe E. Gierka: od nas samych, od naszej codziennej pracy zależy pomyślność całego narodu' in *II Krajowa Konferencja PZPR, 9–10 stycznia 1978* (Warsaw, Książka i Wiedza, 1978), p. 78.
8 'Referat Biura Politycznego na IV Plenum wygłoszony przez E. Gierka: o pełną realizację uchwały VII Zjazdu PZPR w dziedzinie rozwoju rolnictwa', *ND*, no. 9 (September 1976), pp. 21–2.
9 'Tezy VII Plenum: zadania partii w pogłębieniu socjalistycznej świadomości i patriotycznej jedności narodu', *ND*, no. 5 (May 1977), pp. 41–4.
10 'Przemówienie E. Gierka na XVI Plenum', *ND*, no. 11 (November 1979), p. 17.
11 'Referat programowy Biura Politycznego wygłoszony przez E. Gierka: o dalszy rozwój socjalistycznej Polski, o pomyślność narodu polskiego: założenia rozwoju społeczno-gospodarczego kraju w latach 1981–85' in *VIII Zjazd Polskiej Zjednoczonej Partii Robotniczej, 11–15 lutego 1980* (Warsaw, Książka i Wiedza, 1980), p. 155.
12 J. Kowalski, 'Urzeczywistnienie demokracji socjalistycznej', *ND*, no. 2 (February 1980), p. 157.
13 J. Urbański, 'Leninowski styl pracy', *ND*, no. 4 (April 1980), p. 128.
14 W. Kruczek, 'Na straży norm partyjności i zasad socjalizmu', *ND*, no. 5 (May 1980). p. 45.
15 E. Erazmus, 'Istotne treści kultury politycznej', *ND*, no. 8 (August 1980), p. 124–6.
16 'Referat Biura Politycznego na III Plenum wygłoszony przez E. Gierka: o pogłębianie patriotycznej jedności narodu, o umacnianie państwa i rozwój demokracji socjalistycznej', *ND*, no. 3 (March 1976), p. 11.
17 'Narada I sekretarzy', p. 11.
18 'Tezy VII Plenum', p. 43.
19 H. Jankowski and J. Malanowski, 'Socjalistyczny sposób życia a problemy moralne', *ND*, no. 3 (March 1978), p. 90.
20 E. Babiuch, 'Polska Zjednoczona Partia Robotnicza przed VIII Zjazdem', *ND*, no. 1 (January 1980), p. 9.
21 Kruczek, 'Na straży norm', p. 42.
22 'Droga skutecznego działania', *ND*, no. 3 (March 1980), p. 155.
23 'Sprawozdanie Komitetu Centralnego PZPR za okres od VII do VIII Zjazdu'; 'Sprawozdanie Centralnej Komisji Rewizyjnej PZPR za okres od VII do VIII Zjazdu'; 'Referat programowy'; 'Uchwała VIII Zjazdu PZPR'; 'Zadania partii w dalszym rozwoju socjalistycznej Polski, w kształtowaniu pomyślności narodu polskiego'; in *VIII Zjazd*, pp. 59–61, 85, 155, 209–11.
24 Karpinski, *Countdown*, p. 186.
25 Karpinski, *Countdown*, p. 187.
26 S. Starski, *Class struggle in classless Poland* (Boston, South End Press, 1982), p. 48.
27 'Przemówienie E. Gierka na spotkaniu z aktywem robotniczym woj. katowickiego: miłość Ojczyzny przekuwajmy w czyn', *ND*, no. 7 (July 1976), p. 45.
28 'Referat Biura Politycznego na IV Plenum', p. 22.

29 'Przemówienie E. Gierka na VII Plenum', *ND*, no. 5 (May 1977), p. 13; 'Tezy VII Plenum', pp. 23–41.
30 'To co najważniejsze', *ND*, no. 7 (July 1980), p. 35. See also E. Gierek, 'Jedność narodu: źródłem siły i podstawą przyszłości socjalistycznej Polski', *ND*, no. 9 (September 1979), p. 5.
31 'Referat Biura Politycznego na III Plenum', pp. 17–18.
32 K. Rokoszewski, 'Prasa, radio i telewizja po VII Zjezdzie PZPR', *ND*, no. 3 (March 1976), p. 45.
33 'Referat Biura Politycznego na V Plenum wygłoszony przez E. Gierka: o konsekwentną realizację społeczno-ekonomicznego programu VII Zjazdu PZPR, o wyższą efektywność gospodarowania', *ND*, no. 12 (December 1976), p. 27.
34 W. Klimczak, 'Nad realizacją programu VII Zjazdu', *ND*, no. 2 (February 1977), pp. 38–40.
35 'Przemówienie E. Gierka na VII Plenum', pp. 9–11.
36 'Sprawozdanie Komitetu Centralnego' and 'Referat programowy' in *VIII Zjazd*, pp. 52, 61–3, 124–6.
37 'Referat programowy' in *VIII Zjazd*, p. 124.
38 For a historical account of one-person management, see J. Azrael, *Managerial power and Soviet politics* (Cambridge, Mass., Harvard Univ. Press, 1966), pp. 90–5.
39 'Referat Biura Politycznego na III Plenum', pp. 15–16.
40 'Exposé prezesa Rady Ministrów P. Jaroszewicza: pierwsza sesja Sejmu VII kadencji', *ND*, no. 4 (April 1976), p. 20.
41 'Przemówienie E. Gierka na wspólnym posiedzeniu Biura Politycznego, Rady Państwa, Prezydium Rządu i Prezydium CRZZ w sprawie samorząda robotniczego', *Trybuna Ludu*, 8 April 1977.
42 W. Rogowski, 'Społeczne funkcje samorządu robotniczego', *ND*, no. 6 (June 1977), pp. 66, 70.
43 S. Szkraba, 'Problemy rozwoju samorządu', *ND*, no. 8 (August 1978), p. 10.
44 'Referat Biura Politycznego wygłoszony przez E. Gierka na naradzie przedstawicieli samorządu robotniczego', *Trybuna Ludu*, 4 July 1978.
45 'Sprawozdanie Komitetu Centralnego'; 'Referat programowy'; 'Uchwała VIII Zjazdu'; in *VIII Zjazd*, pp. 42–3, 131–3, 201–2.
46 Z. Grudzień, 'Udział samorządu robotniczego w rozwijaniu demokracji socjalistycznej, w podnoszeniu jakości życia i pracy załog', *ND*, no. 5 (May 1980), p. 56. See also S. Zawadzki, 'Demokracja socjalistyczna: cele, kierunki, zadania', *ND*, no. 4 (April 1980), pp. 65–75.
47 K. Kloc, 'Miejsce samorządu robotniczego', *ND*, no. 6 (June 1980), p. 137.
48 See 'VI Plenum: dyskusja', *ND*, nos. 10–11 (October–November 1980).
49 'Referat Biura Politycznego na III Plenum', p. 11.
50 'Exposé prezesa Rady Ministrów', p. 20.
51 'Referat Biura Politycznego' in *II Krajowa Konferencja PZPR*, p. 39.
52 H. Korotyński, 'Fundamenty i warunki jedności narodu', *ND*, no. 5 (May 1979), p. 59.
53 W. Mysłek, 'Państwo i kościół', *ND*, no. 5 (May 1979), pp. 68–70.

54 This account is based on V. Chrypinski, 'Church and state in Gierek's Poland' in M. Simon and R. Kanet (eds.), *Background to crisis: policy and politics in Gierek's Poland* (Boulder, Colorado, Westview Press, 1981), pp. 239–64.

55 'Referat programowy' in *VIII Zjazd*, pp. 127, 157.

56 'Droga skutecznego działania', p. 156.

57 'Exposé prezesa Rady Ministrów E. Babiucha wygłoszone 3 kwietnia b.r. na posiedzeniu Sejmu PRL', *ND*, no. 4 (April 1980), p. 35.

58 Chrypinski, 'Church and state', p. 248.

59 H. Chołaj, 'O zespalanie się polityki społecznej i ekonomicznej w rozwoju socjalizmu', *ND*, no. 2 (February 1977), p. 59.

60 'Referat Biura Politycznego na XII Plenum wygłoszony przez E. Gierka: o dalsze umocnienie roli nauki w społeczno-gospodarczym rozwoju kraju', *ND*, no. 7 (July 1978), pp. 9, 21.

61 W. Nowacki, 'Nauka polska u progu lat osiemdziesiątych', *ND*, no. 2 (February 1980), pp. 33–4.

62 Klimczak, 'Nad realizacją programu', p. 41.

63 'Tezy VII Plenum', p. 32.

64 'Referat Biura Politycznego' in *II Krajowa Konferencja PZPR*, p. 48.

65 A. Werblan, 'Zagadnienia polityki naukowej', *ND*, no. 6 (June 1978), p. 30.

66 'Referat programowy' in *VIII Zjazd*, p. 144.

67 A. Kłoskowska, 'Nauki społeczne: obowiązki i odpowiedzialność', *ND*, no. 5 (May 1978), p. 58.

68 'Referat Biura Politycznego na III Plenum', p. 11.

69 'Przemówienie E. Gierka na VII Plenum', p. 14; 'Tezy VII Plenum', pp. 33–4.

70 J. Kossak, 'Społeczna rola kultury', *ND*, no. 8 (August 1977), pp. 165–9.

71 W. Kaczocha, 'Polityka kulturalna a wartości kulturowe', *ND*, no. 9 (September 1977), p. 176. See also J. Maciszewski, 'Rola kultury w tworzeniu się nowoczesnego narodu polskiego', *ND*, no. 12 (December 1979), p. 14.

72 'Sprawozdanie Komitetu Centralnego' and 'Referat programowy' in *VIII Zjazd*, pp. 55, 146.

73 'Referat Biura Politycznego na III Plenum', p. 20.

74 'Uchwała Biura Politycznego z 22 lutego 1977: o dalsze doskonalenie działalności informacyjno-publicystycznej oraz umocnienie ideowo-wychowawczej roli krytyki w prasie, radiu i telewizji', *ND*, no. 3 (March 1977), p. 42.

75 'Przemówienie E. Gierka na VII Plenum', no. 9; 'Tezy VII Plenum', p. 29.

76 'Referat Biura Politycznego na IX Plenum wygłoszony przez E. Gierka: o wyższa efektywność gospodarowania, o lepsze zaspokojenie potrzeb ludzi pracy', *ND*, no. 11 (November 1977), pp. 21–2.

77 Z. Oleniak, 'O rzetelny i wnikliwy stosunek do ludzkich spraw i bolączek', *ND*, no. 6 (June 1979), p. 27.

78 K. Marszał, 'Ideowo-wychowawcze funkcje organizacji partynych w wielkim zakładzie przemysłowym', *ND*, no. 4 (April 1976), p. 81.

79 'Referat Biura Politycznego' in *II Krajowa Konferencja PZPR*, p. 46.
80 'Sprawozdanie Komitetu Centralnego' in *VIII Zjazd*, p. 49.
81 'Referat Biura Politycznego' in *II Krajowa Konferencja PZPR*, pp. 44–5.
82 'Referat Biura Politycznego na III Plenum', pp. 21–2; 'Referat Biura Politycznego na IX Plenum', p. 26.
83 'Referat Biura Politycznego na IX Plenum', p. 18; 'To co najważniejsze', p. 34; 'Referat Biura Politycznego' in *II Krajowa Konferencja PZPR*, p.19.
84 M. Kabaj, 'Efektywność wzrostu płac', *ND* no. 2 (February 1980), p. 139; A. Melich, 'Efektywność a płace', *ND*, no. 5 (May 1980), p. 119.
85 'Referat programowy' and 'Uchwała VIII Zjazdu' in *VIII Zjazd*, pp. 115, 177.
86 Z. Sufin, 'Długofalowe cele i bieżące potrzeby', *ND*, no. 4 (April 1976), p. 111.
87 'Przemówienie E. Gierka na wojewódzkiej konferencji PZPR w Katowicach', *Trybuna Ludu*, 17 October 1975.
88 'Referat Biura Politycznego na XIII Plenum wygłoszony przez E. Gierka: o pełne wykonanie zadań społeczno-gospodarczych w 1979, o partyjną i obywatelską odpowiedzialność w kształtowaniu wyższej jakości pracy i warunków życia narodu', *ND*, no. 1 (January 1979), pp. 15–16.
89 A. Tymowski, 'Wokół zagadnień minimum socjalnego', *ND*, no. 7 (July 1979), p. 117.
90 'Przemówienie E. Gierka wygłoszone 2 kwietnia b.r. na posiedzeniu Sejmu PRL', *ND*, no. 4 (April 1980), p. 10.
91 'Uchwała VIII Zjazdu' in *VIII Zjazd*, p. 202.
92 H. Jankowski, 'Z zagadnień sprawiedliwości społecznej', *ND*, no. 8 (August 1980), p. 108.
93 M. Fritzhand, 'Socjalistyczny sposób życia jako problem teoretyczny', *ND*, no. 5 (May 1976), p. 99. See also A. Butenko, 'W sprawie socjalistycznego stylu życia', *ND*, no. 8 (August 1976), p. 78.
94 'Przemówienie E. Gierka na VII Plenum', pp. 9–10.
95 'Referat programowy' in *VIII Zjazd*, p. 145.
96 T. Jaroszewski 'Perspektywa: rozwinięte społeczeństwo socjalistyczne', *ND*, no. 2 (February 1976), pp. 56–7.
97 'Narada I sekretarzy', p. 10.
98 'Referat Biura Politycznego na V Plenum', p. 15; 'Sprawozdanie Komitetu Centralnego' in *VIII Zjazd*, p. 39.
99 Dobieszewski, 'Obiektywne i subiektywne czynniki', p. 128.
100 S. Widerszpil, 'Z problemów teorii rozwiniętego społeczeństwa socjalistycznego', *ND*, no. 3 (March 1977), p. 118.
101 W. Wesołowski and J. Wiatr, 'Nowe aspekty struktury społecznej przesłanką rozwoju demokracji socjalistycznej', *ND*, no. 9 (September 1977), p. 127.
102 M. Orzechowski, 'Socjalistyczny naród polski: jedność i sprzeczności', *ND*, no. 2 (February 1980), pp. 62–4.
103 W. Wesołowski, 'Interesy klas i warstw a jedność moralno-polityczna

narodu', *ND*, no. 1 (January 1980), p. 110; Kloc, 'Miejsce samorządu', p. 136.
104 'Droga skutecznego działania', p. 156.
105 K. Janowski, 'Demokracja socjalistyczna a świadomość społeczna', *ND*, no. 11 (November 1977), p. 94.

7. INTERLUDE I: SOLIDARITY 1980–81

1 'Biuro polityczne: informacja o przebiegu i tle wydarzeń strajkowych', *ND*, nos. 10–11 (October–November 1980), pp. 43–5. See also W. F. Robinson (ed.), *The strikes in Poland* (Munich, Radio Free Europe Research, 1980).
2 The most important studies include: N. Ascherson, *The Polish August* (Harmondsworth, Penguin, 1982); D. MacShane, *Solidarity: Poland's independent trade union* (Nottingham, Spokesman, 1981); J. Woodall (ed.), *Policy and politics in contemporary Poland* (London, Frances Pinter, 1982); D. Singer, *The road to Gdansk* (London, Monthly Review Press, 1982); J.-Y. Potel, *The promise of Solidarity* (New York, Praeger, 1982); J. Staniszkis, *Pologne: la révolution autolimitée* (Paris, Presses Universitaires de France, 1982); Starski, *Class struggle in classless Poland*. See also the special issue 'Poland and the future of socialism', *Telos*, no. 47 (spring 1981).
3 'Przemówienie S. Kani na VI Plenum', *ND*, no. 9 (September 1980), p. 69. See also 'Przemówienie S. Kani po ogłoszeniu wyników wyborów I sekretarza' in *IX Nadzwyczajny Zjazd Polskiej Zjednoczonej Partii Robotniczej, 14–20 lipca 1981* (Warsaw, Książka i Wiedza, 1981), p. 74.
4 For example, G. Sanford, 'The response of the Polish Communist leadership to the continuing crisis' in Woodall (ed.), *Policy and politics in contemporary Poland*, pp. 36–7; J. de Weydenthal, 'Poland' in R. F. Staar (ed.), *Yearbook on international Communist affairs 1982* (Stanford, Hoover Institution Press, 1982), pp. 434–43.
5 W. Lebiedziński, 'Refleksje o demokracji wewnątrzpartyjnej', *ND*, nos. 1–2 (January–February 1981), pp. 265–6.
6 'Wystąpienie E. Gierka na IV Plenum', *ND*, no. 9 (September 1980), p. 24; E. Gierek, 'List do KC PZPR', *ND*, no. 12 (December 1980), p. 65.
7 'Przemówienie S. Kani na zakończenie VII Plenum', *ND*, no. 12 (December 1980), p. 61.
8 'Dyskusja na VI Plenum', *ND*, nos. 10–11 (October–November 1980), pp. 133–4; 'Uchwała XII Plenum w sprawie przyjęcia do wiadomości sprawozdania i wniosków komisji powołanej przez X Plenum', *ND*, no. 8 (August 1981), p. 187.
9 Lebiedziński, 'Refleksje', p. 268.
10 'Wystąpienie E. Gierka na IV Plenum', p. 27; 'Dyskusja na IV Plenum', *ND*, no. 9 (September 1980), p. 55.
11 Lebiedziński, 'Refleksje', p. 267.
12 T. Fiszbach, 'W obliczu nowych zadań', *Polityka*, 30 August 1980. See also W. Rogowski, 'Związki zawodowe: partnerzy czy oponenci', *ND*, no. 9 (September 1981), p. 54; 'Referat Komitetu Centralnego PZPR wygłoszony przez S. Kanię' in *IX Zjazd*, p. 33.

13 'Założenia programowe rozwoju socjalistycznej demokracji, umacniania przewodniej roli PZPR w budownictwie socjalistycznym i stabilizacji społeczno-gospodarczej kraju', *ND*, nos. 5–6 (May–June 1981), p. 204; 'Biuro polityczne: informacja', p. 55.

14 'Dyskusja na VII Plenum', *ND*, nos. 1–2 (January–February 1981), pp. 23, 141.

15 'Referat Biura Politycznego na IX Plenum wygłoszony przez K. Barcikowskiego: podstawowe problemy sytuacji w kraju i zadania partii w toku przygotowań do IX Zjazdu'; 'Przemówienie S. Kani na zakończenie IX Plenum', *ND*, no. 4 (April 1981), pp. 17–18, 31.

16 'Dyskusja na X Plenum', *ND*, nos. 5–6 (May–June 1981), pp. 87, 120.

17 G. Kolankiewicz, 'The politics of "socialist renewal"' in Woodall, (ed.) *Policy and politics in contemporary Poland*, p. 71.

18 *Trybuna Ludu*, 27 February 1981.

19 'Dyskusja na XI Plenum', *ND*, no. 7 (July 1981), p. 51.

20 *Życie Warszawy*, 14 July 1981; Warsaw domestic service, 2 April 1981; reported in *Foreign broadcasting information service*, 6 April 1981.

21 'Referat Komitetu Centralnego' in *IX Zjazd*, p. 25.

22 Data for the May 1981 poll are from 'Siedem dni' in *Kultura*, 21 June 1981, and from A. Jasińska and R. Siemieńska, 'The socialist personality: a case study of Poland', *International Journal of Sociology*, vol. 13, no. 1 (spring 1983). Data for the November polls were obtained privately by the author. See also D. Mason, 'Solidarity: the regime and the public', *Soviet Studies*, vol. 35, no. 10 (October 1983).

23 See G. S. Sher, *Praxis* (Bloomington, Indiana Univ. Press, 1977), pp. 11–12; H. G. Skilling, *Czechoslovakia's interrupted revolution* (Princeton Univ. Press, 1976), p. 219.

24 'Referat Komitetu Centralnego' and 'Uchwała IX Zjazdu: program rozwoju socjalistycznej demokracji, umacniania przewodniej roli PZPR w budownictwie socjalistycznym i stabilizacji społeczno-gospodarczej kraju' in *IX Zjazd*, pp. 34–5, 42, 106.

25 *Kurier Polski*, 15 August 1981.

26 'Przemówienie W. Jaruzelskiego na V Plenum', *ND*, no. 11 (November 1981), p. 233.

27 'W sprawie opracowania perspektywicznego programu PZPR' in *IX Zjazd*, p. 163.

28 J. Doliński, 'Rozmyślania o partii', *ND*, no. 10 (October 1981), pp. 88–9.

29 S. Olszowski, 'Niektóre problemy i kierunki ideowo-wychowawczej działalności partii w obecnej sytuacji', *ND*, no. 11 (November 1981), pp. 36–8.

30 Doliński, 'Rozmyślania o partii', p. 95.

31 'Referat Biura Politycznego na VI Plenum wygłoszony przez S. Kanię: sytuacja polityczna kraju i aktualne zadania partii'; 'Przemówienie S. Kani na zakończenie VI Plenum'; *ND*, nos. 10–11 (October–November 1980), pp. 19, 41; *Trybuna Ludu*, 2 and 4 February 1981.

32 M. Jarosz, 'Nierówności społeczne w świetle badań', *ND*, no. 10 (October 1981), p. 100.

33 Z. Sufin, 'Społeczne uwarunkowania i konsekwencje kryzysu', *ND*, no. 12 (December 1980), p. 71.

34 M. Pohorille, 'Jeszcze raz o minimum socjalnym', *ND*, nos. 1–2 (January–February 1981), p. 201.

35 *Dagens Nyheter*, 25 February 1981; reported in *Foreign broadcasting information service*, 2 March 1981.

36 *Życie Warszawy*, 18 February 1981. For the text of the Łódź agreement, see *Sztandar Młodych*, 19 February 1981.

37 Ascherson, *The Polish August*, p. 185.

38 'Referat Biura Politycznego na IX Plenum' and 'Dyskusja na IX Plenum', *ND*, no. 4 (April 1981), pp. 12, 137; *Trybuna Ludu*, 26 March 1981.

39 *Życie Warszawy*, 2 April 1981.

40 *Życie Warszawy*, 16 July 1981.

41 'Referat Komitetu Centralnego' and 'Uchwała IX Zjazdu' in *IX Zjazd*, pp. 28–32, 114.

42 *Trybuna Ludu*, 1 September 1981.

43 *Życie Warszawy*, 4 and 7 September 1981.

44 *Kurier Polski*, 18–20 September 1981.

45 *Życie Warszawy*, 17, 18 and 22 September 1981.

46 *Życie Warszawy*, 29 September 1981.

47 *Trybuna Ludu*, 17 November 1981; *Życie Warszawy*, 4 November 1981.

48 'Przemówienie W. Jaruzelskiego na V Plenum', p. 230.

49 *Trybuna Ludu*, 30 November 1981; *Życie Warszawy*, 20 November 1981.

50 *Kurier Polski*, 2–4 November 1981

51 *Trybuna Ludu*, 7 December 1981.

52 'Dyskusja na VI Plenum', *ND*, no. 12 (December 1981), p. 103.

53 'Referat Biura Politycznego na III Plenum wygłoszony przez J. Głowczyka'; 'Przemówienie S. Kani na zakończenie obrad III Plenum'; *ND*, no. 10 (October 1981), pp. 8–21, 29.

54 *Życie Warszawy*, 27 August 1980.

55 *Słowo Powszechne*, 4 September 1980. The meeting was held on 26 August.

56 *Kurier Polski*, 16 August 1981.

57 *Kurier Polski*, 30 September 1981.

58 'Referat Komitetu Centralnego' and 'Uchwała IX Zjazdu' in *IX Zjazd*, pp. 35, 110–11.

59 *Życie Warszawy*, 6 November 1981.

60 *Le Figaro*, 11 September 1980.

61 *Życie Warszawy*, 29 December 1980.

62 *Tygodnik Solidarność*, 17 April 1981.

63 See J. Bielasiak (ed.), *Poland today: the state of the Republic* (White Plains, NY, Sharpe, 1982).

64 M. Simon, 'Developed socialism and the Polish crisis' in J. Seroka and M. Simon (eds.), *Developed socialism in the Soviet bloc* (Boulder, Colorado, Westview Press, 1982), p. 112.

65 D. Horodyński, 'Niebezpieczeństwa', *Kultura*, 21 September 1980.

66 A. Wróblewski, 'Jak Polak z Polakiem', *Polityka*, 13 September 1981.

8. INTERLUDE II: MARTIAL LAW, 1981–82

1 Z. Gitelman, 'The limits of organisation and enthusiasm: the double failure of the Solidarity movement and the PUWP', in K. Lawson and P. Merkl (eds.), *When parties fail* (forthcoming).
2 R. Stefanowski, 'Poland: a chronology of events August–December 1981', Radio Free Europe Research, RAD Chronology, 16 July 1982, p. 43.
3 *Trybuna Ludu*, 10 December 1981.
4 Staniszkis, *Pologne; la révolution autolimitée*, pp. 26–35.
5 See A. Bromke, 'Socialism with a martial face', *The World Today*, vol. 38 (July–August 1982), p. 265.
6 *Rzeczpospolita*, 22 July 1982.
7 *Expres Wieczorny*, 11–13 December 1981.
8 *Trybuna Ludu*, 30–31 October–1 November 1982. See also M. Rakowski, 'W obronie słowa "tak"' and 'Kto bardziej cierpliwy', *Polityka*, 13 and 20 November 1982.
9 'Nie ma próżni', *Polityka*, 26 February 1983.
10 'Referat Biura Politycznego na VII Plenum wygłoszony przez W. Jaruzelskiego: zadania PZPR w walce o jedność partii, o umocnienie władzy ludowej, o pełną społeczną akceptację socjalizmu', *ND*, no. 3 (March 1982), pp. 28–9.
11 *Trybuna Ludu*, 8 January 1982.
12 J. Ładosz, 'Źródła i charakter naszego kryzysu', *ND*, nos. 1–2 (January–February 1982), p. 136.
13 *Trybuna Ludu*, 21 April and 12 July 1982.
14 'Referat Biura Politycznego na VII Plenum', p. 22.
15 *Żołnierz Wolności*, 30–31 January 1982.
16 *Trybuna Ludu*, 12 July 1982.
17 E. Erazmus, 'Refleksje o jedności partii', *ND*, no. 5 (May 1982), pp. 45–51.
18 *Le Monde*, 31 October–1 November 1982.
19 *Trybuna Ludu*, 18–19 December 1982.
20 'Deklaracja ideowo-programowa KC PZPR (projekt): o co walczymy, dokąd zmierzamy', *ND*, no. 3 (March 1982), pp. 46–7.
21 J. Wawrzyniak, 'Dialektyka kierowniczej roli partii i demokracji socjalistycznej', *ND*, no. 9 (September 1982), p. 124.
22 *Życie Warszawy*, 4 August 1982.
23 J. Staniszkis, 'Martial law in Poland', *Telos*, no. 54 (winter 1982–3), pp. 95–7.
24 A. Wajda, 'Polityczne jutro PZPR', *ND*, nos. 7–8 (July–August 1982), p. 28.
25 'Referat Biura Politycznego na VII Plenum', p. 13.
26 S. Olszowski, 'Konsolidacja partii: warunkiem jej odrodzenia', *ND*, nos. 1–2 (January–February 1982), p. 7; idem, 'Bieżące i perspektywiczne zadania frontu ideologicznego partii', *ND*, no. 4 (April 1982), pp. 10–35.
27 *Trybuna Ludu*, 2 March 1982.

28 J. Wiatr, 'The sources of crises', *Polish Perspectives*, no. 4 (autumn 1982), pp. 18–21.
29 *Trybuna Ludu*, 8 October 1982.
30 *Życie Warszawy*, 28 December 1981.
31 *Trybuna Ludu*, 22 February 1982.
32 *Trybuna Ludu*, 22 July 1982.
33 *Trybuna Ludu*, 26 October 1982.
34 K. Kąkol, 'Mistyfikacja: instrument kontrrewolucji', *ND*, no. 12 (December 1982), p. 27. See also *Życie Warszawy*, 23–24 October 1982.
35 *Życie Warszawy*, 8 and 26 April 1982.
36 *Polacy 80* (Warsaw, Polska Akademia Nauk, 1981).
37 *Rzeczpospolita*, 8 September 1982. See also *Rzeczpospolita*, 13 September 1982 and *Żołnierz Wolności*, 21 September 1982.
38 W. Mysłek, 'Z problematyki światopoglądowej konfrontacji w warunkach kryzysu', *ND*, nos. 1–2 (January–February 1982), p. 154; S. Markiewicz, 'Kościół rzymskokatolicki w procesie przystosowywania się do nowych warunków społecznych', *ND*, no. 6 (June 1982), p. 48. See also J. Godlewski, 'Stosunek kościoła rzymskokatolickiego do inteligencji i jej społecznej roli', *ND*, no. 12 (December 1982), pp. 129–37.
39 *Trybuna Ludu*, 10 October 1982.
40 *La Republica*, 25 February 1983; reported in *Foreign broadcasting information service*, 3 March 1983.
41 *Kongres kultury polskiej* (Stockholm, mimeograph, 1982), p. 9
42 *Życie Warszawy*, 5 January 1982; *Trybuna Ludu*, 9–10 January 1982.
43 H. Kubiak, 'Ideologiczne funkcje kultury i nauki', *ND*, no. 4 (April 1982), pp. 36–42.
44 *Trybuna Ludu*, 4 May 1982.
45 J. Górski, 'Drogi i bezdroża nauk społecznych', *ND*, nos. 7–8 (July–August 1982), pp. 132–41.
46 *Rzeczpospolita*, 23–24 October 1982.
47 *Słowo Powszechne*, 5–7 March 1982.
48 *Trybuna Ludu*, 26 October 1982.
49 J. Głowczyk, 'Społeczne problemy reformy gospodarczej', *ND*, no. 4 (April 1982), p. 66.
50 *Trybuna Ludu*, 16 and 19 July 1982.
51 P. Zwick, *National communism* (Boulder, Colorado, Westview Press, 1983), p. 135.

9. OPERATIVE IDEOLOGY, FUNDAMENTAL PRINCIPLES AND SOCIAL REALITY

1 A. B. Evans, 'Developed socialism in Soviet ideology', *Soviet Studies*, vol. 29, no. 3 (July 1977), pp. 409, 426–7.
2 H. Dahm, 'The function and efficacy of ideology', *Studies in Soviet Thought*, vol. 21, no. 2 (May 1980), pp. 110–12.
3 B. Russell, *Bolshevism: practice and theory* (New York, Arno Press, 1972); R. N. Carew Hunt, *The theory and practice of Communism* (Harmondsworth, Penguin, 1973); H. Marcuse, *Soviet Marxism* (Harmondsworth, Penguin,

1971); R. Schlesinger, *Marx: his time and ours* (London, Routledge and Paul, 1950).

4 K. Marx and F. Engels, 'Address of the Central Committee to the Communist League' in *Selected works*, 3 vols. (Moscow, Progress, 1969–70), vol. 1, p. 175.

5 V. I. Lenin, 'What is to be done?' in *Collected works*, vol. 5, pp. 467–73.

6 V. I. Lenin, 'Party organisation and party literature' in *Collected works*, vol. 10, p. 46.

7 V. I. Lenin, 'Freedom to criticise and unity of action' in *Collected works*, vol. 10, p. 443.

8 V. I. Lenin, 'Preliminary draft resolution of the X Congress of the RCP (b) on party unity' in *Collected works*, vol. 32, p. 243.

9 K. Marx and F. Engels, 'Manifesto of the Communist Party' in *Selected works*, vol. 1, p. 120.

10 V. I. Lenin, 'The state and revolution' in *Selected works*, 12 vols. (London, M. Lawrence, 1936–9), vol. 7; *idem*, 'Foreword to the published speech "Deception of the people with slogans of freedom and equality"' in *Collected works*, vol. 29, p. 381.

11 V. I. Lenin, 'Left-wing Communism: an infantile disorder' in *Collected works*, vol. 31, pp. 70–1, 95.

12 D. McLellan, *Marx's Grundrisse* (London, Macmillan, 1971), pp. 124, 152; K. Marx, 'Critique of the Gotha programme' in Marx and Engels, *Selected works*, vol. 3, p. 17.

13 Marx and Engels, 'Manifesto of the Communist Party', p. 116.

14 K. Marx, 'Speech to a delegation of German trade unionists' (1869) in D. McLellan (ed.), *Karl Marx: selected writings* (Oxford Univ. Press, 1977), p. 538.

15 V. I. Lenin, 'The role and functions of the trade unions under the New Economic Policy' in *Collected works*, vol. 33, pp. 188–93. See also his *On trade unions* (Moscow, Progress, 1970).

16 V. I. Lenin, 'International Socialist Congress in Stuttgart' in *Selected works*, vol. 4, p. 319.

17 V. I. Lenin, 'Once again on the trade unions, the present situation, and the mistakes of Trotsky and Bukharin' in *Selected works*, vol. 9, pp. 36, 57.

18 Lenin, 'Once again on the trade unions', pp. 12, 53.

19 V. I. Lenin, 'Political report of the Central Committee to the XI Congress of the RCP (b)' in *Selected works*, vol. 9, pp. 324ff.

20 V. I. Lenin, 'The work of the Council of People's Commissars' in *Selected works*, vol. 8, p. 261.

21 K. Marx, 'Contribution to the critique of Hegel's philosophy of law' in *Collected works*, 12 vols. (New York, International Publishers, 1975–9), vol. 3, p. 175.

22 Marx and Engels, 'Manifesto of the Communist Party', p. 129.

23 V. I. Lenin, 'Socialism and revolution' in *Selected works*, vol. 11, pp. 661–2.

24 V. I. Lenin, 'The attitude of the workers' party towards religion' in *Selected works*, vol. 11, pp. 668–71.

25 McLellan, *Marx's Grundrisse*, p. 142.

26 K. Marx, *The German ideology*, 2nd edn (Moscow, Progress, 1968), p. 441.

27 V. I. Lenin, 'The three sources and three component parts of Marxism' in *Selected works*, vol. 11, p. 3.

28 Lenin, 'The three sources', p. 3.

29 V. I. Lenin, 'What the friends of the people are' in *Selected works*, vol. 11, p. 422.

30 V. I. Lenin, 'The achievements and difficulties of the Soviet government' in *Collected works*, vol. 29, p. 74; *idem*, 'How does Bishop Nikon defend the Ukrainians?' in *Collected works*, vol. 19, p. 380.

31 V. I. Lenin, 'Tolstoy and the proletarian struggle' in *Collected works*, vol. 16, pp. 353–4.

32 J. Stalin, 'Concerning Marxism in linguistics' in *Marxism and problems of linguistics* (Peking, Foreign Languages Press, 1972).

33 V. I. Lenin, 'Constitutional illusions' in *Selected works*, vol. 6, p. 180.

34 V. I. Lenin, 'Report delivered at the first session of the All-Russia Central Executive Committee, seventh convocation' in *Collected works*, vol. 30, pp. 327–8; *idem*, 'The state and revolution', p. 75.

35 V. I. Lenin, 'The New Economic Policy and the tasks of the political education departments' in *Collected works*, vol. 33, p. 70; *idem*, 'Resolutions of the IX Congress of the RCP (b)' in *Collected works*, vol. 26, pp. 550–1.

36 Marx, 'Critique of the Gotha programme', pp. 18–19.

37 D. Lane, *Leninism: a sociological interpretation* (Cambridge Univ. Press, 1981), pp. 127–9.

38 R. E. Lane, 'Waiting for lefty: the capitalist genesis of socialist man', *Theory and Society*, vol. 6, no. 1 (July 1978), p. 24.

39 G. Kolankiewicz and R. Taras, 'Poland: socialism for everyman?' in A. Brown and J. Gray (eds.), *Political culture and political change in Communist states*, (London, Macmillan, 1977), p. 109.

40 L. Kolakowski, *Main currents of Marxism*, 3 vols. (Oxford Univ. Press, 1978), vol. 3, pp. 460–7.

41 Z. Bauman, *Socialism: the active utopia* (New York, Holmes and Meier, 1976), pp. 71–2.

42 J. Staniszkis, 'On some contradictions of socialist society', *Soviet Studies*, vol. 31, no. 2 (April 1979), pp. 167–87.

43 F. G. Casals, *The syncretic society* (White Plains, NY, Sharpe, 1980), p. 60.

44 *Trybuna Ludu*, 15–16 October 1983.

Bibliography

This is a select bibliography based on general books in three fields of study: (1) the theory of ideology; (2) empirical analyses of ideology in socialist states; and (3) ideological and political developments in Poland. Only English, French and Polish sources are included.

Althusser, L., *Lenin and philosophy*, London, New Left Books, 1977.
For Marx, London, Verso, 1979.
Apter, D. (ed.), *Ideology and discontent*, New York, Free Press of Glencoe, 1964.
Armstrong, J. A., *Ideology, politics and government in the Soviet Union*, 3rd edn, New York, Praeger, 1975.
Aron, R., *The opium of the intellectuals*, New York, Norton Co., 1962.
Ascherson, N., *The Polish August*, Harmondsworth, Penguin, 1982.
Bauman, Z., *Socialism: the active utopia*, New York, Holmes and Meier, 1976.
Bell, D., *The end of ideology*, New York, Free Press of Glencoe, 1960.
The coming of post-industrial society, New York, Basic Books, 1973.
Bethell, N., *Gomulka*, Harmondsworth, Penguin, 1972.
Bienkowski, W., *Motory i hamulce socjalizmu*, Paris, Instytut Literacki, 1969.
Theory and reality, London, Allison and Busby, 1981.
Błażyński, G., *Flashpoint Poland*, New York, Pergamon, 1979.
Bodnar, A., *Ekonomia i polityka*, Warsaw, Państwowe Wydawn. Naukowe, 1978.
Breslauer, G., *Khrushchev and Brezhnev as leaders*, London, Allen and Unwin, 1982.
Bromke, A., *Poland: the last decade*, Oakville, Ontario, Mosaic Press, 1981.
Bromke, A and Strong, J. W. (eds.), *Gierek's Poland*, New York, Praeger, 1973.
Brumberg, A. (ed.), *Poland: genesis of a revolution*, New York, Vintage Books, 1983.
Brus, W., *Socialist ownership and political systems*, London, Routledge and Kegan Paul, 1975.
Brzezinski, Z., *Ideology and power in Soviet politics*, New York, Praeger, 1962.
The Soviet bloc: unity and conflict, rev. edn, Cambridge, Mass., Harvard Univ. Press, 1967.
Brzezinski, Z and Huntington, S., *Political power: USA/USSR*, New York, Viking Press, 1965.

Carew Hunt, R. N., *The theory and practice of Communism*, Harmondsworth, Penguin, 1973.

Casals, F. G., *The syncretic society*, White Plains, NY, Sharpe, 1980.

Checinski, M., *Poland: Communism, nationalism, anti-semitism*, New York, Karz-Cohl, 1982.

Chołaj, H., *O rozwiniętym społeczeństwie socjalistycznym*, Warsaw, Wiedza Powszechna, 1977.

Dobieszewski, A. and Gołębiowski, J. W. (eds.), *PZPR (1948–78)*, Warsaw, Państwowe Wydawn. Naukowe, 1978.

Drucker, H. M., *The political uses of ideology*, London, Macmillan, 1974.

Dziewanowski, M. K., *The Communist party of Poland*, Cambridge, Mass., Harvard Univ. Press, 1959.

Foucault, M., *The archaeology of knowledge*, London, Tavistock Publications, 1972.

Golan, G., *The Czechoslovak reform movement*, Cambridge Univ. Press, 1971.

Gouldner, A. W., *The dialectic of ideology and technology*, London, Macmillan, 1976.

The two Marxisms, New York, Seabury Press, 1980.

Habermas, J., *Toward a rational society*, Boston, Beacon Press, 1971.

Legitimation crisis, London, Heinemann, 1976.

Hertz, A., *Szkice o ideologiach*, Paris, Instytut Literacki, 1967.

Hirszowicz, M., *The bureaucratic leviathan*, New York Univ. Press, 1980.

Hochfeld, J., *Studia o marksowskiej teorii społeczeństwa*, Warsaw, Państwowe Wydawn. Naukowe, 1963.

Hsiung, J. C., *Ideology and practice*, New York, Praeger, 1972.

Johnson, A. R., *The transformation of Communist ideology*, Cambridge, Mass., MIT Press, 1972.

Jordan, Z. A., *Philosophy and ideology*, Dordrecht, D. Reidel, 1963.

Karpinski, J., *Countdown*, New York, Karz-Cohl, 1982.

Kolakowski, L., *Main currents of Marxism*, 3 vols., Oxford Univ. Press, 1978.

Kortunow, W., *Ideologia i polityka*, Warsaw, Państwowe Wydawn. Naukowe, 1976.

Kozyr-Kowalski, S., and Ładosz, J., *Dialektyka a społeczeństwo*, 2nd edn, Warsaw, Państwowe Wydawn. Naukowe, 1974.

Kusin, V., *The intellectual origins of the Prague spring*, Cambridge Univ. Press. 1971.

Labbé, D., *Le Discours communiste*, Paris, Presses de la Fondation nationale des sciences politiques, 1977.

Lane, R. E., *Political ideology*, New York, Free Press of Glencoe, 1962.

Larrain, J., *The concept of ideology*, London, Hutchinson, 1979.

Laszlo, E., *The Communist ideology in Hungary*, Dordrecht, D. Reidel, 1966.

Lenin, V. I., *Collected works*, 45 vols., London, Lawrence and Wishart, 1960–6.

Leslie, R. F., *et al.*, *The history of Poland since 1863*, Cambridge Univ. Press, 1983.

McCauley, M., *Marxism–Leninism in the German Democratic Republic*, London, Macmillan, 1979.

MacShane, D., *Solidarity: Poland's independent trade union*, Nottingham, Spokesman, 1981.

Mannheim, K., *Ideology and Utopia*, New York, Harcourt, Brace and World, 1955.

Marx, K. and Engels, F., *Collected works*, 12 vols., New York, International Publishers, 1975–9.

Moore, B. Jr., *Soviet politics: the dilemma of power*, New York, Harper Torchbooks, 1965.

Morawski, *Nowe społeczeństwo przemysłowe*, Warsaw, Państwowe Wydawn. Naukowe, 1975.

Mucha, J., *Konflikt i społeczeństwo*, Warsaw, Państwowe Wydawn. Naukowe, 1978.

Naess, A., Christophersen, J and Kvalø, K., *Democracy, ideology and objectivity*, Oslo Univ. Press, 1956.

Narojek, W., *Społeczeństwo planujące*, Warsaw, Państwowe Wydawn. Naukowe, 1973.

Ossowski, S., *Class structure in the social consciousness*, New York, Free Press of Glencoe, 1963.

Parekh, B., *Marx's theory of ideology*, Baltimore, Johns Hopkins Univ. Press, 1982.

Pomian, K., *Pologne, défi à l'impossible?* Paris, Editions ouvrières, 1982.

Potel, J-Y., *The promise of Solidarity*, New York, Praeger, 1982.

PZPR, *Third Congress of the Polish United Workers' Party, March 10–19, 1959*, Warsaw, Central Committee of the PUWP, 1959.

IV Zjazd Polskiej Zjednoczonej Partii Robotniczej, Warsaw, Książka i Wiedza, 1964.

V Zjazd Polskiej Zjednoczonej Partii Robotniczej, Warsaw, Książka i Wiedza, 1969.

VI Zjazd Polskiej Zjednoczonej Partii Robotniczej, Warsaw, Książka i Wiedza, 1972.

VII Zjazd Polskiej Zjednoczonej Partii Robotniczej. Warsaw, Książka i Wiedza, 1975.

VIII Zjazd Polskiej Zjednoczonej Partii Robotniczej, Warsaw, Książka i Wiedza, 1980.

IX Nadzwyczajny Zjazd Polskiej Zjednoczonej Partii Robotniczej, Warsaw, Książka i Wiedza, 1981.

I Krajowa Konferencja PZPR, Warsaw, Książka i Wiedza, 1973.

II Krajowa Konferencja PZPR, Warsaw, Książka i Wiedza, 1978.

Podstawy ideologii i polityki PZPR, Warsaw, Książka i Wiedza, 1976.

Raina, P., *Political opposition in Poland 1954–77*, London, Poets and Painters Press, 1978.

Rainko, S., *Świadomość i historia*, Warsaw, Czytelnik, 1978.

Świadomość i determinizm, Warsaw, Czytelnik, 1981.

Rakowski, M., *Od sierpnia do grudnia*, Warsaw, Czytelnik, 1981.

Przesilenie grudniowe, Warsaw, Państwowy Instytut Wydawn., 1981.

Rzeczypospolita na progu lat osiemdziesiątych, Warsaw, Państwowy Instytut Wydawn., 1981.

Richta, R., *Cywilizacja na rozdrożu*, Warsaw, Książka i Wiedza, 1971.

Robinson, W. (ed.), *The strikes in Poland*, Munich, Radio Free Europe Research, 1980.

Ruane, K., *The Polish challenge*, London, BBC, 1982.
Russell, B., *Bolshevism: practice and theory*, New York, Arno Press, 1972.
Schaff, A., *Marxism and the human individual*, New York, McGraw-Hill, 1970.
Schurmann, F., *Ideology and organisation in Communist China*, 2nd edn, Berkeley, Univ. of California Press, 1968.
Seliger, M., *Ideology and politics*, London, Allen and Unwin, 1976.
The Marxist conception of ideology, Cambridge Univ. Press, 1977.
Seroka, J. and Simon, M. (eds.), *Developed socialism in the Soviet bloc*, Boulder, Colorado, Westview Press, 1982.
Shapiro, M. J., *Language and political understanding*, New Haven, Yale Univ. Press, 1981.
Simon, M. and Kanet, R. (eds.), *Background to crisis: policy and politics in Gierek's Poland*, Boulder, Colorado, Westview Press, 1981.
Singer, D., *The road to Gdansk*, London, Monthly Review Press, 1982.
Sokolewicz, W., *Konstytucja PRL po zmianach z 1976 r.*, Warsaw, Państwowe Wydawn. Naukowe, 1978.
Stalin, J., *Works*, Moscow, Foreign Languages Publishing House, 1952–5.
Staniszkis, J., *Pologne: la révolution autolimitée*, Paris, Presses Universitaires de France, 1982.
Starski, S., *Class struggle in classless Poland*, Boston, South End Press, 1982.
Steven, S., *The Poles*, New York Macmillan, 1982.
Strzelecki, J., *Kontynuacje (2)*, Warsaw, Państwowy Instytut Wydawn., 1974.
Szczepański, J., *Zmiany społeczeństwa polskiego w procesie uprzemysłowienia*, Warsaw, Instytut Wydawn. CRZZ, 1973.
Therborn, G., *The ideology of power and the power of ideology*, London, Verso. 1980.
Tokes, R. (ed.), *Opposition in Eastern Europe*, London, Macmillan, 1979.
Topolski, J., *Methodology of history*, Warsaw, Polish Scientific Publishers, 1976.
Touraine, A., *et al.*, *Solidarité*, Paris, Fayard, 1982.
Triska, J. and Gati, C. (eds.), *Blue-collar workers in Eastern Europe*, London, Allen and Unwin, 1981.
Ulam, A., *Ideologies and illusions*, Cambridge, Mass., Harvard Univ. Press, 1976.
Wesołowski, W., (ed.), *Marksizm i procesy rozwoju społecznego*, Warsaw, Książka i Wiedza, 1979.
Wiatr, J. J., *Czy zmierzch ery ideologii?* Warsaw, Książka i Wiedza, 1968.
Marksistowska teoria rozwoju społecznego Warsaw, Książka i Wiedza, 1973.
Przyczynek do zagadnienia rozwoju społecznego w formacji socjalistycznej, Warsaw, Książka i Wiedza, 1979.
(ed.), *Polish essays in the methodology of the social sciences*, Dordrecht, D. Reidel, 1979.
Woodall, J., *The socialist corporation and technocratic power*, Cambridge Univ. Press, 1982.
(ed.), *Policy and politics in contemporary Poland*, London, Frances Pinter, 1982.

Index

293